CATALOGING SAMPLER

A COMPARATIVE AND INTERPRETIVE GUIDE

by

Laura C. Colvin

Professor, School of Library Science
Simmons College

ARCHON BOOKS
The Shoe String Press, Inc.
Hamden, Connecticut

Sole Agents in the United Kingdom & British Commonwealth
Bailey Bros. & Swinfen Ltd.
Hyde House
West Central Street
London WC 1, England

Library of Congress Catalog Card No. 62-20998
Printed in the United States of America

TO

M   M

as she was affectionately known by her students

CONTENTS

CONTENTS

PREFACE

The Cataloging Sampler, a Comparative and Interpretive Guide, developed as a visual reference manual of the cataloging process, was conceived primarily for use in the cataloging courses of the Simmons College graduate library school. However, it is hoped other library schools may find it effective in teaching cataloging, and that it will also prove valuable in cataloging departments.

Charles Ammi Cutter's oft-quoted statement, "Cataloging is an art, not a science," which appeared in the preface to the fourth edition of his Rules, has been the essence of American cataloging practice. This heritage, the privilege to be unique to meet individual tastes and requirements, continues to be reflected in the many differences and in the varieties of style which exist from library to library. However, because of the standards evolved by the Library of Congress and its impress upon American catalogs, this Cataloging Sampler contains predominantly LC printed cards. To illustrate comparative cataloging, Wilson printed cards, and typed catalog cards, which may serve as a pattern or which may be adapted for any library, have also been included. The limited and scattered cataloging examples solicited primarily from Greater Boston libraries and from a few in other parts of the country broaden the comparative approach. Together the Sampler reveals a potpourri or garden varieties of American cataloging practice; traditional, original, and experimental.

Reflected chiefly in this volume, however, is current standard practice, summarizing in a sense an era of six decades of cataloging. Significant changes are in progress; draft editions of the proposed Code of Cataloging Rules, continued improvements in facsimile, and experiments in punched card, cataloging, development of additional commercial card services, wide-spread growth of regional processing centers in two-thirds of the states. Catalog card policies, practices, styles, etc., may tend toward much less individuality and toward much more conformity to standardization in catalogs. We shall likely prepare manuals for electronic cataloging before another decade!

Organized with respect to the cataloging process, this Cataloging Sampler is designed to demonstrate the various records which may be involved. The different patterns of entry, descriptive data, and style of catalog cards may serve to supplement the theoretical approach to cataloging and to provide a vehicle for discussion of the values and limitations of policies and practices. Included are selective examples for books and nonbook materials, which illustrate many of the principles in the 1949 ALA Cataloging Rules and Library of Congress Rules for Descriptive Cataloging. The intent has been neither to collect exhaustive examples nor to illustrate every rule and exception. Coverage is uneven; for some areas comprehensive, while for others perhaps thin. Because cards have been collected over a period of several years, changes of practice as well as errors and omissions — the human element — will undoubtedly be represented in this volume.

This work is also planned with a concise, interpretive outline, rather than with an explanatory or evaluative text (which is part of the teaching function) to accompany the sample cataloging records, cards, forms, etc. Because the outline precedes and introduces each section of the work, captions do not appear on all pages. However, the introduction which follows the preface serves as a commentary to clarify the content, organization, and special features of each section. The layout of the volume, perforce limited by page area, proved to be an absorbing adventure in which the compiler would not be thwarted either by the plethora (or the paucity) of the samples collected, or by the intent to provide a functional presentation. Facing pages (verso and recto) serve instructional objectives whenever possible. Typed card copy made in the School of Library Science was done on an unpredictable manual typewriter over a considerable period. Variations in reproduction of typed cards from many sources are to be expected. The lining of the cards and the insertion of captions and numerals have been the responsibility of the Press to which I am indebted.

Although originally proposed as a joint production with Andrew D. Osborn, librarian of the University of Sydney, Australia (professor, University of Pittsburgh Graduate Library School, 1962/63-   ) and conceived as a systematic development and broad comparative study of catalog cards from many different types of library installations, with a text and recommended examples and practice, this volume has been constructed along simpler lines. The envisioned volume did not materialize; nevertheless, I should like to thank Dr. Osborn for our thinking and planning together.

Indeed, I am especially thankful to the many catalogers and other librarians or representatives of agencies who have cordially responded to requests for samples and for information. Continued interest and support of many colleagues have been of immeasurable value. Sincere appreciation is extended to the Library of Congress for its generous cooperation in providing samples of its cataloging procedures and for its prompt service in sending printed cards. Acknowledgment of permission granted to me by the libraries and agencies to reproduce materials follows the preface.

In 1957/58 for an excellent seminar paper, Arlene Kupis collected approximately 200 cards. Some of her examples have proved particularly appropriate for this volume. Students and graduates have been cooperative in responding to requests. To them all, but most especially to Barbara P. Andrews, administrative assistant, Descriptive Cataloging Division, Processing Department, Library of Congress, for locating my many varied requests and for answering my many questions always with understanding and patience, I am very grateful. David R. Proper, graduate assistant in Library Science, has been diligent in searching and gathering samples and in the detailed work of typing cards, which meticulous contribution I appreciate. Miss M. Ruth MacDonald, assistant to the director, National Library of Medicine, has graciously given permission to reproduce the visual study (Appendix H) which illustrated her working paper presented at the Stanford Institute on Cataloging Code Revision, 1958.

For her constant and loyal support, cogent criticisms and suggestions, invaluable editorial assistance, and careful checklisting of the layout, I am greatly indebted and warmly grateful to Ruth S. Leonard, associate professor and esteemed colleague. Kenneth R. Shaffer, director of the Simmons College School of Library Science for some years has encouraged and stimulated me to compile this publication, sharing the hope that it will become an effective teaching instrument and also a reference volume in cataloging departments. Concerning whatever omissions, disproportions, or bias it contains, I shall welcome suggestions.

Laura C. Colvin
Professor of Library Science
Simmons College
15 June 1962

ACKNOWLEDGMENTS

Below are listed the libraries and agencies which contributed cards, forms, and other cataloging records for this work. Identifying symbols, most of which represent those used in the National Union Catalog, have been added to the examples whenever necessary.

Armed Services Technical Information Agency, U. S. Air Force, Arlington, Va. ASTIA

Boston University Libraries. MBU

Bro-Dart Industries, Newark, N. J. ALANAR

Boston Public Library:
    Division of Home Reading and Community Services. MB
    Division of Reference and Research Services. MB

Brookline (Mass.) Public Library. MBr

Demco Library Supplies, Madison, Wis.

Enoch Pratt Free Library, Baltimore. MdBE

Dartmouth College, Baker Library. NhD

Framingham (Mass.) Public Library. MFm

Gaylord Bros., Inc., Syracuse, N. Y.

Harvard University:
    William Hayes Fogg Museum of Art Library. MH-FA
    Harvard-Yenching Institute, Chinese-Japanese Library. MH-HY
    Graduate School of Business Administration, Baker Library. MH-BA
    Harvard College Library. MH
    Houghton Library. MH

Library of Congress. LC

Library of Hawaii, Honolulu. HL

Massachusetts Institute of Technology Libraries. MCM

Mitre Corporation, Bedford, Mass. MITRE

Montgomery County Public Schools, Division of Instructional Materials, Rockville, Md. MdMCPS

Museum of Fine Arts, Boston:
    Division of Education, Slide Library. MBMu
    Library. MBMu

National Library of Medicine. DNLM, NLM

Perkins School for the Blind, Watertown, Mass. MWatP

Simmons College Library. MBSi

University of California Library, Los Angeles. CLU

University of California Library, Berkeley. CU

University of Michigan Library, Ann Arbor. MiU

Wayne County Library, Wayne, Mich. MiWC

Wellesley College Library. MWelC

Wilson (H. W.) Company, New York.

Yale University Library. CtY

In addition, permission to include sample styles from the following books or manuals is gratefully acknowledged:

Boggs, Samuel W. and Lewis, Dorothy C. The classification and cataloging of maps and atlases. New York, Special Libraries Association, 1945. Boggs & Lewis

Columbia University. School of Library Service. Sample catalog cards, for use in connection with courses in technical services in libraries and organization of materials. 3d ed. New York, 1958. COL

Markley, A. Ethelyn. Introduction to classification and cataloging, Librarianship 210 [by] Anne Ethelyn Markley, Grete W. Frugé, reviser. Berkeley, University of California Press, 1960. UCB

---- Special problems in classification and cataloging, Librarianship 214 [by] Anne Ethelyn Markley, Grete W. Frugé, reviser. Berkeley, University of California, 1959. UCB

Cover design for student edition, by Virginia L. Bratton, Assistant Professor of Graphic Arts, Simmons College.

INTRODUCTION

The function of the introduction, which is arranged according to the sections of the outline, is to provide supplementary information, particularly when content and arrangements may not be obvious. It amplifies the objectives and organization of the work; it is not intended to be an interpretive text. Since it is difficult to demonstrate through visual means alone the systematic development of the cataloging process, each section outline reveals the organization of the layout which follows. Whenever possible throughout the outline, the use of the diagonal or slash designates, in general, related terms, near synonyms, terms in succession, etc. for the sake of brevity. Conciseness is also apparent in the use of initialisms and shortened forms. Similarly, cryptic statements in the introduction assume its use with the outline and with the samples.

The samples (verso as well as recto) have been numbered continuously within each section, a few inclusively, most individually. These numbers for the samples have been added to the outline for each section, and the outline symbols have been added to each page. Thus each outline constitutes a key to the samples which follow. Because of this index feature, captions have not been added to each page and to each item. For convenience, however, captions are used to introduce sections and subdivisions. Relationships among sections or subdivisions of the work are indicated in the outlines by both see and see also references, which serve as a general guide to related samples.

Samples collected from various libraries (except in the appendices) usually are not identified in the outline or in the captions, but identifying symbols have been typed on these cards. Since color cannot be shown, it is indicated on appropriate samples. Some pages have been arranged vertically, others horizontally; some pages are to be read from bottom to top, others top to bottom. The latter is the general design. Space is available on many pages for students' and catalogers' notes.

I. Cataloging control records

Section I includes multiple order forms, preliminary, and interim records based upon their use in and/or referral to some aspect of the cataloging process. Since these forms appear self-explanatory, or information has been added, few captions are used. As an example, however, detailed procedures for multiple order forms in one library are described.

Sources identified only by initialisms or abbreviations on the sample authority cards are not listed. Each cataloging department will have its own list. To economize space, as may also be practical in libraries,

name, title, etc. references have been made only for the public catalog.
A few references are included in the LC official catalog sampling. Most of
these samples obtained from the LC official catalog are Xeroxed copies.

Subdivision E, Authority records for subjects and references, is designed
as a controlled demonstration of records and procedures. Scope notes are
optional on subject authority cards. References as well as tracing of references are included in the subject authority file. The LC file is merely a
token display.

II. The dictionary card catalog

Section II shows comparative styles of printed and typed catalog card
sets, or unit cards. Subdivisions F-G in the outline represent an analysis
of entries in the catalog and descriptive data on catalog cards, specified
examples of which are available through the index.

Subdivision H lists in one sequence the references (except the topical
subject references provided in another section) which would be interfiled
in the dictionary catalog. These references are highly selective; some
have been traced in the authority file, some in the LC official catalog, some
in the dictionary catalog, some in the shelf list. Every name, title, subject,
etc. reference (except LC printed random samples) displayed has been
traced somewhere in the volume.

III. Monograph publications

Section III, a long one, illustrates not only choice of entry for single,
multiple, unknown or complex, and corporate authorship, but also various
types of names. Equally pertinent names may be found in other sections.
The European names, generally middle European, are included mainly because of the languages represented. Under Chinese names an unusual study
is inserted. Transliterated or romanized titles appear in this section, as
well as in others, but access to transliteration or romanization is through
the index.

While texts for anonymous classics appear in this section, their adaptations appear in another section. Both Bible texts and criticism, etc. appear
here and in several other sections as well. General societies and institutions have not been differentiated but interfiled. However, certain types of
corporate bodies are grouped separately. Again, highly selective samples
of government publications are represented.

Some subdivisions are more complete than others. In gathering samples,
except for a special reason, exact duplicates which appear in cataloging codes
or in other manuals have been omitted. When it has not been possible to ar-
range samples in exact order of the outline, card numbers serve as guides.

IV. Serial publications

Section IV represents a very limited sampling of serials; however, referral is made to supplementary examples in other sections. Several methods of showing, or referral to, holdings records are demonstrated, such as in the public catalog, the shelf list, or the serial check list. Use of the skeleton card for secondary entries is shown.

V. Publications issued in series

Section V demonstrates variant styles and arrangements for publisher's and monograph series on a comparative basis because series present controversial problems. Generally, editors are not given by LC in the series note, and LC in its present limited cataloging policy omits tracing for series.

VI. Analytical entries

Section VI displays Wilson's printed analytics in contrast to the use of LC unit cards. Several brief styles are also exhibited.

VII. Works related

Section VII consists of works related in diverse ways which are evident in the outline. Translations which appear in many sections are indexed. To illustrate works bound together three title pages have been reproduced as an added visual presentation.

VIII. Relationships in the catalog

Section VIII is divided to demonstrate catalog relationships through main and secondary entries, and references as contrasted with arrangement devices. Full treatment of filing titles would require more numerous and varied examples.

IX. Works of special type and special collections

Section IX brings together unlike materials, each of which needs specialized treatment. The division of the outline is arbitrary. LC card numbers reveal the vintage of cataloging style.

X. Nonbook materials

Section X, with outline divided, is devoted to diverse treatment, since nonbook materials lend themselves to more individualized cataloging and arrangements. Some subdivisions, however, exhibit LC style primarily. Because specialized cataloging of two art museums is compared, the outline is detailed. Coverage for each type of material in this section is not uniform.

XI. Shelf list

Section XI is designed to demonstrate functional aspects of the shelf list, styles of cards and of call numbers, and use of book numbers. The LCC shelf list includes three NLMC shelf list cards. Nonbook materials are separated to indicate comparative arrangements. Each item in the shelf list has a main entry card in some section of the work.

APPENDICES

The appendices consist of separate studies which, with the exception of the first and the last, treat of cataloging in individual libraries, or systems. The outline preceding each study explains the content.

Appendix A displays in shelf list arrangement a sampling of book numbers to express differentiation and/or bibliographic features of works, based on the assumption of an extensive collection.

Appendix B demonstrates steps in the cataloging process at the Library of Congress in 1959 when the samples were secured. The accompanying outline of LC current practice lists the steps, which are virtually the same.

Appendix C shows records and style of the Boston Public Library for its branch cataloging, which also illustrates brief/simplified style of cataloging. Stamp to show copies in branches is an interesting feature.

Appendix D is devoted to the classified catalog of Boston University Libraries. In order to visualize related cataloging records, the authority file and the shelf list have been included to supplement the classified and the main catalogs.

Appendix E on brieflisting cataloging represents UCLA's experiments in coping with backlogs of uncataloged materials. Would the attractive title-page cards tempt one to take them out to look at?

Appendix F on synchronized book processing is another experiment. Wayne County Public Library uses PW and BPR catalog entries as a substitute for what CIS plus the cataloger's camera could be! What do you think of a unit catalog card serving also as a book pocket?

Appendix G, the color band card system for nonbook materials in the Montgomery County Public School libraries, reveals the values of cross media interfiled in the dictionary catalog. How fortunate for teachers in this system to find all media together on a subject!

Appendix H represents the visual analysis of National Library of Medicine entries to demonstrate Ruth MacDonald's study of corporate body under successive names. This combined study of entries has not appeared previously in any publication.

INDEX

The index features of the outline are both complemented and supplemented by the index which provides the alphabetic approach. Where collocation is provided in the outline, it is usually not duplicated in the index. Therefore, the index must be used with the outline, and vice versa.

Referrals in the index are of two types—indirect and direct. The indirect access—to page numbers in the outline where subjects are analyzed and inclusive numbers for sample cards, forms, etc. are given—has obvious values. Direct access—to the samples—is made by use of the key symbols for the sections, derived from the outline, followed by numbers for the samples.

By design double entry indexing is minimal. See references are also kept to a minimum to conserve space. See also references are made from general classes of headings to specific types of headings, and from general terms to more specific. Plural terms are generally the pattern. The notes within quotation marks indicate their use on LC catalog cards.

Where numerous samples are located either in one section of the volume or in different sections, the usual plan is to give a sampling of illustrations followed by "etc." at the end of the sections. "Etc." may refer to further samples within the section and/or to samples, which may be found upon search throughout the volume. Widely distributed throughout the volume, also, are samples for some five subdivisions of the outline, such as Catalog cards: descriptive data; analysis; etc., which have the statement, "access through Index."

Since the index is selective, omissions are generally intentional. Names of individual libraries which have contributed samples are listed only in ACKNOWLEDGMENTS. Societies and institutions are not identified separately. The index, however, refers to page numbers of the outline where corporate bodies are treated. For nonbook materials and works of special type, bibliographic and descriptive data are indexed by sections only. These data, specifically indexed under their respective headings, are reserved for monographs and serials. In the Appendices which represent separate studies, all items have not been individually indexed. Details of abbreviation, capitalization, and punctuation (except for brackets and ellipses) are not indexed because they may be found in the cataloging codes.

Because of the character of the outline and the comprehensive nature of the Sampler, the index is not exhaustive. Nuggets are still available upon further search!

ABBREVIATED CITATIONS

American book publishing record. v. 1+ Feb. 1, 1960+ New York,
   Bowker.   BPR

American Library Association. Division of Cataloging and Classification. A. L. A. cataloging rules for author and title entries.
   2d ed., edited by Clara Beetle. Chicago, 1949.   ALA

Cataloging rules of the American Library Association and the Library
   of Congress. Additions and changes, 1949-1958. Washington,
   Library of Congress, 1959.   A&C

Cutter, Charles A. C. A. Cutter's three figure alphabetic-order
   table. Chicopee Falls, Mass., H. R. Huntting Co. [n. d.]   Cutter

Dewey, Melvil. Dewey decimal classification and relative index.
   16th ed. Lake Placid Club, N. Y., Forest Press [1958]   DDC

Publishers' weekly. v. 1+ Jan. 18, 1872+ New York, Bowker.   PW

Sears, Minnie E. List of subject headings; with Suggestions for the
   beginner in subject heading work. 8th ed. by Bertha Margaret
   Frick. New York, Wilson, 1959.   Sears

U. S. Library of Congress. Descriptive Cataloging Division. Rules
   for descriptive cataloging in the Library of Congress. Washington,
   1949.   RDC

---- Subject Cataloging Division. Classification. [Classes A-Z]
   Washington, 1901+   LCC

---- Subject headings used in the dictionary catalogs of the Library
   of Congress [from 1897 through December 1955] 6th ed., edited
   by Marguerite V. Quattlebaum. Washington, 1957.   LCSH

CATALOGING SAMPLER
A COMPARATIVE AND INTERPRETIVE GUIDE

I. Cataloging control records (1-218)

  A. Multiple order forms (1-55)

  B. Printed card orders (56-62)

    1. LC (56-61)
    2. Wilson (62)

  C. Preliminary/interim/temporary records: serials and monographs (63-120) see also I-A

    1. Routing and priority slips: LC (Priorities 1-4, etc.)
    2. Search/decision/process/specifications/work/records: see also I-A
    3. Form cards/slips for corrections, changes, etc. (115-120)

  D. Authority records for names, titles, etc.: variant styles (121-193) see also X-G

    1. Authority file, without references, arranged in alphabetic sequence (121-163)
      a. Personal names
      b. Corporate names
      c. Phrases; title
      d. Form cards (159-163)
      e. References: see II-H
    2. Official catalog: LC, arranged in alphabetic sequence (164-193)
      a. Authority cards
      b. History cards: see II-H
      c. References: see also II-H
      d. Series treatment cards
      e. Arrangement form cards
      f. Filing titles/ corner marks
      g. Other form cards (190-193)
    3. Public catalog, incorporating name and/or title authority information; references traced on main entry: see II; III; IV; V; VIII
    4. Shelf list, incorporating name authority information; references traced for fiction: see XI-A

I.   Cataloging control records (continued)

   E.   Authority records for subjects and references (194-218)

      1.   Subject authority card file, alternative to checking subject heading list as official record
      2.   Case demonstration based on <u>Sears</u>, 8th ed., and <u>LC</u>, 6th ed.: see also VIII-B

CATALOGING CONTROL RECORDS

SHELF 206323

7 pink   AUTHOR

1-8

DEALER

CATALOG 206323

6 yellow   AUTHOR

DEALER

TEMPORARY 206323

5 orange   AUTHOR

ORDER DATE   TITLE

REC'D

FUND

EST. OR LIST PRICE   VOLS.
PLACE   PUBLISHER

BILL DATE

COST

DEPT.   RECOMMENDED BY

DEALER   **FUND SLIP** 206323

4 white   AUTHOR

ORDER DATE   TITLE

REC'D

FUND

EST. OR LIST PRICE   VOLS.   EDITION
PLACE   PUBLISHER   YEAR

BILL DATE

COST

LIQUIDATED

IF BOOK IS NOT AVAILABLE RETURN
3 (verso)   **TO YALE UNIVERSITY LIBRA**
WITH YOUR ANSWER

Underline your answer, or fill in correct information.
1. Complete; discontinued; suspended; not yet published; according
2. Sold; out of print and unavailable; can probably supply in_____
   Has been claimed repeatedly; shall we continue our efforts?_____
3. Please confirm your order.
   Book forms part of series:_____
   Author's correct name is:_____
   Correct title reads:_____
4. Not available separately. Shall we order complete set or volum
5. Costs_____ Pric
   Remarks:_____

DEALER   **REPORT SLIP** 206323

3 green   AUTHOR

ORDER DATE   TITLE

REC'D

FUND   **RETURN THIS SLIP**
WITH BOOK

EST. OR LIST PRICE   VOLS.   EDITION
PLACE   PUBLISHER   YEAR

BILL DATE

COST

DEPT.   **NOTE:** USE THE REVERSE OF THIS SLIP TO REPORT AT ONCE IF UNABLE TO SUPPLY.

DEALER   **ORDER SLIP**

2 white   AUTHOR

ORDER DATE   TITLE

REC'D

FUND

EST. OR LIST PRICE   VOLS.
PLACE   PUBLISHER

BILL DATE

COST

DEPT.   **YALE UNIVERSITY LIBRARY**

DEALER   **ACCESSION FILE** 206323

1 white   AUTHOR

  (No carbon required)

ORDER DATE   TITLE

REC'D

FUND

EST. OR LIST PRICE   VOLS.   EDITION
PLACE   PUBLISHER   YEAR

BILL DATE

COST

DEPT.   RECOMMENDED BY   P.C.

9-12

HARVARD COLLEGE LIBRARY
DEPARTMENT OF RESOURCES AND ACQUISITIONS
CAMBRIDGE 38, MASSACHUSETTS

B- 14442

1 blue: to dealer

ORDERED: SOURCE: FOR:

FUND:

[FO]LLOW INSTRUCTIONS ON REVERSE

1 (verso)   INSTRUCTIONS

INVOICE: Bill in duplicate referring to our **order**
number. Enclose original with shipment
and send copy by airmail.

SHIPPING: RETURN REPORT SLIP inside front cover of
book. Address all shipments and correspondence
to:
Acquisition Division, Harvard College Library
Cambridge 38, Mass.

REPORT: USE REPORT SLIP if order cannot be filled **or**
will be delayed.
Report before sending:
1. Any item which is a reprint or part of
a series if we have not so indicated.
2. Author's name and /or title if different
from that used on our order slip.
4. Juveniles and text books.
5. Any item whose cost exceeds $50.00 unless
we quote price.

HARVARD COLLEGE LIBRARY
DEPARTMENT OF RESOURCES AND ACQUISITIONS
CAMBRIDGE 38, MASSACHUSETTS

B- 14442

2 green: to dealer and returned with book, or
used by dealer as report form

ORDERED: SOURCE: FOR:

RECEIVED: FUND:

RETURN INSIDE FRONT COVER OF BOOK OR REPORT ON REVERSE

If Book Is Not Available Return This Slip To

Acquisition Division
2 (verso)   Harvard College Library
Cambridge 38, Mass.

☐ Sold. Order Cancelled
☐ Out of Print. Searching for 2nd hand copy
☐ Out of Print. Order Cancelled
☐ Not Yet Published. Order on File.   ☐ Not Yet Published-Cancelled
Please confirm order:

☐ Series
☐ Reprint
☐ Author's Correct Name
☐ Juvenile   ☐ Cost
☐ Other

HARVARD COLLEGE LIBRARY
DEPARTMENT OF RESOURCES AND ACQUISITIONS
CAMBRIDGE 38, MASSACHUSETTS

B- 14442

13-15

3 yellow (card stock): for "tub" (combined orders
outstanding and received)
until cards for book in
official catalog

ORDERED: SOURCE: FOR:
RECEIVED: FUND:

HARVARD COLLEGE LIBRARY
DEPARTMENT OF RESOURCES AND ACQUISITIONS
CAMBRIDGE 38, MASSACHUSETTS

B- 14442

4 yellow: for agent file (includes accession
information); with book until cataloged

ORDERED: SOURCE: FOR:
RECEIVED: FUND:

HARVARD COLLEGE LIBRARY
DEPARTMENT OF RESOURCES AND ACQUISITIONS
CAMBRIDGE 38, MASSACHUSETTS

B- 14442

5 white: departmental record and/or personal order
record (potential discard)

ORDERED: SOURCE: FOR:
RECEIVED: FUND:

DO NOT WRITE IN THIS SPACE

Author, Inverted:

Title:

(1 blue: to catalog dept. with publication)

CHECK LEVEL AT PRIMARY USE

FRESH - SOPH.
JUNIOR - SENIOR
MASTERS'
DOCTORS'
RESEARCH

Date of Pub.:
Replacement?:
Is Book Being Held?:
Call No.:

Series:

Place:
Edition:
Sources

Publisher:
No. of Copies:
Price:

No. of Vols.:

Library:
Authorized By:

Fund:
Recommended By:

U of M LIBRARY ORDER REQUEST

SEND TO ORDER DEPT. UNIV. LIB.-REPORT ON ITEMS NOT PURCHASED WILL BE MADE ON REVERSE SIDE.

SEARCHING RECORD

OOF	
OFF	
Dep-Lc	
BIP	
RC	
PW	
CBI	
BNB	
DB	
BIB	
CL-CCL	
ULS-NST	

REPORT: 1-verso

ANOTHER ED.
Another Cop.
ADDED COP.
ADDED VOL.
CALL NO.

☐ IN GENERAL LIBRARY
☐ IN DIV. LIBRARY:
☐ ON ORDER FOR GENERAL LIBRARY
☐ ON ORDER FOR DIV. LIBRARY:
☐ FUNDS EXHAUSTED
☐ DUE ON STANDING ORDER OR EXCHANGE IN
☐ DEALER INFORMED US BOOK WAS SOLD
☐ BOOK REPORTED OUT-OF-PRINT. SHALL WE LIST WITH SECOND HAND DEALER?
☐ WE CANNOT IDENTIFY. DO YOU HAVE MORE INFORMATION?

SEARCHER:
Replacement?:
Is Book Being Held?:
Call No.:

Edition:
Sources

No. of Vols.:
No. of Copies:
Price:

Fund:
Recommended By:

Library:
Authorized By:

(2 pink)

THIS COPY MAY BE RETAINED BY DEPARTMENT INITIATING ORDER REQUEST

Fund:
Recommended By:

Library:
Authorized By:

(3 yellow)

THIS COPY FOR DIVISIONAL LIBRARIAN

16
-
23

ORDER DEPARTMENT
THE UNIVERSITY OF MICHIGAN LIBRARY
ANN ARBOR, MICHIGAN

ORDER NO. 275599
FUND:

DEALER:

CAT. & ITEM:
ORDERED: ☐
EST. PRICE:

DESTINATION:
RECOMMENDED BY:

OUTSTANDING ORDER FILE

1 white

DEALER:

CAT. & ITEM:
ORDERED: ☐

2 yellow

THIS IS A PURCHASE ORDER – SEE OTHER SIDE FOR INSTRUCTIONS

2-verso

INVOICE: BILL IN **DUPLICATE**, REFERRING TO ORDER NUMBER. BILL ITEMS ON SAME FUND ON ONE INVOICE (FUND IS DIRECTLY UNDER ORDER NUMBER ON REVERSE SIDE OF THIS FORM.)

SHIPPING: SEND ACCOMPANYING REPORT SLIP INSIDE FRONT COVER OF BOOK; SHOW FULL ORDER NUMBER ON ALL PACKAGES. ADDRESS SHIPMENTS TO:

ORDER DEPARTMENT
THE UNIVERSITY OF MICHIGAN LIBRARY
ANN ARBOR, MICHIGAN

REPORT: REPORT SLIP IS ENCLOSED FOR YOUR CONVENIENCE IN REPORTING ON ORDERS THAT CAN NOT BE FILLED.

SERIES: IF AN ITEM IS A PART OF A SERIES AND WE HAVE NOT SO INDICATED, PLEASE REPORT ON PINK SLIP BEFORE SENDING.

3 green

RECEIVED:
COST: ☐

ENCUMBRANCE RELEASE SLIP

8-verso

If Book Is Not Available Return This Slip To:
ORDER DEPARTMENT
THE UNIVERSITY OF MICHIGAN LIBRARY
ANN ARBOR, MICHIGAN

□ Sold. Order Cancelled
□ Not Yet Published } Due _____
□ Out of Stock At Publisher
□ Out Of Print, Order Cancelled
□ Please Confirm Order:
  1. Author's correct name is:
  2. Series:
□ Other:

□ Order Cancelled
□ Will Send

9 yellow

9-verso

We have not as yet received the title indicated on the reverse side of this slip. Please report by checking the appropriate box below. If the title has already been sent, please do not duplicate shipment.

□ Shipped on _____ _____ Will send.
□ Not yet published. Due _____
□ Out of print. Cancelling.
□ Out of print. Searching.
□ Out of stock. Will send.
  (Please give approximate date if possible.)
□ Sold. Cancelling.
□ Other:

10 yellow

FUND SLIP

ORDER NO. 275599
FUND:

4 – 7 to catalog dept. with publication (integral part of temporary record process)

24 – 32

4 pink
OFFICIAL CATALOG

5 pink
PUBLIC CATALOG

6 white
LABELING GUIDE

THIS TITLE HAS BEEN

7 blue
ARRIVAL NOTICE – THE UNIVERSITY OF MICHIGAN LIBRARY

DESTINATION:
RECOMMENDED BY:
DEALER:

8 pink
RETURN INSIDE FRONT COVER OF BOOK OR REPORT ON REVERSE

Author				Class No.	Off. Ref. 016
Walford, Arthur John, ed.					
Title				Remarks	Bklist 6-1-60 p.581
Guide to reference materials					
Edition	Publisher	Year	Price	Type	A T S-1
	Library Assoc.	1959	12.15		
Ordered For	From		Date		
Merr	Bowker		9-20-61		

1 white: a) in open order file; b) with book until cards typed; c) with cards until revised

Framingham Town Library (Merriam)

L C No. 59-16733

Date Ordered Oct. 9 1961

2 yellow: a) in open order file; b) in books received file

L C No.

Date Ordered

3 pink: to dealer

Date Ordered

4 blue: to Edgell Library (branch) for a) open order file; b) books received file; c) monthly accessions list (reader interest arrangement)

L C No.

Date Ordered

33-41

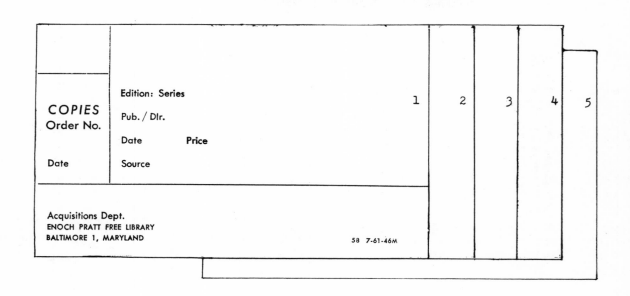

COPIES Order No. Date	Edition: Series Pub. / Dlr. Date Price Source	1	2	3	4	5

Acquisitions Dept.
ENOCH PRATT FREE LIBRARY
BALTIMORE 1, MARYLAND   58 7-61-46M

ENOCH PRATT FREE LIBRARY

THE MULTIPLE ORDER CARD

The Enoch Pratt Free Library uses a multiple order card: an original and four carbons, each of which is a different color.

(1) The first copy (a white slip) is sent to the dealer.

(2) The second copy (a green slip) is retained by the agency (department or branch) ordering the book. If the order card is typed in the Acquisitions Department, the green slip is returned to the originator of the order. For combined orders, the green slip is held in the Book Selection Room or Appropriate Coordinator's office.

(3) The third slip (yellow) is kept in the Acquisitions Department as a record of orders placed. The file of these slips is arranged by our order number and, within order number, alphabetically by author. When the book is received, the yellow slip is pulled and sent to the agency originating the order, thus serving as a notification that the book has arrived. At regular intervals the yellow slips of a certain date remaining in the file are checked, and necessary progress reports are requested from the dealer.

(4) The fourth copy (a pink slip) has various uses. If the book is for the Central Library, the pink slip is clipped to the official order card until the book arrives, then it is placed in the book for forwarding to the Catalog Department. For new titles it is returned to Acquisitions when the book is fully processed and is used to pull the order card from the order file. This carbon also furnishes the Catalog Department with the price of the book which is given on the shelf list card and on the book card.

In the case of a book ordered for a branch, this pink slip is sent to the branch cataloger at the time the order is placed. The branch cataloger inserts this carbon in the Official Catalog as a temporary card (in place of the main entry) during the processing period. Its early receipt also gives the Branch Catalog section an opportunity to get catalog cards prepared, anticipating the arrival of the book.

(5) The official order card (the fifth card copy, bluish in color) is retained in the Acquisitions Department, interfiled alphabetically by author. It remains in the Order File until the book is received (or order cancelled); and, in the case of new titles, it is retained until the book is processed and catalog cards are filed. The order cards for duplicate books are sent through to the Catalog Department with the books. Since they have call numbers, they serve as temporary shelf list cards. The call number on the order card also gives the assistant handling duplicates a quick approach to the card in the shelf list.

The cards are printed four to a strip on "NCR" (no carbon Required) paper. Best results in typing are obtained with the use of an electric typewriter.

2/25/58 (Revised)

SAMPLE COMMERCIAL MULTIPLE COPY BOOK ORDER FORMS
(6/5/5 - PART SETS OF COLORED SLIPS, WITH LC CARD ORDER FORM)

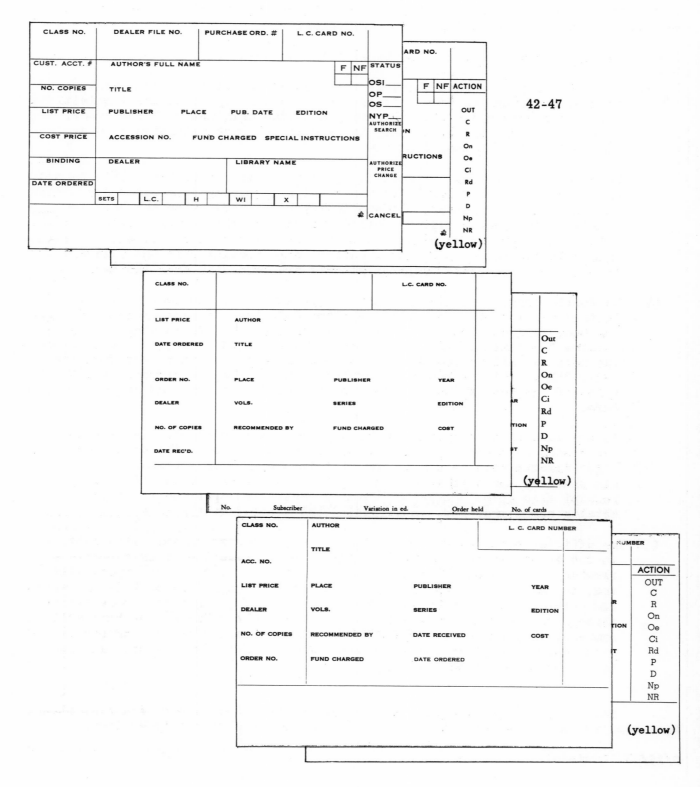

7 orange: for notice to faculty

6 blue: temporary card for catalog

5 pink: for books received file (from order to
         cataloging); for in process file

4 lemon: duplicate of LC card order form; dated;
          awaiting cards

3 yellow: LC card order form	L. C. CARD NUMBER

Action

Out
C
Ci
R
On
Oe
Rd
P
Np

1275   2 white: by dealer (number, date)

1-verso

ORIGINAL ORDER — WELLESLEY COLLEGE LIBRARY

1. MAKE OUT ALL BILLS IN DUPLICATE. QUOTE OUR ORDER NUMBER(S) AND ADDRESS TO WELLESLEY COLLEGE LIBRARY, ACQUISITION DEPARTMENT. WELLESLEY 81, MASS.
2. It is understood that this order is subject to the usual Library discount.
3. Report on items which cannot be sent or which will be delayed.
4. Report before sending on every item which proves to be part of a series or of a society publication, unless our order gives series.
5. Report before supplying on items for which our information differs from your trade information.
6. Report before supplying on price of expensive items if our order does not give price.
7. Always send the latest edition unless otherwise particularly specified.
8. It is understood that unfilled orders are automatically cancelled one year from the date of this order unless otherwise specified or order is renewed.

L. LIB.   a — d   Out — Ci   2 sa + 1

48-55

This is an order from	WELLESLEY COLLEGE LIBRARY WELLESLEY 81, MASS.	L. C. CARD NUMBER
Order No. 1275		
Date Ordered	Author	
Dealer	Title	
	(1 white: to dealer)	
No. of copies		
	Edition: Imprint:	
List Price		
	Series:	
Fund		
	Recommended by:	
PLEASE FOLLOW INSTRUCTIONS ON THE BACK OF THIS SLIP		

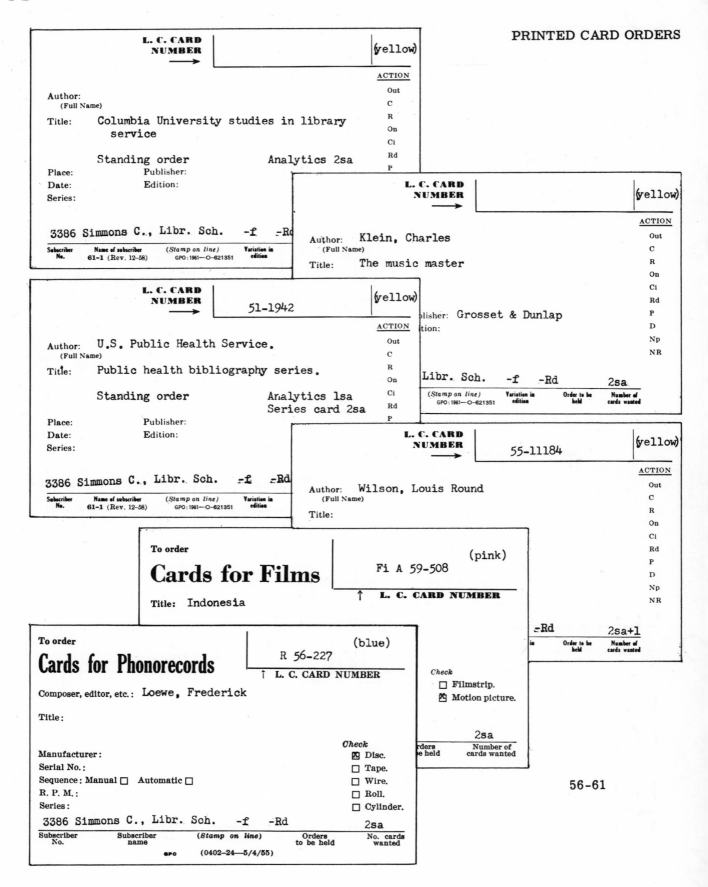

L. C. CARD NUMBER ⟶ (yellow)

ACTION
Out
C
R
On
Ci
Rd
P

Author:
(Full Name)

Title: Columbia University studies in library service

Standing order   Analytics 2sa

Place: Publisher:
Date: Edition:
Series:

3386 Simmons C., Libr. Sch.   -f   -Rd

Subscriber No.	Name of subscriber 61-1 (Rev. 12-58)	(Stamp on line) GPO:1961—O—621351	Variation in edition

L. C. CARD NUMBER ⟶ (yellow)

ACTION
Out
C
R
On
Ci
Rd
P
D
Np
NR

Author: Klein, Charles
(Full Name)

Title: The music master

Publisher: Grosset & Dunlap
Edition:

Libr. Sch.   -f   -Rd   2sa

(Stamp on line) GPO:1961—O—621351	Variation in edition	Order to be held	Number of cards wanted

L. C. CARD NUMBER ⟶ 51-1942 (yellow)

ACTION
Out
C
R
On
Ci
Rd
P

Author: U.S. Public Health Service.
(Full Name)

Title: Public health bibliography series.

Standing order   Analytics 1sa
                        Series card 2sa

Place: Publisher:
Date: Edition:
Series:

3386 Simmons C., Libr. Sch.   -f   -Rd

Subscriber No.	Name of subscriber 61-1 (Rev. 12-58)	(Stamp on line) GPO:1961—O—621351	Variation in edition

L. C. CARD NUMBER ⟶ 55-11184 (yellow)

ACTION
Out
C
R
On
Ci
Rd
P
D
Np
NR

Author: Wilson, Louis Round
(Full Name)

Title:

-Rd   2sa+1

in	Order to be held	Number of cards wanted

To order

Cards for Films

Fi A 59-508   (pink)

↑ **L. C. CARD NUMBER**

Title: Indonesia

Check
☐ Filmstrip.
☒ Motion picture.

          2sa

To order

Cards for Phonorecords

R 56-227   (blue)

↑ **L. C. CARD NUMBER**

Composer, editor, etc.: Loewe, Frederick

Title:

Manufacturer:
Serial No.:
Sequence: Manual ☐   Automatic ☐
R. P. M.:
Series:

Check
☒ Disc.
☐ Tape.
☐ Wire.
☐ Roll.
☐ Cylinder.

3386 Simmons C., Libr. Sch.   -f   -Rd   2sa

Subscriber No.	Subscriber name	(Stamp on line) GPO (0402-24—5/4/55)	Orders to be held	No. cards wanted

56-61

CATALOG CARD ORDER FORM

**FOR PROMPT DELIVERY
PLEASE FILL OUT
PERFORATED MAILING FORM**

SEND CARDS—(CHECK ONE!)
xⓍ WITH subject headings and classi-
    fication numbers at top of cards
Ⓧ WITHOUT

Contents • Merchandise
POSTMASTER: This parcel may be opened for postal inspection if necessary.

FROM
**THE H. W. WILSON CO.
950 University Avenue
New York 52, N. Y.**

(PLEASE PRINT)

62

TO
LIBRARIAN

School of Library Science

Simmons College

Boston 15, Massachusetts

☝ IMPORTANT: PRINT YOUR NAME & ADDRESS BELOW — ALSO! ☝

HOW TO ORDER PRINTED CATALOG CARDS. Enclose 1 coupon for each set ordered plus 1 additional coupon for the entire order.

For example: If you order *10* sets send *11* coupons; for *20* sets send *21* coupons.

List the cards desired in alphabetical order by author and title and consult our checklists when ordering IT WILL BE NECESSARY TO CHARGE 20c FOR EACH SET SUPPLIED IF YOUR ORDER IS NOT IN ALPHABETICAL ARRANGEMENT BY AUTHOR OR IT CONTAINS TITLES NOT LISTED IN OUR CHECKLISTS. Only those titles listed in The H. W. Wilson Checklists are available.

LIST ALPHABETICALLY — BY AUTHOR PLEASE

xx   American Library Association. Subject and title index to short
        stories for children

xx   The best plays of 1959-1960 to include 21 analytics   (4 coupons
        extra)

xx   Forrester, G. Occupational literature. 1958 edition

x   Havighurst, W. The Midwest. 1958 edition

x   Hilton, J. H. R. H.

xx   Lyle, G. R. The administration of the college library. 1961
        edition

ORDERED BY — (PLEASE FILL OUT!)

School of Library Science
NAME
        Simmons College
ADDRESS
        Boston 15, Massachusetts

**COUPONS ENCLOSED
NUMBER OF**

11

PLEASE USE OTHER SIDE FOR ADDITIONAL ORDERS

2-61—360M(292)E.D.

Notice of SERIAL DISCONTINUED

Call no.

Author

Title

Pub. discontinued ☐ Date   Pub. suspended ☐ Date
Subs. discontinued ☐ Date   Transferred to monographs ☐

Route 2 copies Acq. Dept. as follows:
1. Original. To Coll. and Binding Dept. To Catalog Dept. Then return to Acq. Dept. (Serial check list.)
2. Carbon. To Coll. and Binding Dept. To Catalog Dept. Then return to Coll. and Binding Dept.

Merged into with

and continued as

This is no. .... as indicated above.   (verso)

If publication discontinued is discovered by Catalog Dept., send all copies to Acq. Dept. to be routed as above.

Authority

If a change of location of the back file is also involved, use Notice of Serial Change for only, noting discontinuance under "Remarks."

Date of our last issue

INSTRUCTIONS REGARDING LIBRARY HOLDINGS

Keep back file ☐   Discard complete file ☐   Discard current unbound issues only ☐
Keep incomplete file, discarding the following

From Acquisition Dept.   Per   Date

BS-2-8347-5-51-3000

ORDER NO. 5120

DATE

g   gt   pd

AUTHOR

SERIES TITLE

ITEMS REQUESTED

DEALER

Please Address
1 white: to dealer

Baker Library
Harvard University
Graduate School of Business Administration
Boston 63, Mass.

DEALER   *(to simplify checking and checking-in process)

Please Address
2 blue: to dealer and returned*

Baker Library
Harvard University
Graduate School of Business Administration
Boston 63, Mass.

DEALER

Please Address
3 orange: by order number

Baker Library
Harvard University
Graduate School of Business Administration
Boston 63, Mass.

Catalog Entry   Serial ☐   Incomplete Mon. ☐   Mon. Ed. ☐

Location
Cur. unb. iss.

various colors (off-white/blue/yellow,etc.)

Monograph ☐

Mon. Ser.
Class. Sep. ☐

Cat. Dept.
does not
record
Ser. ☐

(verso)

63-69

TEMPORARY ENTRY FROM ACQUISITION DEPT.

Author

Title

First issue added.   Vol.   No.   Date   Short form cataloging ☐
Library keeps complete file ☐   on basis of specific issues as follows: Complete or back file ☐

Full cataloging ☐
Location: Current unb. issues   Latest vol.
Cop. 1
Cop.

Source (VT)   Date

SM-12-50

70   71

SERIAL ☐	
MONOGRAPH EDITION ☐ INCOMPLETE MONOGRAPH ☐	
☐ CHANGE — COMPLETION ☐	

CHANGED TO

Author

Title

Call no.   Holdings

If current unbound issues
Location

Frequency of publication
Publication resumed.   Date   Vol.   No.
Library keeps complete file ☐   on basis of specific issues as follows:

Short form cataloging ☐   Full cataloging ☐
Total number of copies   Complete or
Location   Current unb. issues   Latest vol.   Back file
Cop. 1
Cop.

| Last issue before change.   Date   Vol.   No. |
| First issue after change.   Date   Vol.   No. |
| Authority for publication change |

FORMERLY

Author

Title

Call no.   Holdings

If current unbound issues
Location

Frequency of publication
Publication suspended.   Date   Vol.   No.
Library keeps complete file ☐   on basis of specific issues as follows:

Short form cataloging ☐   Full cataloging ☐
Total number of copies   Complete or
Location   Current unb. issues   Latest vol.   Back file
Cop. 1
Cop.

                          Date
                          From   Dept.

3M—4—52   (over)

REMARKS   (verso)

Send 2 copies (with serial) to Catalog Dept. by way
    of the Coll. and Bind. Dept.

From Catalog Dept. distribute copies as follows:
    1. Original. To Acq. Dept.

    2. Carbon. To Coll. and Bind. Dept. to be sent
       to Circ. Desk and then returned to Catalog
       Dept.

This is no.......................as indicated above.

Baker Library, Harvard University
Graduate School of Business Administration

72

73

S E R I A L

Total no. of copies .... This is decision for cop. ....

SERIES
Do not collect
Analyze series ☐ Do not analyze series ☐
Refer to Catalog Dept. ☐
(If "analyze series" is checked, do not indicate any preliminary shelving for current unbound issues)
Short-form cataloging ☐

ACQUISITION DECISION

ON HAND or DRIFT IN	BACK ISSUES	FUTURE ISSUES
Keep all	☐	☐
last only	☐	☐
2d year or issue	☐	☐
3d	☐	☐
5th	☐	☐
approved issues only	☐	☐
	☐	☐
Discard	☐	☐
Discard if H. C. L. has	☐	☐
if .... has	☐	☐

SEEK

	BACK ISSUES	FUTURE ISSUES
if paid	☐	☐
if free	☐	☐
Do not seek	☐	☐
every year or issue	☐	☐
2d	☐	☐
3d	☐	☐
5th	☐	☐
only if requested	☐	☐
	☐	☐
back issues		
over complete period of time	☐	☐
over partial period of time	☐	☐
earlier than	☐	☐
from		

After...............................get new decision
....

SHELVING DECISION

	Curr. unb. issues	Latest vol. or vols.	Complete or Back file
Baker Room	☐	☐	☐
Current Magazines	☐	☐	☐
Reference	☐	☐	☐
Vertical File	☐	☐	☐
	☐	☐	☐
Kress Room	☐	☐	☐
Collating shelves	☐	☐	☐
Corp. Rec. Div.	☐	☐	☐
Aviation Collection	☐	☐	☐
Vertical File	☐	☐	☐
Reg. loc. for class	☐	☐	☐
	☐	☐	☐
	☐	☐	☐

....
....
....

BINDING DECISION

Cloth ☐   Prefer paper ☐   Minimum preparation ☐

Decision of

Date

(over)

Serial Decision Slip
2–52–5M

(verso) **DATA ON THIS TITLE**

Requested by

Author

Title

Price

Frequency of issue

Additional information

Date

Baker Library, Harvard University
Graduate School of Business
    Administration

SERIAL/JOURNAL/REPORT DECISION SLIP

Title:

The attached material has been received:

☐ Drift — availability of future issues questionable

☐ First number on your order

☐ Sample issue, offered on:
    ☐ subscription
    ☐ exchange
    ☐ free mailing list

☐ Duplicate report. Check below if this is to be cataloged.

☐ This number is one of a series not being completely analyzed.

If this number is to be cataloged, check below.

(to be filled in by S & J)

ORDER AND CLAIM INSTRUCTIONS

☐ Standing order. (Send order form if not already done.)

☐ Each issue to be ordered separately by Div. Library.

☐ Do not claim or back order.

☐ Current year only kept.

PROCESSING INSTRUCTIONS

☐ Detailed cataloging; series to be analyzed and/or record of each number entered in catalog.

☐ Open entry cataloging; catalog cards to read "to date," or have a dash after the recorded date with record of holdings at Serials/Journals.

☐ Do not catalog or keep record of holdings; send each number direct to:_____

☐ Discard this number and future issues.

BINDING INSTRUCTIONS

☐ Regular binding

☐ Special preparation as follows:

(to be filled in by Div. Lib.)

MIT/8/61   (over)

SERIAL/JOURNAL/REPORT DECISION SLIP

Title:

The attached material has been received:

☐ Drift — availability of future issues questionable

☐ First number on your order

☐ Sample issue, offered on:
    ☐ subscription
    ☐ exchange
    ☐ free mailing list

☐ Duplicate report. Check below if this is to be cataloged.

☐ This number is one of a series not being completely analyzed.

If this number is to be cataloged, check below.

(to be filled in by S & J)

REMARKS

carbon copy (buff) duplicate maintained at SERIALS/JOURNALS for follow-up purposes

74-76

ROUTING SLIP (verso)

PLEASE ROUTE THIS MATERIAL TO:

☐ Humanities
☐ Science
☐ Dewey
☐ Rotch
☐ Engineering
☐ Aeronautics
☐ Music
☐ Reference
☐ Other

Use the space below for signature. When signing, specify library and fund on all material to be added to the collection.

Library   Fund

Signature

Date

REMARKS

Indicate your decision on this slip and return with material to

ACQUISITIONS DEPT.

I-C

NEW SERIAL TITLE

☐ Series   ☐ Subseries   ☐ Sub-subseries

Routing   **Cleared**

.... Selection Officer ....

.... For recommendation ....

.... Wanted for the Library .... Not wanted for the Library ....

Keep .... sets .... Review before binding

.... Retain current issues only .... Retain this issue only

Acquire .... Back numbers .... Bound vols. only .... Continuation

.... By purchase .... By exchange or gift

.... Recommendation review shelf, Ser. Rec. Div. ....

.... Subject Cataloging decision shelf ....

.... Sets collected .... Sets monograph

Analyzed .... In full .... In part { .... This part / .... Not this part

Not analyzed ....

.... Descriptive Cataloging decision shelf ....

.... Serials Section, Desc. Cat. Div. for form card ....

.... Slavic Languages Sect., Desc. Cat. Div. for form card ....

.... Cataloging Section, Ser. Rec. Div. ....

.... New Serial Titles Section, Ser. Rec. Div. ....

.... Monthly Checklist of State Publications, E & G Div. ....

.... Monthly Index of Russian Accessions ....

.... Exchange and Gift Division ....

.... Order Division ....

.... Copyright Office—for claiming ....

.... Card Division ....

.... Preliminary Cataloging Section, Desc. Cat. Div. ....

.... Serials Section, Desc. Cat. Div. ....

.... Slavic Languages Sect., Desc. Cat. Div. ....

....

Custody

.... Periodical R. R.   .... Law Library   .... Nat. Lib. of Med.

.... G. P. R. R.   .... Orientalia Div.   .... Dept. of Agr. Lib.

.... Slavic Room   .... Ser. Div. Sample File   ....

Searched in ☐ SR ☐ OC ☐ FF ☐ ULS

Author not established ☐ SR ☐ OC ☐ ULS

Author established ☐ SR ☐ OC ☐ ULS

67–4 (Rev. 11/61)   SERIAL RECORD DIVISION / LIBRARY OF CONGRESS   U.S. GOVERNMENT PRINTING OFFICE

ANALYZED IN FULL

( ) SERIES   ( ) SUBSERIES
_____ SET
                    ( ) Search for call no.

___1. Selection Officer

___2. Monthly Checklist of State Publ.

___3. Monthly List of Russian Accessions

___4. East European Accessions List

___5. Card Division

___6. Preliminary Cataloging Section

___7. Slavic Languages Section

___8. Subject Cat. (General Series Unit)
       (Note: Sent here only second or
       further sets, when received
       separately, of collected sets,
       add to cards.)

___9. Labeling. (Note: Send here bound
       issues of second or further sets
       if collected, in progress.)

___10. Service Division. (Note: Send
        here unbound issues of second
        or further sets if collected, in
        progress.) Check Service Div. below

Monographs_____sets   Call nos. on slip
Collected_____sets   if any set collected
(check appropriate box
below)
( ) In progress
    For unbound, check
    Service Division below
    For bound, add call no.
    and set no. in book
( ) Add to cards
    Call no. on slip, not in book

Service Division

___GPRR

___Periodicals

0174-1 (rev 10/56)

Library of Congress
Serial Record Division

ANALYZED IN PART

( ) SERIES   ( ) SUBSERIES
_____ SET
                    ( ) Search for call no.

___1. Subject Cataloging Decision Shelf

This Part
( ) Analyzed   ( ) Not Analyzed

___2. Selection Officer

___3. Monthly Checklist of State Publications

___4. Monthly Index of Russian Accessions

___5. East European Accessions Index

___6. Card Division

___7. Prel. Cat. Sect. (Send here all 1st sets
       to be anal. & all 2nd and further sets
       treated as Mono., Anal. nos. only)

___8. Slavic Cat. Sect. (Send here all 1st sets
       to be anal. & all 2nd and further sets
       treated as Mono., Anal. nos. only)

___9. Subj. Cat. (General Serials Unit)
       (Send here only 2nd or further sets
       when rec'd. separately and when
       class. as coll. set, Add to cards)

Collected_____sets (Call no. on slip in all
                           cases)

   ( ) In progress
       Unbound Check Service Div. below
       Bound Add call no. & set no. in book

   ( ) Add to cards
       Call no. on slip only

Monographs____sets (Anal nos. only)

Service Division
___GPRR
___Periodicals

(Send unbound 2nd & all further sets when
 rec'd. separately and class. as coll.
 sets, in progress to Service Division

(Send bound 2nd & all further sets when
 rec'd. separately & class. as coll. sets,
 in progress to Labeling)

67-2 (rev. 8/61)
Library of Congress   (green)
Serial Record Division

RUSH

80–81

For.....................................

To.......................................

Authorized by.........................

	Initials	Date	Time
Slip inserted			

(orange)

Basic slip for PRIORITY 1

Additional instructions
may be handwritten on
any priority slip.

RUSH

FOR CARDS

Authorized by *Chief, Card Div.*

	Initials	Date	Time
Slip inserted			

Used when Card Division
has many card orders.

LC 0402–72 (8/57) **(orange)** GPO

HASTEN

For......Rare Books........
          Division

....

Report of searcher.......................

Date......JUL 8 1959.......

Call No.

Title not in

   Official Cat.

   Process File

Another edition

   Card no.

   In process

Author not established

   No conflict

Author established as

Basic slip for PRIORITY 2

3/57)

LC 0173–31 (11/58) **(pink)** GPO

COPYRIGHT HASTEN

82–84

HASTEN

For—LATIN AMERICAN STUDIES
HANDBOOK OF
HISPANIC FOUNDATION

To..........*anr*..........

PRIORITY 2

LC 0126–11 (8/58)

	INITIALS	DATE	TIME
Slip inserted			
Searched			
Temporary card made			
Descriptive Cataloger			
Reviser			
Subject Cataloger			
Reviser			
Shelflister			
Decimal Classifier			
Labeled and delivered			

L.C. 15-1
LC 0126–11 (8/58) **(pink)** GPO

85-87

(0174-3—7/22/53)   (blue)

SPECIAL ATTENTION

☐ Assign to
☐ If other than 1st copy
assign to

Authorized by

☐ For examination by

Completed by

Report of searcher..........................

Date.......................................

Call No.

Title not in

   Official Cat.

   Process File

Another edition

   Card No.

   In process

Author not established

   No conflict

Author established as

Only slip used in PRIORITY
   3; inserted in reference
   works to insure handling
   before others in PRIORITY
   3 (regular cataloging)

GPO

PRIORITY
4

REPORT OF SEARCHER

Initials................. Rev...................
Date............................ 19...... USE

This work is NOT in
   Off. Cat............ Proc. File..........
L. C. has:
   Original.............................ed.
   Translation: Eng........................
      Fr........... Ger.......... Sp...........
   other.......................................

Classified in:

Author NOT established..............

Unadapted cooperative authority
   card for another title..................
   Form:

Name problem........................
Author ESTABLISHED as:

x-ref............ Pseud. x-ref...........
(yellow)

MUS   HISP   MAP   LAW

4   (verso)

Copy in process..................................
   Location:

Other ed. in:

   Off. Cat............ Proc. File..........

   Classified in:

   Variations:

      Title—

      Ed. statement—

      Place of publication—

      Publisher—

      Imprint date—

      Collation—

      Series—

Open entry in process...................
   Location:

Discard..
Keep   2   3   4   all..................
Keep if lacking in set...................
L. C. has required no...................

LIBRARY OF CONGRESS
DESCRIPTIVE CATALOGING
DIVISION

64-16   (Rev. 4/61)   (yellow)   GPO

88

(buff)

LIMITED
CATALOGING
(red)

(red) Subject Cat. Div.

(red) Descriptive Cat. Div.

CATEGORIES

1b*

Material of secondary im-
portance

2a

Groups of material

2b

Minor materials

Cf. LC Departmental & di-
visional manuals, no.
13. Processing Dept.
Office, 1950, p. 15.

Cf. Cataloging rules of
ALA and LC: additions
and changes, 1959, p.
69-76.

89

REPORT OF SEARCHER
NEW WORK

Initials................ Rev.............

Date................. 19...... USE

BOOK not in L. C...............

   Location:

Searched in

   Off. Cat............. Proc. File........

Main entry NOT established:

   Name problem.......................

Main entry ESTABLISHED as:

x-ref............ Pseud. x-ref............

LC 64–29 (rev. 12/61) (yellow) GPO

90

REPORT OF SEARCHER
ADDED VOLUME

Initials...............................

Date............................. 19........

Covered by card no.

Call no.

Open entry in process..................
   Location:

Send to DESC. CAT. DIV. if:

   Add to cards........................
      (Cataloger's initials)

   Dash entry........................
      (Cataloger's initials)

   Open to include?..................
      (Cataloger's initials)

Send to SER. REC. DIV. if:

   In progress (serial).......................

   Form card.......................

Send for SHELFLISTING if:

   Kept up to date by
   replacement or
   revised volumes.........................

   Contents added
   to shelflist only.........................

Main entry:

LC 64–2 (rev. 12/61)   GPO

REPORT OF SEARCHER
EDITION

Initials.................... Rev..................

Date.................... 19...... USE

L. C. has:

   Original ....ed.

   Translation: Eng.......................

      Fr.......... Ger.......... Sp..........

   other............................

Card no. for most similar edition in L. C.:

....

Other edition in

   Off. Cat............. Proc. File..........

Variations:

   Title—

   Ed. statement—

   Place of publication—

   Publisher—

   Imprint date—

   Collation—

   Series—

Main entry ESTABLISHED as:

x-ref.......... Pseud. x-ref..........

Discard....................

Keep....................

LC 64–48 (rev. 12/61) (green) GPO

REPORT OF SEARCHER
DUPLICATE

MUS HISP MAP LAW

Initials....................................

Date.................................. 19........

In Off. Cat..............................

   Call no.

Official card needs attention of descriptive cataloger

....

In process.............................

   Location:

Main entry removed

   to adapt...........................
               (Cataloger's initials)

Main entry for works classified in Law:

Discard.....................................

Keep   2   3   4   all

Keep if lacking in set....................

L. C. has required no....................

LC 64–32 (rev. 12/61) (pink) GPO

REPORT OF SEARCHER
CARD TO BE ADAPTED

Initials....................................

Date.. 19........

First word of entry:

....

Card no..

No printed card, but an un-adapted cooperative authority card for this title from:

   Library....................................

   Cataloger....................................

   Date..

LC 64–31 (rev. 12/61) (blue) GPO

94

SIMMONS COLLEGE LIBRARY
AUTHOR
TITLE
DATE RECEIVED
ACCESSIONED
L.C. CARD
CATALOGUED
REVISED
PLATED
POCKETED
DATE DUE SLIP
MARKED
OTHER DIRECTIONS
ROUTE TO

PROCESS SLIP   (orange)

95

Date

MONOGRAPH

Requested   by...
....
....

When cataloged send to..
....
    Faculty Club Shelf..

Catalog for...
    General use...
    Reference...
    Reserve...
    Archives..
    Transportation..
    Kress...
    Pamphlet Vol..

Send uncataloged to...
    RR Vertical File..
    Transportation..
    Aldrich Room..
    Personnel File..
    Corporation Records...
    Archives..
    ....

Not wanted..
    Send to...
    ....

Decision of...

Baker Library, Harvard University
Graduate School of Business
        Administration

96

97

SEARCHING REPORT

Heading (Check **one** box only)

☐ Identification guaranteed
☐ Identification **not** guaranteed
☐ Conflict
☐ No conflict

Other headings searched and Comments:

Edition Report

Latest Widener edition

Year

Call number

☐ Only edition

☐ No edition
☐ Earlier ⎫
☐ Later   ⎬ editions in Widener
☐ 5 or more ⎭

☐ Earlier ⎫
☐ Later   ⎬ editions in K

Author number (unless shown above)

(Cataloging searching with book in
hand)

HARVARD COLLEGE LIBRARY

DUPLICATE

☐ * Widener (Give call number)

☐ * K
☐ * Lamont
☐ * Houghton
☐ * Dept. Lib. (Give location)

* Omit this information if card is pulled

Edition Report

☐ Only edition
☐ No edition in Widener
☐ 5 or more editions in Widener

Later editions:
☐ Widener
☐ K
☐ Other libraries (Give location)

Latest Widener edition (unless shown above)

Year

Call number:

Comments

(pink)   HARVARD COLLEGE LIBRARY

I-C

98   99

(recto fold)   (verso fold)

CLASSED INDIVIDUALLY   Heading:

ANALYZE   Author cd. only
                                  cat. LC   Other
Series:
 Added entry   x ref. in LC from:
                                            cat.

 No added entry   H or I call no.:

 Enters under: Alternate heading:

 Adds to subseries   cat. LC   Other

                                  Added information:

(YALE)   No. P2

Heading as given, or   Subjects:

Call no.   Added entries: x refs.:

26

100

```
┌─────────────────────────────────────────────────────────────────────┐
│                          (inside fold)                                │
│                                                                       │
│    2d copy for:        Copy 2                                         │
│                                                                       │
│        OTHER COPIES IN YALE            OTHER EDITIONS IN YALE          │
│                                                                       │
│    Heading:                        Heading:                           │
│                                                                       │
│                                                                       │
│    Location:                       Location:                          │
│                                                                       │
│        AOS        L & B                AOS        L & B               │
│        Art        Med.                 Art        Med.                │
│        Div.       YCAL                 Div.       YCAL                │
│        Law        YCGL                 Law        YCGL                │
│           Other:                          Other:                      │
│                                                                       │
│                                                                       │
│    LC card in cat.                 LC                                 │
│                                                                       │
│                                    Date of 1st or nearest edition     │
│                                                                       │
│                                                                       │
│  H                                                                    │
│  e                                                                    │
│  a                                                                    │
│  d                                                                    │
│  i                                                                    │
│  n                                                                    │
│  g                                                                    │
│                S                                                      │
│  a             u                                                      │
│  s             b                                                      │
│                j                                                      │
│  g             e                                                      │
│  i             c                                                      │
│  v             t                                                      │
│  e             s                                                      │
│  n             :                                                      │
│  ,      ┌──────────┐  A                                              │
│         │          │  d                                              │
│  o      │          │  d                                              │
│  r      │          │  e         x        N                          │
│         │          │  d                  o                          │
│  C      │          │            r        t                          │
│  a      │          │  e         e        e                          │
│  l      │          │  n         f        s                          │
│  l      │          │  t         s        :                          │
│         │          │  r         :                                   │
│  n      │          │  i                                             │
│  o      │          │  e                          No. P2             │
│  .      │          │  s                                             │
│         └──────────┘  :                                             │
└─────────────────────────────────────────────────────────────────────┘
```

(yellow)

SET A
no shelf
OFFICIAL

STAMP

Public
Div1
Eds

MAIN E.
Est.
X Not est.

```
891.806
B515v
v.21

      Striedter, Jurij.
          Der Schelmenroman in Russland; ein
      Beitrag zur Geschichte des russischen
      Romans vor Gogol'. Berlin, In Kommis-
      sion bei O.Harrassowitz,Wiesbaden, 1961.
          296 p. (Berlin. Freie Universität.
      Osteuropa-Institut. Veröffentlichungen
      der Abteilung für Slavische Sprachen und
      Literaturen, Bd.21)

                              4sa + a
          Series.
          (Copy slip prepared as an author-title order
              for LC cards.)
                                            TYPING GUIDE
UNIV. OF MICHIGAN LIBRARIES
      UL 152
```

101
-
102

103-108

(Temporary fanfold in
catalog dept.)

UNIV. OF MICHIGAN LIBRARIES	PUBLIC CATALOG
UNIV. OF MICHIGAN LIBRARIES	OFFICIAL CATALOG
310 MICHIGAN U. a, c-e -Rd	CARDS WANTED
UNIV. OF MICHIGAN LIBRARIES	SHELF-LIST
UNIV. OF MICHIGAN LIBRARIES	LABELING GUIDE
UNIV. OF MICHIGAN LIBRARIES	DIVISIONAL LIBRARY COPY

MIU SEARCH SLIP.

1. MONOGRAPHS (INCL.ANALS)   (yellow)

Author: Striedter,Jurij

	yes	no	
Official			Holdings in Official
Div.	✓		New title
Dep.	✓		Added vol.
Auth.cd.			Added copy
Conflict			Another ed.
			Title changed
			Copy for new location

Series (Unnumbered):
Used   Not used
New   Use   Do not use

2. SERIALS.   NUMBERED SERIES.

Entry:

	yes	no	
Official			First no.rec'd.
Div.			Copy for new location
C.L.			Class set ✓
C.C.L.			Class sep.
Dep.			Extracted set
Auth.cd.			Open entry anal.
			Anal O. Anal ✓
			Do not anal.

Series (Numbered):
Used ✓
Not used

Do not use; do not record

NEW
Use

Do not use

Do not use; do not record

Class.sep.hldgs.in Div.

Added vols.

3. TYPE OF CARD:

LC	LCPC	NC	IU	NJP	AUTH.-TITLE	OTHER
					✓	

MiU SEARCH SLIP.   109-111   (verso/yellow)

(Searching performed for an English translation
of a German work, two editions of which are
in our collections.)

1. MONOGRAPHS (INCL.ANALS)   (yellow)

Author: Gröber,Heinrich,1880-1949.

	yes	no		
Official			Holdings in Official	
Div.			New title	Added vol.
Dep.				Added copy
Auth.cd.			Another ed.	
Conflict			Title changed	
			Copy for new location	

Series (Unnumbered):

Used   Not used
New   Use   Do not use

2. SERIALS.   NUMBERED SERIES.

Entry:

	yes	no	
			First no.rec'd.
Official			Copy for new location
Div.			
C.L.			Class set
C.C.L.			Class sep
Dep.			
Auth.cd.			
			Extracted set
			Open entry anal.

Series (Numbered):

Used   Anal O.   Anal

Not used   Do not anal.

Do not use; do not record

NEW
Use
Do not use

Do not use; do not record

Class.sep.hldgs.in Div.

3. TYPE OF CARD:

LC	LCPC	NC	IU	NJP	AUTH.-TITLE	OTHER
✓						

4. CALL NUMBERS.   TRACINGS.

(For all eds. in library being searched, as well as
earliest & latest eds. anywhere)

GL

QC   Die Grundgesetze der Wärmeleitung und des
321   Wärmenbergangen ... Berlin, J.S.Springer, 1921.
.G87

East
Engin.
QC   ... Berlin, Springer, 1955.
321   1.Heat--Transmission.   I.Erk,Sigmund,1895-   joint
.G87   author.   II.Grigull,Ulrich,ed.
1955

5. SECONDARY ENTRIES.   PARTS OF CORPORATE NAMES.

	yes	no		yes	no		yes	no
Official			Official			Official		
Div.			Div.			Div.		
Dep.			Dep.			Dep.		
C.L.			C.L.			C.L.		
C.C.L.			C.C.L.			C.C.L.		
Auth.cd.			Auth.cd.			Auth.cd.		
Conflict			Conflict			Conflict		

6. MISCELLANEOUS NOTES.

(manila proof sheet)

QC
320
.G86   Gröber, Heinrich, 1880-1949.
1961   Fundamentals of heat transfer [by] H. Gröber [and] S.
Erk. 3d ed., rev. by Ulrich Grigull. Translated by Jerzy
R. Moszynski. New York, McGraw-Hill, 1961.

527 p. illus. 24 cm. (McGraw-Hill series in mechanical engineering.)

Includes bibliography.

1. Heat—Transmission.   I. Erk, Sigmund, 1895-   joint
author.

QC320.G86   1961   ◯   536.2   60-53219 ‡
       [15]

Library of Congress

(verso
top
left:)

RD.2-23-62
87-268639

Added
vols.

…hed by:

112

113

(verso/yellow)

RA
960
.A52
no.M41

American Hospital Association.
    Manual of hospital planning procedures.
    Chicago ₍1959₎
    72 p.   illus.   (Its ₍Publication, M41-59)

    1.Hospitals—Construction. I.Title: Hospital
planning procedures.
(Copy slip for standard original cataloging; slip
    ready to be typed on multilith master)

114

M1U SEARCH SLIP.   (Search slip shows searching for the monograph,
                         and also for the monograph as an item in
                         an analyzed series, classed as a set.)   (yellow)

1. MONOGRAPHS (INCL.ANALS)

Author: American Hospital Association.

	yes	no
Official		
Div.		
Dep.		
Auth.cd.		
Conflict		

Holdings in Official   New title   Added vol.   Added copy
Another ed.   Title changed   Copy for new location

Series (Unnumbered):
Used   Not used
New   Use   Do not use

2. SERIALS.   NUMBERED SERIES.

Entry:

	yes	no
Official		
Div.		
C.L.		
C.C.L.		
Dep.		
Auth.cd.		

First no.rec'd.   Copy for new location   Class set   Class sep.

Extracted set   Open entry anal.   Anal O.   Anal   Do not anal.

Series (Numbered):
Used   Not used
Do not use; do not record

NEW
Use
Do not use
Do not use; do not record
Class.sep.hldgs.in Div.

Added vols.

3. TYPE OF CARD:

LC	LCPC	NC	IU	NJP	AUTH.-TITLE	OTHER

118

To...

We have received your note in regard to the catalog entry for

According to the current policy of the Library of Congress, this information has been recorded for the present in the Official Catalog only. Thank you for supplying it.

Descriptive Cataloging Division
Library of Congress

119

CARD NUMBER_____

CORRECTION HAS BEEN MADE. SEE OFFICIAL MAIN CARD BEFORE REPRINTING.

NAME_____ DATE_____

TO BE USED FOR TWO CURRENT SERIES OF CARDS

120

ADD-TO-CARDS   MH

Pull full set and return to _____

Change to agree with OC card:

☑ Full set □ PC main card
□ Call number
□ Imprint date □ Series card
□ Volume statement □ Contents Book
□ Series note
□ Contents note
□ Other notes
□ Other (specify):

Typing □ 1 for K Other (see over)
(yellow)

115

To Card Preparation Section
Catalog Maintenance Division

Add dates
Change heading as on cards herewith
Change heading to agree with tracing I, II, III, IV
Type cross references
Cancel this card
Stamp headings
Add filing title
Add to contents
Send references to Public Catalogs
Other:

Make corrections in:
Official Catalog
Main Catalog
Annex Catalog

From
Date
0165-9 (Rev. 6/56)   GPO

116

TO CARD DIVISION
REPRINT UNIT

To be reprinted revised _____ (Card number)

_____ (First word of heading)

_____ (Name)

(Date forwarded)

Check (√) □ DESCRIPTIVE CATALOGING DIVISION
Division □ SUBJECT CATALOGING DIVISION

61-108 (8/60)   16-76047-1   GPO

117

(green)

TO CARD DIVISION
REPRINT UNIT

PLEASE CANCEL _____ (Card Number)

_____ (First Word of Heading)

COVERED BY _____ (Card number)

_____ (Cataloger's Name)

_____ (Date)

AUTHORITY FILE

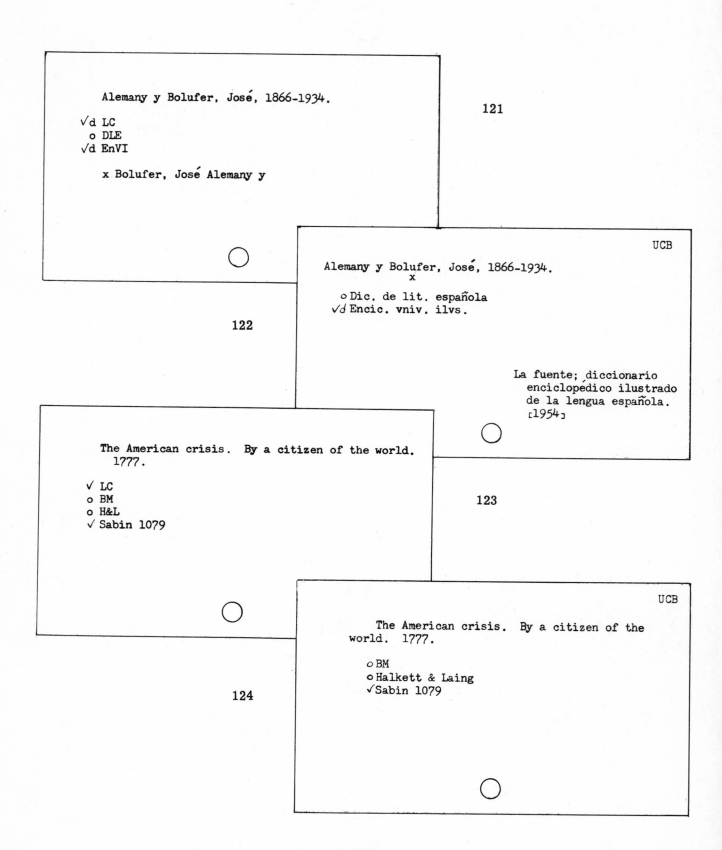

Alemany y Bolufer, José, 1866-1934.

√d LC
 o DLE
√d EnVI

x Bolufer, José Alemany y

121

122

UCB

Alemany y Bolufer, José, 1866-1934.
                    x
 o Dic. de lit. española
√d Encic. vniv. ilvs.

La fuente; diccionario
enciclopédico ilustrado
de la lengua española.
[1954]

123

The American crisis. By a citizen of the world.
   1777.

√ LC
o BM
o H&L
√ Sabin 1079

124

UCB

The American crisis. By a citizen of the
world. 1777.

o BM
o Halkett & Laing
√ Sabin 1079

American Library Association. Cataloging and
    Classification Section.

✓LC
✓ALA Bulletin Dec. 1957 (established Jan. 1, 1957)
✓ALA Bulletin Dec. 1960 (established July 1, 1957)

    History card
  x American Library Association. Resources and
      Technical Services Division. Cataloging and
      Classification Section
 xx American Library Association. Division of
      Cataloging and Classification

125

American Library Association. Division of Cata-
    loging and Classification.

✓ LC

 gx ALA
 gx Chicago. American Library Association
 xx American Library Association. Cataloging and
     Classification Section
  x American Library Association. Catalog Section

126

Arnold, Benedict, 1741-1801.

✓d USC 1928
✓d DAB

127

Arnold, Benedict, 1741-1801.

  ✓d USC, 1928
  ✓d DAB

UCB

      subj anal in: Bradford,
        Gamaliel. Damaged souls.
        1931[c1923]

128

Basilius, Saint, the Great, Abp. of Caesarea,
    330 (ca.)-379.

√d CBI 1949-52 (Basil the Great ...)
√d LC
√d Bu (St. Basil ... Doctor of the Church, Patriarch
    of Eastern Monks ... b. 329)

    x Basil, Saint, the Great, Abp. of Caesarea
    x Basil the Great, Saint

129

Beeding, Francis, pseud.

√LC (Francis Beeding, pseud. of John Leslie Palmer
    and Hilary Aidan St. George Saunders)
√Web (Beeding, Francis, pseudonym; see John Leslie
    Palmer ... collaborator with Hilary Aidan
    St. George Saunders under joint pseudonym
    Francis Beeding)

    x Palmer, John Leslie, 1885-1944.
    x Saunders, Hilary Aidan St. George, 1898-1951.

130

131

Beeding, Francis, pseud.
    Pseud. of John Leslie Palmer and Hilary
    St. George Saunders
                                    x
√CBI, 1943-48
√Halkett & Laing

UCB

La maison du Dr Edwardes
    (Spellbound) [1948]

Bochow, Martin

√ LC (Full name: Theodor Martin Bochow)
o Br
o W ist W
o IWW

    x Bochow, Theodor Martin
    x ** Krieg dem Hunger!

132

133

NLM

British Medical Association

   Founded 1832 as Provincial Medical and
Surgical Association.
   Name changed 1856 to British Medical
Association.

   x British Medical Association. Spa
      Practitioners Group Committee
   x British Medical Association. Public
      Relations Dept.
   x British Medical Association. Shropshire
      Ethical Branch

                                    (over)

134

√ Book cat.
√ LC

                           ... Toronto meeting,
                           1906

135

A citizen of the world.
   The American crisis. 1777.

√ LC
o BM
o H&L
√ Sabin 1079

UCB

A citizen of the world

   o BM
   o Halkett & Laing
   √ Sabin 1079

136

137

Dolores, Sister.

√   NUC (Secular name: Marie Elisabeth Letterhouse)
o RoCa
√d Com Ctr, Boston. Sisters of the Blessed Sacra-
      ment (Sister Mary Dolores, 1880-1953)

   x Letterhouse, Marie Elisabeth, 1880-1953

            added entry: The American
               crisis. 1777.

Doolittle, Hilda, 1886-1961.

√d CBI 1957-58 (H. D.); 1961 (d. 1961)
√d LC (Aldington, Mrs. Hilda (Doolittle)
√d NUC 1958 (b. 1886)
√d ColE (pseud. H. D. ... 1913 ... m. Richard
    Aldington ... later divorced)

  x Aldington, Hilda (Doolittle)
  x D., H. Tribute to Freud

138

Eliot, George, pseud., i.e. Marian Evans, after-
    wards Cross, 1819-1880.

√d CBI 1961 (pseud. of Mary Ann (Evans) Cross)
√d KuBr (Mary Ann Evans Cross ... born Mary Ann (or
    Marian) Evans)
√d NUC

  x Eliot, George, pseud. of Mary Ann (Evans) Cross
  x Evans, Marian
  x Evans, Mary Ann
  x Cross, Marian (Evans)

139

UCB

Haydn, Joseph, 1732-1809.
    ⌞Mass, C major (1773?)⌟
    Full name: Franz Joseph Haydn
                 x
  x Haydn, Joseph, 1732-1809. St. Cecilia's mass.
  x St. Cecilia's mass. Haydn, Joseph, 1732-1809.

√√d Grove

              Missa Sanctae Caeciliae.
              ⌞c1951⌟

140

Horatius Flaccus, Quintus

√ LC P-PA (65-8 B. C.)
√ OCD (Horace, 65-8 B. C.)

  x Horace

141

Maurois, André, 1885-

√d IWW 1951 (pseud. of André Herzog)
√d OFL (... name originally Émile Herzog ...)
√d NUC (Name originally: Émile Salomon Wilhelm
    Herzog)

   x Herzog, Émile Salomon Wilhelm
   x Herzog, André, pseud.

142

NLM

Miyazaki, Saburō

宮崎 三郎

  ○ Complete cat. of Jap. pub. 1952
  ○ 会員氏名簿 1942

    Yakurigaku. 1948

143

Petersham, Maud (Fuller) 1890-

√ CBI 1928-32
√d LC (Full name: Mrs. Maud Sylvia (Fuller) Peter-
    sham)
√d WWAmA (b. 1889)
√d WWAmW 1958/59 (b. 1889; Mrs. Miska Petersham)

   x Petersham, Mrs. Miska

144

COL

Petersham, Maud (Fuller) 1890-
  illus. Lamb, C. Tales from Shakespeare. [c1932]

√d C.B.I. 1928-32; 1957-58
√d Who's who of Amer. women 1958/59 (b. 1889)
√d Who's who in Amer. art (b. 1889)

145

37

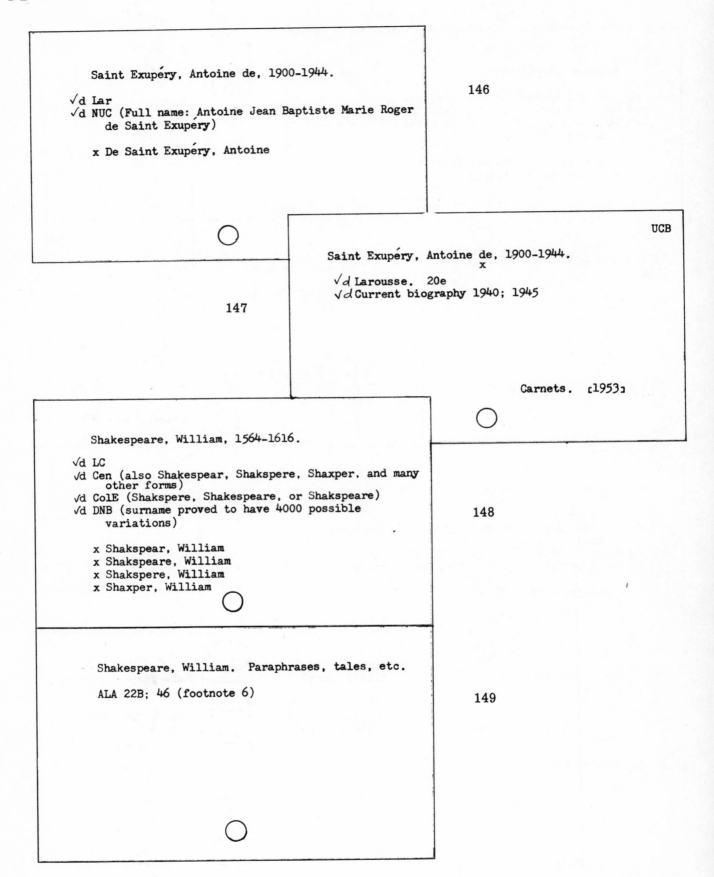

Saint Exupéry, Antoine de, 1900-1944.

√d Lar
√d NUC (Full name: Antoine Jean Baptiste Marie Roger
de Saint Exupéry)

x De Saint Exupéry, Antoine

146

UCB

Saint Exupéry, Antoine de, 1900-1944.
x

√d Larousse. 20e
√d Current biography 1940; 1945

147

Carnets. ₁1953₃

Shakespeare, William, 1564-1616.

√d LC
√d Cen (also Shakespear, Shakspere, Shaxper, and many
other forms)
√d ColE (Shakspere, Shakespeare, or Shakspeare)
√d DNB (surname proved to have 4000 possible
variations)

x Shakspear, William
x Shakspeare, William
x Shakspere, William
x Shaxper, William

148

Shakespeare, William. Paraphrases, tales, etc.

ALA 22B; 46 (footnote 6)

149

Simmons College, Boston.

✓ CBI 1943-48; 1959
✓ NUC 1959

  x Boston. Simmons College

150

    ◯

151

      SIMMONS COLLEGE, BOSTON.
Mark, Kenneth Lamartine, 1947-1958.
   Delayed by fire. 1945.

  x Boston. Simmons College

  CBI 1943; 1959
  NUC 1959

    ◯

152

Virginia. Civil War Commission.

✓ USLCMoC 1961
✓ NUC 1961

  x Civil War Commission of Virginia

    ◯

153

United Nations Educational, Scientific, and
   Cultural Organization.

✓ UNY 1960
✓ CBI 1961

  x UNESCO
  x Paris. United Nations Educational, Scientific,
    and Cultural Organization

    ◯

154

U.S. Congress. House. Committee on the Judiciary.

✓ LC
o USG
✓ CongD

  gx Congress
  gx U.S. House of Representatives
  gx House of Representatives of the U.S. Congress
   x Judiciary Committee of U.S. House

    ◯

Wellington, Dorothy Violet (Ashton) Wellesley,
  duchess of, 1889-1956.

✓ LC (Wellesley, Dorothy (Ashton) lady)
✓d ChCEL (Wellesley, Dorothy Violet, Lady Gerald,
    b. 1889)
✓ NUC
✓d WW 1962 (Wellington, 7th duke of, Gerald Wellesley
    m. Dorothy Violet (d. 1956) dau. of late Robert
    Ashton, Croughton, Cheshire, and late Countess
    Scarborough)
✓ BNB 1955 (Wellesley, Dorothy, Duchess of Welling-
    ton)
⬡ (Continued on next card)

155

Wellington, Dorothy Violet (Ashton) Wellesley,
  duchess of, 1889-1956. (Card 2)

x Wellesley, Dorothy Violet (Ashton) duchess of
    Wellington
x Wellesley, Lady Gerald

156

⬡

COL

Wellington, Dorothy Violet (Ashton) Wellesley, duchess
  of, 1889-1956.
  Early light. 1955.

✓   L.C. (Wellesley, D ---- (A ----) lady)
✓d Chambers cyc. of Eng. lit. (Wellesley, D ----
      V ----, Lady Gerald, b. 1889)
✓✓ N.U.C.
✓d W.W. (1962) (W ----, 7th duke of, Gerald Wellesley
      m. D ---- V ---- (d. 1956) dau. of late Robert
      Ashton, Croughton, Cheshire, and late Countess
      Scarborough)
⬡ (Continued on next card)

157

Wellington, Dorothy Violet (Ashton) Wellesley, duchess
  of, 1889-1956. (Card 2)

✓ B.N.B. (1955) (Wellesley, D ----, Duchess of W ----)

    (s) Wellesley, Dorothy Violet (Ashton) duchess
        of Wellington
    (s) Wellesley, Lady Gerald

158

⬡

AUTHORITY
FORM CARDS

AUTHORITIES

159

160

REFERENCES

See ref. from | See also ref. from

Authorities:

Work cataloged:

161-
162

Name

Book

Authorities: Refer from

163

American college and university series.

Classified as a collection
✓ Classified as monographs
✓ Analyzed in full
Analyzed in part
Not analyzed
Analytics supplied by an outside library
Form of series note: ' [American college and
university series. v.1]

(blue)   ◯ BR 7 Mar 47

164

165

American Library Association. Cataloging
and Classification Section.
✗ x American Library Association. Resources and Technical Services Division.
Cataloging and Classification Section
✗ x (see also) American Library Association.
Division of Cataloging and Classification
✓ ALA bulletin, Dec. 1957. p. 862: The Resources and Technical Services Division ... established on January 1, 1957 ... combined
the former Division of Cataloging and (Over)

EMP 9Jun58   ◯ made for subdivision

Classification ... the former Board on Acquisition of Library Materials ... and
the former Serials Round Table. p. 863:
Sections ... Cataloging and Classification Section.

166

Avila Lozada, Ricardo.
   †x
   †x Avila, Ricardo
✓✓ Work cat.: Ricardo Avila Lozada. p. [1] padres:
Ricardo Avila Flores y Esther Lozada de
Avila. Cover: R. Avila.

No conflict

167

                Autocomposición.
        sh 4apr57 LJ   ◯ 1956.
(0165-7—12/7/53)
   (yellow)

Bacon, Robert Sargent.

√√ Work cat.

No conflict

168

Resistance to extinction of a learned fear drive
... ₁1955₃

0165—No. 7—(12/7/53)
(yellow)

JEH 28 Nov 56

169

Burns, Robert, 1759–1796   *Arrangement* ▼

Works, by date of publication, followed by translations alphabetically
   by language.
Selected works, arranged like Works.
Poems, arranged like Works.
Correspondence, arranged like Works.

Individual works and other titles, alphabetically by title.
   Under each title the arrangement is as follows:
      1. Editions in the original language, by date.
      2. Translations, by language and date.
      3. Related works; e. g. adaptations.
      4. Works about the publication.
Secondary entries, representing works edited or translated by this
   author or works to which he contributed in some other manner.
Subject entries for works   about this author or his
   writings.

BJ214   √×De officiis. Ger.
C6D44

Cicero, Marcus Tullius.
      Vom rechten Handeln; eingeleitet und neu übers. von Karl
   Bücher. Zürich, Artemis-Verlag ₁1953₃
      217 p. 18 cm. (Die Bibliothek der alten Welt. Römische Reihe)
   Translation of De officiis.

170

      1. Ethics.   I. Title.

BJ214.C6D44   54–18258 rev

Library of Congress   ₁r56b⅜₃   OCAT

171

Cicero, Marcus Tullius.
   Vom rechten Handeln
   see his
   De officiis.

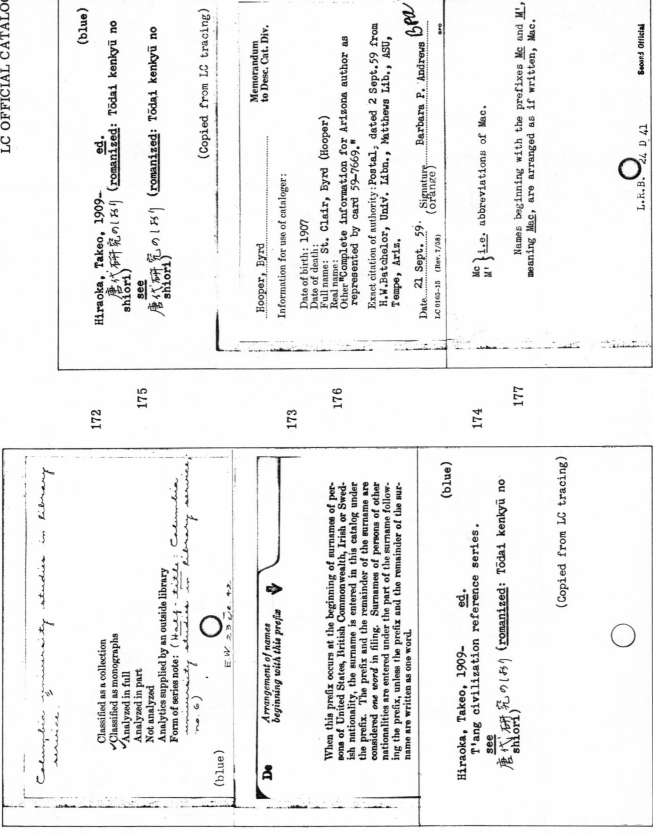

175

Hiraoka, Takeo, 1909- ed. (romanized: Tōdai kenkyū no shiori)
唐代研究のしおり)
see
唐代研究のしおり (romanized: Tōdai kenkyū no shiori)

(Copied from LC tracing)

(blue)

176

Memorandum
to Desc. Cat. Div.

Hooper, Byrd

Information for use of cataloger:

Date of birth: 1907
Date of death:
Full name: St. Clair, Byrd (Hooper)
Real name:
Other"Complete information for Arizona author as represented by card 59-7669."

Exact citation of authority:Postal, dated 2 Sept.59 from H.W.Batchelor, Univ. Libn., Matthews Lib., ASU, Tempe, Ariz.

Date. 21 Sept. 59. Signature. Barbara P. Andrews
LC 0105-15 (Rev. 7/58)

(orange)

177

Mc } i.e. abbreviations of Mac.
M'

Names beginning with the prefixes Mc and M', meaning Mac, are arranged as if written, Mac.

L.R.B. 24 D 41

Second Official

172

Columbia university studies in library science

Classified as a collection
✓Classified as monographs
Analyzed in full
Analyzed in part
Not analyzed
Analytics supplied by an outside library
Form of series note: (Half-title: Columbia university studies in library science, no.6).

E.W. 23 Ju. 42.

(blue)

173

De

Arrangement of names beginning with this prefix

When this prefix occurs at the beginning of surnames of persons of United States, British Commonwealth, Irish or Swedish nationality, the surname is entered in this catalog under the prefix. The prefix and the remainder of the surname are considered one word in filing. Surnames of persons of other nationalities are entered under the part of the surname following the prefix, unless the prefix and the remainder of the surname are written as one word.

174

Hiraoka, Takeo, 1909- ed.
T'ang civilization reference series.
see
唐代研究のしおり (romanized: Tōdai kenkyū no shiori)

(Copied from LC tracing)

(blue)

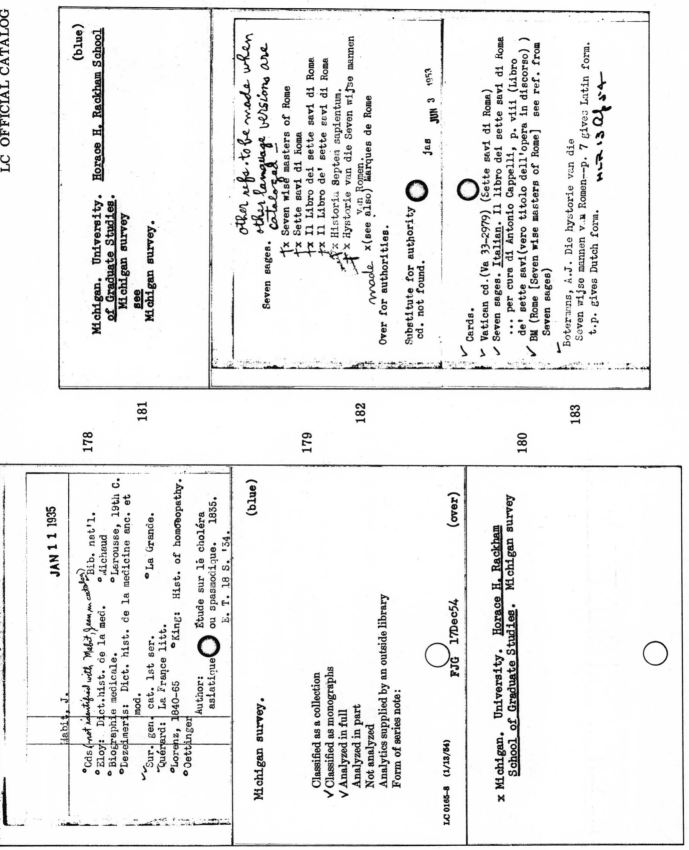

181

Michigan. University. Horace H. Rackham School (blue)
of Graduate Studies.
Michigan survey
see
Michigan survey.

182

Seven sages.

Other refs. to be made when
other language versions are
catalogued.

+x Seven wise masters of Rome
+x Sette savi di Roma
x Il Libro dei sette savi di Rome.
x Il Libro de' sette savi di Rome
x Historia Septem sapientum.
x Hystorie van die Seven wijse mannen
van Romen.
made x(see also) Marques de Rome

Over for authorities.

Substitute for authority
cd. not found.

jas   JUN 3 1953

183

Cards.
Vatican cd. (Va 33-2979) (Sette savi di Roma)
Seven sages. Italian. Il libro dei sette savi di Rome
... per cura di Antonio Cappelli, p. viii (Libro
de' sette savi (vero titolo dell'opera in discorso))
BM (Rome [Seven wise masters of Rome]   see ref. from
Seven sages)

Botermans, A.J. Die hystorie van die
Seven wijse mannen van Romen--p. 7 gives Latin form.
t.p. gives Dutch form.

178

Mabit, J.   JAN 1 1 1935

Cds (not identified with Mabit, Jean, m cataloger) Bib. nat'l.
Eloy: Dict.hist. de la méd.   Michaud
Biographie medicale.   Larousse, 19th C.
Dezeimeris: Dict. hist. de la medicine anc. et
                              mod.
                              La Grande.
Sur. gen. cat. 1st ser.
Quérard: La France litt.
Lorenz, 1840-65   King: Hist. of homoeopathy.
Oettinger

Author: Étude sur le choléra
asiatique   ou spasmodique. 1835.
             E. T. 18 S. '34.

179

Michigan survey.   (blue)

Classified as a collection
✓ Classified as monographs
✓ Analyzed in full
  Analyzed in part
  Not analyzed
  Analytics supplied by an outside library
  Form of series note:

FJG 17Dec54   (over)

LC 0165-8 (1/13/54)

180

x Michigan. University. Horace H. Rackham
School of Graduate Studies. Michigan survey

45

187

Von	*Arrangement of names beginning with this prefix*

When this prefix occurs at the beginning of surnames of persons of United States, British Commonwealth or Irish nationality, the surname is entered in this catalog under the prefix. The prefix and the remainder of the surname are considered *one word* in filing. Surnames of persons of other nationalities are entered under the part of the surname following the prefix, unless the prefix and the remainder of the surname are written as one word.

188

Von Braun, Wernher, von 1912–

  Braun, Wernher von

x† Braun, Wernher von.

✓ Work cat.: Prof. Dr. Wernher von Braun.

✓d © appl. A 113615 for his The Mars project. 1953. RL 18 nn 54

No conflict

189

  Das Marsprojekt. 1952.

(Over)

FW6SI553

✓d CBI, 1953/54 = Von Braun, Wernher; incl. x-ref. from Braun, Wernher von.; Jan.–July 1956 = Von Braun, Wernher, with no x-ref. from Braun.

✓d Biogr. Index, 1955/56 = Von Braun, Wernher, with x-ref. from Braun, Wernher von.

✓d WWA, 1958/59 = Von Braun, Wernher, with no x-ref. from Braun. *natur-alized U.S.S.*

IG 9 Ny 58

SL

184

唐代研究のしおり (romanized: Tōdai kenkyū no shiori)　　　　(blue)

 Classified as a collection
✓Classified as monographs
✓Analyzed in full
 Analyzed in part
 Not analyzed
 Analytics supplied by an outside library
 Form of series note:

185

made for:
Hiraoka, Takeo:
Tōdai no koyomi. 1954.

188

Hiraoka, Takeo, 1909– ed.
唐代研究のしおり (romanized: Tōdai kenkyū no shiori)

x Hiraoka, Takeo, 1909– ed.
 T'ang civilization reference series.

x T'ang civilization reference series.

186

T'ang civilization reference series. (blue)
 see
唐代研究のしおり (romanized: Tōdai kenkyū no shiori)

189

(Copied from LC tracing)

LC FORM CARDS

OFFICIAL CATALOG MEMO

190

CARD OUT

Entry:...
....
....
....

Imprint date... Card number...........................

Call number...

Purpose of removal..

Date.. Name..

LW 14/54 (rev. 4/61)   (green) GPO

191

192

....   **Memorandum to Desc. Cat. Div.**

Information for use of cataloger:

    Date of birth:
    Date of death:
    Full name:
    Real name:
    Other

    Exact citation of authority:

Date........................... Signature...

LC 0165–15 (Rev. 7/58)   (orange) GPO

193

    Classified as a collection
    Classified as monographs
    Analyzed in full
    Analyzed in part
    Not analyzed
    Analytics supplied by an outside library
    Form of series note:

LC 0165–8 (1/13/54)   (blue)

SUBJECT AUTHORITY CARD FILE

194

Addresses
    see

    and general subjects with the subdivision
Addresses and essays, e.g. Library science -
Addresses and essays

Sears:8:59

195

Bibliography
    see also
Library science

xx Library science

Sears:8:59

196

Business libraries

 x Libraries, Business
xx Libraries

Sears:8:59

197

Directories
    Use for works about directories and for
       bibliographies of directories

    see also names of countries, cities, etc. with
the subdivision Directories (e.g. U. S. - Directories; Boston - Directories); classes of institutions with the subdivision Directories (e.g. Libraries - Directories); and classes of persons
with the subdivision Directories (e.g. Librarians
- Directories)

Sears:8:59

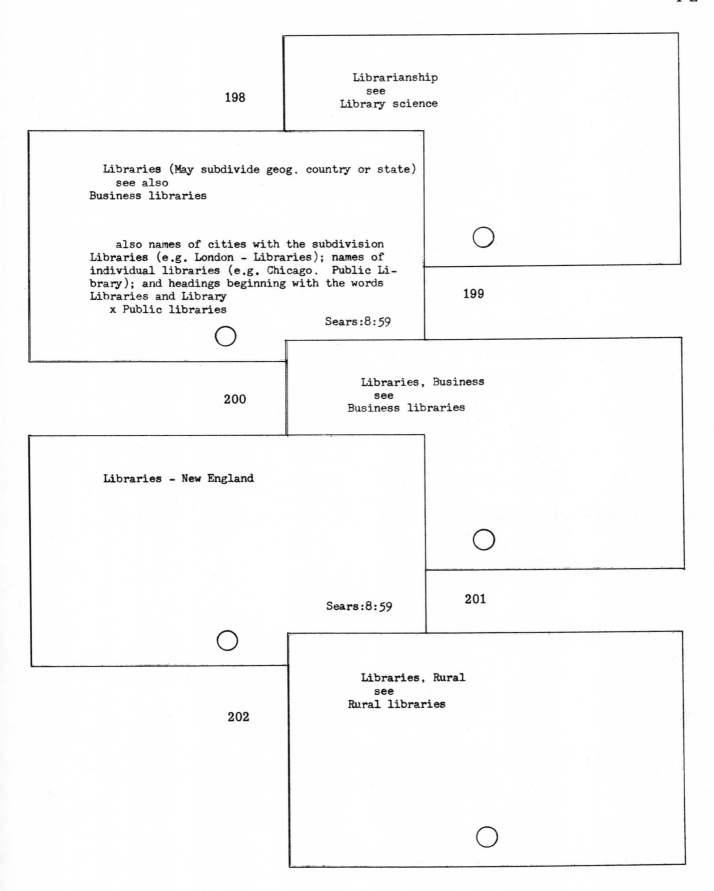

198

Librarianship
see
Library science

199

Libraries (May subdivide geog. country or state)
see also
Business libraries

also names of cities with the subdivision
Libraries (e.g. London - Libraries); names of
individual libraries (e.g. Chicago. Public Library); and headings beginning with the words
Libraries and Library
x Public libraries

Sears:8:59

200

Libraries, Business
see
Business libraries

201

Libraries - New England

Sears:8:59

202

Libraries, Rural
see
Rural libraries

203

Library science
    Use for general works on the organization and
       administration of libraries. Works about
       services offered by libraries to patrons are
       entered under Library service
    see also
Bibliography
Library service
Library surveys
    also headings beginning with the words Librar-
ies and Library
   x Librarianship
   xx Bibliography   Sears:8:59
   gxx Libraries

204

Library science - Addresses and essays

Sears:8:59

205

Library service
  see note under Library science

  xx Library science
  gxx Libraries   Sears:8:59

206

Library surveys

  x Surveys, Library
  xx Library science
              Sears:8:59

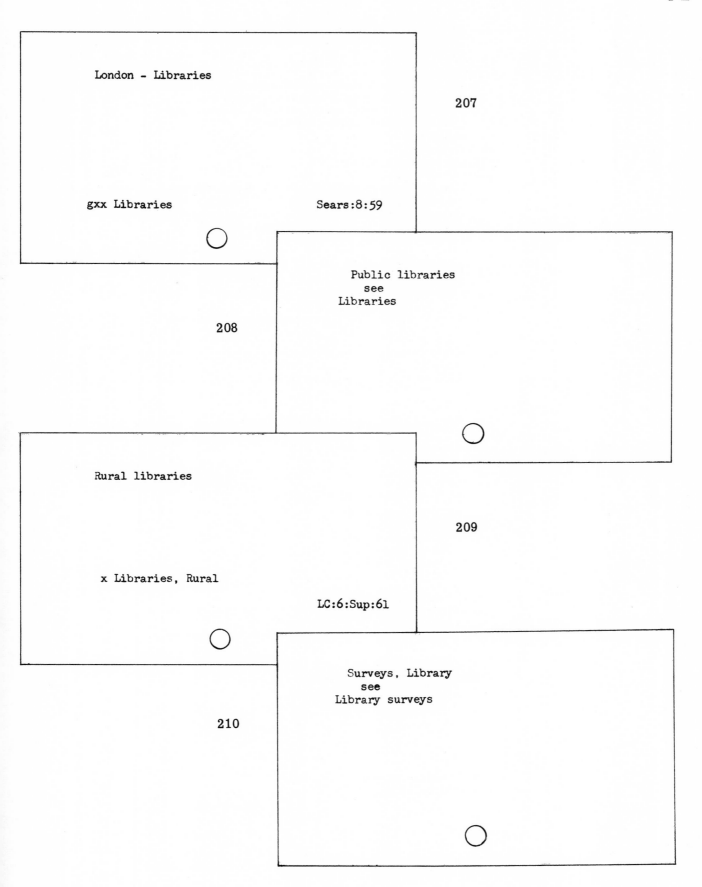

London - Libraries

207

gxx Libraries   Sears:8:59

208

Public libraries
see
Libraries

Rural libraries

209

x Libraries, Rural

LC:6:Sup:61

210

Surveys, Library
see
Library surveys

SUBJECT AUTHORITY CARD FILE

211

Church music (Indirect)

Here are entered works on church music and on
    sacred vocal music in general. Sacred vocal
    compositions are entered under the heading
    Sacred vocal music and headings referred to
    under that heading.

Subdivided, when desirable, by denomination as
    well as by locality, e.g. 1. Church music -
    Church of England. 2. Church music - England.

(Continued on next card)

212

Church music (Indirect)   (Card 2)

sa Music in churches

    x Music, Religious
    x Music, Sacred
    x Religious music
    x Sacred music
    xx Music in churches

213

Church music - Hesse - Mainz

214

Music, Religious
see
Church music

215

Music, Sacred
see
Church music

Music in churches

Here are entered discussions as to the desira-
bility, etc. of having music in the church.

sa Church music

xx Church music

216

217

Religious music
see
Church music

218

Sacred music
see
Church music

II.

II. The dictionary card catalog: demonstration: A-E (1-115)

A. Catalog cards: LC unit card with sets prepared for catalog (1-8)

1. Monograph (1-4)
2. Serial: periodical (5-8)

B. Catalog cards: typed sets: comparative styles (9-58)

1. Monographs (9-45)
   a. Personal author main entries with tracing on recto or verso (9-31)
   b. Corporate main entry and subject heading with tracing on recto or verso (32-37)
   c. Title main entry with tracing on verso (38-44)
   d. Monograph set: LC unit card (45)
2. Serials (46-58)
   a. Corporate main entry (closed) with tracing on verso for references and secondary entries (46-53)
   b. Title main entry (open) with tracing on verso for references and secondary entries: skeleton cards (54-58)

C. Catalog cards: LC compared with Wilson (59-102)

1. Monographs: full sets vs. unit cards (59-75, 98-102)
2. Serials: full sets vs. unit cards (76-97)

D. Alanar standard catalog cards (103-109)

E. LC cards tailored to work: variant styles (110-115)

F. Catalog cards: entries in the catalog: analysis: access through Index

1. Main entries
   a. Names
      (1) Personal
      (2) Corporate
   b. Titles
      (1) Monograph and serial
      (2) Anonymous work
      (3) Conventionalized/uniform heading
2. Secondary entries
   a. Subject headings
      (1) Names: personal and corporate
      (2) Geographic names: nonjurisdictional
      (3) Topics
      (4) Form
      (5) Subdivisions

II. The dictionary card catalog (continued)

    F. 2. b. Added entries
          (1) Names
             (a) Joint author, collaborator
             (b) Editor
             (c) Compiler
             (d) Translator
             (e) Illustrator
             (f) General added/secondary
          (2) Titles: common/nondistinctive vs. striking/distinctive
             (a) Alternative, cover, subtitle, etc.
             (b) Partial, shortened
             (c) Multiple
             (d) Transliterated/romanized
             (e) Author and title
             (f) Title vs. subject
          (3) Series: see also II; V
          (4) Analytical entries: see VI
      3. Tracing of secondary entries

    G. Catalog cards: descriptive data: analysis: access through Index

      1. Monographs
        a. Headings
        b. Body of the entry: statements for
          (1) Title
          (2) Author
          (3) Edition
          (4) Imprint
             (a) Place
             (b) Publisher
             (c) Date(s)
        c. Collation
          (1) Pagination, volumes, etc.
          (2) Illustrative matter
          (3) Size
        d. Notes: conventional: order and style
          (1) Series: conventional location on card
          (2) At head of title
          (3) Bound with
          (4) Sequel
          (5) Thesis; Inaug.-Diss.; etc.
          (6) Contents; Partial contents; Bibliography
          (7) Title transliterated; Title romanized
          (8) Full, Real, Secular name; Name originally, etc.
        e. Notes: informal
          (1) Identification
          (2) Physical description
          (3) Authorship
          (4) Bibliographic history
          (5) Other

II. The dictionary card catalog (continued)

    G. 2. Serials
        a. Headings: title vs. corporate entry
        b. Body of the entry: statements for
            (1) Title
            (2) Author
            (3) Holdings
            (4) Edition
            (5) Imprint: place, publisher
        c. Collation
            (1) Volumes, numbers, etc.
            (2) Illustrative matter
            (3) Size
        d. Notes
            (1) Frequency
            (2) Report year
            (3) Duration of publication
            (4) Suspension of publication
            (5) Numbering
            (6) Connection with preceding publications
            (7) Organ
            (8) Variations in title
            (9) Variations in author's name; changes in authorship
            (10) Issuing bodies
            (11) Edition
            (12) Variations in imprint
            (13) Titles absorbed; mergers, unions, etc.
            (14) "No more published?"
            (15) Contents
        e. Supplements: see IV-F
        f. Indexes: see II-B; IV-B

    H. Catalog cards: history, reference, form, etc. (116-241)

      1. History cards (116-126)
        a. Sample (116)
        b. LC (117-126)
        c. Corporate body under successive names: NLM study: see App. H
      2. References (see, see also) general, specific, explanatory, in alphabetic
          sequence (127-221) see also I-D; X-G
        a. Monographs
            (1) Names: personal and corporate
            (2) Pseudonyms
            (3) Author and title
            (4) Titles: changed, conventional, etc.
            (5) Anonymous works
            (6) Uniform heading/traditional title: anonymous classics,
                 Bible, etc.
            (7) Series
        b. Serials: corporate entries; titles
        c. Miscellaneous: LC printed references (222-233)
      3. Subject references: see VIII-B
      4. Form cards: LC and others (234-241)

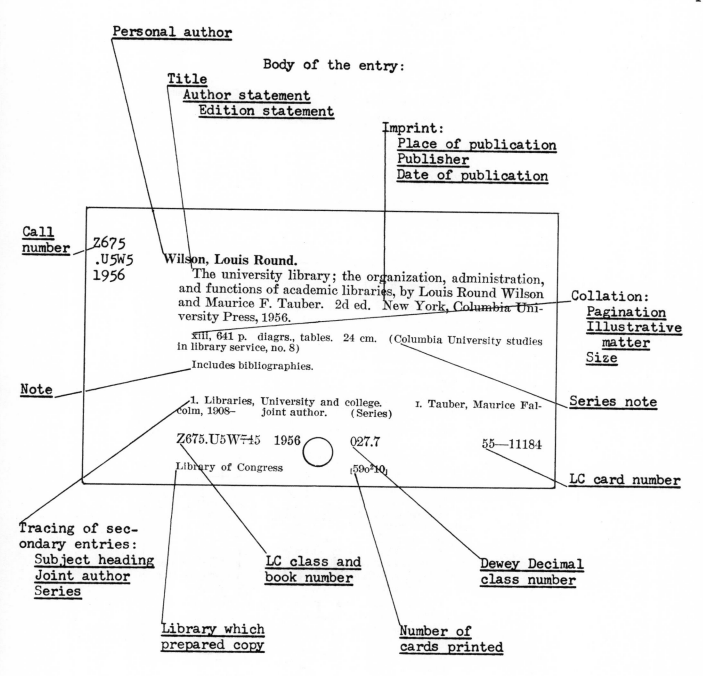

Personal author

Body of the entry:

Title
Author statement
Edition statement

Imprint:
Place of publication
Publisher
Date of publication

Call number
Z675
.U5W5
1956

Wilson, Louis Round.
    The university library; the organization, administration, and functions of academic libraries, by Louis Round Wilson and Maurice F. Tauber. 2d ed. New York, Columbia University Press, 1956.

    xiii, 641 p. diagrs., tables. 24 cm. (Columbia University studies in library service, no. 8)

    Includes bibliographies.

Note

    1. Libraries, University and college. colm, 1908– joint author. (Series)

    I. Tauber, Maurice Fal-

Z675.U5W745 1956   027.7

Library of Congress   [59o²10]

55—11184

Collation:
Pagination
Illustrative matter
Size

Series note

LC card number

Tracing of secondary entries:
Subject heading
Joint author
Series

LC class and book number

Dewey Decimal class number

Library which prepared copy

Number of cards printed

2

```
Z675
.U5W5
1956
```
LIBRARIES, UNIVERSITY AND COLLEGE
Wilson, Louis Round.
    The university library; the organization, administration, and functions of academic libraries, by Louis Round Wilson and Maurice F. Tauber. 2d ed. New York, Columbia University Press, 1956.

    xiii, 641 p. diagrs., tables. 24 cm. (Columbia University studies in library service, no. 8)

    Includes bibliographies.

    1. Libraries, University and college.   I. Tauber, Maurice Falcolm, 1908–   joint author.   (Series)

Z675.U5W745 1956   027.7   55—11184

Library of Congress   [590²10]

3

```
Z675
.U5W5
1956
```
Tauber, Maurice Falcolm, 1908–   joint
    author
Wilson, Louis Round.
    The university library; the organization, administration, and functions of academic libraries, by Louis Round Wilson and Maurice F. Tauber. 2d ed. New York, Columbia University Press, 1956.

    xiii, 641 p. diagrs., tables. 24 cm. (Columbia University studies in library service, no. 8)

    Includes bibliographies.

    1. Libraries, University and college.   I. Tauber, Maurice Falcolm, 1908–   joint author.   (Series)

Z675.U5W745 1956   027.7   55—11184

Library of Congress   [590²10]

4

```
Z675
.U5W5
1956
```
Columbia University studies in library
    service, no.8
Wilson, Louis Round.
    The university library; the organization, administration, and functions of academic libraries, by Louis Round Wilson and Maurice F. Tauber. 2d ed. New York, Columbia University Press, 1956.

    xiii, 641 p. diagrs., tables. 24 cm. (Columbia University studies in library service, no. 8)

    Includes bibliographies.

    1. Libraries, University and college.   I. Tauber, Maurice Falcolm, 1908–   joint author.   (Series)

Z675.U5W745 1956   027.7   55—11184

Library of Congress   [590²10]

HC101
.N45
LIBRARY HAS: Challenge, the magazine of economic affairs.

VOL. OR NO.	PERIOD COVERED		VOL. OR NO.	PERIOD COVERED	
7	1958/59				
8	1959/60				
9	1960/61				

HOW ISSUED: monthly

5

6

SET OF LC CARDS

HC101
.N45

Challenge; the magazine of economic affairs. v. 1–
Oct. 1952–
[New York]

v. illus. 20 cm. monthly.

Title varies: Oct. 1952–Jan. 1954, Challenge magazine.
Published by the Institute of Economic Affairs, New York University.
Supersedes the Institute's Popular economics
(Oct. 1950–June 1952)

1. U. S.—Econ. condit.—Period.   I. New York University. Institute of Economic Affairs.
x Challenge magazine

HC101.N533   330.5   55–36370
⁴⁵

Library of Congress   [3]

7

HC101
.N45

U. S. - ECONOMIC CONDITIONS - PERIODICALS
Challenge; the magazine of economic affairs. v. 1–
Oct. 1952–
[New York]

v. illus. 20 cm. monthly.

Title varies: Oct. 1952–Jan. 1954, Challenge magazine.
Published by the Institute of Economic Affairs, New York University.
Supersedes the Institute's Popular economics
(Oct. 1950–June 1952)

1. U. S.—Econ. condit.—Period.   I. New York University. Institute of Economic Affairs.

8

HC101
.N45

New York University. Institute of Economic
Affairs.
Challenge; the magazine of economic affairs. v. 1–
Oct. 1952–
[New York]

v. illus. 20 cm. monthly.

Title varies: Oct. 1952–Jan. 1954, Challenge magazine.
Published by the Institute of Economic Affairs, New York University.
Supersedes the Institute's Popular economics
(Oct. 1950–June 1952)

1. U. S.—Econ. condit.—Period.   I. New York University. Institute of Economic Affairs.

HC101.N533   330.5   55–36370

Library of Congress   [3]

```
 R
PC4625
.A4    Alemany y Bolufer, José, 1866-1934.
1954     La fuente; diccionario enciclopédico ilustrado
       de la lengua española, publicado bajo la dirección
       de José Alemany y Bolufer y de varios reputados
       especialistas.  Esta obra contiene todas las voces
       de uso corriente y numerosos americanismos,
       tecnicismos, neologismos y artículos enciclopédicos
       de biografía ... etc., etc. 80,000 artículos, 1,300
       grabados, 600 retratos, 100 cuadros.  Barcelona,
       R. Sopena [1954]
         viii,1431p.  illus.,ports.  19cm.
         "Despues del Diccionario enciclopedico ilustrado
                 ◯ (Continued on next card)
```

9

```
 R
PC4625
.A4    Alemany y Bolufer, José, 1866-1934.  La fuente ...
1954     [1954]  (Card 2)

       publicamos ahora éste, con el mismo carácter ...
       pero limitando, hasta donde nos ha sido posible
       su extensión y su precio" - Prólogo.


         1. Spanish language - Dictionaries  2. Encyclo-
       pedias and dictionaries, Spanish  I. Title
                      ◯
```

10

```
 R                 SPANISH LANGUAGE - DICTIONARIES
PC4625   Alemany y Bolufer, José, 1866-1934.  La fuente ...
         .A4              (Card 2)
```

```
 R         SPANISH LANGUAGE - DICTIONARIES
PC4625
.A4    Alemany y Bolufer, José, 186
1954     La fuente; diccionario enci
       de la lengua española, publi
       de José Alemany y Bolufer y d
```

```
 R          ENCYCLOPEDIAS AND DICTIONARIES, SPANISH
PC4625   Alemany y Bolufer, José, 1866-1934.  La fuente ...
         .A4              [1954]  (Card 2)

              hora éste, con el mismo carácter ...
              do, hasta donde nos ha sido posible
```

```
 R         ENCYCLOPEDIAS AND DICTIONARIES, SPANISH
PC4625
.A4    Alemany y Bolufer, José, 1866-1934.
1954     La fuente; diccionario encicl
       de la lengua española, publicad
       de José Alemany y Bolufer y de
       especialistas.  Esta obra conti
```

```
 R         La fuente
PC4625   Alemany y Bolufer, José, 1866-1934.  La fuente ...
.A4              (Card 2)
         [1954]

              ahora éste, con el mismo carácter ...
              ando, hasta donde nos ha sido posible
              ion y su precio" - Prologo.
```

```
 R         La fuente
PC4625
.A4    Alemany y Bolufer, José, 1866-1934.
1954     La fuente; diccionario enciclopédico ilustrado
       de la lengua española, publicado bajo la dirección
       de José Alemany y Bolufer y de varios reputados
       especialistas.  Esta obra contiene todas las voces
       de uso corriente y numerosos americanismos,
       tecnicismos, neologismos y artículos enciclopédicos
       de biografia ... etc., etc. 80,000 artículos, 1,300
       grabados, 600 retratos, 100 cuadros.  Barcelona,
       R. Sopena [1954]
         viii,1431p.  illus.,ports.  19cm.
         "Despues del Diccionario enciclopedico ilustrado
                 ◯ (Continued on next card)
```

11-16

60

940.549
C153m   Caniff, Milton Arthur, 1907-
     Male call [comic strip] The first complete
collection of the uninhibited adventures of every
GI's dream girl - Miss Lace. New, enl. ed. New
York, Grosset & Dunlap [1959]
     unpaged. illus. 19 x 26cm.

17

     1. World War, 1939-1945 - Humor, caricatures,
etc. 2. U. S. Army - Military life I. Title

○

940.549   WORLD WAR, 1939-1945 - HUMOR, CARICATURES, ETC.   18
C153m   Caniff, Milton Arthur, 1907-
     Male call [comic strip] The first complete

940.549   U. S. ARMY - MILITARY LIFE   19
C153m   Caniff, Milton Arthur, 1907-
     Male call [comic strip] The first complete

940.549   Male call   20
C153m   Caniff, Milton Arthur, 1907-
     Male call [comic strip] The first complete
collection of the uninhibited adventures of every
GI's dream girl - Miss Lace. New, enl. ed. New
York, Grosset & Dunlap [1959]
     unpaged. illus. 19 x 26cm.

○

21

Caniff, Milton Arthur, 1907–
     Male call; [comic strip] The first complete collection of
the uninhibited adventures of every GI's dream girl—Miss
Lace. New, enl. ed. New York, Grosset & Dunlap [1959]
     unpaged. illus. 19 x 26 cm.

     1. World War, 1939-1945—Humor, caricatures, etc. 2. U. S.
Army—Military life. I. Title.

D745.2.C24 1959   ○   940.549   59–3089 ‡

Library of Congress   [5]

JOINT AUTHORSHIP

```
823
L165tam Lamb, Charles, 1775-1834.
          Tales from Shakespeare [by] Charles and Mary
       Lamb, edited by the Rev. Alfred Ainger, revised
       by H. Y. Moffett; illustrated by Maud and Miska
       Petersham.  [New York] Macmillan [c1932]
          xix,441p.  illus.  17cm.  (New pocket classics)
```

22

```
                          LCC
```

TRACING
COMPARATIVE STYLES

```
     I. Shakespeare, William.  Paraphrases, tales, etc.
    II. Lamb, Mary Ann, 1764-1847, joint author
   III. Ainger, Alfred, 1837-1904, ed.
    IV. Moffett, Harold Young
     V. Petersham, Maud (Fuller) 1890-      illus.
    VI. Petersham, Miska, 1888-      joint illus.
   VII. Title
```

23

24

```
                                          UCB


       Shakespeare, William.  Paraphrases, tales, etc.
       Lamb, Mary Ann, 1764-1847, joint author
       Ainger, Alfred, 1837-1904, ed.
       Moffett, Harold Young
       Petersham, Maud (Fuller) 1890-      illus.
       Petersham, Miska, 1888-      joint illus.
       Title
```

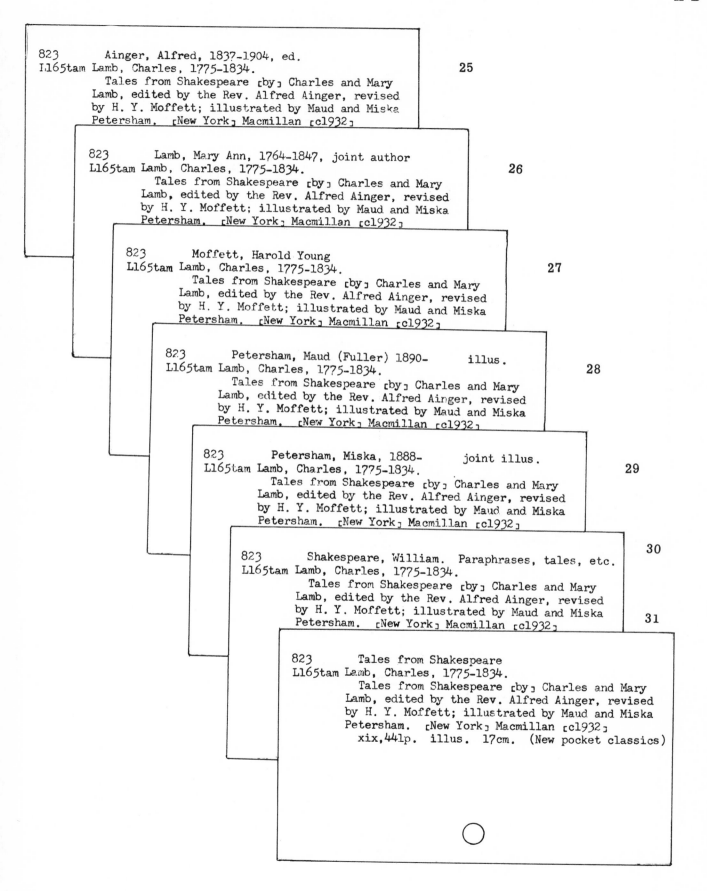

823   Ainger, Alfred, 1837-1904, ed.   25
L165tam Lamb, Charles, 1775-1834.
   Tales from Shakespeare ₍by₎ Charles and Mary
Lamb, edited by the Rev. Alfred Ainger, revised
by H. Y. Moffett; illustrated by Maud and Miska
Petersham. ₍New York₎ Macmillan ₍c1932₎

823   Lamb, Mary Ann, 1764-1847, joint author   26
L165tam Lamb, Charles, 1775-1834.
   Tales from Shakespeare ₍by₎ Charles and Mary
Lamb, edited by the Rev. Alfred Ainger, revised
by H. Y. Moffett; illustrated by Maud and Miska
Petersham. ₍New York₎ Macmillan ₍c1932₎

823   Moffett, Harold Young   27
L165tam Lamb, Charles, 1775-1834.
   Tales from Shakespeare ₍by₎ Charles and Mary
Lamb, edited by the Rev. Alfred Ainger, revised
by H. Y. Moffett; illustrated by Maud and Miska
Petersham. ₍New York₎ Macmillan ₍c1932₎

823   Petersham, Maud (Fuller) 1890- illus. 28
L165tam Lamb, Charles, 1775-1834.
   Tales from Shakespeare ₍by₎ Charles and Mary
Lamb, edited by the Rev. Alfred Ainger, revised
by H. Y. Moffett; illustrated by Maud and Miska
Petersham. ₍New York₎ Macmillan ₍c1932₎

823   Petersham, Miska, 1888- joint illus. 29
L165tam Lamb, Charles, 1775-1834.
   Tales from Shakespeare ₍by₎ Charles and Mary
Lamb, edited by the Rev. Alfred Ainger, revised
by H. Y. Moffett; illustrated by Maud and Miska
Petersham. ₍New York₎ Macmillan ₍c1932₎

823   Shakespeare, William. Paraphrases, tales, etc. 30
L165tam Lamb, Charles, 1775-1834.
   Tales from Shakespeare ₍by₎ Charles and Mary
Lamb, edited by the Rev. Alfred Ainger, revised
by H. Y. Moffett; illustrated by Maud and Miska
Petersham. ₍New York₎ Macmillan ₍c1932₎ 31

823   Tales from Shakespeare
L165tam Lamb, Charles, 1775-1834.
   Tales from Shakespeare ₍by₎ Charles and Mary
Lamb, edited by the Rev. Alfred Ainger, revised
by H. Y. Moffett; illustrated by Maud and Miska
Petersham. ₍New York₎ Macmillan ₍c1932₎
   xix,441p. illus. 17cm. (New pocket classics)

```
711.517446
B657+   Boston.  City Planning Board.
           Proposed zoning; a report.  Boston, 1958.
           51p.  illus.,12 fold.maps.  31cm.




           1. Zoning
```

32

```
711.517446  ZONING
B657+      Boston.  City Planning Board.
              Proposed zoning; a report.  Boston, 1958.
              51p.  illus.,12 fold.maps.  31cm.
```

33

```
378.7446
Si47m    Mark, Kenneth Lamartine, 1874-1958.
           Delayed by fire, being the early history of
         Simmons College.  ⌐Concord, N. H.⌐ Priv. print.
         ⌐Rumford Press⌐ 1945.
              vii,163p.  illus.,ports.  24cm.
```

34

```
           1. Simmons College, Boston.
           I. Title
```

35   36

```
378.7446  Delayed by fire
Si47m    Mark, Kenneth Lamartine, 1874-1958.
           Delayed by fire, being the early history of
         Simmons College.  ⌐Concord, N. H.⌐ Priv. print.
         ⌐Rumford Press⌐ 1945.
              vii,163p.  illus.,ports.  24cm.
```

37

```
378.7446  SIMMONS COLLEGE, BOSTON.
Si47m    Mark, Kenneth Lamartine, 1874-1958.
           Delayed by fire, being the early history of
         Simmons College.  ⌐Concord, N. H.⌐ Priv. print.
         ⌐Rumford Press⌐ 1945.
              vii,163p.  illus.,ports.  24cm.
```

```
LC1011
.F7      Freedom and the university; the responsibility of
            the university for the maintenance of freedom in
            the American way of life ⌐by⌐ Edgar N. Johnson
            ⌐and others⌐ Ithaca ⌐N.Y.⌐ Cornell University
            Press, 1950.
            ix,129p.  23cm.
            "These essays were originally presented - during
         the spring of 1949 - as lectures in the third part
         of the Cornell symposium on "American freedom and
         responsibility in the contemporary crisis."
            Contents.-The background of the university tra-
         dition, by E. N. Johnson.-Liberal arts and

                ◯(Continued on next card)
```

                                                    ◯
                                                    LCC

38   39

```
                    1. Education, Humanistic - Addresses, essays, lectures
                    I. Johnson, Edgar Nathaniel, 1901-
```

```
LC1011
.F7      Freedom and the university ... 1950.  (Card 2)

            Contents - continued
         professional training, by R. D. Calkins.-Liberal
         education and the law, by E. V. Rostow.-Liberal
         education and medicine, by J. L. Lilienthal, Jr.-
         The relation of research to the liberal univer-
         sity, by J. R. Oppenheimer.-Academic freedom and
         the community, by E. C. Kirkland.
```

TITLE MAIN ENTRY

40

                                    ◯

```
                        EDUCATION, HUMANISTIC - ADDRESSES, ESSAYS,
LC1011              LECTURES
.F7      Freedom and the university ... 1950.  (Card 2)

         ontents - continued
         . N. Johnson.-Liberal arts and
          training, by R. D. Calkins.-Liberal
```

```
                EDUCATION, HUMANISTIC - ADDRESSES, ESSAYS,
LC1011              LECTURES
.F7      Freedom and the university; th⌐
            the university for the maint⌐
            the American way of life ⌐by⌐
```

```
LC1011      Johnson, Edgar Nathaniel, 1901-
.F7      Freedom and the university ... 1950.  (Card 2)

         ontents - continued
          training, by R. D. Calkins.-Liberal
         d the law, by E. V. Rostow.-Liberal
         d medicine, by J. L. Lilienthal, Jr.-
          of research to the liberal univer-
         R. Oppenheimer.-Academic freedom and
         y, by E. C. Kirkland.
```

```
LC1011      Johnson, Edgar Nathaniel, 1901-
.F7      Freedom and the university; the responsibility of
            the university for the maintenance of freedom in
            the American way of life ⌐by⌐ Edgar N. Johnson
            ⌐and others⌐ Ithaca ⌐N.Y.⌐ Cornell University
            Press, 1950.
            ix,129p.  23cm.
            "These essays were originally presented - during
         the spring of 1949 - as lectures in the third part
         of the Cornell symposium on "American freedom and
         responsibility in the contemporary crisis."
            Contents.-The background of the university tra-
         dition, by E. N. Johnson.-Liberal arts and

              ◯ (Continued on next card)
```

                                    ◯

41-44

MONOGRAPH SET

45

Burke, Edmund, 1729?–1797.
    The correspondence of Edmund Burke. Edited by
Thomas W. Copeland. Cambridge, University Press; Chicago, University of Chicago Press, 1958–

        v. port. 24 cm.

    Bibliography: v. 1, p. xxiii–₍xxvi₎ Bibliographical footnotes.

        DA506.B9A18   923.242   58–5615
        Library of Congress   ₍10₎

46

020.5
C28   American Library Association. Division of Cata-
            loging and Classification.
            Catalogers' and classifiers' yearbook. no. ₍1₎–
         11; 1929-45. Chicago.
            11 no. ports. 23cm.
            Title varies: 1929, Proceedings.
            No. 1-8 (1929-39) issued by the Division under
         an earlier name: Catalog Section.
            Index for no. 1-5, 1929-36 in no. 5.

SERIAL
CLOSED
ENTRY

47

         xx Journal of cataloging and classification (1944-56)
         xx Serial slants (1950-56)
         xx Library resources & technical services (1957-
         1. Cataloging - Yearbooks
         2. Classification - Books - Yearbooks
         3. Library conferences
         I. American Library Association. Division of Cata-
               loging and Classification. Proceedings.
         II. Title

```
020.5    CATALOGING - YEARBOOKS
C28      American Library Association.  Division of Cata-
            loging and Classification.                              48
         Catalogers' and classifiers' yearbook.  no. ₍1₎-
         11; 1929-45.  Chicago.
```

```
020.5    CLASSIFICATION - BOOKS - YEARBOOKS
C28      American Library Association.  Division of Cata-           49
            loging and Classification.
         Catalogers' and classifiers' yearbook.  no. ₍1₎-
         11; 1929-45.  Chicago.
```

```
020.5    Catalogers' and classifiers' yearbook.
C28      American Library Association.  Division of Cata-
            loging and Classification.                              50
         Catalogers' and classifiers' yearbook.  no. ₍1₎-
         11; 1929-45.  Chicago.
```

```
020.5    LIBRARY CONFERENCES
C28      American Library Association.  Division of Cata-           51
            loging and Classification.
         Catalogers' and classifiers' yearbook.  no. ₍1₎-
         11; 1929-45.  Chicago.
```

```
         American Library Association.  Division of Cata-           52
020.5       loging and Classification.  Proceedings.
C28      American Library Association.  Division of Cata-
            loging and Classification.
         Catalogers' and classifiers' yearbook.  no. ₍1₎-
         11; 1929-45.  Chicago.
         11 no.  ports.  23cm.
         Title varies: 1929, Proceedings.
         No. 1-8 (1929-39) issued by the Division under
         an earlier name: Catalog Section.
         Index for no. 1-5, 1929-36 in no. 5.
```

53

```
020.5
C28    American Library Association.  Division of Cataloging and
          Classification.
          Catalogers' and classifiers' yearbook.  no. ₍1₎–11; 1929–45.
       Chicago, American Library Association.
          11 no.  ports.  23 cm.

          Title varies: 1929, Proceedings.
          No. 1-8 (1929–39) issued by the division under an earlier name:
       Catalog Section.
          Index for no. 1-5, 1929-36, in no. 5.

          1. Cataloging—Yearbooks.  2. Classification—Books—Yearbooks.
       3. Library conferences.   i. American Library Association.  Division
       of Cataloging and Classification.  Proceedings.  ii. Title.

       Z695.A58                        025.3058            29—22649*

       Library of Congress          ₍59r52d³3₎
```

```
020.5
L616    Library resources & technical services.
            v. 1-
            winter 1957-
            [Richmond]
              v. in      24cm.   quarterly.
          Formed by the union of Serial slants and the
        Journal of cataloging and classification.
          Official publication of the Resources and
        Technical Services Division of the American
        Library Association.

        For statement of holdings, see shelf list
```

54

LCC

55

```
        xx American Library Association.  Division of Cata-
              loging and Classification.  Catalogers' and
              classifiers' yearbook (1929-45)
        xx Journal of cataloging and classification (1944-56)
        xx Serial slants (1950-56)
        1. Library science - Periodicals
        I. American Library Association.  Resources and
              Technical Services Division
```

```
020.5     LIBRARY SCIENCE - PERIODICALS
L616      Library resources & technical services.

            For further information see

          Library resources & technical services.
```

56

```
            American Library Association.  Resources and
020.5             Technical Services Division.
L616      Library resources & technical services.

            For further information see

          Library resources & technical services.
```

57

58

```
020.5
L616    Library resources & technical services.  v. 1-
            winter 1957-
            [Richmond]
                 v. in      24 cm.   quarterly.
            Formed by the union of Serial slants and the Journal of cataloging
        and classification.
            Official publication of the Resources and Technical Services Divi-
        sion of the American Library Association.


            1. Library science—Period.     I. American Library Association.
        Resources and Technical Services Division.

        Z671.L7154                      025.06273              59-3198

        Library of Congress                   [10]
```

JR
028.5
Am35s **American Library Association.** *Editorial Committee.*
Subject and title index to short stories for children. Compiled by a subcommittee; Julia F. Carter, chairman. Chicago, American Library Association, 1955.

59

JR
028.5
Am35s CHILDREN'S STORIES - INDEXES
American Library Association. *Editorial Committee.*
Subject and title index to short stories for children. Compiled by a subcommittee; Julia F. Carter, chairman. Chicago, American Library Association, 1955.

60

JR
028.5
Am35s Subject and title index to short stories for children
American Library Association. *Editorial Committee.*
Subject and title index to short stories for children. Compiled by a subcommittee; Julia F. Carter, chairman. Chicago, American Library Association, 1955.

vi, 333 p. 25 cm.

61

1. Children's stories—Indexes.   I. Title.

Z1037.A4924   028.5   55—10208

Library of Congress   [561*20]

62

jr 808.83   **American Library Association**
Subject and title index to short stories for children; Compiled by a subcommittee of the A.L.A. Editorial Committee, Julia F. Carter, Chairman.   A.L.A. 1955

63

SHORT STORIES—INDEXES

jr 808.83   **American Library Association**
Subject and title index to short stories for children; Compiled by a subcommittee of the A.L.A. Editorial Committee, Julia F. Carter, Chairman.   A.L.A. 1955

64

Subject and title index to short stories for children

jr 808.83   **American Library Association**
Subject and title index to short stories for children; Compiled by a subcommittee of the A.L.A. Editorial Committee, Julia F. Carter, Chairman.   A.L.A. 1955
333p
"A tool to assist . . . in locating stories on specific or related subjects, and in tracing hard-to-find stories . . . the index has been planned for the use of public and school librarians and teachers who work with boys and girls from the third grade through junior high school." Foreword
Divided into 3 parts: List of books indexed; Subject index to short stories for children; List of stories indexed
1 Short stories—In-   dexes   I Title   808.83

59W5,442   (W)   The H. W. Wilson Company

Forrester, Gertrude, 1895–
    Occupational literature; an annotated bibliography.
1958 ed. New York, Wilson, 1958.

    603 p. 34 cm.

    First published in 1946 under title: Occupations, a selected list
of pamphlets.

    1. Occupations—Bibl.   I. Title.

Z7164.C81F6 1958   ◯   016.371425   58—7288

Library of Congress   ₍59x20₎

65

66

371.42   Forrester, Gertrude, 1895-
    Occupational literature ; an annotated bibliography. 1958 ed.
Wilson, H.W. 1958
    603p

    First published under this title in 1954 as an expansion of the author's
"Occupations: A selected list of pamphlets." The 1958 edition has
been expanded to include approximately 3500 pamphlets and 900
references to books

67

OCCUPATIONS—BIBLIOGRAPHY

371.42   Forrester, Gertrude, 1895-
    Occupational literature ; an annotated bibliography. 1958 ed.
Wilson, H.W. 1958
    603p

68

PROFESSIONS—BIBLIOGRAPHY

371.42   Forrester, Gertrude, 1895-
    Occupational literature ; an annotated bibliography. 1958 ed.
Wilson, H.W. 1958
    603p

    First published under this title in 1954 as an expansion of the author's
"Occupations: A selected list of pamphlets." The 1958 edition has
been expanded to include approximately 3500 pamphlets and 900
references to books
    Includes references to material in books, pamphlets, textbooks, charts,
posters and graphic aids

69

Occupational literature

371.42   Forrester, Gertrude, 1895-
    Occupational literature ; an annotated bibliography. 1958 ed.
Wilson, H.W. 1958
    603p

    First published under this title in 1954 as an expansion of the author's
"Occupations: A selected list of pamphlets." The 1958 edition has
been expanded to include approximately 3500 pamphlets and 900
references to books
    Includes references to material in books, pamphlets, textbooks, charts,
posters and graphic aids

1 Occupations—Bibliography   2 Professions—Bibliography   I Title
                                      371.42

58W2528   (W)   The H. W. Wilson Company

Hilton, James, 1900–1954.
    H. R. H., the story of Philip, duke of Edinburgh. With photos. Boston, Little, Brown ₍1956₎

    71 p. illus. 20 cm. (An Atlantic Monthly Press book)

    "A condensation ... appeared in the American weekly under the title of England's uncrowned King."

    1. Philip, duke of Edinburgh, 1921–

DA591.A2H5   923.242

Library of Congress   ₍30₎

70

Hilton, James, 1900-1954
    H.R.H. The story of Philip, Duke of Edinburgh. Little 1956
    71p illus

    At an early age Philip came under the wing of his uncle, Earl Mountbatten, who supervised his education. This biography tells briefly of his training at the Royal Naval Academy, his World War II service in the British Navy, his courtship, engagement and marriage, the coronation, and his children, Prince Charles and Princess Anne. (Publisher)

   1 Philip, consort of   Elizabeth II, Queen of Great Britain, 1921-   I Title   92

      (W)   The H. W. Wilson Company

71

Lyle, Guy Redvers, 1907–
    The administration of the college library, by Guy R. Lyle with the collaboration of Paul H. Bixler, Marjorie Hood, and Arnold H. Trotier. 3d ed. New York, Wilson, 1961.

    xiii, 419 p. diagrs., forms, tables. 24 cm.

    Includes bibliographies.

    1. Libraries, University and college. 2. Library administration. I. Title.

Z675.U5L88   1961   027.7   61–11121

Library of Congress   ₍40₎

72

73

027.7   Lyle, Guy R
    The administration of the college library ₍by₎ Guy R.

74

          LIBRARIES, COLLEGE AND UNIVERSITY
027.7   Lyle, Guy R
    The administration of the college library ₍by₎ Guy R. Lyle with the collaboration of Paul H. Bixler. Marjorie

75

      The administration of the college library
027.7   Lyle, Guy R
    The administration of the college library ₍by₎ Guy R. Lyle with the collaboration of Paul H. Bixler, Marjorie Hood and Arnold H. Trotier. 3d ed. Wilson, H.W. 1961
    419p illus

    First published 1944. The 1961 edition has been revised by the authors, bringing it up-to-date
    "While this book is planned as a text in the teaching of college library administration, I hope that it will also be found useful for independent professional reading." Preface to the third edition
    "Additional references" at the end of most of the chapters

   1 Libraries, College and university   I Title   027.7

61W11,540   (W)   The H. W. Wilson Company

SERIAL: SUCCESSIVE TITLE ENTRY FOR LATEST REVISION

76

Z731
.A5

American library & book trade annual. 1955/56-1961.
  New York, R. R. Bowker.
  6 v. 25 cm.

  Title varies: 1955/56-1958, American library annual.—1959, American library annual and book trade almanac.
  Sponsored by the Council of National Library Associations and the Library Journal.
  Editors: 1955/56-1961, W. E. Wright and the editorial staff of R. R. Bowker Company.
  Vols. for 1958-1960 include indexes cumulative from 1955/56.

  I. Libraries—U. S.—Direct.   I. Wright, Wyllis Eaton, 1903-
  ed. II. Bowker (R. R.) Company, firm, publishers, New York. III. Council of National Library Associations. IV. Library journal.

Z731.A4 5

020.58   55—12484
Library of Congress   (Continued on next card)
                                    [61r61z²30]

79

Z731
.A5

LIBRARIES - U. S. - DIRECTORIES

American library & book trade annual. 1955/56-1961.
  New York, R. R. Bowker.
  6 v. 25 cm.

  Title varies: 1955/56-1958, American library annual.—1959, American library annual and book trade almanac.
  Sponsored by the Council of National Library Associations and the Library Journal.
  Editors: 1955/56-1961, W. E. Wright and the editorial staff of R. R. Bowker Company.
  Vols. for 1958-1960 include indexes cumulative from 1955/56.
  Continued by The Bowker annual of library and book trade information, 1962-

  I. Libraries—U. S.—Direct.   I. Wright, Wyllis Eaton, 1903-
  ed. II. Bowker (R. R.) Company, firm, publishers, New York. III. Council of National Library Associations. IV. Library journal.

80

Z731
.A5

Wright, Wyllis Eaton, 1903-   ed.

American library & book trade annual. 1955/56-1961.
  New York, R. R. Bowker.

81

Z731
.A5

Bowker (R. R.) Company, firm, publishers, New York.

American library & book trade annual. 1955/56-1961.
  New York, R. R. Bowker.

82

Z731
.A5

Council of National Library Associations.

American library & book trade annual. 1955/56-1961.
  New York, R. R. Bowker.

83

Z731
.A5

Library journal

American library & book trade annual. 1955/56-1961.
  New York, R. R. Bowker.
  6 v. 25 cm.

  Title varies: 1955/56-1958, American library annual.—1959, American library annual and book trade almanac.
  Sponsored by the Council of National Library Associations and the Library Journal.
  Editors: 1955/56-1961, W. E. Wright and the editorial staff of R. R. Bowker Company.
  Vols. for 1958-1960 include indexes cumulative from 1955/56.
  Continued by The Bowker annual of library and book trade information, 1962-

  I. Libraries—U. S.—Direct.   I. Wright, Wyllis Eaton, 1903-
  ed. II. Bowker (R. R.) Company, firm, publishers, New York. III. Council of National Library Associations. IV. Library journal.

Z731.A47   020.58   55—12484
Library of Congress   [61r61z²30]

77

x American library annual
x American library annual and book trade almanac
xx The Bowker annual of library and book trade information
x to II. R. R. Bowker Company
x to II. New York. Bowker (R. R.) Company, firm, publishers

78

Z731
.A5

American library & book trade annual. 1955/56-1961. (Card 2)

Continued by The Bowker annual of library and book trade information, 1962-

(or, preferably, note typed in, as below, to reduce number of cards required for successive entry)

Z731
.A5 — 87

BOOK INDUSTRIES AND TRADE - U. S. - YEARBOOKS
The Bowker annual of library and book trade information.

Z731
.A5 — 88

LIBRARIES - U. S. - DIRECTORIES
The Bowker annual of library and book trade information.

Z731
.A5 — 89

Wright, Wyllis Eaton, 1903-   ed.
The Bowker annual of library and book trade information.

85

For further information, see

The Bowker annual of library and book trade information.

Z731
.A5 — 90

Bowker (R. R.) Company, firm, publishers, New York.
The Bowker annual of library and book trade information.

Z731
.A5 — 91

Council of National Library Associations.
The Bowker annual of library and book trade information.

86

For further information, see

The Bowker annual of library and book trade information.

84

Z731
.A5

The Bowker annual of library and book trade information.
1962-
New York, R. R. Bowker
v.   24cm.
Continues American library & book trade annual.
Sponsored by the Council of National Library Associations.
Editors: 1962-   W. E. Wright and the editorial staff of R. R. Bowker Company.
For statement of holdings, see shelf list

The Bowker annual of library and book trade annual
xx American library & book trade annual
1. Book industries and trade - U. S. - Yearbooks
2. Libraries - U. S. - Directories
I. Wright, Wyllis Eaton, 1903-   ed.
II. Bowker (R. R.) Company, firm, publishers, New York.
III. Council of National Library Associations.

The Bowker annual of library and book trade information.
1955/56-
New York, R. R. Bowker.
v.   25 cm.
Title varies: 1955/56-1958, American library annual.—1959, American library annual and book trade almanac.—1960-61, American library and book trade annual.
Vols. for 1955/56-   sponsored by the Council of National Library Associations (with Library Journal, 1955/56-1961)
Editors: 1955/56-   W. E. Wright and the editorial staff of R. R. Bowker Company.
Vols. for 1958-60 include indexes cumulative from 1955/56.
1. Book industries and trade—U. S.—Yearbooks. 2. Libraries—U. S.—Yearbooks.   I. Wright, Wyllis Eaton, 1903-   ed.   II. Bowker (R. R.) Company, firm, publishers, New York.   III. Council of National Library Associations.   IV. Library journal.
Z731.A47   020.58   55—12434
Library of Congress   [62r62e5]

WILSON
LC
SERIALS

92

020.58 **American** library annual. 1955/56- Bowker 1956-

v

93

LIBRARIES—U. S.—DIRECTORIES

020.58 **American** library annual. 1955/56- Bowker 1956-

v

94

Wright, Wyllis Eaton, 1903-   ed.

020.58 **American** library annual. 1955/56- Bowker 1956-

v

    Sponsored by the Council of National Library Associations and the Library journal
    Editors: 1955/56-   W. E. Wright and editorial staff of R. R. Bowker Company
    "This volume revives publication of an annual last issued in 1918. A directory of national and regional library associations of the U.S., Canada, and Latin American and joint committees in these organizations, and a subject index of activities of the groups are followed by a miscellany of data and statistics on libraries and the book trade." Bkl.

    1 Libraries—U.S.—Di-   rectories ɪ Wright, Wyllis Eaton, 1903-   ed.   020.58

12-28-56   ◯   (W) The H. W. Wilson Company

Look.
    Look at America, by the editors of Look. Boston, Houghton Mifflin Co. ₍1946–

    v. illus. (part col.) maps. 21 cm. (₍v. 1₎ : 31 cm.)

    Contents.—₍1₎ The country you know, and don't know.—₍2₎ The Southwest.—₍3₎ New England.—₍4₎ The Central Northwest.—₍5₎ The South.—₍6₎ The Midwest.—₍7₎ The Far West.—₍8₎ The Central Northeast.—₍9₎ New York City.

95

    1. U. S.—Descr. & trav.—Views. 2. U. S.—Descr. & trav.—Guidebooks. ɪ. Title.

E169.L84   ◯   917.3   46—8215*
Library of Congress   ₍54r48c^{10}30₎

96

Look (Periodical)
    New York City, by the editors of Look; with an introduction by Frederick Lewis Allen. New and rev. ed. A handbook in pictures, maps and text for the vacationist, the traveler and the stay-at-home. . . Houghton 1956
    375p illus (Look at America)

917.471

7-27-56   ◯   (W) The H. W. Wilson Company

The **Best** plays. 1894/99–
New York [etc.] Dodd, Mead [etc.]
 v. illus. 21 cm.
 Title varies: 1947/48–1949/50, The Burns Mantle best plays and
the year book of the drama in America.—1950/51–1951/52, The Best
plays and the year book of the drama in America.—1952/53, The
Burns Mantle yearbook. The Best plays.
 Other slight variations in title.
 Added t. p., 1953/54–   The Burns Mantle yearbook.
 Editors: 1894/99, G. P. Sherwood, J. Chapman.—1899/1909–1946/
47, B. Mantle (with G. P. Sherwood, 1899/1909–1909/19).—1947/48–
1951/52, J. Chapman.—1952/53–   L. Kronenberger.
 INDEXES:
 1899/1909–1949/50. 1 v.
 1. Drama—20th cent. 2. Theater—U. S.—Yearbooks. 3. Drama—
Bibl.   I. Mantle, Rob-   ert Burns, 1873–1948, ed. II. Chap-
man, John Arthur, 1900–   ed. III. Sherwood, Garrison P., ed.
IV. Kronenberger, Louis,   1904–   ed.
PN6112.B45   812.5082   20—21432*
Library of Congress   [61r56i⁵¹60]

97

98

808.82 The **best** plays of 1959-1960; the Burns Mantle yearbook;
 ed. by Louis Kronenberger; illus. with photographs, and
 with drawings by Hirschfeld. Dodd 1960
 435p illus

99

DRAMA

808.82 The **best** plays of 1959-1960; the Burns Mantle yearbook;
 ed. by Louis Kronenberger; illus. with photographs, and
 with drawings by Hirschfeld. Dodd 1960
 435p illus

100

DRAMA—COLLECTIONS

808.82 The **best** plays of 1959-1960; the Burns Mantle yearbook;
 ed. by Louis Kronenberger; illus. with photographs, and
 with drawings by Hirschfeld. Dodd 1960
 435p illus

101

THEATER—YEARBOOKS

808.82 The **best** plays of 1959-1960; the Burns Mantle yearbook;
 ed. by Louis Kronenberger; illus. with photographs, and
 with drawings by Hirschfeld. Dodd 1960
 435p illus

102

Kronenberger, Louis, ed.

808.82 The **best** plays of 1959-1960; the Burns Mantle yearbook;
 ed. by Louis Kronenberger; illus. with photographs, and
 with drawings by Hirschfeld. Dodd 1960
 435p illus

 Contains the following plays, abridged: The tenth man, by P. Chayefsky;
Five finger exercise, by P. Shaffer; The Andersonville trial, by
S. Levitt; The deadly game, by F. Duerrenmatt; Caligula, by A. Camus;
Toys in the attic, by L. Hellman; The best man, by G. Vidal; Duel of
angels, by J. Giraudoux; A Thurber carnival, by J. Thurber; Fiorello!
by J. Weidman and G. Abbott

 1 Drama 2 Drama—   Collections 3 Theater—Yearbooks
 I Kronenberger, Louis, ed.   (21 author and title anals) 808.82

 60W10,163   (W) The H. W. Wilson Company

B
SMITH   **Al Smith and his America**
Handlin, Oscar, 1915–
    Al Smith and his America. ₍1st ed.₎ Boston, Little,
Brown ₍1958₎

105

B
SMITH   **SMITH, ALFRED EMANUEL, 1873– 1944**
Handlin, Oscar, 1915–
    Al Smith and his America. ₍1st ed.₎ Boston, Little,
Brown ₍1958₎

104

B
SMITH

Handlin, Oscar, 1915–
    Al Smith and his America. ₍1st ed.₎ Boston, Little,
Brown ₍1958₎

    207 p. 21 cm. (The Library of American biography)

    Includes bibliography.

103

    1. Smith, Alfred Emanuel, 1873–1944.   ɪ. Title.

E748.S63H16   ◯   923.273   57–6446 ‡

Library of Congress   ₍30₎

539.721   **High energy nuclear physics.**
L   **Lock, W**   **O**
    High energy nuclear physics. London, Methuen; New
York, Wiley ₍1960₎

109

539.721   **NUCLEAR PHYSICS**
L   **Lock, W**   **O**
    High energy nuclear physics. London, Methuen; New
York, Wiley ₍1960₎

108

539.721   **MESONS**
L   **Lock, W**   **O**
    High energy nuclear physics. London, Methuen; New
York, Wiley ₍1960₎

107

539.721
L   **Lock, W**   **O**
    High energy nuclear physics. London, Methuen; New
York, Wiley ₍1960₎

    190 p. illus. 20 cm. (Methuen's monographs on physical subjects)

    Includes bibliography.

106

    1. Mesons. 2. Nuclear physics.   ɪ. Title.

QC721.L76   ◯   539.7216   60–50435 ‡

LC CARDS
TAILORED TO WORK

Card 110:

SCL

891.73
G67z3
(red)

Gor′kiĭ, Maksim, 1868–1936.
    My universities. ₍Translated from the Russian by Helen Altschuler₎ Moscow, Foreign Languages Pub. House, 1952.
    301 p. illus. 17 cm. (Library of selected Soviet literature)

    Library copy: 3d ed. ₍n.d.₎ 286p.

        Title.

        Real name: Alekseĭ Maksimovich Peshkov.

PG3465.A34A5   928.917   52–36326 ‡

Library of Congress   ₍1₎

Card 111:

Gor′kiĭ, Maksim, 1868–1936.
    My universities. 3d ed. ₍Translated from the Russian by Helen Altschuler₎ Moscow, Foreign Languages Pub. House, 1952. ₍n.d.₎
    301 p. illus. 17 cm. (Library of selected Soviet literature)
286 port.

    ɪ. Title.

        Real name: Alekseĭ Maks

PG3465.A34A5   928.917

Library of Congress   ₍1₎

Card 112:

SCL

BR
355
H87e
(red)

Huie, William Bradford, 1910–
    The execution of Private Slovik; the hitherto secret story of the only American soldier since 1864 to be shot for desertion. ₍1st ed.₎ New York, Duell, Sloan and Pearce ₍1954₎
    247 p. 21 cm.

    Library copy: ₍N.Y.₎ New American Library. 152p. (A Signet book, 1113)

    1. Slovik, Edward Donald, 1920–1945.   2. Desertion, Military—U. S.   ɪ. Title.

         355.133   54—5099 ‡

Library of Congress   ₍54x10₎

Card 113:

Huie, William Bradford, 1910–
    The execution of Private Slovik; the hitherto secret story of the only American soldier since 1864 to be shot for desertion. ₍1st ed.₎ New York, Duell, Sloan and Pearce ₍1954₎
New American Library
    247 p. 21 cm. (A Signet book, 1113)
152

    1. Slovik, Edward Donald, 1920–1945.   2. Dese
U. S.   ɪ. Title.

         355.133

Library of Congress   ₍54x10₎

Card 114:

SCL

946.08
T36s
(red)

Thomas, Hugh, 1931–
    The Spanish Civil War. New York, Harper ₍1961₎
    720 p. illus. 23 cm.
    Includes bibliography.

    Copy 2: London, Eyre & Spottiswoode.

    Spain—Hist.—Civil War, 1936–1939.   ɪ. Title.

        Full name: Hugh Swynnerton Thomas.

269.T5   946.081   61—6177 ‡

Library of Congress   ₍62g³5₎

Card 115:

Thomas, Hugh, 1931–
    The Spanish Civil War. New York, Harper ₍1961₎
London, Eyre & Spottiswoode
    720 p. illus. 23 cm.
    Includes bibliography.

    1. Spain—Hist.—Civil War, 1936–1939.   ɪ. Title.

        Full name: Hugh Swynnerton Thomas.

DP269.T5   946.081   61—6177 ‡

Library of Congress   ₍62g³5₎

116

American Library Association. Cataloging and
Classification Section.

The Cataloging and Classification Section of the
American Library Association is one of the sections of the Resources and Technical Services Division, established Jan.-July 1, 1957. It combines the former Division of Cataloging and Classification (established in 1900 and until 1940
called the Catalog Section), the former Board on
Acquisition of Library Materials (created by the
ALA Council in 1951), and the former Serials
Round Table (created by the ALA Council in 1929)

117

**Berlin. Biologische Zentralanstalt für Land- und Forst-
wirtschaft,** *West Berlin.*

Founded in 1898 in Berlin as the Abteilung für Land- und Forstwirtschaft of the German Gesundheitsamt. Moved to Berlin-Dahlem
Apr. 1, 1905, becoming an independent institution called Kaiserliche
Biologische Anstalt für Land- und Forstwirtschaft. In 1920 name
was changed to Biologische Reichsanstalt für Land- und Forstwirtschaft, and in 1945 to Biologische Zentralanstalt für Land- und Forstwirtschaft.
Until 1949 the Zentralanstalt was responsible for activity in Berlin and the Russian Zone of Occupation. In that year East German
officials established an institution with the same name (later called
Biologische Zentralanstalt Berlin) in Berlin-Kleinmachnow (East

(Continued on next card)

[2]

58–1257

118

**Berlin. Biologische Zentralanstalt für Land- und Forst-
wirtschaft,** *West Berlin.* (Card 2)

Berlin), transferring personnel and projects from Berlin-Dahlem
(West Berlin) to Berlin-Kleinmachnow.
The Zentralanstalt in West Berlin maintained an independent
existence until 1954 when it merged with the Biologische Bundesanstalt für Land- und Forstwirtschaft in Brunswick to form the new
Biologische Bundesanstalt für Land- und Forstwirtschaft, Berlin
and Brunswick.
The branches of the Reichsanstalt (i. e. Zentralanstalt) in the
British and U. S. Zones were affiliated with the Biologische Zentralanstalt (later Biologische Bundesanstalt) für Land- und Forstwirtschaft in Brunswick, which had itself been a branch of the Reichsanstalt. The Bernkastel-Kues branch in the French Zone of Occupation remained inde-   pendent until after the establishment
of the German Federal   Republic when it too became affiliated with the Biologi-   sche Bundesanstalt.

Library of Congress   -2,   58–1257

Church of the Nazarene.

Organized in Oct. 1907 as the Pentecostal Church of the Nazarene through a union of the Church of the Nazarene (founded 1895) and the Association of Pentecostal Churches of America. There were united with this organization the Holiness Church of Christ in 1908, the Pentecostal Mission in Feb. 1915 and the Pentecostal Church of Scotland in Nov. 1915. At the general assembly of 1919 it was voted to change the name to Church of the Nazarene.

119

International Railway Congress Association.

Formed as a result of the first International Railway Congress, held in Brussels, 1885; definitely organized at the second congress, held in Milan, 1887. The association is represented by an International Commission, having its seat at Brussels. The first meeting of the commission was held Feb. 20, 1886.

The organization continued to function until Oct. 1914, when, owing to the European War, it was forced to discontinue its activities, and it was formally dissolved Aug. 1, 1919. A new association was immediately constituted under the title International Railway Association, including only the allied and neutral countries as existing at that time.

In 1922 the earlier name, International Railway Congress Association was resumed. Publications of the original association and the one formed in 1919 are cataloged in the Library of Congress under the heading International   Railway Congress Association.

Library of Congress   [r48c1]   21–22049 rev*

120

Malaya (*Federation*)

Established Feb. 1, 1948, succeeding the Malayan Union and comprising the same territories: Johore, Kedah, Perlis, Kelantan, and Trengganu (formerly known collectively as the unfederated Malay States); the former Federated Malay States (Perak, Selangor, Negri Sembilan, and Pahang); and Penang and Malacca of the former Straits Settlements.

See also Malay States, Federated; Malayan Union.

121

Malayan Union.

Established Apr. 1, 1946, comprised of Johore, Kedah, Kelantan, Perlis, and Trengganu (known collectively as the unfederated Malay States); the Federated Malay States (Negri Sembilan, Pahang, Perak, and Selangor); and Penang and Malacca of the Straits Settlements. Succeeded Feb. 1, 1948 by the Federation of Malaya.

See also **Johore; Kedah; Kelantan; Malay States, Federated; Malaya** (*Federation*); **Perlis; Straits Settlements; Trengganu.**

Library of Congress   [r56c1]   56–4510 rev

122

123

U. S. *Board on Geographic Names.*
    Established by law in the Dept. of the Interior July 25, 1947, succeeding the Board on Geographical Names.
See also **U. S.** *Board on Geographical Names;* **U. S.** *Geographic Board.*

124

U. S. *Board on Geographical Names.*
    Created by Departmental order no. 1010 of the Dept. of the Interior Dec. 10, 1935, combining the department's Division of Geographic Names and its Advisory Committee on Geographic Names. Abolished by the law of July 25, 1947 which created the Board on Geographic Names in the same department.

    See also **U. S.** *Board on Geographic Names;* **U. S.** *Geographic Board.*

39–7518 rev

Library of Congress   [r48c1]

125

U. S. *National Institutes of Health.*
    Established Aug. 1887 as the laboratory of the Public Health Service and called the Hygienic Laboratory. Name changed to National Institute of Health by Public act no. 251, 71st Cong., May 26, 1930; to National Institutes of Health by Public law 655, 80th Cong., approved June 16, 1948.

126

U. S. *National Library of Medicine.*

    Publications of this body are included in the Microprint edition, U. S. Government publications (depository) New York, Readex Microprint Corporation, which contains all depository publications cataloged in the Monthly catalog of United States Government publications, issued by the U. S. Superintendent of Documents, from Jan. 1956 (no. 7) to date.
    The items are arranged according to their numbers in the Monthly catalog.

56–31726 rev

Library of Congress   [r57b2]

REFERENCES

```
** Krieg dem Hunger!
    see
Bochow, Martin                                    127



    ALA
      see
American Library Association.                      128



    Aldington, Hilda (Doolittle)
      see
Doolittle, Hilda, 1886-1961.                       129



    American library & book trade annual
        see also
The Bowker annual of library and book trade        130
    information



    American library annual
      see
American library & book trade annual.              131



    American library annual and book trade almanac
      see
American library & book trade annual               132
```

○

133

American Library Association. Catalog Section
   see
American Library Association. Division of Cataloging and Classification.

134

American Library Association. Cataloging and
   Classification Section
   see also
American Library Association. Division of Cataloging and Classification.

135

American Library Association. Division of
   Cataloging and Classification
   see also
American Library Association. Cataloging and
   Classification Section.

136

American Library Association. Division of Cataloging and Classification. Catalogers' and
   classifiers' yearbook (1929-45)
   see also
Journal of cataloging and classification (1944-56)
Serial slants (1950-56)
Library resources & technical services (1957-

137

American Library Association. Resources and
   Technical Services Division. Cataloging and
   Classification Section
   see
American Library Association. Cataloging and
   Classification Section.

138

Amleto
Shakespeare, William, 1564-1616.

   For editions and translations of this title,
   see
Shakespeare, William, 1564-1616.
   Hamlet

Basil the Great, Saint
   see
Basilius, Saint, the Great, Abp. of Caesarea,
   330 (ca.)-379.

139

Basil, Saint, the Great, Abp. of Caesarea
   see
Basilius, Saint, the Great, Abp. of Caesarea,
   330 (ca.)-379.

140

Bochow, Theodor Martin
   see
Bochow, Martin

141

Bolufer, José Alemany y
   see
Alemany y Bolufer, José, 1866-1934.

142

(blue)   MB

143

Boston advertiser. Sunday edition

    see

Boston Sunday advertiser.

144

Boston. Simmons College
   see
Simmons College, Boston.

145

The Bowker annual of library and book trade
   information
   see also
American library & book trade annual

146

Braun, Wernher von
   see
Von Braun, Wernher, 1912-

147   **Catholic Church.** *Pope, 1958–*   (*Joannes XXIII*)
              see also
        Joannes XXIII, *Pope,* 1881–

148   Challenge magazine
              see
        Challenge; the magazine of economic affairs.

149   Chicago. American Library Association
              see
        American Library Association.

150   Cicero, Marcus Tullius
              Vom rechten Handeln
                see his
                De officiis.

151   **Civil War Commission of Virginia**
              see
        Virginia. Civil War Commission.

152   Congress
              see
        U.S. Congress.

153   Les contes des sept sages
              see
        Seven sages. French.

Cross, Marian (Evans)
   see
Eliot, George, pseud., i.e. Marian Evans, afterwards Cross, 1819-1880.

154

D., H.
   Tribute to Freud
   see
Doolittle, Hilda, 1886-1961.

155

De Saint Exupéry, Antoine
   see
Saint Exupéry, Antoine de, 1900-1944.

156

Douai version of the Bible
   see
Bible. English. Date. Douai.

157

Douay version of the Bible
   see
Bible. English. Date. Douai.

158

   *

Eliot
   see also
Elliot
Elliott

159

Eliot, George, pseud. of Mary Ann (Evans) Cross
   see
Eliot, George, pseud., i.e. Marian Evans, afterwards Cross, 1819-1880.

160

161
> Elizabeth II, Queen of Great Britain, 1926-
> > see also
> Gt. Brit. Sovereigns, etc., 1952-   (Elizabeth
> II)

162
> Evans, Marian
> > see
> Eliot, George, pseud., i.e. Marian Evans, after-
> wards Cross, 1819-1880.

163
> Evans, Mary Ann
> > see
> Eliot, George, pseud., i.e. Marian Evans, after-
> wards Cross, 1819-1880.

> Gamlet
> Shakespeare, William, 1564-1616.

164
> > For editions and translations of this title,
> > > see
> > Shakespeare, William, 1564-1616.
> > > Hamlet

165
> Gt. Brit. Sovereigns, etc., 1952-
> > (Elizabeth II)
> > see
> Elizabeth II, Queen of Great Britain, 1926-

166
> Greek New Testament
> > see
> Bible. N.T. Greek.

167
> Hamlet
> Shakespeare, William, 1564-1616.

> > For editions and translations of this title,
> > > see
> > Shakespeare, William, 1564-1616.
> > > Hamlet

HL

168
> Hay, Timothy, pseud.
> > see
> Brown, Margaret Wise, 1910-1952.

Haydn, Franz Joseph
  see
Haydn, Joseph, 1732-1809.

     169

Haydn, Joseph, 1732-1809.
  St. Cecilia's mass
    see his
  Mass, C major (1773?)

     170

Herzog, André, pseud.
    see
Maurois, André, 1885-

     171

Herzog, Émile Salomon Wilhelm
    see
Maurois, André, 1885-

     172

                 (Copied from LC tracing)
Hiraoka, Takeo, 1909-   ed.
  T'ang civilization reference series.
    <u>see</u>
唐代研究のしおり (<u>romanized</u>:Tōdai kenkyū no
  shiori)

     173

                                     LC
Hiraoka, Takeo, 1909-   <u>ed.</u>
  唐代研究のしおり(<u>romanized</u>: Tōdai kenkyū no
  shiori)
    <u>see</u>
唐代研究のしおり(<u>romanized</u>: Tōdai kenkyū no
  shiori)

     174

     175

Historia Septem sapientum
    see
Seven sages. Latin.

Holy Bible
    see
Bible. English

     176

177
      Horace
        see
  Horatius Flaccus, Quintus

178
      House of Representatives of the U.S. Congress
        see
  U.S. Congress. House.

                                              *

179
      Hystorie van die Seven wijse mannen van Romen
        see
  Seven sages. Dutch.

180
      Joannes XXIII, Pope, 1881-
        see also
  Catholic Church. Pope, 1958-   (Joannes
    XXIII)

181
      Journal of cataloging and classification (1944-
        56)
        see also
  American Library Association. Division of Cata-
    loging and Classification. Catalogers' and
    classifiers' yearbook (1929-45)
  Serial slants (1950-56)
  Library resources & technical services (1957-

182
      Judiciary Committee of U.S. House
        see
  U.S. Congress. House. Committee on the Judiciary.

183
      Kennedy, John Fitzgerald, Pres. U.S., 1917-
        see also
  U.S. President, 1961-   (Kennedy)

184
      Larsen, Egon, pseud.
        see
  Lehrburger, Egon, 1904-

Letterhouse, Marie Elisabeth, 1880-1953
   see
Dolores, Sister.

                               *

185

Il Libro de' sette savi di Roma
   see
Seven sages. Italian .

                              *

186

Il Libro dei sette savi di Roma
   see
Seven sages. Italian.

187

Library resources & technical services (1957-
   see also
American Library Association. Division of Cataloging and Classification. Catalogers' and
   classifiers' yearbook (1929-45)
Journal of cataloging and classification (1944-56)
Serial slants (1950-56)

                           HL

188

MacDonald, Golden, pseud.
   see
Brown, Margaret Wise, 1910-1952.

189

Man on the moon
Von Braun, Wernher, 1912-
   see his
   Conquest of the moon

   The same work published under both titles.

                           *

190

Marques de Rome
   see also
Seven sages. German.

                           LC

191

Michigan. University. Horace H. Rackham School
   of Graduate Studies.
     Michigan survey
     see
   Michigan survey.

192

193   Minnesota. University.
         The Gideon D. Seymour memorial lecture series
         see
     The Gideon D. Seymour memorial lecture series

194   New Testament
         see
     Bible. N.T.

195   New York. Bowker (R. R.) Company, firm, pub-
         lishers
         see
     Bowker (R. R.) Company, firm, publishers, New York.

196   An observer
         A Chinese village and its early change under
         communism
         see
      Yang, Ching-kun

       O'Connor, Frank   MFm

197   see

    O'Donovan, Michael

198   Palmer, John Leslie, 1885-1944.
         For works written in collaboration with
        Hilary Aidan St. George Saunders, under the
        name Francis Beeding
         see
     Beeding, Francis, pseud.

199   Paris. United Nations Educational, Scientific,
         and Cultural Organization
         see
     United Nations Educational, Scientific, and
        Cultural Organization.

200   Pentateuch (Book of the Old Testament)
         see
     Bible. O.T. Pentateuch.

Petersham, Mrs. Miska
  see
Petersham, Maud (Fuller) 1890-

                                                                  201

Queen

    Names of queens may be found in this catalog
under their forenames; e.g., Queen Victoria is
found under Victoria, Queen of Great Britain, etc.

                                                                    202

R. R. Bowker Company
  see
Bowker (R. R.) Company, firm, publishers, New York.

                                                                    203

Revised standard version of the Bible
  see
Bible. English. 1952. Revised standard.

                                                                    204

Saint

    **Names which include the designation, Saint, may
generally be found in this catalog under the fore-
name, e.g., Basilius, Saint; Paul, Saint, apostle;
Jeanne d'Arc, Saint, etc.**

                                                                    205

St. Cecilia's mass
Haydn, Joseph, 1732-1809.
  see his
Mass, C major (1773?)

                                                                    206

Saunders, Hilary Aidan St. George, 1898-1951.
    For works written in collaboration with
John Leslie Palmer, under the name Francis
Beeding
  see
Beeding, Francis, pseud.

                                                                    207

208   Serial slants (1950-56)
    see also
American Library Association. Division of Cata-
  loging and Classification. Catalogers' and
  classifiers' yearbook (1929-45)
Journal of cataloging and classification (1944-56)
Library resources & technical services (1957-

                                                *

209   Sette savi di Roma
    see
Seven sages. Italian.

                                                *

210   Seven wise masters of Rome
    see
Seven sages.

211   Shakspear, William
    see
Shakespeare, William, 1564-1616.

212   Shakspeare, William
    see
Shakespeare, William, 1564-1616.

213   Shakspere, William
    see
Shakespeare, William, 1564-1616.

214   Shaxper, William
    see
Shakespeare, William, 1564-1616.

(Copied from LC tracing)

T'ang civilization reference series.   215
   <u>see</u>
  唐代研究のしおり (<u>romanized</u>: Tōdai kenkyū no
  shiori)

    UNESCO   216
      see
  United Nations Educational, Scientific, and
    Cultural Organization.

    U.S. House of Representatives   217
      see
  U.S. Congress. House.

    U.S. President, 1961-   (Kennedy)   218
      see also
  Kennedy, John Fitzgerald, Pres. U.S., 1917-

  Von Braun, Wernher, 1912-   219
    Man on the moon
      see his
  Conquest of the moon

    The same work published under both titles.

  Wellesley, Dorothy Violet (Ashton) duchess of   220
    Wellington
      see
  Wellington, Dorothy Violet (Ashton) Wellesley,
    duchess of, 1889-1956.

  Wellesley, Lady Gerald   221
      see
  Wellington, Dorothy Violet (Ashton) Wellesley,
    duchess of, 1889-1956.

LC PRINTED REFERENCES

222

American Library Association. *Cataloging and Classification Section*
  see also
American Library Association. *Division of Cataloging and Classification.*
Institute on Cataloging Code Revision, *Stanford University, 1958.*
Institute on Cataloging Code Revision, McGill University, 1960.

LIBRARY OF CONGRESS REFERENCE

Users of depository catalogs should note that references may be to Library of Congress secondary entries which do not appear as headings in depository catalogs.

X 58–8299 rev

[r59b½]

223

American Library Association. *Resources and Technical Services Division. Cataloging and Classification Section*
  see
American Library Association. *Cataloging and Classification Section.*

LIBRARY OF CONGRESS REFERENCE

Users of depository catalogs should note that references may be to Library of Congress secondary entries which do not appear as headings in depository catalogs.

X 58–8298

224

American railroad journal. Richmond
  see
The **Railroad** journal.

225

Dolle, Frank A
  see
Dolle, Francis Anthony, 1923–

LIBRARY OF CONGRESS REFERENCE

Users of depository catalogs should note that references may be to Library of Congress secondary entries which do not appear as headings in depository catalogs.

X 55–8016

ESOMAR
see
European Society for Opinion Surveys and Market Research.

226

Laurence, John, *pseud.*
The single woman
see
McCauley, Laurence James, 1915–

227

Paris. Conference, *1954*
see
Four-Power Conference, *Paris, 1954.*

228

Raiz, Gilles de
see
Rais, Gilles de Laval, *seigneur* **de,** 1404–1440.

229

Rays, Gilles de
see
Rais, Gilles de Laval, *seigneur* **de,** 1404–1440.

230

Tag manual for inspectors of petroleum
see
Fisher/Tag manual for inspectors of petroleum.

231

Television factbook
see
Television digest with electronics reports.

232

TV directory
see
Television digest with electronics reports.

233

LIBRARY OF CONGRESS REFERENCE

Users of depository catalogs should note that references may be to Library of Congress secondary entries which do not appear as headings in depository catalogs.

X 55–7995

95

MH   Afr 2030.340.5

Algerian Front of National Liberation

A collection of miscellaneous papers

238

MH   HUH 751

Rogers, Francis Millet, 1914-

A collection of miscellaneous papers

239

FORM

Catalogs, circulars, and other announcements of courses, faculty, etc., of this institution are entered here under the general title Catalog, without mention of individual and varying titles.

In asking for a specific catalog give the call number above and the year covered by the catalog.

GPO

LC 0165-25 (4/57)

240

CARDS

Temporary cataloging. To be cataloged in full when volume is complete. Unbound numbers may be found

not LC

241

234

LC

Additional material on this subject, not individually cataloged, is classified in

235

LC

Pamphlets and other miscellaneous matter by or relating to this person, not separately cataloged, are classified in

236

Miscellaneous printed matter published by or relating to this body is classified in

LC 0165-25 (12/56)

237

Until bound and cataloged, issues of the above will be found in the

GPO 904659

III. Monograph publications: main and/or secondary entries (1-248)

A. Works of individual/personal authorship (1-83) see also II

1. Surnames (1-24, 27, 29-30, 34, 45)
   a. Names with designation (1-3)
   b. Unused forenames vs. full name: see III-A
   c. Compound names (4-6)
   d. Prefix names (7-11)
   e. Married women's names (12-14)
   f. Changed names: pseudonyms; original; secular names, etc. (13-23) access also through Index
2. Titles of nobility vs. family name (24-33)
3. Forenames (35-44, 47, 49-54)
   a. Secular names: sovereigns, consorts, princess, etc. (35-43)
   b. Religious names: pope, sister, saints, Biblical names, etc. (47, 49-54)
4. Personal name vs. title of office (34, 43-49)
5. Classical names: Greek and Latin (55-58)
6. Medieval names: see IX-D-E
7. European names (59-67)
   a. Finnish (59)
   b. Gaelic (60)
   c. Hungarian (61)
   d. Polish (62)
   e. Russian (63-65)
   f. Serbo-Croatian (66)
   g. Slovenian (67)
8. Oriental names (68-83)
   a. Arabic (68-70)
   b. Hebrew (71-72)
   c. Indic (73-75)
   d. Chinese (76-79)
      (1) Card for title in Harvard's Classified Book Catalogue of Chinese Books, 1938-1940
      (2) Card for title produced for LC Card Reproduction Project, 1949-1958
      (3) Card for title produced by Harvard for its own use
      (4) Card for title produced for LC Cooperative Cataloging Project since 1958
   e. Japanese (80-81) see also I-D; V-C
   f. Korean (82-83)

III.

NAMES WITH DESIGNATION

194
D453l **Lefèvre, Roger,** *of Grenoble.*
Le criticisme de Descartes. [1. éd.] Paris, Presses universitaires de France, 1958.

340 p. 23 cm. (Bibliothèque de philosophie contemporaine. Histoire de la philosophie et philosophie générale)

Bibliographical footnotes.

1. Descartes, René, 1596–1650. 2. Criticism (Philosophy)

A 59—4195

Chicago. Univ. Libr.   B1878
for Library of Congress   [60c2]

1

Meyer, Paul, *Swiss physician.*
Medizinischer Leitfaden zur privaten Unfall- und Haftpflichtversicherung für Ärzte und Versicherungsfachleute. Mit einem Anhang Schadenregulierung von H. J. Jung. Bern, H. Huber [1958]

178 p. 22 cm.

Bibliographical footnotes.

1. Insurance, Accident—Switzerland. 2. Insurance, Liability—Switzerland. I. Jung, Hans Jakob. II. Title. III. Title: Schadenregulierung.

A 59–3814

New York Univ.   Libraries HG9343
for Library of Congress   [$\frac{3}{8}$]

2

Mulder, R   *writer on salesmanship.*
Van marktsituatie tot offerte; enkele beschouwingen over verkooporganisatie en verkooptechniek. Alphen aan den Rijn, N. Samsom [1958]

99 p. illus. 21 cm.

"Erratum" slip laid in.

1. Salesmen and salesmanship.

HF5438.M868   A 59–4112

New York Univ.   Libraries
for Library of Congress   [$\frac{3}{8}$]†

3

Alemany y Bolufer, José, 1866–1934.
La fuente; diccionario enciclopédico ilustrado de la lengua española, publicado bajo la dirección de José Alemany y Bolufer y de varios reputados especialistas. Esta obra contiene todas las voces de uso corriente y numerosos americanismos, tecnicismos, neologismos y artículos enciclopédicos de biografía ... etc., etc. 80,000 artículos, 1,300 grabados, 600 retratos, 100 cuadros. Barcelona, R. Sopena ₁1954₎

viii, 1431 p. illus., ports. 19 cm.

"Después del Diccionario enciclopédico ilustrado publicamos ahora éste, con el mismo carácter ... pero limitando, hasta donde nos ha sido posible zu extensión y su precio."—Prólogo.

1. Spanish language—Dictionaries. 2. Encyclopedias and dictionaries, Spanish.   I. Title.

PC4625.A52   1954

Library of Congress   ₁¾₎   55–28286

4

Martins Pereira e Sousa, María de Lourdes, 1900–
Asia Maior; o planêta China. Pref. de Oswaldo Aranha. Rio de Janeiro, Editôra Civilização Brasileira ₁1958₎

330 p. illus. 22 cm.

1. China—Descr. & trav.—1949–

DS711.M28

Library of Congress   ₁¾₎   59–30990 ‡

5

Yeats-Brown, Francis Charles Claypon, 1886–1944.
The lives of a Bengal lancer. ₁Bantam ed.₎ New York, Bantam Books ₁1946, °1930₎

217 p. illus. 17 cm. (Bantam books, 43. Personal adventure)

Autobiographical.
London ed. (Gollancz) has title: Bengal lancer.

1. India—Soc. life & cust.   I. Title.

DS421.Y4   1946   915.4

Library of Congress   ₁¾₎

6

PREFIX NAMES

7

Du Pasquier, Jacqueline.
Guide de l'élégance. Illustrations de Louis Moles. Paris, Larousse ₁1954₎

250 p. illus. 18 cm. ₁Collection pratique₎

1. Beauty, Personal. 2. Clothing and dress.   I. Title.

RA778.D93

Library of Congress   ₁¾₎   55–29435 ‡

Escalante, Bernardino de.
　　B. de Escalante y del Hoyo; selección y estudio de Agustín
Pérez de Regules.　Santander, Imp. y Enc. de la Librería
Moderna, 1952.

　　lxix, 117 p.　18 cm.　(Antología de escritores y artistas montañeses,
25)

　　I. Pérez de Regules, Agustín, ed.

　　　　　Full name: Bernardino de Escalante y del Hoyo.

AC71.E8

Library of Congress　　　　　[3]

8

Saint Exupéry, Antoine de, 1900–1944.
　　Carnets.　[Paris] Gallimard [1953]
　　221 p.　illus.　19 cm.

　　I. Title.

　　　　　Full name: Antoine Jean Baptiste Marie
　　　　　Roger de Saint Exupéry.

PQ2637.A274C3　　　848.91　　　54–174 ‡

Library of Congress　　　[2]

9

Braun, Wernher von.
　　Conquest of the moon, by Wernher von Braun, Fred L.
Whipple [and] Willy Ley; illustrated by Chesley Bonestell,
Fred Freeman [and] Rolf Klep.　Edited by Cornelius Ryan.
New York, Viking Press, 1953.

　　126 p.　illus. (part col.) map.　28 cm.

　　"Expanded version of a series of scientific articles which appeared
in Colliers under the title 'Man on the moon.'"

　　1. Space flight to the moon.　　I. Ryan, Cornelius, ed.　II. Title.

TL799.M6B7　　　　　　　53—8620

Library of Congress　　　*629.1435
　　　　　　　　　[550*10]

10

Von Braun, Wernher, 1912–
　　Conquest of the moon, by Wernher von Braun, Fred L.
Whipple [and] Willy Ley; illustrated by Chesley Bonestell,
Fred Freeman [and] Rolf Klep.　Edited by Cornelius Ryan.
New York, Viking Press, 1953.

　　126 p.　illus. (part col.) map.　28 cm.

　　"Expanded version of a series of scientific articles which appeared
in Colliers under the title 'Man on the moon.'"
　　London ed. (Sidgwick and Jackson) has title: Man on the moon.
　　　　　　　　　　　　x

　　1. Space flight to the moon.　　I. Ryan, Cornelius, ed.　II. Title.

TL799.M6V6　1953　　　　　　　53–8620 rev

Library of Congress　　　*629.14353　629.1388
　　　　　　　　　[r59x19]

11

MARRIED WOMEN

Fremantle, Elizabeth (Wynne) 1779–1857.
The Wynne diaries, 1789–1820; passages selected and edited by Anne Fremantle.   London, New York, Oxford University Press ₍1952₎

xvi, 551 p.   geneal. tables.   16 cm.   (The World's classics, 522)

Diaries of Elizabeth and Eugenia Wynne.

12

1. Europe—Soc. life & cust.   2. Europe—Descr. & trav.—1800–1918.
3. Wynn family.   4. Europe—Hist.—1789–1900.   ɪ. Campbell, Eugenia (Wynne) b. 1780.   ɪɪ. Fremantle, Anne (Jackson) 1909– ed.   ɪɪɪ. Title.

D360.F72   920.7   53–3163
Library of Congress   ₍3₎

Best, Allena (Champlin) 1892–
The wavering flame: Connecticut, 1776; written and illustrated by Erick Berry ₍pseud.₎   New York, Scribner ₍1953₎

266 p.   illus.   21 cm.   (The Strength of the Union)

PSEUDONYMS

1. Connecticut—Hist.—Revolution—Fiction.   ɪ. Title.
Full name: Evangel Allena (Champlin) Best.

13

PZ7.B4656Wav   53—12261 ↕
Library of Congress   ₍54h5₎

823
Eℓ44s   Eliot, George, pseud., i.e. Marian Evans, afterwards Cross, 1819-1880.
Silas Marner; with critical and biographical material by G. Robert Strange. New York, Harper ₍1961₎
ix,259p. 21cm. (Harper's modern classics)
"Bibliographical and textual note": p. 259.

14

I. Title

Crow, Dox, *pseud.*
Hunry Shakespeare, an American novel, by Dox and John Crow ₍pseud. 1st ed.₎   New York, Exposition Press ₍1955₎

84 p.   21 cm.

15

ɪ. Crow, John, pseud., joint author.   ɪɪ. Title.

PZ4.C9529Hu   55–9398 ↕
Library of Congress   ₍2₎

Beeding, Francis, *pseud.*
    La maison du Dr Edwardes (Spellbound) tr. de l'anglais par Jean Foras. Paris, A. Michel ₁1948₎

    309 p. 18 cm. (Collection "Le Limier," 9)

16

    ɪ. Title.   (Series)
            Francis Beeding, *pseud. of* John Leslie Palmer
            and Hilary Aidan St. George Saunders.

PR6003.E3H63   48–21821*‡

Library of Congress   ₁1₎

Stevens, Peter, *pseud.*
    The noisy baby animals. Pictures by Glen Thomas. Philadelphia, Winston ₁1955₎

    unpaged. illus. 21 cm. (Magic talking books, T–7)

    "Old MacDonald had a farm" (phonodisc. 78 rpm.) on cover. James Macklin, vocalist; full orchestra and sound effects; Jimmy Carroll, musical director.

17

    ɪ. Old MacDonald had a farm. Phonodisc. ɪɪ. Title.
                Peter Stevens, *pseud. of* Bernard
                    and Darlene Geis.

    PZ10.3.S837No   55–2680 ‡

Congress   ₁3₎

926.08
L529m Lehrburger, Egon, 1904–
    Men who changed the world; stories of invention and discovery, by Egon Larsen ₁pseud. 2d ed.₎ New York, Roy Publishers ₁1953₎

    224 p. illus. 22 cm.

18

    x Larsen, Egon, pseud.
    1. Inventors.   ɪ. Title.

    T39.L43 1953   926   52–11610 rev ‡

Library of Congress   ₁r55o5₎

Larsen, Egon, pseud.
    Men who changed the world; stories of invention and discovery; with 38 photographs. Roy Pubs. 1952
    224p illus

    Contents: Alexander Graham Bell; Thomas Alva Edison; William Friese-Greene; Charles A. Parsons; John Boyd Dunlop; Guglielmo Marconi; Wilbur and Orville Wright; Henry Ford; Lord Rutherford; John Logie Baird; Sir Frank Whittle; Sir Robert Watson-Watt
    Bibliography: p218

19

    1 Inventions 2 Inventors ɪ Title   920

    5-8-53   (W) The H. W. Wilson Company

Dodgson, Charles Lutwidge, 1832–1898.
    Alice's adventures in Wonderland, and Through the look-
ing glass, by Lewis Carroll [pseud.] Illustrated by Roberta
Paflin. Racine, Wis., Whitman Pub. Co. [1955]

    284 p. illus. 21 cm. (Whitman famous classics)

    ɪ. Title. ɪɪ. Title: Through the looking glass.

PZ8.D666A 96

Library of Congress   [2]

55–2241 ↕

20

Fisher, Clay, 1912–
    Yellowstone Kelly. Boston, Houghton Mifflin, 1957.
    246 p. 21 cm.
    Fictionized biography.

    1. Kelly, Luther Sage, 1849–1928—Fiction.   ɪ. Title.

Yg

Congress   [7]

57–6945 ↕

21

Allen, Henry, 1912–
    Yellowstone Kelly [by] Clay Fisher [pseud.] Boston,
Houghton Mifflin, 1957.
    246 p. 21 cm.

    1. Kelly, Luther Sage, 1849–1928—Fiction.   ɪ. Title.

PZ3.A4256Yg

Library of Congress   [r58h6]

57–6945 rev ↕

22

Allen, Henry, 1912–
    Yellowstone Kelly [by] Clay Fisher [pseud]. Houghton
1957
    246p
    "The author has built his story around Luther S. Kelly, a romantic
figure with vast frontier experience and considerable learning. The
action takes place during the winter of 1875-76 during the Battle of the
Little Big Horn. A novel of hardship, fighting, love and inevitable
tragedy." Huntting

    1 Kelly, Luther Sage, 1849–1928—Fiction   2 Little Big Horn, Battle
of the, 1876—Fiction   ɪ Title   Fic

5-24-57   (W)   The H. W. Wilson Company

23

1889–1956.
Wellington, Dorothy Violet (Ashton) Wellesley, *duchess of,* ∧
　　Early light; the collected poems of Dorothy Wellesley.
London, R. Hart-Davis, 1955.

　　255 p.　23 cm.

24

　　ɪ. Title.

　　PR6045.E53E2　　　◯　　　821.91　　　　　56–414 ‡

　Library of Congress　　　　₍2₎

25

Queensberry, Francis Archibald Kelhead Douglas, *10th*
marquis, 1896–
　　Oscar Wilde and the Black Douglas, by the Marquess of
Queensberry in collaboration with Percy Colson.　London,
Hutchinson ₍1949₎

　　181 p.　port.　24 cm.
　　Bibliography: p. 169.

　　1. Wilde, Oscar, 1854–1900.　2. Douglas, Lord Alfred Bruce, 1870–
1945.

　　PR5823.Q4　　　◯　　　928.2　　　　　50—1975

　Congress　　　　₍5₎

Attlee, Clement Richard Attlee, *1st earl,* 1883–
　　Empire into Commonwealth; the Chichele lectures delivered at Oxford in May 1960 on Changes in the conception
and structure of the British Empire during the last half
century.　London, New York, Oxford University Press,
1961.

　　53 p.　20 cm.

26

　　1. Commonwealth of Nations—Hist.　ɪ. Title.

　　JN276.A76　　　◯　　　342.42　　　　　61–1497 ‡

　Library of Congress　　　　₍10₎

Bacon, Francis, *viscount St. Albans,* 1561–1626.
　　The New organon, and related writings.　Edited with an
introd. by Fulton H. Anderson.　New York, Liberal Arts
Press ₍1960₎

　　292 p.　21 cm.　(The Library of liberal arts, no. 97)

27

　　1. Science—Methodology.　ɪ. Anderson, Fulton Henry, 1895–
ed.　ɪɪ. Title.

　　B1168.E5A5　　　◯　　　112　　　　　59–11682 rev 2 ‡

　Library of Congress　　　　₍r61k9₎

28

Henley, Dorothy (Howard) Eden, *baroness*, 1881–
　　Rosalind Howard, countess of Carlisle. London, Hogarth Press, 1958.

　　147 p. illus. 21 cm.

　　1. Carlisle, Rosalind Frances (Stanley) Howard, countess of, 1845–1921.

CT788.C257H4　　　　　　　920.7　　　　　59–31156 ‡
Library of Congress　　　　　　[8]

29

354.42092
Sm97　　**Smyth,** *Sir* **John George,** *bart.*, 1893–
　　The only enemy; an autobiography. London, Hutchinson [1959]

　　352 p. illus. 22 cm.

　　ɪ. Title.

DA574.S55A3　　　　　　923.542　　　　　59–3160 ‡
Library of Congress　　　　　[2]

30

Churchill, *Sir* **Winston Leonard Spencer,** 1874–
　　A history of the English-speaking peoples. [1st ed.] New York, Dodd, Mead, 1956–58.

　　4 v. maps, tables. 22 cm.

　　CONTENTS.—v. 1. The birth of Britain.—v. 2. The New World.—v. 3. The age of revolution.—v. 4. The great democracies.

　　1. Gt. Brit.—Hist.　　ɪ. Title.

DA16.C47　　　　　　942　　　　　56—6868
Library of Congress　　　　[58r58v⁵20]

Caulaincourt, Armand Augustin Louis, *marquis* de, *duc de Vicence*, 1773–1827.
　　With Napoleon in Russia; the memoirs of General de Caulaincourt, duke of Vicenza. From the original memoirs as edited by Jean Hanoteau. Abridged, edited, and with an introd. by George Libaire. New York, Grosset & Dunlap [1959, °1935]

　　422 p. illus. 21 cm. (The Universal library, UL–55)

　　Translation of Mémoires du général de Caulaincourt.

　　1. Napoléon I—Invasion of Russia, 1812. 2. France—Hist.—Consulate and Empire, 1799–1815. I. Title.

DC198.C35A33　　1959　　　　923.544　　　　　　59–2924 ‡

Library of Congress　　　　　[10]

31

La Rochefoucauld, Edmée (de Fels) *duchesse de*, 1895–
　　Choix de poèmes [par] Gilbert Mauge [pseud. Paris] Gallimard [1955]

　　93 p. 19 cm.

A 56–2591

Illinois. Univ. Library
for Library of Congress　　　　[8]

32

843
H874Wm　Maurois, André, 1885–
　　Olympio; the life of Victor Hugo; translated from the French by Gerard Hopkins. [1st American ed.] New York, Harper [1956]

　　xii, 498 p. illus., ports. 25 cm.

　　Bibliography: p. 447–458.

　　1. Hugo, Victor Marie, comte, 1802–1885. I. Title.

　　Name originally: Émile Salomon Wilhelm Herzog.

PQ2293.M353　　1956a　　　　928.4　　　　　　55—8026

Library of Congress　　　　　[57v²20]

33

TITLE OF OFFICE

Nasser, Gamal Abdel, *Pres. United Arab Republic*, 1918–
　　The philosophy of the revolution. With an introd. by John S. Badeau, and biographical sketch by John Gunther. Buffalo, Smith, Keynes & Marshall [1959]

　　102 p. illus. 21 cm. (Economica books, E–16)

　　1. Egypt—Hist.—Philosophy. 2. Egypt—Pol. & govt.—1952–
I. Title.

DT107.83.N333　　1959　　　　962.05　　　　　　59–9190 rev ‡

Library of Congress　　　　[r59h6]

34

Edward VIII, *King of Great Britain,* 1894–
    A family album, by the Duke of Windsor. London, Cassell ₁1960₎

    151 p. illus. 22 cm.

35

    ɪ. Title.

DA580.A34   923.142   61–1626 ‡

Library of Congress   ₁5₎

948.905092
F873p   **Palsbo, Susanne,** *ed.*
    The daily life of the King of Denmark. Editors: Susanne Palsbo ₁and₎ Ernst Mentze. ₁Copenhagen? Press Dept. of the Ministry for Foreign Affairs, 1957.

    unpaged (chiefly illus.) 26 cm.

36

    1. Frederik ɪx, King of Denmark, 1899–   ɪ. Mentze, Ernst, joint ed. ɪɪ. Title.

DL258.P313   923.1489   58–37631 ‡

₍ Congress   ₁8₎

Tokioka, Takashi.
    Ascidians of Sagami Bay, collected by His Majesty the Emperor of Japan. Described and illustrated by Takasi Tokioka. Edited by Hirotaro Hattori. Tokyo, Iwanami Shoten, 1953.

    3, 4, 315 p. illus., 79 plates, map. 31 cm.

    English and Japanese; Japanese title (transliterated): Sagami-wan-san kaishō-rui zufu.
    Bibliography: p. 299–305.

37

    1. Tunicata—Sagami Bay.   ɪ. Hirohito, Emperor of Japan, 1901–
ɪɪ. Hattori, Hirotarō, 1875–   ed. ɪɪɪ. Title. ɪv. Title: Sagami-wan-
san kaishō-rui zufu.

QL613.T6   594.91   53—39480

Library of Congress   ₁a55b½₎

Muḥammad V, *King of Morocco,* 1909–
    Le Maroc à l'heure de l'indépendance. Traduit de l'arabe. Rabat, Ministère de l'information et du tourisme ₁1957–

    v. illus. 23 cm.

    Speeches and addresses.

    Contents.—t. 1. 1955–1957.

38

    1. Morocco—Pol. & govt.—Addresses, essays, lectures.

DT324.M814   59–31299 ‡

Library of Congress   ₁8₎

Alice, *consort of Louis IV, grand duke of Hesse-Darmstadt,*
1843–1878.

Alice, grand duchess of Hesse, princess of Great Britain
and Ireland, biographical sketch and letters. With portrait.
New York & London, G. P. Putnam's sons, 1884.

x, 11–407 p. 21ᶜᵐ.

A memoir, by Dr. K. Sell, with a translation of the letters of the princess to her mother, was published anonymously in German, Darmstadt, 1883. The letters in the original with a translation, by Princess Christian, of the memoir, were published at London, 1884.

Appendix: A watcher by the dead.—A sketch in memoriam Dec. 14, 1878. By Sir Theodore Martin.—Lines in memoriam.

I. Helena, Augusta Victoria, princess Christian of Schleswig-Holstein, 1846–1923. II. Sell, Karl, 1845–1914.

39

Library of Congress   DA559.A3A4   1884 b

16—1908

[a41b1]

40

Aleksandra, *consort of Peter II, King of Yugoslavia,* 1921–
For love of a king. [1st ed.] Garden City, N. Y., Doubleday, 1956.

318 p. illus. 22 cm.

1. Peter II, King of Yugoslavia, 1923–   I. Title.

DR369.A6   923.1497   56–7529 ‡

41

Lofts, Norah (Robinson) 1904–
Eleanor the queen; the story of the most famous woman
of the Middle Ages. [1st ed.] Garden City, N. Y., Doubleday, 1955.

249 p. 22 cm. (Cavalcade books)

1. Eleanor of Aquitaine, consort of Henry II, 1122?–1204—Fiction.
I. Title.

Full name: Norah Ethel (Robinson) Lofts.

PZ3.L825El   55–5509 ‡

42

Clapham, John, *b.* 1566.
Elizabeth of England; certain observations concerning the
life and reign of Queen Elizabeth. Edited by Evelyn Plummer Read and Conyers Read. Philadelphia, University of
Pennsylvania Press, 1951.

vii, 125 p. ports. 21 cm. (University of Pennsylvania. Dept. of History. Translations and reprints from the original sources of history, 3d ser., v. 6)

"The text printed is that of the second draft in Additional manuscripts 22295, in the British Museum."—p. 26.

1. Elizabeth, Queen of England, 1533–1603. 2. Gt. Brit.—Hist.—Elizabeth, 1558–1603. 3. Gt. Brit.—Hist.—Tudors, 1485–1603. (Series: Pennsylvania. University. Dept. of History. Translations and reprints from the original sources of history, 3d ser., v. 6)

D101.P4   ser. 3,   vol. 6   942.05   51–10140
——— ——— Copy 2.   DA355.C5

Library of Congress   [53q10]

Elizabeth II, *Queen of Great Britain, 1926–*
 Dedication; a selection from the public speeches of Her Majesty Queen Elizabeth II, compiled by Joan Werner Laurie. London, Heinemann [1953]

 unpaged. illus. 25 cm.

 I. Title.   xx Gt. Brit. Sovereigns, etc., 1952–
 (Elizabeth II)
 DA590.A35   *942.085   54–16075 ‡

43

Gt. Brit. *Sovereigns, etc., 1952–*   (*Elizabeth II*)
 Royal warrant to amend the Royal warrant of the 24th May, 1949, concerning retired pay, pensions and other grants for members of the military forces and of the nursing and auxiliary services thereof disabled, and for the widows, children, parents, and other dependants of such members deceased, in consequence of service after the 2nd September, 1939. London, H. M. Stationery Off. [1955]
 12 p. 25 cm. ([Gt. Brit. Parliament. Papers by command] cmd. 9362)
 At head of title: Ministry of Pensions and National Insurance.
 1. Pensions, Military—Gt. Brit.   I. Gt. Brit. Ministry of Pensions and National Insurance.   (Series)   xx Elizabeth II,
Queen of Great Britain, 1926–
          351.5   55–2369

 Library of Congress   [2]

44

Kennedy, John Fitzgerald, *Pres. U. S., 1917–*
 To turn the tide; a selection from President Kennedy's public statements from his election through the 1961 adjournment of Congress, setting forth the goals of his first legislative year. Edited by John W. Gardner. Foreword by Carl Sandburg. Introd. by President Kennedy. [1st ed.] New York, Harper [1962]

 235 p. 22 cm.

 1. U. S.—Pol. & govt.—1961–   2. U. S.—For. rel.—1961–
 I. Title.   xx U.S. President, 1961–   (Kennedy)

 E841.K43   973.922   61—12221 ‡

45

U. S. *President, 1961–*   (*Kennedy*)
 Inaugural address, delivered at the Capitol, January 20, 1961. [Washington, Dept. of State, 1961]
 6 p. 20 cm. ([U. S.] Dept. of State. Publication 7137. General foreign policy series, 161)

 1. U. S.—Pol. & govt.—1961–   (Series: U. S. Dept. of State. Publication 7137. Series: U. S. Dept. of State. General foreign policy series, 161)   xx Kennedy, John Fitzgerald, Pres.
U.S., 1917–   S D 61–5
 U. S. Dept. of State.   Library E183.7
 for Library of Congress   [5]

46

Joannes XXIII, *pope*, 1881–   *comp.*
    Gli atti della visita apostolica di s. Carlo Borromeo a Ber-
gamo (1575) ... a cura di Angelo Giuseppe Roncalli ... con
la collaborazione di don Pietro Forno.   Firenze, L. S.
Olschki, 1936–
        v. pl. 26½ cm. (*Added t.-p.:* Fontes ambrosiani in lucem editi
cura et studio Bybliothecae ambrosianae, moderante Iohanne Galbiati.
XIII–XIV)
        Added title-pages have imprint: Mediolani, in aedibus ambrosianis.
        Bibliographical foot-notes.
        CONTENTS.—I. La città. 2 v.
        1. Carlo Borromeo, Saint, 1538–1584. 2. Visitations, Ecclesiastical—
Bergamo. 3. Bergamo—Church history.   I. Forno, Pietro, joint
comp.   xx Catholic Church. Pope, 1958–
(Joannes XXIII)

                                                                A C 39–567 rev 2

Yale Univ.   Library   ◯
for Library of Congress   [r59d8]

47

Catholic Church. *Pope, 1958–*   (*Joannes xxiii*) *Sacer-*
dotii nostri primordia (1 Aug. 1959) English.
    From the beginning of our priesthood, "Sacerdotii nostri
primordia."   As provided by N. C. W. C. [Boston] St. Paul
Editions [1959]
        32 p. 19 cm.

        1. Vianney, Jean Baptiste Marie, Saint, 1786–1859. 2. Clergy—
Religious life.   I. Title.   xx Joannes XXIII, Pope,
1881–

BX4700.V5C3   ◯   253.2   60–197 ‡
Library of Congress   [2]

48

Murphy, Francis Xavier, 1914–
    Pope John XXIII comes to the Vatican. [1st ed.]   New
York, R. M. McBride Co. [1959]
        242 p. illus. 21 cm.

49

        1. Joannes XXIII, Pope, 1881–   I. Title.   xx to 1.
Catholic Church. Pope, 1958–   (Joannes XXIII)
BX1378.2.M8   ◯   922.21   59–8871 ‡
Library of Congress   [30]

50

Dolores, *Sister.*
    The Francis A. Drexel family.   Cornwells Heights, Pa.,
Sisters of the Blessed Sacrament [1955, °1939]
        418 p. illus. 22 cm.

        1. Drexel family.
                        Secular name: Marie Elisabeth Letterhouse.

CS71.D7685 1955   ◯   55–31204 ‡
Library of Congress   [1]

Justinus *Martyr, Saint.*
Христомаθіа; или, Выбранныя мѣста, служащія полез-
нымъ нравоученіемъ. Съ присовокупленіемъ Письма св.
Василія Великаго ко св. Григорію Богослову о пустын-
ножительствѣ. Въ Москвѣ, Иждивеніемъ Н. Новикова,
въ Унив. тип., 1783.

146 p. 20 cm.

Translated by hieromonk Mefodiĭ.

1. Theology—Collected works—Early church. ɪ. Gregorius
Nazianzenus, Saint, Patriarch of Constantinople. ɪɪ. Basilius, Saint,
the Great, Abp. of Caesarea, 330 (ca.)–379. ɪɪɪ. Title.
Title transliterated: Khristomafĭa.

BR65.J8 1783   55–51173

51

Anouilh, Jean, 1910–
The lark; ₍play₎ Translated by Christopher Fry. New
York, Oxford University Press, 1956 ₍°1955₎

103 p. 20 cm.

1. Jeanne d'Arc, Saint, 1412–1431—Drama.   ɪ. Title.
PQ2601.N67A692   1956   842.91   56—5472 ‡

Library of Congress   ₍59c²3₎

52

53

BIBLICAL NAMES

Allen, Roland, 1869–1947.
Missionary methods: St. Paul's or ours? ₍3d ed.₎ London,
World Dominion Press, 1953.

230 p. 19 cm.

Companion vol. to the author's The spontaneous expansion of the
church.

1. Missions, Foreign. 2. Paul, Saint, apostle.   ɪ. Title.
BV2110.A5 1953   54–32915 ‡

54

Fleg, Edmond, 1874–
Moïse, raconté par les sages. Éd. définitive. Paris, A.
Michel ₍1956₎

220 p. 20 cm.

1. Moses.
BS580.M6F6   57–24405 ‡

Library of Congress   ₍8₎

Archimedes.
Works. Edited in modern notation, with introductory chapters by T. L. Heath. With a supplement, The method of Archimedes, recently discovered by Heiberg. New York, Dover Publications [195–?]

clxxxvi, 326, 51 p. illus. 21 cm.

Bibliography: p. [xi]–xii.

55

1. Mathematics, Greek. 2. Geometry—Early works to 1800. 3. Mechanics—Early works to 1800. I. Heath, Sir Thomas Little, 1861–1940, ed.

QA31.A692   510.81   53—3224

Sophocles.
König Ödipus. Deutsch von Wolfgang Schadewaldt. Berlin, Suhrkamp Verlag [1955]

95 p. 21 cm.

56

I. Schadewaldt, Wolfgang, 1900–   tr. II. Title.

PA4415.G5O7   1955

Library of Congress   [¾]

Horatius Flaccus, Quintus.
Odes and Epodes, a modern English verse translation by Joseph P. Clancy. [Chicago] University of Chicago Press [1960]

v, 257 p. 21 cm.

Bibliography: p. 8–9.

57

1. Clancy, Joseph P., 1928–   ed. and tr.

PA6395.C48   1960a   874   60–2404

Vergilius Maro, Publius.
The Aeneid. A new translation by Patric Dickinson. [New York] New American Library [1961]

319 p. fold. map. 18 cm. (A Mentor book, MT348)

A Mentor classic.

58

I. Dickinson, Patric, 1914–   tr. II. Title.

PA6807.A5D5   873   61–10759

Library of Congress   [2]

Leinonen, Artturi Aleksanteri, 1888–
Johannes Jussoila; historiallinen romaani. 3. painos. Helsinki, W. Söderström [1944]

548 p. 21 cm.

59

1. Jussoila, Johannes, d. 1604—Fiction.   I. Title.

PH355.L45J6   1944

Library of Congress   [₈³]

60–55222   ‡

60

Diolún, Eilís.
Oscar agus an cóiste sé neasóg. Patricia Ní Laighin a rinne na pictiúirí. Baile Áta Cliat, Oifig an tSoláťair [1952]

106 p. illus. 22 cm.

I. Title.

Title transliterated: Oscar agus an cóiste sé neasóg.

PZ90.G2D53

Congress   [₈³]

59–40510

Markos, György.
Az orosz ipar fejlődése Nagy Pétertől Sztálinig. [Budapest] Cserépfalvi [ᶜ1940]

189 p. illus. 20 cm. (Kék könyvek, 9)

61

1. Russia—Indus.   I. Title.

HC333.M3

Library of Congress   [₈³]

60–55169   ‡

62

Stahl, Zdzisław, 1901–
Istota budżetu na tle rozwoju historycznego i współczesnych tendencyj konstytucyjnych. We Lwowie, Nakł. Tow. Naukowego; skł. gł.: Gubrynowicz, 1934.

94 p. 26 cm. (Archiwum Towarzystwa Naukowego we Lwowie. Dział II., t. 14, zesz. 4)

Also paged [277]–368.

1. Finance, Public.   (Series: Towarzystwo Naukowe we Lwowie. Wydział II. Historyczno-Filozoficzny. Archiwum, t. 14, zesz. 4)

D1.T68   t. 14, zesz. 4

Library of Congress   [₈³]

60–55078

SAMPLE

WC
320
A366d
1957

ALEKSANÍAN, Arto Bogdanovich
    Дифтерия; эпидемилогия [sic]
профилактика.   Москва, Медгиз,
1957.
        206 p. illus.
        Title transliterated: Difteriíà.
        1. Diphtheria
    W C320 A366d   59-3321

63

CtY

Kirsanov, Semen Isaakovich, 1906-
    Избранные произведения. Москва, Гос.
Изд-во Худож. Лит-ры, 1961.
    2 v. port. 21 cm.
    Title transliterated: Izbrannye proizve-
deniíà.

64

Val'dman, Andreĭ Robertovich.
    Значение витаминов в питании сельскохозяйственных
животных и птиц. Рига, Изд-во Академии наук Латвий-
ской ССР, 1957.

    271 p. illus. 23 cm.

    At head of title: Академия наук Латвийской ССР. Институт
биологии.
    Bibliography: p. 259-269.

    1. Vitamins. 2. Feeds.
                    Title transliterated: Znachenie vitaminov v pi-
                tanii sel'skokhozíaĭstvennykh zhivotnykh.

SF203.V26   60-22997

Library of Congress   [8]

65

FA 2568.27   MH

Kreševljaković, Hamdija, 1890-
    Banje u Bosni i Hercegovini, 1462-1916. Drugo popr.
i prošireno izd. Sarajevo, Svjetlost, 1952

    148 p. illus., map, plans

66

Slav 8871.1.8   MH

Vraz, Stanko, 1810-51
    Slovenska korespondenca Vraz-Kočevar, 1833-1838.
[Uredil] Ljubomir Andrej Lisac. Ljubljana, 1961

    131 p. (Slovenska akademija znanosti in umetnosti.
Razred za filološke in literarne vede. Korespondence
pomembnih Slovencev, 3)

67

Averroës, 1126–1198.

تلخيص كتاب النفس لابى الوليد بن رشد، وأربع رسائل:
رسالة الاتصال لابن الصائغ ‏(و)‏ كتاب النفس لاسحق بن حنين
‏(و)‏ رسالة الاتصال لابن رشد ‏(و)‏ رسالة العقل ليعقوب الكندى.
نشرها وحققها وقدم لها احمد فؤاد الاهوانى. الطبعة الاولى.
القاهرة، مكتبة النهضة المصرية، ١٩٥٠. ‏[1950]‏

188 p. facsim. 25 cm.
Cover title: Talkhiç Kitab al nafs (Paraphrase du "De anima")
suivi de quatre textes: 1. L'union avec l'intellect agent, d'Avempace.
2. L'union avec l'intellect agent, du fils d'Ibn Rochd. 3. Le "De
anima" d'Ishaq ibn Hunayn. 4. L'intellect d'al-Kindi.

(Continued on next card)
58–42947

[1]

68

Averroës, 1126–1198.

تلخيص كتاب النفس ... (Card 2)

Summary in French.
Bibliographical footnotes.

I. Aristoteles. De anima. II. Avempace, d. 1138 or 9. Risālat
al-ittişāl. III. Ishāq ibn Hunayn, d. 910 or 11, supposed author.
Kitāb al-nafs. IV. 'Abd 'Allāh ibn Muhammad ibn Rushd. Risālat
al-ittişāl. V. al-Kindī, d. ca. 873. Risālat al-'aql. VI. al-Ahwānī,
Ahmad Fu'ād, ed. VII. Title.

Title transliterated: Talkhīş Kitāb al-nafs.

B749.T3 1950

Library of Congress [1]

69

al-Karkhī, 'Abbūd, 1861–1946.

ديوان الكرخى. عنى بطبعه حسين حاتم الكرخى. بغداد،
مطبعة المعارف، ١٩٥٥- ‏[الجزء الاول: ١٩٥٦]‏
‏[1955-]‏

v. illus., ports. 25 cm.
At head of title: عبود الكرخى
Vol. 1: الطبعة الثانية، منقحة ومزيدة

I. Title.

Title transliterated: Dīwān.

PJ7842.A7A17 1955
Library of Congress [2]

59–36689

70

Judah ben Samuel, *he-Ḥasid, d.* 1217.

ספר חסידים, עם פירוש מלוקט מפירושי סעדיה חלאוונה, דוד
גרינהוט ‏[ו]‏ דוד אפטרוד, ‏[עם]‏ ברית עולם ממרן אזולאי. ונלוה
להם הגהות מקור חסד והערות ממני ראובן מרגליות.
‏[Lwów, 192-]‏

1 v. (various pagings) 24 cm.

1. Ethics, Jewish. I. Title.

Title transliterated: Sefer ḥasidim.

BJ1287.J83S4
Library of Congress [3]

53–54682

71

Kazenelson, Judah Loeb Benjamin, 1847–1917.

שירת הזמיר, ספור מאת בוקי בן יגלי [pseud.] ווארשא,
אחיאסף, תרנ"ה. Варшава, 1895.

75 p. 17 cm. (ספורי בוקי בן יגלי (ל. קאצנלסאהן] חוברת א)

72

I. Title. *Title transliterated:* Shirat ha-zamir.

PJ5053.K42S5 1895

Library of Congress

60–56476

73

Pant, Sumitra Nandan, 1900–

श्रीसुमित्रानन्दन पंत. [तृतीय संस्करण] प्रयाग,
हिन्दी साहित्य सम्मेलन, संवत् २००३ [1946?]

37, 101, 2 p. port. 19 cm. (आधुनिक कवि, २)

देवपुरस्कार ग्रंथावली, २.

In Hindi.
Poems.
(Series: Ādhunika kavi, 2. Dĕva-puraskāra granthāvalī, 2)
Title transliterated: Śrīsumitrānandana Panta.

PK2098.P32S7

Library of Congress

S A 61–5

MH

IndL 3045.7
ed.

74

Shastri, Vishva Bandhu, 1896–
     Veda mēṃ asita śabda. [Lāhaura, Bhīmadeva Śāstrī, 1932?]

     19 p.
Verses in Sanskrit with Hindi translation

MH

IndL 2800.870.5

75

Vīrabhadra Śivācārya
     Śrī Jagadguru Viśvarādhya aṣtottaraśata nāmvalih. Kāśī [Ramachandra Prasad, 1946]

     19 p. ports.
T.p. & text in Sanskrit

Card 1

4932/1344
(MH-HY call number)

Chang, Chiu-ju, 1896–
三民主義教育學　張九如編　上海　商務印書館
民國18 [1929]
4, 186 p. 19 cm. （新時代三民主義教育叢書）

79

Card 2 (SAMPLE DNLM)

86–1925.　San min chu i.
min chu i chiao yü hsüeh.
brary 4932　C 60–5393
(MH-HY class no)

Card 3 (SAMPLE DNLM)

QV
4
M685ya
1935

MIYAZAKI, Saburō
[Yakurigaku, yakugakusei no tame ni]
藥理學　藥學學生のために　Tōkyō, Hakusen Shobō,
1935.
8, 11, 676, 43 p.　illus., ports.
1. Pharmacology
QV4 M685ya　59–7858

Card 4

J4361.9/9322
(MH-HY call number)

Obama, Toshie, 1889–
現代日本財界人物論　小汀利得著　東京　ダイ
ヤモンド社
4, 227 p.

1. Capitalis
jimbutsu ron.
HG188.J3O
Harvard Univ
for Library of

76–
78

Card 5

K4346/2128.2
(MH-HY call number)

Ch'oe, Ho-jin, 1914–
一般經濟史　崔虎鎭著　新稿
檀紀 4287 [1954]
7, 306 p.　22 cm.
Appendices (p. 273–294)：一般經濟史에關한主要文獻─朝鮮社
會經濟史에關한研究文獻─朝鮮社會經濟史에關한主要文獻
1. Capitalis

80–
81

Card 6

Chŏng, T'ae-hyŏn.
韓國植物圖鑑　鄭台鉉著　서울　新志社
4289–90 [1956–57；v. 1, 1957]
2 v.　illus., maps (1 col.)　21 cm.
Korean and Latin; added title: Korean flora.
Errata slips inserted.

1. Botany—Korea.　I. Title.　II. Title: Korean flora.
Title romanized: Hanguk singmul togam.

QK370.C48　　　K 59–16
Library of Congress　　[8]

82–
83

Card 7 (letterpress)

MH-HY
柯劭忞字仲勉慇鳳蓀(1850–1933)撰
春秋穀梁傳補注 十五卷　　民國二四年(1935)北京
大學研究院文史部鉛印本(柯劭忞先生遺著第一種)
四册，一函
Ko, Shao-min
Ch'un ch'iu ku liang chuan pu chu

(letterpress)　　(card number) (call number)
2609　　779/4210.2

Harvard-Yenching Institute

Card 8 (offset)

MH-HY
4924/3193

江恬源，字問漁(1885–)撰
職教論改革言論　民國二八年(1939)重慶
正中書局影印本(教育"叢書)
三六面　圓　計六分

Chiang, Hêng-yüan.
Hsüeh chih kai ko lun.
4924/3193
(offset)　(call number)　Harvard Univ. Library
for Library of Congress

C54–5600
(card number)

Card 9 (lithomat)

MH-HY
6129/2147.2B

康有為号長素廣夏康長素(1818–1927)撰
廣藝舟雙楫 六卷　　民國二六年(1937)
上海商務縮印本（國學基本叢書之一）
一七八面　七公分

K'ang, Yu-wei.
Kuang i chou shuang chi.

(lithomat) Harvard Univ.
(card number)
61C 646

Stevenson, Fanny (Van de Grift) 1840–1914.
Our Samoan adventure, by Fanny and Robert Louis Stevenson. With a three-year diary by Mrs. Stevenson, now published for the first time, together with rare photos. from family albums. Edited, with an introd. and notes, by Charles Neider. ₁1st ed.₁ New York, Harper ₁1955₁

xxii, 264 p. illus., ports., map, facsims. 22 cm.

1. Samoan Islands—Descr. & trav.   I. Stevenson, Robert Louis, 1850–1894.   II. Title.

PR5499.S1Z5   928.2

Library of Congress   ₁50₁

84

Kay, Herbert Davenport, 1893–
Milk pasteurization: planning, plant, operation, and control ₁by₁ H. D. Kay ₁and others₁ Geneva, World Health Organization, 1953.

204 p. illus., diagrs. 24 cm. (World Health Organization. Monograph series, no. 14)

"Published jointly by FAO and WHO and issued also as FAO agricultural studies, no. 23."
Bibliography : p. 203–204.

1. Milk—Pasteurization.   (Series)

SF259.K3   637.1333   53—3453

Library of Congress   ₁58c½₁

85

Foucault, Marc, 1902–
Le Mont-Saint-Michel; photos de Marc Foucault et Emmanuel Boudot-Lamotte. ₁Paris₁ Éditions Tel ₁1952₁

54 p. (p. 9–54 illus., map) 31 cm. (Collection des cathédrales et des sanctuaires du moyen âge)

Introductory text by Marc Thibout in French and English.

1. Mont St. Michel, France.   2. Mont St. Michel, France (Benedictine abbey)   I. Boudot-Lamotte, Emmanuel.   II. Thibout, Marc.

NA5551.M7F6   1952   726.771   53–33466

Library of Congress   ₁¾₁

86

Montesquieu, Charles Louis de Secondat, *baron* **de La Brède et de,** 1689–1755.
The spirit of laws, by Charles de Secondat, baron de Montesquieu. ₁Translated by Thomas Nugent, rev. by J. V. Prichard₁ On the origin of inequality. On political economy. The social contract. By Jean Jacques Rousseau. ₁Translated by G. D. H. Cole₁ Chicago, Encyclopædia Britannica ₁1955, ᶜ1952₁

xxii, 439 p. 25 cm. (Great books of the Western World, v. 38)

Bibliographical footnotes.

(Continued on next card)
55–10345
₁252₁

87

...esquieu, Charles Louis de Secondat, *baron* de La Brède ...de, 1689–1755.   The spirit of laws ... ₁1955, ᶜ1952₁ ...ard 2)

1. Political science.   2. State, The.   3. Law—Philosophy.   4. Jurisprudence.   I. Rousseau, Jean Jacques, 1712–1778.   On the origin of inequality.   II. Rousseau, Jean Jacques, 1712–1778.   On political economy.   III. Rousseau, Jean Jacques, 1712–1778.   The social contract.   IV. Nugent, Thomas, 1700?–1772, tr.   V. Prichard, J. V., ed.   VI. Cole, George Douglas Howard, 1889–   tr.   VII. Title.

AC1.G72   vol. 38   320.1   55–10345

Library of Congress   ₁252₁

88

119

The **Symposia** read at the joint session of the Aristotelian Society and the Mind Association at St. Andrews, 10th to 12th July, 1959. London, Harrison, 1959.

232 p. diagr. 22 cm. (Aristotelian Society ₍for the Systematic Study of Philosophy. Proceedings₎ Supplementary volume 33)

CONTENTS.—Address: Mind and the concept of mind, by J. N. Wright.—Symposium: Is there only one correct system of modal logic? 1. By E. J. Lemmon. 2. By G. P. Henderson.—Symposium: Pleasure and belief. 1. By B. A. Williams. 2. By E. Bedford.—Symposium: Phenomenology and linguistic analysis. 1. By C. Taylor. 2. By A. J. Ayer.—Symposium: On determinables and resemblance. 1. By S. Körner. 2. By J. Searle.—Symposium: Rules and morality. 1. By N. Cooper. 2. By R. J. Edgley.—Symposium: Paradox in religion. 1. By I. T. Ramsey. 2. By N. Smart.

1. Philosophy—Addresses, essays, lectures.   I. Mind Association. (Series)

B11.A72 vol. 33   104   A 59–8069

Virginia. Univ. Libr.
for Library of Congress   ₍5₎†

89

90

Essays honoring Lawrence C. Wroth. Portland, Me., 1951.

xxi, 515 p. illus., port. 27 cm.

Bibliographical footnotes.

CONTENTS.—Introduction, by W. S. Lewis.—Richard Eden's copy of the 1533 Decades of Peter Martyr, by E. Baer.—Columbus in sixteenth-century poetry, by L. Bradner. — American booksellers' catalogues, 1734–1800, by C. S. Brigham. — The river in the ocean, by L. A. Brown.—Novello Cattannio: un viaggio fatto alli paesi del continente nuovo, by C. F. Bühler.—The first decade of the Federal act for copyright, 1790–1800, by F. R. Goff. — Not in Harrisse, by E. P. Goldschmidt.—The Historia de las Indias of Bartolmé de las Casas, by L. Hanke.—The melody of "The Star Spangled Banner" in the United States before 1820, by R. S. Hill.—Tunc et nunc; or, The Pepys and

91

Essays honoring Lawrence C. Wroth. 1951. (Card 2)

CONTENTS—Continued.

Taylor collections of early English books on navigation, by W. A. Jackson.—John Carter Brown and America, by G. Kubler.—William Bradford's book trade and John Bowne, Long Island Quaker, as his book agent, 1686–1691, by G. D. McDonald.—King James takes a collection, by J. G. McManaway.—The Browns and Brown University, by W. G. Roelker.—The bibliographical press at Yale University, by C. P. Rollins.—The beginnings of systematic bibliography in America, 1642–1799, by J. H. Shera.—The Boston book trade, 1790–1799, by R. G. Silver.—Comparative cartography exemplified in an analytical & bibliographical description of nearly one hundred maps and charts of the American continent published in Great Britain during the years 1600–1850, by H. Stevens and R. Tree.—The first printing in

(Continued on next card)

52–834

92

Essays honoring Lawrence C. Wroth. 1951. (Card 3)

CONTENTS—Continued.

Providence, by B. F. Swan. — A half-century of Canadian life and print, 1751–1800, by M. Tremaine. — A patriotic pair of peripatetic printers, the up-state imprints of John Holt and Samuel Loudon, 1776–1783, by R. W. G. Vail.—Hispanic Americana in the John Carter Brown Library, by H. R. Wagner.—Eighteenth-century American fiction, by L. H. Wright.—The first Maryland tract: a reconsideration of the date of printing of the Maryland Charter, by J. C. Wyllie.—A list of published writings of Lawrence C. Wroth to Decemebr 31, 1950, by M. W. Adams and J. D. Black (p. 485–504)

1. Wroth, Lawrence Counselman, 1884–   2. Bibliography—Collections.

Z1009.Z3W7   010.4   52–834

Library of Congress   ₍3₎

Festschrift... Jones, Percy Mansell

MH

37566.135

Austin, Lloyd James, 1915-　　ed.
　Studies in modern French literature presented to P.
Mansell Jones by pupils, colleagues and friends, edited
by L.J.Austin, G.Rees and E.Vinaver. [Manchester]
Manchester UP [1961]

　xix, 343 p.　illus.

93

94

Μεγάλη παγκόσμιος γεωγραφία καὶ ἄτλας μετὰ πολλῶν εἰκόνων καὶ
χαρτῶν μονοχρώμων καὶ πολυχρώμων· ἐπιμελείᾳ Παν. Γαβρεσέα,
συνεργασίᾳ Γ. Γεωργαλᾶ, Ἰ. Κούμαρη, Ἠλ. Μαριολοπούλου καὶ
πολλῶν ἄλλων εἰδικῶν ἐπιστημόνων καὶ λογοτεχνῶν. Ἀθῆναι,
Ἐκδοτικὸς Οἶκος Π. Δημητράκου [1957?]

　3 v.　illus. (part col.) ports., maps (part fold., part col.)　29 cm.

1. Geography.　ɪ. Gabreseas, Pan., ed.
　　　　　　　　Title transliterated: Megalē pankosmios
　　　　　　　　　geōgraphia kai atlas.

G115.M49

57–35774

Congress　　　　　[⅜]

וועלט אײַן וועלט אויס [א זאמעלבוך.　פערלאג "אמעריקא"[
[New York, 1916]

　159 p.　illus.　27 cm.

　"Copyright by David Ignatoff."

95

1. Yiddish literature—U. S.　ɪ. Ignatoff, David, 1886–
　　　　Title transliterated: Velt ayn, velt oys.

PJ5125.V45

54–53283

Library of Congress　　　[⅜]

96

The **American** spectator, or Matrimonial preceptor.　A collection (with additions and variations) of essays, epistles,
precepts and examples, relating to the married state, from
the most celebrated writers, ancient and modern.　Adapted
to the state of society in the American republic ...　Boston,
D. West, 1797.

　xii, [13]–286 p.　front.　17½ cm.

1. Marriage.

HQ31.A5

9—5376

Library of Congress　　　[61d½]

AUTHORSHIP

99

R
032
En19

Encyclopaedia Britannica; a new survey of universal knowledge. ₍Walter Yust, editor in chief₎ Chicago, Encyclopaedia Britannica ₍°1959₎

24 v. illus. (part col.) ports, maps (part fold, part col.) 29 cm.

Includes bibliographies.

1. Encyclopedias and dictionaries.   ɪ. Yust, Walter, 1894–   ed.

AE5.E363 1959   032   59—1044

Library of Congress   ₍59e5₎

100

750.3

Encyclopedia of painting; painters and painting of the world from prehistoric times to the present day: Bernard S. Myers, editor.   Contributing associates: Milton W. Brown ₍and others₎.   Crown 1955

Contains more than 3000 entries including biographical sketches of great painters, sections on Japanese, Chinese, Persian and Indian paintings, and discussions of the various schools of art arranged in one alphabet.   The illustrations are integrated with the text.   (Publisher) Quarto volume

1 Painters — Dictionaries   2 Paintings — Dictionaries   750.3
ɪ Myers, Bernard S 1908-   ed.

10-21-55   (W) The H. W. Wilson Company

97

Bildwörterbuch, Deutsch und Tschechisch. ₍Deutscher Text und Bildredaktion: Dudenredaktion des Bibliographisches Institut.   Tschechischer Text: Josef Beneš₎ Leipzig, Bibliographisches Institut, 1956.

xv, 508 p. illus. (part col.) 19 cm.

1. Picture dictionaries, German.   2. Picture dictionaries, Czech.   3. German language—Dictionaries—Czech.   4. Czech language—Dictionaries—German.   ɪ. Beneš, Josef.

PG4645.G5B5   57—22820

Library of Congress   ₍3₎

98

The **Golden** geographic encyclopedia.   Adapted and edited by Theodore Shabad and Peter M. Stern.   Based on a compilation by Erich Kaden, Harry Garms, and Werner Diederich.   Picture maps and illus. by Wilhelm Eigener and August Eigener.   New York, Simon and Schuster ₍1958₎

228 p.   col. illus., col. maps. 25 cm.

"Adapted from the Westermann Bildkarten Lexicon."

1. Encyclopedias and dictionaries.   ɪ. Shabad, Theodore, ed.
ɪɪ. Stern, Peter M., ed.

AG6.W4 1958   910.3   58—4519

Library of Congress   ₍20₎

MULTIPLE

101

LSR
020.92
W62

Who's who in library service; a biographical directory of professional librarians of the United States and Canada. 3d ed.   Dorothy Ethlyn Cole, editor.   Prepared under the direction of the Council on Who's Who in Library Service for the School of Library Service, Columbia University. New York, Grolier Society, 1955.

xxiii, 546 p. 26 cm.

1. Librarians—U. S.   ɪ. Cole, Dorothy Ethlyn, 1907–   ed.
ɪɪ. Columbia University.   School of Library Service.

Z720.A4U58 1955   920.2   55—7959

Library of Congress   ₍55t°30₎

[Bochow, Martin]
    Krieg dem Hunger! Von ******. Berlin, Brunnen-Verlag,
W. Bischoff [°1931]
    142 p. 21 cm.

102

1. Food supply—Germany.   I. Title.
                          Full name: Theodor Martin Bochow.

HD9013.6.B56   ◯   54–52159 ‡
Library of Congress   [³₄]

103

131.34092
F895d   [Doolittle, Hilda] 1886–1961.
        Tribute to Freud, by H. D. With unpublished letters by
Freud to the author. [New York] Pantheon [1956]
    180 p. 21 cm.

1. Freud, Sigmund, 1856–1939. 2. Psychoanalysis—Cases, clinical
reports, statistics.   I. Title.

PS3507.O726T68   ◯   928.1   56–10963 rev ‡
Library of Congress   [r59q14]

104

```
x Aldington, Hilda (Doolittle)
x D., H.  Tribute to Freud
```

[Hoole, Samuel] 1757?–1839.
    Thoughts on the farther improvement of aerostation; or,
The art of travelling in the atmosphere: with a description
of a machine, now constructing, on different principles from
those hitherto adopted. By the inventor of the machine.
London, Printed for the author; sold by G. Nicol, 1785.
    32 p. 21 cm.

105

1. Balloons.   I. Title.

TL617.H6   ◯   54–52769
Library of Congress   [³₄]

[Lallū Lāla, *kavi*]
　The Luta[ifi Hindee; or, Hindoostanee jest book, contain-
ing a choice collection of humorous stories, in the Arabic and
Roman characters.　Ed. by William Carmichael Smyth.
London, Printed by W. Bulmer and W. Nicol, and sold by
J. Richardson, Cornhill, 1821.

　　vii, 167 p.　22 cm.

　　"These stories were compiled ... by Shree Lulloo Lal Kub ... and
were published in Calcutta, in ... 1810."

　　1. Hindustani wit and humor.　　I. Smyth, William Carmichael, ed.
II. Title.　III. Title: Hindoostanee jest book.

PK2078.W5L3　1821

106

55–47490

Library of Congress　　　[3⁄4]

107

[Passelecq, Paul]
　Guide to the Bible, by the Monks of Maredsous.　Translated from the French by Gerda R. Blumenthal, with pref.
by John M. T. Barton.　London, Sands [1953; label: distributed by W. S. Heinman, New York]

　　92 p.　illus.　19 cm.

　　1. Bible—Study—Text-books.　　I. Maredsous (Benedictine abbey)
II. Title.

BS606.P383　　　　220　　　53–3189 ‡

Congress　　[2]

[Le Prince de Beaumont, Marie] 1711–1780.
　Записки госпожи баронши де Баттевилль; или, Вдова
совершенная.　Переведено съ французскаго E* A*.　Москва, Въ Унив. тип., у В. Окорокова, 1789.

　　239 p.　20 cm.

108

　　I. A *, E *, tr.　II. Title.

Title transliterated: Zapiski gospo-
zhi baronshi de Battevill'.

PQ1995.L75A738

54–52403 rev

Library of Congress　　　[r55b3⁄4]

109

823
R915f　[Russell, Mary Annette (Beauchamp) Russell, count-
　　　　ess] 1866-1941.
　　　Fräulein Schmidt and Mr. Anstruther, by the
　　author of "Elizabeth and her German garden."　New
　　York, C. Scribner's Sons, 1913[c1907]
　　　332p.　19cm.

　　　　I. Title

[Trory, Ernest]
A catalogue of cylinder flaws on King George VI Great Britain commemoratives. [2d ed. Brighton, Crabtree Press] 1954.

20 p. illus. 23 cm.

110

1. George VI, King of Great Britain, 1895–1952. 2. Commemorative postage stamps—Gt. Brit. I. Title.

HE6185.G6T7 1954

Library of Congress [3]

54–41809 ‡

111

[Yang, Ching-kun]
Summary of A Chinese village and its early change under communism [by an observer; summarized by the CENIS staff. Cambridge] Center for International Studies, Massachusetts Institute of Technology, 1954.

28 p. 28 cm.

x An observer + title
1. Nan-ching. 2. Villages—China—Case studies. I. Massachusetts Institute of Technology. Center for International Studies. II. Title.

HN680.N3Y312

[2]ngress

55–1939 ‡

973.31
Am35

The American crisis, by a citizen of the world; inscribed to those members of the community, vulgarly named patriots. London, Printed for W. Flexney, 1777.
31p. 21cm.

112

1. U.S. - Politics and government - Revolution
I. A citizen of the world

113

A Confederate diary of the retreat from Petersburg, April 3–20, 1865; edited by Richard Barksdale Harwell. Atlanta, The Library, Emory University, 1953.
23 p. 24 cm. (Emory University publications. Sources & reprints, ser. 8, no. 1)
Diary of an anonymous participant in the Appomattox Campaign.
"Has been supposed ... the diary of ... Samuel Howard Gray, 1846–1885."
"Bibliographical note": p. 8–9.
1. U. S.—Hist.—Civil War—Personal narratives—Confederate side. 2. Appomattox Campaign, 1865. I. Gray, Samuel Howard, 1846–1885. II. Harwell, Richard Barksdale, ed. (Series: Emory University, Atlanta. Emory University publications. Sources & reprints, ser. 8, no. 1)

E477.67.C6   973.7384   53–12120

Library of Congress [1]

Learne of a Tvrk; or, Instructions and advise sent from the Turkish Army at Constantinople, to the English Army at London. Faithfully and impartially communicated by M. B., one of the attendants of the English agent there. London, 1660.

22 p.   18 cm.

1. Turkey—Hist.—1453–1683.   I. B., M.

DR511.L4   57–52773

Library of Congress   ◯   [8]

114

115

ANONYMOUS WORKS
UNIDENTIFIED

116

117

821
R349   Rhymes without reason, with reasons for rhym-
          ing; to which are added two prose essays. By the
          author of no other publication!!! London, Rodwell
          & Martin, 1823.
          xviii,77p. illus. 26cm.
          "To the reader" signed: E. G.

Cataloger's initials ◯

I. G., E.

                    G., E.
821
R349   Rhymes without reason, with reasons for rhyming;
          to which are added two prose essays. By the au-
          thor of no other publication!!! London, Rodwell &
          Martin, 1823.
          xviii,77p. illus. 26cm.
          "To the reader" signed: E. G.

◯

Book of O'Hara.

    The Book of O'Hara. Leabhar Í Eadhra. Edited by Lambert McKenna. ₍Dublin₎ Dublin Institute for Advanced Studies, 1951 ₍i. e. 1952₎

    xxxii, 458 p. port., facsim. 23 cm.

    A collection of bardic poems dealing with the Í Eadhra edited with translations into English.

    1. O'Hara family—Poetry.   ɪ. McKenna, Lambert Andrew Joseph, 1870–   ed. and tr.

    PB1397.B65 1952 ◯   54–29711

    Library of Congress   ₍¾₎

118

119

Chanson de Roland.

    La Chanson de Roland, par Raoul Mortier. ₍Paris₎ Bonne Presse ₍1945₎

    186 p. 19 cm. (La Noble France)

    In modern French.

    ɪ. Mortier, Raoul, tr.   (Series)

    PQ1520.M6   ◯   841.11   A F 48–4621*

    Chicago. Univ. Libr.
    for Library of Congress   ₍2₎†

Cuchulain.

    Cuchulain of Muirthemme: the story of the men of the Red Branch of Ulster; arranged and put into English by Lady Gregory. With a preface by W. B. Yeats. London, J. Murray, 1902.

    xix, 360 p. 20½ cm.

    1. Folk-lore—Ireland.   ɪ. Gregory, Isabella Augusta (Persse) lady, 1859–1932, ed. and tr. ɪɪ. Yeats, William Butler, 1865–1939.

                       3—2086

    Library of Congress ◯ PB1423.C8G7

             ₍50p½₎   -891.623

120

121

Orfeo (*Middle English poem*)

    Sir Orfeo; edited by A. J. Bliss. ₍London₎ Oxford University Press, 1954.

    li, 79 p. 23 cm. (Oxford English monographs)

    Contains the text of the poem in three versions: the Auchinleck ms., Ms. Harley 3810, and Ms. Ashmole 61.

    1. Orpheus—Poetry.   ɪ. Bliss, A. J., ed.

    PR2065.O6 1954 ◯   821.19   55—2637

    Library of Congress   ₍58f5₎

La queste del Saint Graal.
    La queste du Saint Graal, translatée des manuscrits du
XIIIᵉ siècle ₍par₎ Albert Pauphilet. Melun, Librairie d'Ar-
gences, 1949.

    108 p. 20 cm. (Bibliothèque elzévirienne, nouv. sér.)

122

    ɪ. Pauphilet, Albert. ɪɪ. Grail. Legend.

PQ1475.A26   A 50—5178

Illinois. Univ. Library
for Library of Congress   ₍a60c½₎†

123

Reynard the Fox. *English.*
    The history of Reynard the Fox. Translated and printed
by William Caxton in 1481. Edited with an introd. and
notes by Donald B. Sands. Cambridge, Harvard University
Press, 1960.

    viii, 224 p. illus., facsims. 22 cm.

    Bibliography: p. 191–200.

    ɪ. Caxton, William, 1422 (ca.)–1491. ɪɪ. Sands, Donald B., ed.

PT5584.E5C35   398.2   60—5884

Library of Congress   ₍61t10₎

Seven sages. *French.*
    Les contes des sept sages, adapted by Hugo Giduz and Ur-
ban T. Holmes ... New York, Farrar & Rinehart, inc. ₍ᶜ1938₎

    2 p. l., iii–ix, 61 p. 19½ᶜᵐ.

124

    1. French language—Chrestomathies and readers. ɪ. Giduz, Hugo, ed.
ɪɪ. Holmes, Urban Tigner, 1900–   ed. ɪɪɪ. Title.

                               38—11399

Library of Congress   PQ1533.S3A35

——— ——— Copy 2.

Copyright A 113762   ₍30d3₎   448.6

Sleeping beauty.
    Sleeping beauty, retold by Evelyn Andreas. Pictures by
Ruth Ives. New York, Wonder Books ₍1956₎

    unpaged. illus. 21 cm. (Wonder books, 635)

125

    ɪ. Andreas, Evelyn.

PZ8.S38An   56—58535 ‡

Library of Congress   ₍2₎

Bible. *English. 1952. Revised standard.*
  The Holy Bible. Revised standard version containing the Old and New Testaments, translated from the original tongues; being the version set forth A. D. 1611, revised A. D. 1881–1885 and A. D. 1901; compared with the most ancient authorities and revised A. D. 1952. New York, T. Nelson, 1952.
    xii, 997, iii, 294 p. 22 cm.
    New Testament has special t. p.: The New Covenant, commonly called the New Testament of Our Lord and Savior Jesus Christ: revised standard version translated from the Greek ... compared with the most ancient authorities and revised 1946 A. D.

  BS191.A1 1952.N4   220.52   52—2922
  Library of Congress   [60p⁴2]

126

gx Holy Bible
 x Revised standard version of the Bible

127

128

Bible. *English. 1953. Douai.*
  The family Rosary edition of the Holy Bible; edited by John P. O'Connell. Chicago, Catholic Press [1953]
    lxii, 909, 304, 288 p. illus. (part col.) col. port., col. maps. 26 cm.
    "A Catholic home encyclopedia": 288 p. at end.

  1. Catholic Church—Dictionaries.   I. O'Connell, John P., ed.
  II. Title.
  BS180 1953a   220.52   54–16101
  Library of Congress   [1]

129

 x Douai version of the Bible
 x Douay version of the Bible

Bible. *English. 1961.*
  The new English Bible. [New York] Oxford University Press, 1961–
    v. 24 cm.
    Translated under the supervision of the Joint Committee on the New Translation of the Bible.
    CONTENTS.—[1] New Testament.

  I. Joint Committee on the New Translation of the Bible. II. Title.
  BS192.A1 1961.N4   220.52   61–16025
  Library of Congress   [25]

130

Bible. *English. Selections. 1953. Authorized.*
 Every man's Bible; selected and arr. from the King James version by Manuel Komroff. New York ₍Lion Books₎ by arrangement with Cornell Pub. Corp. ₍1953₎
 192 p. 17 cm. (A Lion book, 167)

131

ɪ. Komroff, Manuel, 1890– ed. ɪɪ. Title.

BS391.K6 220.52

Library of Congress ₍2₎

Bible. *O. T. Hebrew. 1959.*
תורה נביאים וכתובים. ₍הוגהו על ידי ד. גולדשמידט. א. מ. הברמן, ו.מ. מדן₎ ירושלים, קורן. ₍Jerusalem, 1959–
 v. 35 cm.
"התג"ך הראשון המסודר ומודפס בנקודות וטעמים בארץ-ישראל."
Contents.— ₍א₎ תורה.

132

1. Goldschmidt, Ernst Daniel, ed.

A 60–3377

Hebrew Union College. Library
for Library of Congress ₍⅜₎

Bible. *O. T. Psalms. English. Paraphrases. 1903. Bay Psalm book.*
 The Bay Psalm book; being a facsimile reprint of the first edition, printed by Stephen Daye at Cambridge, in New England in 1640, with an introduction by Wilberforce Eames. New York, Dodd, Mead & company, 1903.
 1 p. l., v–xvii p., facsim.: 1 l., ₍292₎ p., 1 l. 20 cm.
 With reproduction of the original t.-p.
 "The edition of this facsimile reprint of the Bay Psalm book is limited to 1000 copies, of which 25 copies are on Japan paper and 975 on plain paper."
 The introduction contains a list of the 10 copies of the first edition of the Bay Psalm book known to be extant, with their present locations.
 ɪ. Eames, Wilberforce, 1855–1937, ed. ɪɪ. Title.

133

BS1440.B4 1903 4—5974

Library of Congress ₍57r32k½₎

Bible. *O. T. Psalms. English. Paraphrases (1640) 1956. Bay Psalm book.*
 The Bay Psalm book, a facsimile reprint of the first edition of 1640. ₍Chicago₎ University of Chicago Press ₍1956₎
 ₍3₎ p., facsim. (₍295₎ p.), ₍2₎ p. 20 cm.
 Original title page reads: The vvhole booke of psalmes faithfully translated into English metre ... Imprinted 1640.
 "Made from an original copy of the Prince collection in the Boston Public Library ... ₍with some₎ pages from the second copy of the Prince collection."
 Accompanied by a companion volume, The enigma of the Bay Psalm book, by Zoltán Haraszti.
 ɪ. Bay Psalm book.

134

BS1440.B4 1640c 223.5 56—14544 rev

Library of Congress ₍r57u9₎

Bible. *N. T. Danish. 1953. Schindler.*
Det Nye testamente. Gengivet paa dansk af Peter Schindler. København, A. Frost-Hansen, 1953.

714 p. 25 cm.

―――― Nøgle til det Nye testamente. København, A. Frost-Hansen, 1953.

336 p. maps. 25 cm.

BS2121 1953 Suppl.

1. Bible. N. T.—Commentaries. I. Schindler, Peter, 1892– tr.

BS2121 1953 ◯ 54–42460

Library of Congress ₍₃₎

135

Bible. *N. T. English. 1946. Revised standard.*
The new covenant, commonly called the New Testament of Our Lord and Savior Jesus Christ. Revised standard version, translated from the Greek, being the version set forth A. D. 1611, revised A. D. 1881 and A. D. 1901, compared with the most ancient authorities and revised A. D. 1946. New York, T. Nelson & sons ₍1946₎

vi p., 1 l., 553 p. 19 cm.

Cover-title: New Testament. Revised standard version.

I. Title.

BS2091.A1 1946.N4 ◯ 225.52 46—12740

Library of Congress ₍60o³2₎

136

Bible. *N. T. Pastoral epistles. English. 1960. Barclay.*
The letters to Timothy, Titus, and Philemon. Translated, with introductions and interpretations, by William Barclay. ₍2d ed.₎ Philadelphia, Westminster Press ₍1960₎

xv, 324 p. 18 cm. (The Daily study Bible)

1. Bible. N. T. Pastoral epistles—Commentaries. 2. Bible. N. T. Philemon—Commentaries. I. Bible. N. T. Philemon. English. 1960. Barclay. II. Barclay, William, lecturer in the University of Glasgow, ed. and tr. III. Title. (Series: The Daily study Bible series)

BS2735.3.B3 1960 ◯ 227.807 61–5396

Library of Congress ₍3₎

137

Koran.

Der heilige Qur-ân, Arabisch-Deutsch, versehen mit einer ausführlichen Einführung. Unter der Leitung von Hazrat Mirza Bashiruddin Mahmud Ahmad. Herausgeber: Ahmadiyya-Mission des Islams, Zürich und Hamburg. Im Auftrag von The Oriental and Religious Publishing Corporation, Rabwah (Pakistan) ₁1. Aufl. Wiesbaden, O. Harrassowitz, 1954₁

164, 639 p. 22 cm.

ɪ. Koran. German. ɪɪ. Ahmad, Bashiruddin Mahmud, hazrat mirza, 1889–   ed.

138

A 56–6983

Harvard Univ. Library
for Library of Congress   ₁1₁

Koran. *English. Selections.*

The short Koran, designed for easy reading; edited by George M. Lamsa. Chicago, Ziff-Davis Pub. Co. ₁1949₁

xx, 377 p. 21 cm.

"Arrangement ... is based on George Sale's translation."—p. 24.

139

ɪ. Lamsa, George Mamishisho, 1893–   ed.

BP110.L29   297   49–48257*

Library of Congress   ₁10₁

140

Talmud. *Selections.*

מימי קדם, ליקוטי סיפורים ואגדות מן התלמוד והמדרש. סודרו ונערכו, עם תרגום אנגלי ובאורים והערות בעברית ובאנגלית על ידי הרב זאב גוטליב. עם הקדמה מאת נתן מוריס. לונדון, המועצה המרכזית לחינוך דתי בבריטניה הגדולה ואירלנדיה, תש"ח. ₁London, 1948₁

114, 114 p. illus. 22 cm.
Added t. p.: From days of old; stories and sayings from Talmud and Midrash.
Hebrew and English.
1. Talmud—Legends.   ɪ. Midrash. Selections. ɪɪ. Talmud. English. Selections. ɪɪɪ. Midrash. English. Selections. ɪv. Gottlieb, Wolf, ed. and tr.   *Title transliterated:* Mi-yeme kedem.

BM504.5.G6   51–46382

Library of Congress   ₁3₁

Tripiṭaka. *English. Selections.*

The quest of enlightenment; a selection of the Buddhist Scriptures translated from the Sanskrit, by E. J. Thomas. ₁1st ed.₁ London, Murray ₁1950₁

vi, 89 p. 18 cm. (The Wisdom of the East series)

141

ɪ. Thomas, Edward Joseph, 1869–   ed. and tr. ɪɪ. Title.
(Series: The Wisdom of the East series (London))

BL1411.T8E56   294.3   50—8399

Library of Congress   ₁59c½₁

CtY

Akademiia Nauk SSSR. Institut russkoĭ litera-
    tury.
    Былины Печоры и Зимнего Берега, новые за-
писи. Изд. подготовили А.М. Астахова [и др.]
Москва, Изд-во Академии Наук СССР, 1961.
    606 p. ports., music. 27 cm. (Памятни-
ки русского фольклора)
    Title transliterated: Byliny Pechory...

    1. Byliny. I. Astakhova, Anna Mikhaĭlovna,
1886-   II. Title.

142

American Federation of Musicians.
    Eventful decade; cartoonists' version of James C. Petrillo
and the A. F. of M. over the last 10 years. New York [195–?]
    1 v. (unpaged, chiefly illus.) 28 cm.

    1. Petrillo, James Caesar, 1892–   —Portraits, caricatures, etc.
2. American Federation of Musicians—Caricatures and cartoons.   I.
Title.
    ML27.U5A759   331.881178   53–35956
of Congress   [1]

143

Book Club of California, San Francisco.
    Early transportation in southern California. [Edited by
Robert J. Woods. San Francisco] 1954.
    12 no. plates, facsims. 24 cm.
    Illustrative matter inserted.
    CONTENTS.—1. The mule car, by A. D. Mitchell.—2. Military camels,
by A. Woodward.—3. The free harbor contest; or, Citizen versus
railroad, by C. S. Bliss.—4. The first aviation meet in America, by
D. W. Davies.—5. The Orange Dummy, by D. Meadows.—6. The
Uncle Sam at Fort Yuma, by C. N. Rudkin.—7. Orizaba on the Cali-
fornia coast, 1876, by J. H. Kemble.—8. Professor Lowe's planet air-
ship, by W. W. Robinson.—9. Early staging, by R. J. Woods.—10. The
crossing of the Tehachapi by the Southern Pacific, by G. S. Dumke.—
11. The Water Witch, by J. V. Mink.—12. The horse car, by R. J.
Woods.
    1. Transportation—   California, Southern.   I. Woods,
Robert J., ed.   II. Title.
HE213.C2B6
Library of Congress   [56b1]   55—36207

144

708.1446
B657h   Boston. Museum of Fine Arts.
            Handbook. 31st ed. Boston, 1956.
            ix,193p. illus.,ports. 18cm.

145

SAMPLE

W
21
B862h
1958

BRITISH Medical Association
The medical practitioners' handbook.
[New & rev. ed.] London, 1958.
285 p.
1. Medicine as a profession   Title
W21 B862h   59-3380

146

147

British Museum (Natural History)
Mosquitoes and their relation to disease: their life-history, habits, and control. 6th ed. London, Printed by order of the Trustees of the British Museum, 1958.

15 p. illus. 22 cm. (*Its* Economic series, no. 4)

1. Mosquitoes.

RA640.B7   1958   59-30519

Congress   [2/8]

Brünn. Universita. *Knihovna.*
Za rozvoj živočišné výroby. [Sest. R. Trautmann za spolupráce dr. Bednářové a O. Líbala. V Brně] 1956.

[44] p. 20 cm. (*Its* Výběrový seznam, 12)

148

1. Stock and stock-breeding—Bibl. 2. Stock and stock-breeding—Czechoslovak Republic—Bibl. I. Trautmann, R. II. Title. (Series)

Z5074.L7B7   60-55076

Library of Congress   [3/8]

149

Brussels. Bibliothèque royale de Belgique.
Collection voltairienne du comte de Launoit. [Bruxelles? 1955]

131 p. illus., 16 plates, facsims. 26 cm.

350 copies printed. "Trois cents exemplaires numérotés de 1 à 300 sur papier Drury book ... Exemplaire no 226."

1. Voltaire, François Marie Arouet de—Bibl.   I. Launoit, Paul Auguste Cyrille, comte de, 1891–

Z8945.B7   59-28604

Library of Congress   [2/8]

150

California. University. *School of Librarianship.*
The climate of book selection; social influences on school
and public libraries; papers presented at a symposium held
at the University of California, July 10–12, 1958. ₍Sponsored by the School of Librarianship and the Dept. of Conferences and Special Activities of the University of
California₎ Edited, with an introd. by J. Periam Danton.
Berkeley, University of California School of Librarianship,
1959.
vii, 98 p. 24 cm.
Bibliographical footnotes.
1. Book selection—Congresses. I. California. University. Dept.
of Conferences and Special Activities. II. Danton, J. Periam, 1908–
ed. III. Title.

Z689.C17 1958　　◯　　025.2106379467　　59—12887

016.82309
C128c

151

California. University. *University at Los Angeles. Library.*
College life, an exhibit of the English university novel,
1749–1954, UCLA Library, October 14–November 8, 1959.
₍Los Angeles? 1959₎
13 p. illus. 22 cm.

"Mortimer Proctor ... has ... written the notes for the catalogue
of the exhibit."

1. English fiction—Bibl. 2. Universities and colleges in literature—
Bibl. 3. Universities and colleges—England—Bibl. I. Proctor,
Mortimer Robinson, 1916– II. Title.

Z2014.F4C3　　◯　　016.823099　　59—63966 ‡
Congress　　　₍1₎

152

Cambridge. University. *Peterhouse. Library.*
Catalogue of the musical manuscripts at Peterhouse, Cambridge; compiled by Anselm Hughes. Cambridge, University Press, 1953.
xvi, 75 p. 26 cm.
Description of 19 items, 15 of which were fully catalogued in 1856
by John Jebb.
Includes scores of Christ rising again, for SATB and organ, by
Thomas Wilson, and O sapientia, for SSAATB, by Robert Ramsey, the
latter with keyboard reduction.
Bibliographical footnotes.
CONTENTS. — The Henrician set. — The Caroline part-books. — The
organ-book (Ms. 46)—The folio prayer-book.—Index of texts.

153

Cambridge. University. *Peterhouse. Library.* Catalogue
of the musical manuscripts at Peterhouse, Cambridge ...
1953. (Card 2)

1. Church music—Bibl.—Catalogs. 2. Music—Bibl.—Manuscripts.
3. Music—Manuscripts—Gt. Brit. 4. Manuscripts. Gt. Brit.—Catalogs. 5. Church music—England—Bibl. I. Hughes, Anselm, Father,
1889– comp. II. Wilson, Thomas, 17th cent. Christ rising again.
III. Ramsey, Robert, fl. 1616–1644. O sapientia.

ML136.C21P4　　◯　　781.9732　　53—13275
Library of Congress　　₍3₎

135

Conference on the State and Economic Growth, *New York,*
1956.
The state and economic growth; papers, edited by Hugh
G. J. Aitken.   New York, Social Science Research Council,
1959.

x, 389 p. 24 cm.

Bibliographical footnotes.

1. Economic development—Congresses. 2. Economic policy—Congresses.   I. Aitken, Hugh G. J., ed. II. Title.

HC51.C58   1956   338.9082   59—9954

Library of Congress   [60q10]

154

155

Congreso de Institutos de Cultura Hispánica.
2d, Bogotá, 1958.
Itinerarios de cultura hispánica; memoria.
Bogotá, Editorial Kelly, 1958.
164p. ports. 23cm. (Biblioteca del Instituto
Columbiano de Cultura Hispánica)
Ediciones "Ximénez de Quesada."
"Datos biográficos de delegados al Congreso":
p. 143-164.

1. Pan-Hispanism I. Title (Series)

F1414.C8 1958   60-46295

Denver. University. *Social Science Foundation.*
Problem papers prepared for seminars of the World
Affairs Institute on the prospect for freedom in the last half
of the century, July 23–August 22, 1951. [Denver, 1951]

1 v. (various pagings) 29 cm.

Supplement to the Journeys behind the news radio series, given
during the foundation's twenty-fifth anniversary year.
Includes bibliographies.

1. Social problems—Addresses, essays, lectures.

HN18.D45   *301.46 301.153   55–34439

Library of Congress   [3]

156

157

Francis Bacon Foundation, *Pasadena, Calif. Library.*
Wing (Short title catalogue 1641–1700) numbers in the
Library of the Francis Bacon Foundation, incorporated.
Compiled by Elizabeth S. Wrigley. Pasadena, Calif., 1959.

186 l. 29 cm.

1. English literature—Early modern (To 1700)—Bibl.—Catalogs.
I. Wrigley, Elizabeth S., comp.

Z733.P244   59–30931

Library of Congress   [3]

Harvard University.
The behavioral sciences at Harvard; report by a faculty
committee, June, 1954. ₍Cambridge, 1954₎

vi, 518 p.   23 cm.

158

1. Social sciences—Study and teaching.   2. Harvard University—
Curricula.   I. Title.

H67.H23   307

Harvard Univ.   Library
for Library of Congress   ₍2₎†

159

Harvard University. *Law School.*
International problems of financial protection against
nuclear risk; a study under the auspices of Harvard Law
School and Atomic Industrial Forum, inc.   ₍Cambridge,
1959₎

95 p.   28 cm.   (A Forum report)

Bibliographical footnotes.

1. Liability for nuclear damages.   2. Insurance, Atomic hazards.
I. Atomic Industrial Forum.   II. Title.

368.57   59—3162

ongress   ₍60f5₎

708.1446
Islg   Isabella Stewart Gardner Museum, Boston.
Guide. Boston, 1954.
48p.   20cm.

160

Isham Library Conference, *Harvard University, 1957.*
Instrumental music; a conference at Isham Memorial Library, May 4, 1957. Edited by David G. Hughes. Cambridge, Mass., Harvard University Press, 1959.

vi, 152 p.   music.   22 cm.   (Isham Library papers, 1)

CONTENTS.—Introductory address, by A. T. Merritt.—Dance tunes
of the fifteenth century, by O. Kinkeldey.—Problems of authenticity
in eighteenth-century music, by H. C. R. Landon.—Instrumental music
outside the pale of classicism and romanticism, by E. Werner.—Problems of intonation in the performance of contemporary music, by W.
Piston.—Coda, by C. Sachs.

1. Music—Congresses.   2. Musicology—Addresses, essays, lectures.
3. Instrumental music—Hist. & crit.   I. Hughes, David G., ed.

ML38.C17 I 86   785.0637446   59—9275

Congress   ₍60q10₎

162

161

Ku kung po wu yüan, *Peking.   Wên hsien kuan.*
文獻特刊　故宮博物院文獻館編輯　北平　民國
24 ₍1935₎

4, 52, 38, 96 p.   illus., fold. map, facsims.   27 cm.

Cover title.

At head of title: 國立北平故宮博物院十週年紀念

1. China—Hist.—Sources.   I. Title.
Title romanized: Wên hsien t'ê k'an.

C 60—5137

Harvard Univ.   Chinese-   Japanese Library 9241
for Library of Congress   ₍3₎

Los Angeles County Museum, *Los Angeles.*
Woven treasures of Persian art; Persian textiles from the 6th to the 19th century. Exhibition: Los Angeles County Museum, April–May 1959. [Los Angeles, 1959]

65 p. illus. 27 cm.

163

1. Textile industry and fabrics—Iran. 2. Textile industry and fabrics—Exhibitions. I. Title.

NK8974.L6   746.10955   59–3092 ‡

Library of Congress   [2]

Los Angeles. University of Southern California. *School of Library Science.*
Modern trends in documentation; proceedings of a symposium held at the University of Southern California, April 1958. Edited by Martha Boaz. London, New York, Pergamon Press, 1959.

viii, 103 p. illus. 24 cm.

Bibliographical footnotes.

164

1. Information storage and retrieval systems—Congresses. I. Boaz, Martha Terosse, 1913–   ed. II. Title.

Z699.L6   010.78   59—10081

Congress   [60x10]

Massachusetts Memorial Hospitals, *Boston.*
Health for the American people, a symposium presented Monday, November 21, 1955, Massachusetts Memorial Hospitals centennial celebration. [1st ed.] Boston, Published for Massachusetts Memorial Hospitals by Little, Brown [1956]

xii, 105 p. diagr., tables. 21 cm.

165

1. Hygiene, Public—U. S. 2. Medicine—U. S.   I. Title.

RA445.M35 1955   614.0942   56–10611 rev

Library of Congress   [r57k4]

Michigan. University.
Mexican art; pre-Columbian to modern times; [exhibition held at] University of Michigan, Ann Arbor, State University of Iowa, Iowa City, Joslyn Art Museum, Omaha, Nebraska, Indiana University, Bloomington, The Columbus Gallery of Fine Arts, Columbus, Ohio, Syracuse University, Syracuse, New York, Dallas Museum of Fine Arts, Dallas, Texas, 1958–1959. [Ann Arbor] 1958.

55 p. illus. 28 cm.

166

1. Art, Mexican—Exhibitions.

N6550.M52   709.72   58–63069

Library of Congress   [1]

167

New York. Metropolitan Opera.
   Metropolitan Opera House, 70th anniversary, 1883-1953...
Sponsored by the National Council of the Metropolitan
Opera Association. [Editor: Louis Snyder, Jr. New York,
1954]
   36 p. illus. 31 cm.

1. New York. Metropolitan Opera. 2. Opera—New York (City)
ML1711.8.N32M46 1954   782   54-3461 ‡

170

168

813
C786Yn **New York State Historical Association.**
   James Fenimore Cooper, a re-appraisal. Cooperstown,
N.Y., 1954.
   Iv, 194 p. illus., ports. 24 cm.
   "Special issue of New York history."
   Papers presented at the 1951 annual meeting of the association.
   Includes bibliographies.

1. Cooper, James Fenimore, 1789-1851.   I. New York State Historical Association. New York history.
PS1431.N4   813.24   55-2682

171

169

629.28 **New York University. Division of General Education. Center for Safety Education**
   Man and the motor car. 6th ed. Prentice-Hall 1959
   353p illus map
   First edition, 1936, published by the National Conservation Bureau
under the editorship of Albert W. Whitney. The 1959 edition has
been revised to bring it up-to-date
   An illustrated textbook for training automobile drivers, organized
on a unit basis. Discussion topics, projects and problems, and references
are found at the end of each unit

1 Automobile drivers I Title
59W6,132   629.28
                (W) The H. W. Wilson Company

172

J3381/6308   MH-HY

Meiji Bunka Kenkyū Kai.   明治文化研究論叢
   明治文化研究會編
   東京 一元社 昭和9[1934]
   3,2,348p. 23cm.
   On colophon: 編纂代表者 尾佐竹猛
   Contents:--綿貫哲雄 維新前後に於ける傳統意
識——木村毅 明治前期に於けるマルクス認識
の過程——川原次吉郎 加藤弘之と初期の欧洲思想

167 (上段)

Meiji Bunka Kenkyū Kai. 明治文化研究論叢
1934   (Card 2)

   浦井福治 佐賀の創に關する日支南國官憲の交渉——
板澤武雄 傾國及び"負國國論"に就いて——三浦周行
尾佐竹猛 徳川民部大輔巴金帶在歐中に於る日佛條約——
大塚武松 國關係の一考察 笹岡民次郎 日本江戸幕利公使
館假館に於ける系統區入事件——蛭田八郎 文料とに

                          (Continued on next card)
   Harvard Univ.   6LJ-2236

168

Meiji Bunka Kenkyū Kai. 明治文化研究論叢
1934   (Card 3)

   見もる初期の外字新聞——桑平武彦 英國政府と日
本漂流民——田村榮太郎 三重縣地租改正反
對一揆——名井斛堂 明治初期の世相——神田
泉 寛政改革とその小説——神代種亮「パアレイ
英國史」考——齋藤昌三 明治の装劇界

TR: Meiji bun⌃ka kenkyū ronsō.
   Harvard Univ.   6LJ-2236

169

173

Symposium on Problems and Prospects of Democracy in Asian Countries, *Delhi, 1958.*
Future of Asian democracy; report. New Delhi, Indian Bureau of Parliamentary Studies [1959]
92 p. group port. 25 cm.

1. Asia—Politics—Congresses.   I. Title.

JQ3.S87 1958c   59–3145

174

Symposium on Social Psychology, *University of Chicago,* 1947.
Experiments in social process; a symposium on social psychology, edited by James Grier Miller. 1st ed. New York, McGraw-Hill, 1950.
ix, 205 p. diagrs. 24 cm. (McGraw-Hill publications in psychology)

CONTENTS.—Scientific methodology in human relations by D. G. Marquis.—The strategy of sociopsychological research, by R. Lippitt.—Laboratory experiments, the role of group belongingness, by L. Festinger.—Survey research, psychological economics, by D. Cartwright.—Survey techniques in the evaluation of morale, by D. Katz.—Field experiments, changing group productivity, by J. R. P. French,

(Continued on next card)

[59x1]   50—13152

175

Symposium on Social Psychology, *University of Chicago,* 1947.   Experiments in social process ... 1950. (Card 2)

CONTENTS—Continued.

Jr.—A comparative study of national characteristics, by D. V. McGranahan and I. Wayne.—The implications of learning theory for social psychology, by J. J. Gibson.—Social psychology and the atomic bomb, a round-table discussion, by members of the symposium and L. Szilard.

1. Social psychology—Addresses, essays, lectures.   I. Miller, James Grier, ed.   II. Title.

HM251.S9 1947a   301.1504   50—13152
Library of Congress   [59x1]

176

Peabody Institute, *Baltimore. Library.*
Mr. Emerson lectures at the Peabody Institute. Baltimore, 1949.
19 p. port. 20 cm.

1. Emerson, Ralph Waldo, 1803-1882.

Z733.B187   027.47752   51-5510

177

Philadelphia. Library Company.
A catalogue of books belonging to the Library Company of Philadelphia; a facsimile of the edition of 1741, printed by Benjamin Franklin. With an introd. by Edwin Wolf, 2nd. Philadelphia, 1956.
xii p., facsim. (55 p.), [4] p. 18 cm.
Cover title: Catalogue of the Library Company of Philadelphia, 1741.
"Bibliographical note": p. [1]-3, at end.
"This keepsake is issued by the Library Company as its tribute to the memory of Franklin."—Leaf inserted.

Z881.P5424 1741a   018.2   56-3162

178

Rutgers University, *New Brunswick, N. J. Library.*
The Oriole Press; a few comments on the typographical publications exhibited at Rutgers University Library during the month of March 1950. Berkeley Heights [1950?]
16 p. 17 cm.

1. Oriole Press, Berkeley Heights, N. J.

Z232.O68R8   655.1749   59-30866
[8]
Library of Congress

179

Walker Art Center, *Minneapolis.*
School of Paris, 1959: the internationals; Karel Appel, Hans Hartung, André Lanskoy, Jean-Paul Riopelle, Gérard Schneider, Pierre Soulages, Maria Helena Vieira da Silva, Zao Wou-Ki. An exhibition organized by the Walker Art Center, April 5–May 17, 1959. [Minneapolis, 1959]

59 p. illus. 28 cm.

Includes bibliography.

1. Paintings—Exhibitions. 2. Painting—Paris. ɪ. Title.

N5020.M72 759.4 59–2732 ‡

180

759.13
Sa32w

Whitney Museum of American Art, *New York.*
Attilio Salemme. [Exhibition. Whitney Museum of American Art, April 14–May 30, 1959. Boston, Institute of Contemporary Art, 1959]

unpaged. illus. 20 cm.

1. Salemme, Attilio, 1911–1955. ɪ. Boston. Institute of Contemporary Art.

ND237.S2W47 759.13 59–3337

Library of Congress [2]

Steichen, Edward, 1879–   *comp.*
The family of man; the greatest photographic exhibition of all time—503 pictures from 68 countries—created by Edward Steichen for the Museum of Modern Art. New York, Published for the Museum of Modern Art by the Maco Magazine Corp., ᶜ1955.

192 p. (chiefly illus.) 28 cm.

1. Photography—Exhibitions. ɪ. New York. Museum of Modern Art. ɪɪ. Title.

TR6.N55 1955c 779.2 55—11621

181

Whitehill, Walter Muir, 1905–
Boston Public Library; a centennial history. Illus. by Rudolph Ruzicka. Cambridge, Harvard University Press, 1956.

274 p. illus. 24 cm.

1. Boston. Public Library—Hist.

Z733.B752W5 027.444 56–6528 ‡

Library of Congress [20]

182

Catholic Church. *Liturgy and ritual. Missal. Polyglot.*
Polyglot missal; the prayer book in five languages, Latin,
English, French, Spanish, Italian, by Basile G. D'Ouakil.
New York, S. F. Vanni ₁1948, ᶜ1947₎

531 p. 16 cm.

I. Catholic Church.   Liturgy and ritual. Polyglot. II. D'Ouakil,
Basile Gabriel, 1896–   ed. III. Title.

BX2015.A1 1948   264.025   48—4915*‡

Library of Congress   ₁58f½₎

183

184

Church of England. *Liturgy and ritual. Antiphonary.*
The antiphons upon Magnificat & Nunc dimittis from the
Salisbury Antiphoner. The words translated & the music
adapted by G. H. Palmer. New & rev. ed. Wantage, Imprinted at the Convent of S. Mary, 1911.

167 p. 22 cm.

A publication of the Plainsong and Mediæval Music Society.
Plainsong notation.

1. Chants (Anglican)   I. Plainsong and Mediæval Music Society.

M2.P6C54 1911   M 55–1563

ongress   ₁₃₎

Friends, Society of. *Jericho Monthly Meeting, Randolph
Co., Ind.*
Jericho Friend's Meeting and its community, Randolph
County, Indiana, 1818 to 1958. ₁Ann Arbor? Mich., 1958₎

x, 162 p. illus., ports., maps. 24 cm.

Includes bibliography.

I. Title.

BX7780.R2A4   289.677266   59–20240

Library of Congress   ₁₃₎

185

186

Protestant Episcopal Church in the U. S. A. *Book of common prayer.*
The Oxford American prayer book commentary, by Massey Hamilton Shepherd, Jr. New York, Oxford University
Press, 1950.

1 v. (various pagings) 21 cm.

Facsimile reproduction of the Book of common prayer (New York,
Oxford University Press, 1944) with commentary on opposite pages.
Includes bibliography.

1. Protestant Episcopal Church in the U. S. A. Book of common
prayer.   I. Shepherd, Massey Hamilton, 1913–   II. Title.

BX5945.S5   264.03   50–10192

Library of Congress   ₁7₎

Jews. *Liturgy and ritual. Grace after meals.*
עבודת השלחן עם קריאת שמע על המטה.
Home service with translation and transliteration, comp.
by Rabbi and Mrs. Herbert S. Goldstein. New York,
Bloch Pub. Co., 1921.

75 p. 17 cm.

ɪ. Goldstein, Herbert Samuel, 1890–   ed. ɪɪ. Goldstein, Rebecca
(Fischel) 1891–   joint ed.

BM675.G7G64   ◯   21–9005 rev*

Library of Congress   ₍r55c¾₎

187

Columbus, Ohio. Temple Tifereth Israel. *Minnie Oobey
Memorial Library.*
Catalogue. Columbus, 1953.

96 l. 22 x 36 cm.

Ohio State Univ. Libr.   ◯   Z881
for Library of Congress   ₍8₎

188

189

New York. Trinity Church.
Churchyards of Trinity Parish in the City of New York,
1697–1947. Published in observance of the 250th anniversary of the founding of Trinity Church. Enl. ed. ₍New
York, 1955₎

85 p. illus., maps. 22 cm.

1. New York (City)—Cemeteries. 2. Epitaphs—New York (City)
ɪ. Title.

F128.61.T7N4 1955   ◯   929.3   55–59586
Library of Congress   ₍¾₎

190

Gébelin, François, 1884–
The Cathedral of Notre-Dame. Paris, Éditions Alpina
₍1951₎

62 p. illus. 18 cm. (Alpina guide books)

1. Paris. Notre-Dame (Cathedral)
NA5550.N7G4 1951   726.64   52–17673 ‡

Library of Congress   ₍1₎

International Conference on Safety of Life at Sea, *London,*
1948.
    International regulations for preventing collisions at sea,
1948. Approved by the International Conference on Safety
of Life at Sea, at London, June 10, 1948, proclaimed by the
President of the United States of America August 15, 1953,
entered into force January 1, 1954. ₍Washington, U. S.
Govt. Print. Off., 1955₎
    20 p. 24 cm. (U. S. Dept. of State. Publication 5466. Treaties
and other international acts series, 2899)
    1. Rule of the road at sea.   ɪ. Title.   (Series: U. S. Dept. of
State. Publication 5466. Series: U. S. Dept. of State. Treaties and
other international acts series, 2899)

JX235.9.A32   no. 2899   341.57   55–60740

Library of Congress   ₍3₎

191

192

International Federation for Documentation.
    Abstract of the Universal decimal classification for use in
polar libraries, prepared by Brian Roberts. Cambridge
₍Eng.₎ Scott Polar Research Institute, 1956.
    208 p. 33 cm.
    "First supplement (additions and corrections)": 13 p. inserted
at end.

    1. Classification—Books—Arctic regions.   ɪ. Roberts, Brian Bir-
ley. ɪɪ. Scott Polar Research Institute, Cambridge, Eng. ɪɪɪ. Title:
Universal decimal classification.

Z697.A77 I 5 1956   025.43   59–46

₎Congress   ₍2₎

International Ornithological Congress. *10th, Uppsala, 1950.*
    Proceedings. Edited by Sven Hörstadius, general secre-
tary. Uppsala, Printed at Almqvist and Wiksell, 1951.
    662 p. illus., maps. 25 cm.
    Includes bibliographies.

193

    1. Birds—Congresses.

QL671.I 7 1950   598.20631   52–64296

Library of Congress   ₍1₎

194

League of Nations. *Secretariat. Information Section.*
    La Société des Nations: constitution et organisation. Ge-
nève ₍1923₎
    52 p. 18 cm.

    1. League of Nations.

JX1975.A49 1923hd   53—56705

Library of Congress   ₍57b½₎

United Nations. *Secretary-General, 1953-1961* (Hammarskjöld)
Equal pay for equal work. [By Secretary-General of the United Nations and the International Labour Organisation] New York, United Nations, 1960.
ix, 65 p. 23 cm. (United Nations. [Document] E/CN.6/341/rev. 1)
"United Nations publication. Sales no.: 60.IV.4."
1. Wages. 2. Woman—Employment. II. Title. (Series)   I. International Labor Organization.
JX1977.A2 E/CN.6/341/rev.1   331.26   60—2934
Copy 2.   HD6061.U45

195
198

United Nations Educational, Scientific, and Cultural Organization.
The Haiti pilot project, phase one [1947-1949] Paris [1951]
83 p. plates, maps. 22 cm. (*Its* Monographs on fundamental education, 4)
United Nations Educational, Scientific and Cultural Organization. Publication no. 796.
1. Marbial Valley, Haiti—Soc. condit. I. Title. (Series. Series: United Nations Educational, Scientific and Cultural Organization. UNESCO publication no. 796)
[HN214.M3U]   A 55—2883
New York Univ.   Wash.   Sq. Library [2]
for Library of Congress

196
199

United Nations Educational, Scientific, and Cultural Organization.
The teaching of modern languages. [Paris, 1955]
294 p. 22 cm. (*Its* Problems in education, 10)
1. Languages, Modern—Study and teaching. I. Title. (Series)
PB35.U5   407   55—3400
Library of Congress   [60r52]

197
200

United Nations. *Commission on Human Rights.*
Draft international covenants on human rights. New York, United Nations Dept. of Public Information [1955]
16 p. 22 cm.
Cover title.
"Reprinted from the United Nations review, vol. 1, no. 7, January 1955."
1. Civil rights (International law) I. United Nations. Commission on Human Rights. Draft covenant on economic, social and cultural rights. II. United Nations. Commission on Human Rights. Draft covenant on civil and political rights. III. Title.
55—3609

United Nations. *Dept. of Economic and Social Affairs.*
The development of manufacturing industry in Egypt, Israel and Turkey. New York, 1958.
xiv, 131 p. tables. 28 cm. (United Nations. [Document] E/3111, ST/ECA/54)
"United Nations publication. Sales no.: 58.II.B.4."
Bibliographical footnotes.
1. Egypt—Manuf. 2. Israel—Manuf. 3. Turkey—Manuf. I. Title. (Series: United Nations. Document E/3111 [etc.])
JX1977.A2 E/3111, etc.   338.40956   59—813

United Nations. *Secretary-General, 1946-1953* (Lie)
Organization and procedure of United Nations commissions. Lake Success, Interim Committee of the General Assembly, Sub-committee on International Co-operation in the Political Field, 1949-50.
12 v. 21 cm.
1. United Nations—Commissions. I. Title.
JX1977.A37O7   341.132   50—9360 rev
Library of Congress   [r55f1]

International Business Machines Corporation.
Numerical code for States, counties, and cities of the United States. [New York, 1952]

81 p. 28 cm.

1. Punched card systems—Names, Geographical—U. S. I. Title.

G155.U6 I 6   54-43785 ‡

Library of Congress   [1]

201

Horwath and Horwath, *New York.*
Uniform system of accounts for restaurants. Adopted and recommended by the Cost Committee of National Restaurant Association. Including record keeping for the small restaurant. 3d rev. ed. [Chicago, National Restaurant Association, °1958]

113 p. illus. 24 cm.

1. Restaurants, lunch rooms, etc.—Accounting.   I. National Restaurant Association. II. Title.

Denver.   Public Library   A 59-3753
for Library of Congress   [5]

COM-
MER-
CIAL

202

205

Little (Arthur D.) inc., *Cambridge, Mass.*
Management of industrial research; a selected and annotated bibliography.   Cambridge, 1950.

vi, 14 p. illus. 28 cm.

1. Research, Industrial—Abstracts.   2. Research, Industrial—Bibl. I. Title.

T175.L55   016.607   50-8943

Library of Congress   [2]

203

206

Banca popolare di credito, *Bologna.*
I novanta anni della Banca popolare di Bologna, 1865–1955. [A cura di Ernesto Bassanelli con la collaborazione di Umberto Beseghi et al.   Bologna, 1955]

86 p. illus. (part col.) col. diagrs., tables. 26 cm.

Published by the Consiglio di amministrazione of the Banca popolare di Bologna.

The diagrs. are on transparent paper.

CONTENTS.—Cenni storici sulle banche popolari. — L'economia bolognese nel secolo XIX.—Bologna negli anni dell'unificazione.—Storia della Banca popolare di Bologna.—Bilancio dell'attività sociale.—Cenni biografici dei presidenti e direttori.—Tavole statistiche sugli impieghi e depositi nelle aziende di credito.

I. Bassanelli, Ernesto, 1909–

HG2039.I 8 B3   Libraries   A 59-4113

New York Univ.   [3]‡
for Library of Congress

201

Brown, Son and Ferguson, ltd, *Glasgow.*
Flags of all nations. [Rev. by H. Gresham Carr]   London, G. Philip [1952]

col. plate. 59 x 89 cm. fold. to 23 x 15 cm.

1. Flags.   I. Title.

CR109.B73   1952   55-36460 ‡

Library of Congress   [4]

204

Chase Manhattan Bank, *New York.*
Future growth of the west coast petroleum industry, by Kenneth E. Hill [and] John G. Winger.   Paper for presentation at the spring meeting of the API Division of Production, Pacific Coast District, Los Angeles, Calif, May 16, 1957.   New York [1957?]

44 p. illus. 23 cm.

1. Petroleum industry & trade—The West.   I. Hill, Kenneth E. II. Winger, John G. III. Title.

Kentucky. Univ. Libr.   A 59-4219
for Library of Congress   [5]

202

U. S. *Bureau of Foreign Commerce* (1953–   )
A directory of foreign advertising agencies and marketing research organizations for the United States international business community ₍compiled by Helen Biggane. Washington, 1959₎

iv, 135 p.   24 cm.

207

1. Advertising agencies—Direct.   2. Marketing research—Direct.
I. Title.

HF6178.U6   659.112   59—61136

U. S. *Bureau of Foreign Commerce* (*1953–*   ) *Office of Economic Affairs.*
Electric current abroad. ₍Revision₎ Washington, U. S. Dept. of Commerce, Bureau of Foreign Commerce ₍1959₎

77 p. (chiefly tables)   24 cm.

Previous ed. published in 1948, by G. B. Hall, under title: World electrical current characteristics.

208

1. Electric currents—Direct.   2. Electric utilities—Direct.   3. Electric apparatus and appliances.   I. Hall, Guida Berrigan. World electrical current characteristics.   II. Title.

TK12.U47   621.3058

Library of Congress   ₍59d5₎

U. S. *Bureau of Naval Personnel.*
Ship's serviceman tailor handbook. ₍Prepared as a supplement to the Navy training course for ship's serviceman 3 & 2, Navpers 10286–B₎ Washington, U. S. Govt. Print. Off., 1953 ₍i. e. 1954₎

76 p.   illus.   26 cm.

"Navpers 10288–A."

209

1. Tailoring.   2. U. S. Navy—Equipment and supplies.   I. Title.

VC330.U52   1954   687.1   54—61203 ‡

U. S. *Civil Service Commission. Program Planning Division.*
Reduction in force; a statistical analysis of the reduction-in-force experience of 23 military installations. ₍Washington₎ 1958.

1 v. (unpaged)   map, diagrs., tables.   21 x 28 cm.

210

1. U. S. Dept. of Defense—Officials and employees.   2. U. S. Dept. of Defense—Appointments and retirements.   I. Title.

UB193.A525   355.114   59—61048

Library of Congress   ₍2₎

211

U. S. *85th Cong., 2d sess., 1958.*
Memorial services held in the Senate and House of Representatives of the United States, together with remarks presented in eulogy of William Kerr Scott, late a Senator from North Carolina. Washington, U. S. Govt. Print. Off., 1958.

172 p. port. 24 cm.

1. Scott, William Kerr, 1896–1958.

E748.S387U5   923.273   58–62405

212

U. S. *Congress. House. Committee on the Judiciary.*
The television broadcasting industry. Report of the Antitrust Subcommittee (Subcommittee No. 5) of the Committee on the Judiciary, House of Representatives, Eighty-fifth Congress, first session, pursuant to H. Res. 107 ... Washington, U. S. Govt. Print. Off., 1957.

vii, 148 p. tables. 24 cm. (85th Cong., 1st sess. House report no. 607)

Issued also without congressional series numbering under title: Report ... on the television broadcasting industry.

1. Television broadcasting—U. S.   (Series: U. S. 85th Cong., 1st sess., 1957. House. Report no. 607)

HE8698.A425 1957a   384.550973   57–60687

213

U. S. *Congress. Joint Committee on Atomic Energy.*
AEC Report on Indemnity act and Advisory Committee on Reactor Safeguards. Washington, U. S. Govt. Print. Off., 1959.

v, 60 p. 24 cm.

At head of title: 86th Cong., 1st sess. Joint committee print.
"U. S. Atomic Energy Commission ... Report": p. 3–59.

1. Liability for nuclear damages—U. S. 2. Insurance, Atomic hazards—U. S. 3. U. S. Atomic Energy Commission. Advisory Committee on Reactor Safeguards. I. U. S. Atomic Energy Commission. Report on Indemnity act.

368.57   59–61172

214

U. S. *Congress. Senate. Committee on Interstate and Foreign Commerce.*
The television inquiry; the problem of television service for smaller communities; staff report prepared [by Kenneth A. Cox, special counsel] Washington, U. S. Govt. Print. Off., 1959.

v, 54 p. 24 cm.

At head of title: 85th Cong., 2d sess. Committee print.

1. Television broadcasting—U. S.   I. Title.

HE8698.A43 1959   384.55   59–61067

Library of Congress   [2]

U. S. *Dept. of State. Office of Intelligence Research.*
 Postwar monetary and fiscal policies in Western Germany.
₍Washington, 1951₎

 iii, 39 p. tables. 32 cm. (*Its* OIR report no. 5171)

 Cover title.

 1. Currency question—Germany. 2. Finance, Public—Germany.
ɪ. Title.

 JX231.A324 no. 5171   59–23037

 Library of Congress ◯ ₍1₎

215

216

U. S. *Library of Congress. Card division.*
 Handbook of card distribution. 7th ed. Washington, 1944.

 vi, 88 p. illus. (facsims.) 23ᶜᵐ.

 On cover: The Library of Congress. Card division.

 1. Catalogs, Card. 2. Cataloging.

                                              44–40640

 Library of Congress ◯ Z695.U5H3 1944
                            ₍25₎   025.3

217

U. S. *Library of Congress. Descriptive cataloging division.*
 Cooperative cataloging manual, for the use of contributing
libraries. The Library of Congress, Descriptive cataloging
division. Washington, D. C., U. S. Govt. print. off., 1944.

 2 p. l., 104 p. incl. forms. 23½ cm.

 1. Cataloging, Cooperative.

 Z695.U4734 ◯ 025.3   44–41431

218

U. S. *Library of Congress. Processing Dept.*
 The cataloging-in-source experiment; a report to the Li-
brarian of Congress by the Director of the Processing Dept.
Washington, Library of Congress, 1960.

 xxiv, 199 p. illus. 27 cm.

 1. Cataloging. ɪ. Title.

 Z695.U4738   025.3   60–60033
 ———————Copy 3.   Z663.7.C38
 Library of Congress ◯ ₍61j5₎

U. S. *Library of Congress. Subject Cataloging Division.*
Classification. Class H: Social sciences. 3d ed., with supplementary pages, Washington, 1959.

xxxiv, 614, 123 p. 26 cm.

First ed. published in 1910 by the Classification Division of the Library of Congress.
"Additions and changes to December 1958": 123 p. at end.

1. Classification—Books—Social sciences.   I. U. S. Library of Congress. Classification Division. Classification. Class H: Social sciences.

Z696.U5H   1959   025.463   59–60034 rev
———— ———— Copy 3.   Z663.78.C5H 1959

Library of Congress   ₍r59k9₎

219

U. S. *Library of Congress. Subject Cataloging Division.*
Subject headings used in the dictionary catalogs of the Library of Congress ₍from 1897 through December 1955₎ 6th ed., edited by Marguerite V. Quattlebaum. Washington, 1957.

viii, 1357 p. 31 cm.

"Additions to and changes in these headings since 1955 will be found ... in monthly and cumulative supplements."

1. Subject headings.   I. Quattlebaum, Marguerite Rebecca (Vogeding) 1909–

Z695.U4747   025.33   54—60004

Library of Congress   ₍59q²10₎

220

221

U. S. *Treaties, etc., 1953–1961 (Eisenhower)*
German Red Cross hospital in Korea. Agreement between the United States of America and the Federal Republic of Germany signed at Washington February 12, 1954, entered into force February 12, 1954. ₍Washington, U. S. Govt. Print. Off., 1955₎
13 p. 24 cm. (U. S. Dept. of State. Publication 5444. Treaties and other international acts series, 2924)
English and German.
1. Red Cross. Germany. Deutsches Rotes Kreuz. 2 Hospitals—Korea.   I. Germany (Federal Republic, 1949–   ) Treaties, etc., 1949–   (Heuss) II. Title.   (Series: U. S. Dept. of State. Publication 5444. Series: U. S. Dept. of State. Treaties and other international acts series, 2924)

JX235.9.A32   no. 2924   362.11   55–60976

Library of Congress   ₍5₎

222

U. S. *Treaties, etc., 1961–   (Kennedy)*
Mutual defense assistance: disposition of military equipment and materials. Agreement between the United States of America and the Federal Republic of Germany, amending the Agreement of June 30, 1955, effected by exchange of notes signed at Bonn March 9, 1961. ₍Washington, U. S. Govt. Print. Off., 1961₎
3 p. 24 cm. (Treaties and other international acts series, 4703)
1. Surplus military property, American—Germany (Federal Republic, 1949–   )   I. Germany (Federal Republic, 1949–   ) Treaties, etc., 1959–   (Lübke)   (Series: U. S. Dept. of State. Treaties and other international acts series, 4703)

JX235.9.A32   no. 4703   61–61486

Library of Congress   ₍3₎

Georgia. Governor, 1955-1959 (Marvin Griffin)
    Education in Georgia, 1955 through 1958.
    ₍Atlanta, 1958?₎
    63p. illus. 30cm.

223

    1. Education - Georgia I. Title
GU

Maryland. *Governor, 1951–1959 (McKeldin)*
        The Governor reports: 1951–1958. How Maryland met
    the challenge of the 1950's. Annapolis, Govt. House, 1958.
        169 p. illus., port. 24 cm.

224

        1. Maryland—Pol. & govt.—1865–   ɪ. Title.
                                                            A 59–9139
    Enoch Pratt Free Libr.
    for Library of Congress   ₍2₎

Massachusetts. *Dept. of Mental Health.*
        Special report relative to the progress of psychiatric and
    adjunctive services provided for the courts and correction
    facilities. Boston, Wright & Potter Print. Co., legislative
    printers, 1958.
        23 p. 23 cm. (Massachusetts. ₍General Court, 1958₎ House ₍of
    Representatives. Documents₎ no. 2988)

        1. Psychiatric hospitals — Massachusetts. 2. Insanity — Jurispru-
    dence—Massachusetts.   (Series)

    J87.M4   1958g no. 2988   362.209744   58–63821

    Library of Congress   ₍1₎

225

Michigan. *State Highway Dept.*
        The preparation of soil strip maps for Michigan State
    highway projects ₍by₎ A. E. Matthews, engineer of soils
    ₍and₎ L. J. Cook, assistant to the engineer of soils. Pre-
    pared for presentation at the fortieth annual meeting of the
    Highway Research Board, Washington, D. C., January 9–
    13, 1961. Lansing, 1961.
        13 p. illus., map. 28 cm.

226

        1. Roads—Michigan. 2. Soils—Michigan—Maps.   ɪ. Matthews,
    Albert E. ɪɪ. Cook, L. J. ɪɪɪ. Title: Soil strip maps.

    TE24.M5A53   1961   61–63161
    Library of Congress   ₍1₎

Texas. *Laws, statutes, etc.*
 1959 Texas insurance code; with related acts and rules of
procedure. ₍Austin₎ State Board of Insurance, 1959.

 xxi, 500 p. 26 cm.

 "An unofficial revision of the original ₍Insurance₎ code which was
adopted in 1951. It contains all amendments to the date of adjournment of the third called session of the 56th Legislature, August 6,
1959."

 1. Insurance law—Texas.   I. Texas.   State Board of Insurance.
II. Title : Texas insurance code.

                    368.9764   60–20374

Library of Congress   ₍1₎

227

STATE, COUNTY
GOVERNMENT
PUBLICATIONS

228

Virginia. *Civil War Commission.*
 The Civil War Centennial in Virginia, 1961–1965. Plan
now to come to Virginia, capital State of the Confederacy
and chief battleground of the Civil War. ₍Richmond, 1961₎

 ₍4₎ p. illus. 23 x 10 cm. (Virginia Civil War Centennial, 1961–
1965)

 1. Virginia—Hist.—Civil War.   2. Virginia—Hist.—Civil War—
Societies, etc.   3. U. S.—Hist.—Civil War—Societies, etc.   4. Virginia—Descr. & trav.—1951–   I. Title.

                                  A 61–2603

Virginia.   State Library
for Library of Congress   ₍1₎

Virginia. *Supreme Court of Appeals.*
 Rules, February 1, 1950, including amendments effective
May 1, 1961. ₍Richmond, 1961₎

 58 p. 23 cm.

 1. Court rules—Virginia.

                                  A 61–2600

Virginia.   State Library
for Library of Congress   ₍1₎

229

Arlington Co., *Va. County Manager.*
 Arlington County, Virginia, handbook on county government organization. ₍4th ed. Arlington, 1960₎

 115, xxx p. illus. 22 cm.

 1. Arlington Co., Va.—Pol. & govt.

 JS451.V62   1960   352.0755295   61–26586 ↕

Library of Congress   ₍1₎

230

Los Angeles Co., *Calif. Ordinances, etc.*
Los Angeles County building laws. Official compilation. Edited and proofread by the Los Angeles County Division of Building and Safety. Los Angeles, International Conference of Building Officials, 1958.

655 p. diagrs., tables. 21 cm.

1. Building laws—Los Angeles Co., Calif.   I. Los Angeles Co., Calif. Dept. of County Engineer, Division of Building and Safety.

692.9   58–48634

Library of Congress   [3]

231

MUNICIPAL, ETC.
GOVERNMENT
PUBLICATIONS

New York (*City*) *Dept. of Parks.*
26 years of progress, 1934–1960. New York, 1960.

71 p. illus. 23 cm.

1. New York (City)—Parks. 2. New York (City)—Playgrounds. 3. New York (City)—Recreational activities.

SB483.N548A5   1960   61–40122 ‡

Library of Congress   [1]

232

233

Seattle. *City Engineer's Dept.*
Report on condition of street name signs, Seattle, Washington. W. P. A. Project 3478. [Seattle] City Engineer's Dept., Traffic Division, 1940.

[15] l. illus. (part mounted) map. 18 cm.

Cover title.

1. Street signs—Seattle.   I. Title.

HE370.S4   61–55705

Library of Congress   [3]

234

Washington, D. C. Inaugural Committee, *1961.*
Official program, inaugural ceremonies of John F. Kennedy, thirty-fifth President of the United States and Lyndon B. Johnson, thirty-seventh Vice President of the United States. Washington, D. C., January 20, 1961. [Washington] ᶜ1961.

63 p. illus. 28 cm.

1. Kennedy, John Fitzgerald, Pres. U. S., 1917–   —Inauguration. 2. Johnson, Lyndon Baines, 1908–

F200.W3   973.922   61—9828 ‡

Library of Congress   [61c10]

Canada. *Bureau of Statistics.*
Revised index of industrial production, 1935–1957 (1949=
100) Ottawa, Queen's Printer, 1959.

122 p. diagrs., tables. 26 cm.

At head of title: Dominion Bureau of Statistics. Research and
Development Division. Business Statistics Section.
"Reference paper (formerly no. 34, revised)"
Bibliography: p. [49]

1. Canada—Indus.   I. Title: Index of industrial production,
1935–1957.

HC111.A4 1957   338.0971   59—46136

Library of Congress   [a61b½]

235

236

Gt. Brit. *Treaties, etc., 1952–*   *(Elizabeth II)*
Convention between the Government of the United King-
dom of Great Britain and Northern Ireland and the Swiss
Government for the avoidance of double taxation with re-
spect to taxes on income, London, September 30, 1954.
London, H. M. Stationery Off. [1955]
27 p. 25 cm. ([Gt. Brit. Foreign Office] Treaty series, 1955, no. 21)
[Gt. Brit. Parliament. Papers by command] cmd. 9434.
English and French.
1. Taxation, Double—Gt. Brit. 2. Taxation, Double—Switzerland.
3. Income tax—Gt. Brit.—Law. 4. Income tax—Switzerland—Law.
I. Switzerland. Treaties, etc., 1954.   (Series. Series: Gt. Brit.
Parliament. Papers by command, cmd. 9434)
JX636 1892 1955, no. 21   55–3739

Congress   [2]

London. *County Council. Staff Association.*
Progress report, 1909–1959: the first fifty years in the
history of the London County Council Staff Association.
[London? 1959]

128 p. illus. 22 cm.

1. London. County Council. Staff Association.

JS3675.S8   61–28481 ‡

Library of Congress   [8]

237

238

Honduras. *Constitution.*
Constitution of the Republic of Honduras, 1957. [Wash-
ington, Pan American Union] Legal Division, Dept. of International Law, 1958.

v, 51 p. 27 cm. (Pan American Union. Legal Division. [Consti-
tutions series])

I. Pan American Union. General Legal Division. II. Title.

342.728301   P A 58–24

Pan American Union.   Library
for Library of Congress   [2]†

New Zealand. *Consultative Committee on Agricultural Education.*
Report. Wellington, Dept. of Education, 1958.

ix, 97, v p. 25 cm.

1. Agricultural education—New Zealand. 2. Agricultural extension work—New Zealand. 3. Agriculture as a profession.

S535.N45A53 — 630.7 — 59–28835

239
242

Poland. *Ministerstwo Sprawiedliwości.*
Wymiar sprawiedliwości w odrodzonej Polsce, 22. VII. 1944–22. VII. 1945. Warszawa [1945]

122 p. 24 cm.

1. Justice, Administration of—Poland. I. Title.

59–28963

240
243

Spain. *Instituto Nacional de Estadística.*
Reseña estadística de la Provincia de Tarragona. Madrid, 1952.

xvi, 658 p. col. maps (part fold.) diagrs. (part col.) tables. 25 cm.

1. Tarragona, Spain (Province)—Stat. I. Title.

HA1558.T3A53 — 53–33899

Library of Congress — [5]

241
244

India (*Dominion*) *Ministry of Industry and Supply.*
Manual of control orders; a hand-book containing the central control orders in force on March 1, 1949. Delhi, Manager of Publications [1949]

704 p. 24 cm.

Includes legislation.

1. Priorities, Industrial—India. 2. Rationing, Consumer—India. I. India (Dominion) Laws, statutes, etc. II. Title.

59–31307

India (*Republic*) *Tourist Traffic Branch.*
Guide to Kashmir. New Delhi [1954]

51 p. illus. 13 x 20 cm.

1. Kashmir—Descr. & trav.—Guide-books.

DS485.K2 I 65 — 59–28635 ‡

Ireland (*Eire*) *Commission of Inquiry into the Operation of the Laws Relating to the Sale and Supply of Intoxicating Liquor.*
Reports. Dublin, Stationery Office, 1957.

43 p. 25 cm.

1. Liquor traffic—Ireland.

HV5449.I 7A55 — 59–28854

Library of Congress — [3]

Haykin, David Judson, 1896–1959.
 Subject headings; a practical guide. Washington, U. S. Govt. Print. Off., 1951.

v, 140 p. 26 cm.

At head of title: The Library of Congress.

245

1. Subject headings.   I. U. S. Library of Congress.   II. Title.

Z695.H36   025.33   52—60002

Jackson, Sidney Louis, 1914–
 Catalog use study; director's report. Edited by Vaclav Mostecky. Chicago, American Library Association, 1958.

86 p. 28 cm.

At head of title: American Library Association, Resources and Technical Services Division, Cataloging and Classification Section, Policy and Research Committee.

246

1. Library catalogs and readers.   I. American Library Association. Cataloging and Classification Section. Policy and Research Committee. II. Title.

Z711.3.J2   025.3

Library of Congress   [50]

Lubetzky, Seymour.
 Cataloging rules and principles; a critique of the A. L. A. rules for entry and a proposed design for their revision. Prepared for the Board on Cataloging Policy and Research of the A. L. A. Division of Cataloging and Classification. Washington, Processing Dept., Library of Congress, 1953.

ix, 65 p. 24 cm.

Bibliographical footnotes.

1. American Library Association.   Division of Cataloging and Classification. A. L. A. cataloging rules for author and title entries. 2. Cataloging—Addresses, essays, lectures.   I. American Library Association. Board on Cataloging Policy and Research. II. Title.

Z695.L87   025.32   53—60029
———— Copy 3.   Z663.74.C3

247

Lubetzky, Seymour.
 Code of cataloging rules: author and title entry. An unfinished draft for a new edition of cataloging rules prepared for the Catalog Code Revision Committee. With an explanatory commentary by Paul Dunkin. [n. p.] American Library Association, 1960.

xv, 86 p. 28 cm.

At head of title: American Library Association, Resources and Technical Services Division, Cataloging and Classification Section, Catalog Code Revision Committee.

1. Cataloging.   I. American Library Association. Cataloging and Classification Section. Catalog Code Revision Committee. II. Title.

Z695.L872   025.32   60–2990

Library of Congress   [10]

248

IV. Serial publications (1-51) see also V

A. Entries: open vs. closed: main and secondary: comparative styles: holdings records: LC/Wilson/typed: see also II-B-C

B. Title entries for continuations, periodicals, etc.: interfiled (1-26) see also X-E

C. Corporate entries interfiled for (27-35) see also III-D

1. Continuations (27-31,33,35) see also III-D; VI-B
  a. Directories: see IV-B
  b. Proceedings (30)
  c. Reports (35)
  d. Yearbooks (33)

2. Periodicals (32,34)
3. Maps: see X-C
4. Miscellaneous (29)

D. Government publications: entries for (36-46)

1. Federal (36-38) see also VI-B; X-C
2. State (39-41)
3. Municipal (42-43)
4. Foreign (44-46)

E. Corporate body under successive names: NLM study: see App. H

F. Newspapers (47-51) see also X-E

1. Open entry (47)
2. Collection of extracts (48-49)
3. Reprint; special issue (50-51)

690.5
Ar25

Architectural & engineering news.
v. 1-
[New York, Hagen Pub. Co.]
v. illus.,ports. 29cm.
Bimonthly, Nov./Dec. 1958-Jan./Feb. 1959;
monthly, Mar. 1959-

For statement of holdings, see next card

1. Building - Periodicals

6

690.5
Ar25

Architectural & engineering news. (Card 2)

Library has:

v. 1 no. 1, Nov./Dec. 1958; no. 2, Jan./Feb. 1959, no. 3-12, Mar.-Dec. 1959.
v. 2 1960
v. 3 1961

7

C. R. C. standard mathematical tables.

Cleveland, Chemical Rubber Pub. Co.

v. illus. 17-21 cm.

Issues for 1931- called [1st]- ed.
Some editions issued in revised form.
Title varies: 19 Mathematical tables [from Hand-
book of chemistry & physics]
Editor: 19 C. D. Hodgman.

1. Mathematics—Tables, etc. I. Hodgman, Charles David, 1881-
ed. II. Handbook of chemistry and physics. III. Chemical Rubber
Company, Cleveland.

QA47.M315 510.835 [61r54g²20]

Library of Congress 30—4052*

8

1

378.73

American universities and colleges. 1st- ed. American Council on Education 1928-

v

2

378.73

EDUCATION—U. S.—DIRECTORIES

American universities and colleges. 1st- ed. American Council on Education 1928-

3

378.73

UNIVERSITIES AND COLLEGES—U. S.

American universities and colleges. 1st- ed. American Council on Education 1928-

4

378.73

Irwin, Mary, ed.

American universities and colleges. 1st- ed. American Council on Education 1928-

v

Editors: 1928, D. A. Robertson; 1932, J. H. MacCracken; 1936-40,
C. S. Marsh; 1948, A. J. Brumbaugh; 1952, Mary Irwin
Guide to accredited institutions of higher education in the United
States, Alaska, Hawaii, and Puerto Rico

5

378.73

American Council on Education

American universities and colleges. 1st- ed. American Council on Education 1928-

v

Editors: 1928, D. A. Robertson; 1932, J. H. MacCracken; 1936-40,
C. S. Marsh; 1948, A. J. Brumbaugh; 1952, Mary Irwin
Guide to accredited institutions of higher education in the United
States, Alaska, Hawaii, and Puerto Rico

1 Education—U.S.—Directories 2 Universities and colleges—U.S. 378.73
I Irwin, Mary, ed. II American Council on Education 378.73

5-23-52 (W) The H. W. Wilson Company

Le Bulletin lainier.

Paris.

    no. in v. illus. 28 cm. bimonthly.

    Began publication in 1924.

    Beginning with no. 813 the notation "nouv. sér." is omitted.

    "Organe d'information du Comité central de la laine."

    Separately paged supplements accompany some numbers.

——— Supplément. Statistiques du commerce extérieur français des produits lainiers, d'après les statistiques officielles de la Direction générale des douanes.

Paris.

    (Continued on next card)

[55b2]   55-27815 rev

9

Le Bulletin lainier. (Card 2)

    no. 28 cm.

    Quarterly, each issue cumulative from the first of the year. bound with Le Bulletin lainier, no.

No.   HD9930.F7C63 no. 778–852

——— Supplément. Annuaire statistique.

[Paris]

    v. illus.

    Vols. for 1963– In pts.: pte. 1. France.

    HD9930.F7C6312

    1. Linen—France—Period. I. Comité central de la laine.

HD9930.F7C63   55-27815 rev

10

Catalog of reprints in series. [1st]– ed.; 1940–

New York, Scarecrow Press [etc.,]

    v. 22–26 cm. annual (irregular)

    Vols. for 1958–60 never published.

    Editor: 1940– R. M. Orton.

    1. Bibliography—Editions. 2. Bibliography—Books issued in series. I. Orton, Robert Merritt, 1900– ed.

Z1033.S5C3   011   61-8715

[110–5]

Library of Congress

11

The Corporate director. v. 1–
June 1950–

[New York]

    v. illus. 29 cm.

    Includes miscellaneous publications of the American Institute of Management, some called Management audit, Special issue, Special audit, etc.

INDEXES:

    1950–52. (Issued as v. 2, no. 13)

    1. Industrial management—Period. I. American Institute of Management.

HD28.A643   55-27808

12

Explorations in entrepreneurial history.

Cambridge, Mass.

    v. 28 cm. 4 no. a year.

    Began publication with Jan. 1949 issue. Cf. Union list of serials. Published by the Harvard University Research Center in Entrepreneurial History.

INDEXES:

    Author Index.

    Vols. 1–6, Jan. 1949–May 1954, with v. 6.

    1. Entrepreneur—Period. 2. Economic conditions—Period. I. Harvard University. Research Center in Entrepreneurial History.

HB615.E8   55-3944

13

Forum.

Berlin.

    v. illus., ports. 47 cm. biweekly.

    Began publication in 1947. Cf. Sperlings Zeitungs-Adressbuch, 1947.

    Organ of the Freie Deutsch Jugend. Includes special numbers.

——— Wissenschaftliche Beilage.

[Berlin]

    v. 24 cm. biweekly.

    I. Freie Deutsche Jugend.

AP30.F52   AP30.F522

Library of Congress [3]   55-27845

14

RC321
.J6

Journal of clinical and experimental psychopathology ... (Card 2)

Edited for several years by V. C. Branham.
Vols. 9–13, no. 3 published by the Washington Institute of Medicine.

For statement of holdings, see CENTRAL SERIAL RECORD

1. Psychiatry—Period. I. Branham, Vernon Carnegie, 1889– ed. II. Association for the Advancement of Psychotherapy. III. Washington Institute of Medicine.

RC321.J76

43—16472*

15

18

The **Journal** of criminal law, criminology and police science.
v. 1–   May 1910–
[Chicago] Northwestern University School of Law [etc.]

v. illus. 23 cm.

Bimonthly, May 1910–May 1918, May 1931–quarterly, Aug. 1918–Feb. 1931.
Official publication of the International Association of Arson Investigators, Illinois Academy of Criminology and Society for the Advancement of Criminology, 1951/52—
Title varies: May 1910–Mar./Apr. 1942, Journal of the American Institute of Criminal Law and Criminology (cover title, May 1931–Mar./Apr. 1942, The Journal of Criminal law and criminology)—May/June 1942–Mar./Apr. 1951, The Journal of criminal law and criminology.

(Continued on next card)

16

19

The **Journal** of criminal law ...   (Card 2)

INDEXES: Vols. 1–24, 1910/11–1933/34. 1 v.

Absorbed the American journal of police science, July/Aug. 1932.

1. Criminal law—U. S.—Period. 2. Crime and criminals—U. S.—Period. 3. Police—U. S.—Period. I. International Association of Arson [I]nvestigators.

Library of Congress   [61r53p1]

12—27508*

17

20

020.5
J826

Journal of cataloging and classification. v. 1–12; fall 1944–Oct. 1956. [Richmond, etc.]
12 v. in 4. ports. 25 cm. quarterly.
Official organ of the American Library Association, Division of Cataloging and Classification, fall 1948–Oct. 1956.
Title varies: fall 1944–summer 1948, News notes of the Executive Board, A. L. A. Division of Cataloging and Classification (varies slightly)
Vols. 1–4 are photocopies (negative)
Index for v. 1–10, fall 1944–Oct. 1954, in v. 10, no. 4.
Merged with Serial slants to form Library resources and technical services.

1. Library science—Period. I. American Library Association. Division of Cataloging and Classification. II. American Library Association. Division of Cataloging and Classification. News notes.

Z671.J6   025.306273   57—2437

Library of Congress   [2]

---

xx American Library Association. Division of Cataloging and Classification. Catalogers' and classifiers' yearbook (1929–45)
xx Serial slants (1950–56)
xx Library resources & technical services (1957–

RC321
.J6

Journal of clinical and experimental psychopathology & quarterly review of psychiatry and neurology. v. 1–
July 1939–
[Washington, etc., MD Publications, etc.]

v. in   illus. 26 cm. quarterly.

Official organ of the Association for the Advancement of Psychotherapy, July 1944–Apr. 1946.
Title varies: July 1939–Apr. 1944, Journal of criminal psychopathology.—July 1944–Apr. 1946, Journal of clinical psychopathology and psychotherapy.—July 1946–Oct. 1950, Journal of clinical psychopathology.—Jan./Mar. 1951– Journal of clinical and experimental psychopathology.

(Continued on next card)

43—16472*

[60r55h1]

SAMPLE

W 1   Der LEBENSBERATER.
LE312   [1-   Jahrg.] 1957–
Bern.
v. illus.
Supersedes Naturheilkunde.
1. Naturopathy – Period.
W1 LE312
59–3596

NATIONAL LIBRARY OF MEDICINE

The **Record** year; a guide to the year's gramophone records, including a complete guide to long playing records. [1]–
London, Collins [1953–
v. 23 cm.
Compilers: 1951–   E. Sackville-West and D. Shawe-Taylor.

1. Music—Discography.   I. Sackville-West, Hon. Edward, 1901– comp.   II. Shawe-Taylor, Desmond, comp.

ML156.2.S253   *789.913   54–336 rev

21   24

020.5   **Serial** slants.   v. 1–7; July 1950–Oct. 1956. [Lafayette, Ind.]
Se67
7 v. ports. 29 cm. quarterly (irregular)

Editors: July 1950–Apr. 1952, J. Ganfield.—July 1952–Apr. 1955, S. Ford.
E. Kientzle.—July 1955–Oct. 1956, S. Ford.
Edited for American Library Association Serials Round Table.
L. C. set incomplete: v. 4, no. 3–4, v. 7, no. 3 wanting.

1. Periodicals—Period.   I. American Library Association. Serials Round Table.   II. Ganfield, Jane, ed.   III. Kientzle, Elizabeth, ed.
III. Ford, Stephen, ed.

Z692.S5S47   050   52–39844 rev
[r57b8]
Library of Congress

R
920.7
W62

Who's who of American women; a biographical dictionary of notable living American women. v.1– *date*
1958–59—
Chicago, Marquis-Who's Who.
v. 28 cm. biennial.
Accompanied by Geographical-vocational index.

1. Women in the U. S.—Biog.

CT3260.W5   920.7   58–13264 rev

22   25

---

xx American Library Association. Division of Cataloging and Classification. Catalogers' and
classifiers' yearbook (1929–45)
xx Journal of cataloging and classification (1944–56)
xx Library resources & technical services (1957–

Yearbook of youth organisations. Annuaire des organisations de jeunesse. 1st–   ed.; Nov. 1954–
Gauting/München, UNESCO Youth Institute.
v. 24 cm.

1. Youth—Societies, etc.—Direct.   I. United Nations Educational, Scientific and Cultural Organization. Youth Institute.

HQ796.A1U5   [56c5]   55–3943
Library of Congress

23   26

Colston Research Society.
  Proceedings of the symposium. [1st]–
1948–
  New York, Academic Press.
  v. illus., group ports. 26 cm. (Colston papers, v. 1–)

  Vols. for 1948–49 issued as a Special supplement to Research (London)
  Vols. for 1948–51 have only a distinctive title: 1948, Cosmic radiation.—1949, Engineering structures.—1950, Principles and methods of colonial administration.—1951, The universities and the theatre. Vols. for 1952–   have also a distinctive title: 1952, The suprarenal cortex.—1953, Insecticides and colonial agricultural development.—1954, Recent developments in cell physiology.—1956, The neurohypophysis.

(Continued on next card)

30

27

Colston Research Society.
  Proceedings of the symposium.
(Card 2)

  Vols. 1–4 published in London by Butterworths Scientific Publications (v. 4 by Allen & Unwin)
  L. C. set incomplete; v. 1 wanting.

  I. Research (London, 1947–   ) Special supplement. II. Title: Cosmic radiation. III. Title: Engineering structures. IV. Title: Principles and methods of colonial administration. V. Title: The Suprarenal cortex. VI. Title: Insecticides and colonial agricultural development. VII. Title: Recent developments in cell physiology. VIII. Title: The neurohypophysis.   (Series)

AS122.C62   51—259

31

28

New York. Radio Station WQXR.
  Programs.
  New York, Interstate Broadcasting Co.
  nos. in   v. illus., ports. 24 x 11 cm. monthly.

  Title varies:
  Issued   –Dec. 1939, Radio programs.
       –Dec. 1936 by the station under its earlier name: W2XR.

  1. Radio broadcasting—Period. 2. Radio broadcasting—U. S.

TK6540.N43   791.4   49–31113*†

32

29

629
.1335
Am35   **American Helicopter Society.**
             News letter.
             v. [1]–
           [1953]–
             New York.
             v. in   illus. 29cm.
             Irregular, 1953–54; monthly, 1955–
             Issues for 1953–55 have no vol. numbering but constitute v. 1.

             For statement of holdings, see SERIAL CHECK LIST

             1. Helicopters – Societies, etc.

629
.13335
Am35   **HELICOPTERS – SOCIETIES, ETC.**
             American Helicopter Society.
             News letter.

             For further information see
             American Helicopter Society.
             News letter.

Jinkō Mondai Kenkyūjo, *Tokyo.*
  調査研究主要結果
[東京] 厚生省人口問題研究所
  v. diagrs., tables. 25 cm.

  1. Japan—Population.   *Title romanized:* Chōsa kenkyū shuyō kekka.

HB3651.J5   J 60–19

33

U.S. *Central Intelligence Agency.*
Scientific information report. T1–
July 11, 1958–
Washington.

no. in v. illus., diagrs. 28 cm. semimonthly.

Supersedes an earlier publication with the same title published by the agency's Foreign Documents Division.

1. Science—Abstracts—Period. I. Title.

Q1.U45   508.2   61-31435

36

34

U.S. *Library of Congress. Card Division.*
Handbook of card distribution. 1st– ed.
Washington, 1902–

v. illus. 23 cm.

First-3d editions issued by the Division under its earlier name: Catalog Division, Card Section (varies slightly)

1. Catalogs, Card. 2. Cataloging.

Z695.U5H3   -025.3   2-21132 rev 2*

37

35

025.305
Un3c   U.S. *Library of Congress. Processing Dept.*
Cataloging service. Bulletin 1– 56
June 1945– Apr 1961
Washington.

56 no. 27 cm. irregular.

1. Cataloging. 2. Catalogs, Card. I. Title.

Z695.U437   025.305   49-288*
Library of Congress   [6211]

38

United Nations.
Yearbook. 1946/47–
New York, Columbia University Press in co-operation with the United Nations.

v. illus. 28 cm.

United Nations publications. Sales no.: 1947.I.18 [etc.]
Imprint varies: 1946/47-1947/48, Lake Success, Dept. of Public Information, United Nations.
Issue for 1946/47 includes a summary of the organization's activities from its inception to July 1, 1947.

1. United Nations—Yearbooks. 2. International agencies—Yearbooks. I. United Nations. Dept. of Public Information.

JX1977.A37Y4   47-7191

United Nations. *Children's Fund.*
Bulletin. no. 1– Oct. 25, 1949–
New York.

no. in v. 29 cm. monthly (irregular)

UNICEF. UNAC.
At head of title, Oct. 25, 1949–
No. 1– Issued by the Fund under an earlier name: International Children's Emergency Fund.

1. Child welfare—Period.

HV703.U44   59-2033 ‡

United Nations. *Economic Commission for Africa.*
Report. 1st– sess.; Dec. 29, 1958/Jan. 6, 1959–
New York.

v. 28 cm. (United Nations. [Document])

Issued as supplements to the Official records of the Economic and Social Council.

1. Africa—Econ. condit.—Societies, etc. (Series. Series: United Nations. Economic and Social Council. Official records. Supplement)

JX1977.A2   60-50671   [3]
Library of Congress

Alaska. *Division of Sport Fisheries.*
Report of progress. v. 1–   1959/60–
₍Juneau₎

v. maps, diagrs., tables. 28 cm. annual.

Cover title, 1959/60–   Dingell-Johnson project report.
Vols. for 1959/60–   issued by the division under a variant
name: Sport Fish Division.

39

1. Fishing—Alaska.

SH467.A3

Library of Congress   ₍1₎   61–63312

40

Hawaii. Dept. of Accounting and General Services.
Report of the Comptroller.
₍Honolulu₎
v. illus. 28cm. annual.
Report year ends June 30.

1. Finance, Public - Hawaiian Islands

HJ98.H314   61–63265‡

New Jersey. *Treasury Dept. Division of Budget and Accounting.*
Letters, numbers and titles of State appropriations accounts current. 1953/54–
₍Trenton₎

v. 23 cm. annual.

Report year ends June 30.

41

1. Finance, Public—New Jersey.

HJ11.N5127

Library of Congress   ₍1₎   53–62717 ‡

42

Cincinnati. *City Treasurer.*
Report.
₍Cincinnati₎

v. in   tables. 23 cm. annual.

Reports for 1912–   issued in the Annual reports of the city departments of Cincinnati, 1912–

1. Finance, Public—Cincinnati.

HJ9013.C6b   61–55700

Library of Congress   ₍2/8₎

352.0744
H299r   Haverhill, Mass. Municipal Council.
           Report.
           55th-
           1934-
           [Haverhill, Mass.] Record Press.
             1v. ports. 23cm. annual.

43

44

France. *Assemblée nationale, 1871–1942. Chambre des
députés.*
    Tables analytiques des Annales. 3.–16. législature; 1881/
85–1936/40. Paris.
    14 v. in 28. 28 cm.
    Each volume in 2 pts.: ptie. 1. Table des matières; ptie. 2. Table
nominative.
    Includes references to other publications of the Chamber, as Im-
pressions, Fascicules, Feuilletons, and some references to the Journal
officiel.
    L. C. set incomplete : v. 4, pt. 2; v. 6–11 wanting.
    1. France—Pol. & govt.—1870–1940.   I. France. Assemblée na-
tionale, 1871–1942. Chambre des députés. Annales. Débats parlementaires (Indexes) II. France. Assemblée nationale, 1871–1942.
Chambres des députés. Annales. Documents parlementaires. (Indexes)

J341.K212   55–48905
Library of Congress   [3]

45

Rhodesia, Northern. *Dept. of Trade, Transport and Industry.*
    Report. 1951–
Lusaka, Govt. Printer.
        v. 34 cm. annual.

    1. Rhodesia, Northern—Econ. condit.

HC517.R42A32   55–36225
Library of Congress   [3]

46

Seoul, *Korea. Kyoyuk Wiwŏnhoe.*
    서울문교연보
    [서울] 195
        v. illus., tables. 31 cm.
    Began publication with 1957 issue.
    Added title: Annual reports of Seoul education and culture, Board
of Education, city of Seoul.

    1. Seoul, Korea—Public schools.   I. Title.
                Title romanized: Sŏul mungyo yŏnbo.
LA1334.S4A3   K 59–28
Library of Congress   [8]

NEWSPAPERS

Boston globe.
Family boating in New England; a guide for outboard trailer sailors. [Boston, 1957]

184 p. illus. 23 cm.

1. Outboard motor-boats. 2. New England—Descr. & trav.—Guide-books. I. Title.

VM348.B58   797.125   57-3272 ‡

47

49

Boston globe.
A Governor ... but no home for him. [Boston, 1957]
9p. 4°
Mounted reprint from the Boston Sunday Globe of Jan. 6, 1957.

1. Massachusetts - Executive residence (Proposed)

N

50

The Boston Sunday globe.
This is the White House; the story of the executive mansion, its occupants, tragedies, and triumphs. Souvenir ed. [Boston, 1961]

24 p. illus. 34 cm.

1. Washington, D. C. White House.   I. Title.

F204.W5B6   975.3   61-33826 ‡

Library of Congress   [8]

48

51

J4306/6523   (MH-HY call numer)

(Harvard uses this card after slight changes.)

日本経済新聞社
経済新語辞典   年版 –
東京 昭和 ( ) –
冊 19cm

1. 経済一辞書 I. 書名   Japan-National Diet Library

Nihon keizai shinbunsya
Shinbunsha

330.33

国立国会図書館
57-6596(59)

DEC 1 1960

Chung-kuo ch'ing nien pao, *Peking.*
新中国青年的偉大志气—中国青年报社论选辑 中国青年报社论委员会编 北京 中国青年出版社 1958.

80 p. 19 cm.

1. Youth—China (People's Republic of China, 1949–   ) I. Title. *Title romanized:* Hsin Chung-kuo ch'ing nien ti wei ta chih ch'i.

C 60-5135

Harvard Univ. Chinese-for Library of Congress   Japanese Library 9159   [3]

V. Publications issued in series (1-62) see also IV

   A. Series: monograph; publisher's; main entries (1-3, 8-9, 15-17, 31, 38-40, 45-46, 50-51, 56-62)

      1. Note for series
      2. Tracing for series

   B. Series entry

      1. Title (4-7, 10-14, 18-30, 41-44, 59-60, 62)
      2. Corporate author (47-49, 52-55, 61)
         a. Series statement style and tracing: form on work vs. entry form (46, 51, 60-61)
         b. References: see II-H
      3. Editor
         a. Author series classed together with general editor (56-59)
         b. Omission of editor in series note
         c. Tracing for series editor: see I-D
         d. References from editor: see I-D; II-H

   C. Series treatment: variant styles and arrangements

      1. Unit card form: LC/Wilson (5-7, 11-12, 19-21, 24-26, 32, 41-44, 47-49, 52-55)
         a. Cover card/open entry with referral to cards in following arrangements (4, 10, 18, 23, 41, 47, 52-53)
            (1) Alphabetic by author (5-7, 24-26)
            (2) Numerical (11-12, 19-21, 42-44, 48-49, 54-55)
               see also II-A
         b. Shelf list referral for monograph series holdings (53)
      2. Combined or abbreviated form: typed (13-14, 22, 27-30)
         a. Alphabetic by author (13-14)
         b. Alphabetic by subject (28-30)
         c. Chronologic (27)
         d. Numerical (22)
      3. Form referral cards (33-37)
         a. Series of works by one author or by various authors (33-36)
         b. Miscellaneous publications, etc. (37)

SERIES

4

Columbia University studies in library service

For volumes of this series in the library, see cards following.

5

028
H127ℓ

Columbia University studies in library service

Haines, Helen Elizabeth, 1872–
 Living with books; the art of book selection. 2d ed. New York, Columbia University Press, 1950.
  xxiii, 610 p. 24 cm. (Columbia University studies in library service, no. 2)

 Includes bibliographies.

6

025
T191t

Columbia University studies in library service

Tauber, Maurice Falcolm, 1908– ed.
 Technical services in libraries: acquisitions, cataloging, classification, binding, photographic reproduction, and circulation operations, by Maurice F. Tauber and associates. New York, Columbia University Press, 1954 [°1953]
  xvi, 487 p. diagrs. 24 cm. (Columbia University studies in library service, no. 7)

 Includes bibliographies.

7

027.7
W695u2

Columbia University studies in library service

Wilson, Louis Round.
 The university library; the organization, administration, and functions of academic libraries, by Louis Round Wilson and Maurice F. Tauber. 2d ed. New York, Columbia University Press, 1956.
  xiii, 641 p. diagrs., tables. 24 cm. (Columbia University studies in library service, no. 8)

 Includes bibliographies.

  1. Libraries, University and college. (Series)   I. Tauber, Maurice Falcolm, 1908– joint author.

Z675.U5W745 1956   027.7   55—11184
 [59c²10]
Library of Congress

1

028
H127ℓ

Haines, Helen Elizabeth, 1872–
 Living with books; the art of book selection. 2d ed. New York, Columbia University Press, 1950.
  xxiii, 610 p. 24 cm. (Columbia University studies in library service, no. 2)

 Includes bibliographies.

  1. Books and reading. 2. Book selection. 3. Bibliography—Best books. 4. Libraries—Order dept. I. Title. (Series)

Z1003.H15 1950   028   50—4478

2

025
T191t

Tauber, Maurice Falcolm, 1908– ed.
 Technical services in libraries: acquisitions, cataloging, classification, binding, photographic reproduction, and circulation operations, by Maurice F. Tauber and associates. New York, Columbia University Press, 1954 [°1953]
  xvi, 487 p. diagrs. 24 cm. (Columbia University studies in library service, no. 7)

 Bibliographical references included in "Notes" (p. [414]–463)

  1. Library science.   I. Title.   (Series)

Z665.T28 1954   025   54—10328

3

027.7
W695u2

Wilson, Louis Round.
 The university library; the organization, administration, and functions of academic libraries, by Louis Round Wilson and Maurice F. Tauber. 2d ed. New York, Columbia University Press, 1956.
  xiii, 641 p. diagrs., tables. 24 cm. (Columbia University studies in library service, no. 8)

 Includes bibliographies.

  1. Libraries, University and college. (Series)   I. Tauber, Maurice Falcolm, 1908– joint author.

Z675.U5W745 1956   027.7   55—11184
 [59c²10]
Library of Congress

10

Z1003
.H2
1950

Columbia University studies in library service
For volumes of this series in the library,
see cards following.

11

Z1003
.H2
1950

Columbia University studies in library
service, no.2
Haines, Helen Elizabeth, 1872–
 Living with books; the art of book selection. 2d ed. New York, Columbia University Press, 1950.
 xxiii, 610 p. 24 cm. (Columbia University studies in library service, no. 2)

 Includes bibliographies.

12

Z665
.T2
1954

Columbia University studies in library
service, no.7
Tauber, Maurice Falcolm, 1908– *ed.*
 Technical services in libraries: acquisitions, cataloging, classification, binding, photographic reproduction, and circulation operations, by Maurice F. Tauber and associates. New York, Columbia University Press, 1954 [°1953]
 xvi, 487 p. diagrs. 24 cm. (Columbia University studies in library service, no. 7)
 Bibliographical references included in "Notes" (p. [414]–463)

 1. Library science. I. Title. (Series)

14

Columbia University studies in library service

028
H127ℓ Haines, H. E. Living with books. 1950.

025
T191t Tauber, M. F. and associates. Technical services in libraries. 1954.

027.7
W695u2 Wilson, L. R. and Tauber, M. F. The university library. 1956.

8

Z1003
.H2
1950

Haines, Helen Elizabeth, 1872–
 Living with books; the art of book selection. 2d ed. New York, Columbia University Press, 1950.
 xxiii, 610 p. 24 cm. (Columbia University studies in library service, no. 2)

 Includes bibliographies.

 1. Books and reading. 2. Book selection. 3. Bibliography—Best books. 4. Libraries—Order dept. I. Title. (Series)

Z1003.H16 1950   028   50–4478

9

Z665
.T2
1954

Tauber, Maurice Falcolm, 1908– *ed.*
 Technical services in libraries: acquisitions, cataloging, classification, binding, photographic reproduction, and circulation operations, by Maurice F. Tauber and associates. New York, Columbia University Press, 1954 [°1953]
 xvi, 487 p. diagrs. 24 cm. (Columbia University studies in library service, no. 7)
 Bibliographical references included in "Notes" (p. [414]–463)

 1. Library science. I. Title. (Series)

Z665.T2 1954   025   54–10328

13

Columbia University studies in library service

028
H127ℓ Haines, H. E. Living with books. 1950.

025
T191t Tauber, M. F. Technical services in libraries. 1954.

027.7
W695u2 Wilson, L. R. The university library. 1956.

American college and university series
For volumes of this series in the library,
see cards following.

18

378.774   American college and university series, v. 2
M582s   Sagendorph, Kent, 1902–
Michigan, the story of the university. [1st ed.] New York, E. P. Dutton, 1948.
384 p. illus., ports., map (on lining-paper) 22 cm. (American college and university series, v. 2)

19

376.8744   American college and university series, v. 3
W459h   Hackett, Alice Payne, 1900–
Wellesley, part of the American story. [1st ed.] New York, E. P. Dutton, 1949.
320 p. illus., ports. 22 cm. (American college and university series, v. 3)

20

378.744   American college and university series, v. 4
H261w   Wagner, Charles Abraham, 1899–
Harvard; four centuries and freedoms. [1st ed.] New York, Dutton, 1950.
326 p. illus., ports. 23 cm. (American college and university series. v. 4)

21

American college and university series

378.774   v. 2 Sagendorph, K. Michigan. 1948.
M582s
376.8744   v. 3 Hackett, A. P. Wellesley. 1949.
W459h
378.744   v. 4 Wagner, C. A. Harvard. 1950.
H261w

22

15

376.8744
W459h   Hackett, Alice Payne, 1900–
Wellesley, part of the American story. [1st ed.] New York, E. P. Dutton, 1949.
320 p. illus., ports. 22 cm. (American college and university series, v. 3)

1. Wellesley College.   (Series)

LD7213.H3   376.8744   49-3550*

16

378.774
M582s   Sagendorph, Kent, 1902–
Michigan, the story of the university. [1st ed.] New York, E. P. Dutton, 1948.
384 p. illus., ports., map (on lining-paper) 22 cm. (American college and university series, v. 2)

1. Michigan. University—Hist.   I. Title.   (Series)

LD3278.S3   378.774   48-7109*

17

378.744
H261w   Wagner, Charles Abraham, 1899–
Harvard; four centuries and freedoms. [1st ed.] New York, Dutton, 1950.
326 p. illus., ports. 23 cm. (American college and university series. v. 4)

1. Harvard University—Hist. 2. Teaching, Freedom of.
I. Series

LD2151.W25   378.744   50-10560

Library of Congress   [20]

Card 27

American college and university series

378.774	Sagendorph, K.	Michigan. 1948.
M582s		
376.8744	Hackett, A. P.	Wellesley. 1949.
W459h		
378.744	Wagner, C. A.	Harvard. 1950.
H261w		

UCB

Card 28

American college and university series

HARVARD UNIVERSITY.

378.744	Wagner, C. A.	Harvard. 1950.
H261w		

UCB

Card 29

American college and university series

MICHIGAN. UNIVERSITY.

378.774	Sagendorph, K.	Michigan. 1948.
M582s		

UCB

Card 30

American college and university series

WELLESLEY COLLEGE.

376.8744	Hackett, A. P.	Wellesley. 1949.
W459h		

UCB

Card 23

American college and university series
For volumes of this series in the library,
see cards following.

Card 24

376.8744 American college and university series
W459h **Hackett, Alice Payne,** 1900–
Wellesley, part of the American story. [1st ed.] New
York, E. P. Dutton, 1949.

320 p. illus., ports. 22 cm. (American college and university
series, v. 3)

Card 25

378.774 American college and university series
M582s **Sagendorph, Kent,** 1902–
Michigan, the story of the university. [1st ed.] New
York, E. P. Dutton, 1948.

384 p. illus., ports., map (on lining-paper) 22 cm. (American
college and university series, v. 2)

Card 26

378.744 American college and university series
H261w **Wagner, Charles Abraham,** 1899–
Harvard; four centuries and freedoms. [1st ed.] New
York, Dutton, 1950.

326 p. illus., ports. 23 cm. (American college and university
series. v. 4)

1. Harvard University—Hist. 2. Teaching, Freedom of.

LD2151.W25   378.744#   50-10560
                 [20]

Library of Congress

34 — LC

Tireman, Loyd Spencer, 1896–
    Mesaland series.

    The volumes of this series which are in the library are sep-
arately listed under the author.

---

35 — LC

Mesaland series.

    The volumes of this series which are in the library are sep-
arately listed under the author: Tireman, Loyd
Spencer, 1896–

36

    The volumes of this series which are in the library are listed
under their respective authors.

LC 0165-17 (8/19/54)   GPO

---

37 — LC

    The publications belonging to this series are cataloged in
the following ways: some are entered under their individual
authors, those which have an additional series title and numbering are entered under this sub-series, others are cataloged
as the institution's Miscellaneous publications.

    For catalogs, circulars, and other announcements of courses,
faculty, etc., see the general title Catalog under the name of
the school.

FORM

REFERRAL

CARDS

31

917.7   Havighurst, Walter, 1901-
H299m   The Midwest; picture maps by Jessie Miersma. Fideler
         1958
            144p illus maps (Life in America)
            First published 1951. In the 1958 edition the statistics have been
         brought up-to-date
            By means of easy text, more than a hundred photographs, and a series
         of picture maps, this book shows what might be seen on a "geography"
         trip through the Midwestern states of Ohio, Indiana, Illinois, Missouri,
         Michigan, Iowa, Wisconsin and Minnesota. (Publisher)
            Quarto volume

            1 Middle West—Description and travel I Title II Series   917.7

         58W4048   (W) The H. W. Wilson Company

32

917.7   Life in America
H299m   Havighurst, Walter, 1901-
            The Midwest; picture maps by Jessie Miersma. Fideler
         1958
            144p illus maps (Life in America)
            First published 1951. In the 1958 edition the statistics have been
         brought up-to-date
            By means of easy text, more than a hundred photographs, and a series
         of picture maps, this book shows what might be seen on a "geography"
         trip through the Midwestern states of Ohio, Indiana, Illinois, Missouri,
         Michigan, Iowa, Wisconsin and Minnesota. (Publisher)
            Quarto volume

            1 Middle West—Description and travel I Title II Series   917.7

         58W4048   (W) The H. W. Wilson Company

33

MH

Balzac, Honoré de, 1799-1850
    Scènes de la vie militaire

    The volumes of this series that are in the
library are separately recorded among the works
of the author

Z674
.A8

ACRL monograph. no. 1–
Chicago, 1952–
  no. 24-28 cm.
  Title varies slightly.
  Issued by the Association of College and Research Libraries (called in 1952-57 Association of College and Reference Libraries)

For works in this series, see cards following

1. Library science—Collections.

Z674.A8   020.82
                      [r58c2]
Library of Congress   52-4228

41

Z674
.A8
no. 8

ACRL monograph, no. 8
Kinney, Mary Ramon, 1906–
  Bibliographical style manuals; a guide to their use in documentation and research. Chicago, Association of College and Reference Libraries, 1953.
  21 p. 28 cm. (ACRL monographs, no. 8)
  Includes bibliographical references.

42

Z674
.A8
no. 21

ACRL monograph, no. 21
Reagan, Agnes Lytton.
  A study of factors influencing college students to become librarians. Chicago, Association of College and Research Libraries, 1958.
  viii, 110 p. form, tables. 28 cm. (ACRL monographs, no. 21)

43

Z674
.A8
no. 23

ACRL monograph, no. 23
Knapp, Patricia B   1914–
  College teaching and the college library. Chicago, American Library Association, 1959.
  viii, 110 p. illus. 24 cm. (ACRL monograph no. 23)
  Based on thesis, University of Chicago, issued in microfilm form in 1957 under title: The role of the library of a given college in implementing the course and non-course objectives of that college.
  Bibliography: p. 109-110.

1. Knox College, Galesburg, Ill. Library. 2. Libraries, University and college.   I. Title. (Series)

Z674.A75 no. 23   027.777349
                              [59u20]
Library of Congress   59—10356

44

38

39

40

Z674
.A8
no. 8

Kinney, Mary Ramon, 1906–
  Bibliographical style manuals; a guide to their use in documentation and research. Chicago, Association of College and Reference Libraries, 1953.
  21 p. 28 cm. (ACRL monographs, no. 8)
  Includes bibliographical references.

1. Authorship—Handbooks, manuals, etc. I. Title. (Series) Association of College and Reference Libraries. ACRL monographs, no. 8)

Z674.A75 no. 8   029.6
Library of Congress   53—2897

Z674
.A8
no. 23

Knapp, Patricia B   1914—
  College teaching and the college library. Chicago, American Library Association, 1959.
  viii, 110 p. illus. 24 cm. (ACRL monograph no. 23)
  Based on thesis, University of Chicago, issued in microfilm form in 1957 under title: The role of the library of a given college in implementing the course and non-course objectives of that college.
  Bibliography: p. 109-110.

1. Knox College, Galesburg, Ill. Library. 2. Libraries, University and college.   I. Title. (Series)

Z674.A75 no. 23   027.777349
                              [59u20]
Library of Congress   59—10356

Z674
.A8
no. 21

Reagan, Agnes Lytton.
  A study of factors influencing college students to become librarians. Chicago, Association of College and Research Libraries, 1958.
  viii, 110 p. form, tables. 28 cm. (ACRL monographs, no. 21)
  Thesis—University of Illinois.
  Bibliography: p. 100–103.

1. Library science as a profession.   I. Title: Factors influencing college students to become librarians.   (Series) Association of College and Reference Libraries. ACRL monographs, no. 21)

Z674.A75 no. 21   020.69
                              [59u10]
Library of Congress   58—11152

47

Z6673
.U55

U.S. *Public health service.*
... Publications ... Washington, U.S. Govt. print. off., 1908–27.
v. 24cm.
At head of title, 1914–1927, Treasury department. United States Public health service ...
Issued as Miscellaneous publication, no. 12, U.S. Public health service, 1910–1927.
Title varies: 1908–1912, Publications of the United States Public health service ...
1913–1927, Publications of the United States Public health and marine-hospital service ...
1. U.S.—Public health service—Bibl. 2. U.S.—Sanit. affairs—Bibl. 3. Hygiene, Public—U.S.—Bibl. 4. U.S.—Government publications—Bibl. I. Title.

Library of Congress   Z6673.U55
——— 2d set.
12—35198 (rev. '32)

45

48

Z6673
.U55
no.300

U.S. Public Health Service. Publication no. 300
Hyslop, Frances L
  Bibliography of occupational health; occupational health and related publications from the Public Health Service, 1909–1953 [by] Frances L. Hyslop [and] W. M. Gafafer. [Washington] U.S. Dept. of Health, Education, and Welfare, Public Health Service, Division of Occupational Health of the Bureau of State Services [1954]
  vi, 110 p. 23 cm. (U.S. Public Health Service. Publication no. 300. Public health bibliography series, no. 9)
  "Combines and brings up to date two previous bibliographies ... Publications by the Division of Industrial Hygiene, National Institute of Health, and other Public Health Service publications on in-
(Continued on next card)
54–61328

46

49

Z6673
.U55
no.300

U.S. Public Health Service. Publication no. 300
Hyslop, Frances L ... [1954] (Card 2)
  health ...
dustrial hygiene subjects, January 2, 1942, and Publications by Industrial Hygiene Division and other Public Health Service publications on industrial hygiene subjects, 1942–47, inclusive. In part, it also supplements ... Bibliography of industrial hygiene, 1900–1943, a selected list ... published as Public health bulletin no. 289."
1. Industrial hygiene—Bibl. I. Gafafer, William McKinley, 1886– joint author. (Series: U.S. Public Health Service. Publication no. 300. Series: U.S. Public Health Service. Public health bibliography series, no. 9)
Z6673.U515 no. 9   016.331822   54–61328
Library of Congress   [10]

Z6673
.U55
no.300

Hyslop, Frances L
  Bibliography of occupational health; occupational health and related publications from the Public Health Service, 1909–1953 [by] Frances L. Hyslop [and] W. M. Gafafer. [Washington] U.S. Dept. of Health, Education, and Welfare, Public Health Service, Division of Occupational Health of the Bureau of State Services [1954]
  vi, 110 p. 23 cm. (U.S. Public Health Service. Publication no. 300. Public health bibliography series, no. 9)
  "Combines and brings up to date two previous bibliographies ... Publications by the Division of Industrial Hygiene, National Institute of Health, and other Public Health Service publications on in-
(Continued on next card)
54–61328

Z6673
.U55
no.300

Hyslop, Frances L   Bibliography of occupational health ... [1954] (Card 2)
dustrial hygiene subjects, January 2, 1942, and Publications by Industrial Hygiene Division and other Public Health Service publications on industrial hygiene subjects, 1942–47, inclusive. In part, it also supplements ... Bibliography of industrial hygiene, 1900–1943, a selected list ... published as Public health bulletin no. 289."
1. Industrial hygiene—Bibl. I. Gafafer, William McKinley, 1886– joint author. (Series: U.S. Public Health Service. Publication no. 300. Series: U.S. Public Health Service. Public health bibliography series, no. 9)
Z6673.U515 no. 300   016.331822   54–61328
Library of Congress   [10]

Card 50 / 53

Z6673
.U515

U.S. *Public Health Service.*
  Bibliography series. no. 1–
[Washington] 1951–
  no. 23–26 cm. (*Its* Publication)
  Title varies: no. 1– Public health bibliography series.
  Some no. in rev. editions.

For statement of holdings, see shelf list

1. Hygiene, Public—Bibl.   (Series)

Z6673.U515   016.614   51–1942 rev

Card 51 / 54

Z6673
.U515
no. 9

U. S. Public Health Service. Bibliography
  series, no. 9
Hyslop, Frances L
  Bibliography of occupational health; occupational health
and related publications from the Public Health Service,
1909–1953 [by] Frances L. Hyslop [and] W. M. Gafafer.
[Washington] U. S. Dept. of Health, Education, and Welfare, Public Health Service, Division of Occupational
Health of the Bureau of State Services [1954]
  vi, 110 p. 23 cm. (U. S. Public Health Service. Publication no.
300. Public health bibliography series, no. 9)
  "Combines and brings up to date two previous bibliographies ...
Publications by the Division of Industrial Hygiene, National Institute of Health, and other Public Health Service publications on in-

(Continued on next card)

Card 52 / 55

Z6673
.U515
no. 9

U. S. Public Health Service. Bibliography
  series, no. 9
Hyslop, Frances L
  ... [1954] (Card 2)

dustrial hygiene subjects, January 2, 1942, and Publications by Industrial Hygiene Division and other Public Health Service publications on industrial hygiene subjects, 1942–47, inclusive. In part, tt
also supplements ... Bibliography of industrial hygiene, 1900–1943, a
selected list ... published as Public health bulletin no. 289."

1. Industrial hygiene—Bibl.   i, Gafafer, William McKinley,
1896–   joint author.   (Series: U. S. Public Health Service.
Publication no. 300. Series: U. S. Public Health Service. Public
health bibliography series, no. 9)

Z6673.U515 no. 9   016.331822   54–61328

Library of Congress   [10]

Bottom left card

Z6673
.U515
no. 9

Hyslop, Frances L
  Bibliography of occupational health; occupational health
and related publications from the Public Health Service,
1909–1953 [by] Frances L. Hyslop [and] W. M. Gafafer.
[Washington] U. S. Dept. of Health, Education, and Welfare, Public Health Service, Division of Occupational
Health of the Bureau of State Services [1954]
  vi, 110 p. 23 cm. (U. S. Public Health Service. Publication no.
300. Public health bibliography series, no. 9)
  "Combines and brings up to date two previous bibliographies ...
Publications by the Division of Industrial Hygiene, National Institute of Health, and other Public Health Service publications on in-

(Continued on next card)

54–61328

Bottom middle card

Z6673
.U515
no. 9

Hyslop, Frances L   Bibliography of occupational
  health ... [1954] (Card 2)

dustrial hygiene subjects, January 2, 1942, and Publications by Industrial Hygiene Division and other Public Health Service publications on industrial hygiene subjects, 1942–47, inclusive. In part, tt
also supplements ... Bibliography of industrial hygiene, 1900–1943, a
selected list ... published as Public health bulletin no. 289."

1. Industrial hygiene—Bibl.   i, Gafafer, William McKinley,
1896–   joint author.   (Series: U. S. Public Health Service.
Publication no. 300. Series: U. S. Public Health Service. Public
health bibliography series, no. 9)

Z6673.U515 no. 9   016.331822   54–61328

Library of Congress

Bottom right card

Z6673
.U515

U. S. *Public Health Service.*
  Public health bibliography series.
[Washington]
  v. 23 cm.
  No.   issued as Public Health Service publication.

1. Hygiene, Public—Bibl.   (Series: U. S. Public Health Service. Publication)

Z6673.U515   016.614   51—1942

Library of Congress   [52c2]

56 / 60

Conant, James Bryant, 1893–
  The Federal Republic of Germany, our new ally; a lecture delivered at the University of Minnesota, Williams Arena, on February 24, 1957. [Minneapolis, University of Minnesota, 1957]
  20 p. 22 cm. (The Gideon D. Seymour memorial lecture series no. 5])

57

  1. Germany (Federal Republic, 1949–   )   (Series)
x to Series: Minnesota. University. The Gideon D. Seymour memorial lecture series
  Minnesota. Univ. Libr.
    for Library of Congress   57–7856

58 / 61

Rostow, Eugene Victor, 1913–
  Planning for freedom; the public law of American capitalism. New Haven, Yale University Press, 1959.
  x, 437 p. diagr., tables. 25 cm. (University of Michigan. William W. Cook Foundation. Lectures, 9)

  1. Industrial laws and legislation—U. S. 2. Industry and state—U. S. I. Title. (Series: Michigan. University. William W. Cook Foundation. Lectures, 9)
        338.973   59–12701

59 / 62

Thomas, Homer L
  A survey of Land Baden [by] Homer L, Thomas, with assistance and collaboration of James K. Pollock, Willett Ramsdell [and] W. Clark Trow. Ann Arbor, Mich., Horace H. Rackham School of Graduate Studies, 1944.
  iii, 69, 2 l. maps (1 fold.) diagr. 21 cm. (Michigan survey, no. 10)
  Photocopy (positive) of typescript.

  1. Baden.   (Series)
    DD801.B14T5   60–56255
  Library of Congress   [3]

Edwards, Jonathan, 1703–1758.
  Works. Perry Miller, general editor. [New Haven, Yale University Press, 1957–
  v. port., facsim. 24 cm.
  Half title; each vol. has also special t. p.
  Contents.—v. 1. Freedom of the will.—v. 2. Religious affections.

Edwards, Jonathan, 1703–1758.
  Freedom of the will. Edited by Paul Ramsey. New Haven, Yale University Press, 1957.
  xii, 494 p. port., facsim. 24 cm. (His Works, v. 1)

Edwards, Jonathan, 1703–1758.
  Religious affections. Edited by John E. Smith. New Haven, Yale University Press, 1959.
  526 p. facsim. 24 cm. (His Works, v. 2)
  First published in 1746 under title: A treatise concerning religious affections.
  Bibliographical footnotes.

  1. Emotions—Early works to 1850.   I. Title.
    BX7117.E3 1957, vol. 2   241   59–12702
        LC

DS796
.S55H5
Orien
Japan

Hiraoka, Takeo, 1909–   ea...
  長安と洛陽 平岡武夫 [編] 京都
都大學人文科學研究所索引編集委員會 1956.
  3 v. fold. maps, facsims, plans. 26 cm. (唐代研究のしおり)
  第 5-7. Tung civilization reference series, no. 5-7)
  Title on spine:唐代の長安と洛陽
  Added t. p.: Ch'ang-an and Lo-yang.
  Contents.—[1, 索引—[2, 資料—[3, 地圖
  1. Sian, China—Hist. 2. Lo-yang, China (Honan Province)—Hist. I. Imai, Kiyoshi, joint ed. II. Title. III. Title: Tōdai no Chōan to Rakuyō. (Series: Tōdai Kenkyū no shiori, dai 5-7)
    Title romanized: Chōan to Rakuyō.
  DS796.S55H5   AC...   J 61-4293
  Library of Congress   [3]

VI.   Analytical entries: comparative styles (1-90)

    A. Monograph publications (1-18, 20-90)

        1. Single authorship with tracing (1-14)
            a. Collective biography (1-9)
            b. Novels (10-14)
            c. Separate chapter(s) by other author(s) (22-33)
        2. Multiple authorship with tracing (34-90)
            a. Editor entries (34-58)
            b. Title entries (59-90)
        3. Sets of works (15-17)

    B. Serial publications: interfiled (18-21)

        1. Monograph series (18, 20-21)
        2. Periodical (19)

920.073
B727d   **Bradford, Gamaliel,** 1863–1932.
         ... Damaged souls, by Gamaliel Bradford. Boston and
         New York, Houghton Mifflin company, 1931.

           3 p. l., ix–xi, [1] p., 2 l., 3–276 p. 21ᶜᵐ. (The Riverside library)

           "Copyright, 1922 ... eighth impression, October, 1928."
           Contains bibliographies.

           CONTENTS.—Damaged souls. — Benedict Arnold. — Thomas Paine. —
         Aaron Burr.—John Randolph of Roanoke.—John Brown.—Phineas Tay-
         lor Barnum.—Benjamin Franklin Butler.

           1. U. S.—Biog.   I. Title.

                                                          34–29271
           Library of Congress   E176.B8 1931   920.073

COLLECTIVE BIOGRAPHY

1

Arnold, Benedict, 1741-1801.   (subj anal)
Paine, Thomas, 1737-1814.   (subj anal)
Burr, Aaron, 1756-1836.   (subj anal)
Randolph, John, 1773-1833.   (subj anal)
Brown, John, 1800-1859.   (subj anal)
Barnum, Phineas Taylor, 1810-1891.   (subj anal)
Butler, Benjamin Franklin, 1818-1893. (subj anal)

2

3

920.073   ARNOLD, BENEDICT, 1741–1801.
B727d   **Bradford, Gamaliel,** 1863–1932.
         ... Damaged souls, by Gamaliel Bradford. Boston and
         New York, Houghton Mifflin company, 1931.

           3 p. l., ix–xi, [1] p., 2 l., 3–276 p. 21ᶜᵐ. (The Riverside library)

           "Copyright, 1922 ... eighth impression, October, 1928."
           Contains bibliographies.

           CONTENTS.—Damaged souls. — Benedict Arnold. — Thomas Paine. —
         Aaron Burr.—John Randolph of Roanoke.—John Brown.—Phineas Tay-
         lor Barnum.—Benjamin Franklin Butler.

           1. U. S.—Biog.   I. Title.

                                                          34–29271
           Library of Congress   E176.B8 1931   920.073

920.073   ARNOLD, BENEDICT, 1741-1801.
B727d   Bradford, Gamaliel, 1863-1932.   LC
          Benedict Arnold.

          (In his Damaged souls. Boston, 1931[c1923]
        21cm. p. [17]-[50])

4

920.073
B727d Bradford, Gamaliel, 1863-1932.
          Damaged souls. Boston, Houghton Mifflin, 1931
       [c1923]
          276p. 21cm. (The Riverside library)
          Includes bibliographies.
          Contents.-Damaged souls.-Benedict Arnold.-
       Thomas Paine.-Aaron Burr.-John Randolph of
       Roanoke.-John Brown.-Phineas Taylor Barnum.-
       Benjamin Franklin Butler.

5

          U.S. - BIOGRAPHY
          Title
             Subj anals   UCB
                ARNOLD, BENEDICT, 1741-1801.
                PAINE, THOMAS, 1737-1814.
                BURR, AARON, 1756-1836.
                RANDOLPH, JOHN, 1773-1833.
                BROWN, JOHN, 1800-1859.
                BARNUM, PHINEAS TAYLOR, 1810-1891.
                BUTLER, BENJAMIN FRANKLIN, 1818-1893.

6

920.073 ARNOLD, BENEDICT, 1741-1801.
B727d Bradford, Gamaliel, 1863-1932.
          Benedict Arnold.
          (In his Damaged souls. 1931[c1923] p. [17]-
       [50])

7

                                                      COL
920.073 ARNOLD, BENEDICT, 1741-1801.
B727d Bradford, Gamaliel, 1863-1932.
          Benedict Arnold. (In his Damaged souls. 1931
       [c1923] p. [17]-[50])

920.073 ARNOLD, BENEDICT, 1741-1801.
B727d Bradford, Gamaliel, 1863-1932.
          (In his Damaged souls. 1931[c1923] p. [17]-
       [50])

8-
9

823
L435 **Lawrence, David Herbert,** 1885–1930.
　　Short novels. Phoenix ed. London, Heinemann ₁1956₎

　　2 v. 19 cm.

　　CONTENTS.—v. 1. Love among the haystacks. The ladybird. The fox. The captain's doll.—v. 2. St. Mawr. The virgin and the gipsy. The man who died.

Title anals

10

11

823
L435　　Love among the haystacks, v. 1 ₁pt. 1₎ 39p.
Lawrence, David Herbert, 1885–1930.
　　Short novels. Phoenix ed. London, Heinemann ₁1956₎

　　2 v. 19 cm.

　　CONTENTS.—v. 1. Love among the haystacks. The ladybird. The fox. The captain's doll.—v. 2. St. Mawr. The virgin and the gipsy. The man who died.

A 57—1407

12

823
L435　　Lawrence, David Herbert, 1885-1930.
　　Short novels. Phoenix ed. London, Heinemann ₁1956₎
　　2 v. 19cm.

　　Contents.--v. 1. Love among the haystacks.--The ladybird.--The fox.--The captain's doll.--v. 2. St. Mawr.--The virgin and the gipsy.--The man who died.

　　Author and title anals.

UCB

13

823
L435　　Lawrence, David Herbert, 1885-1930.
　　Love among the haystacks

　　(In his Short novels. London ₁1956₎ v. 1 ₁pt. 1₎ 39 p.)

UCB

14

823
L435　　Love among the haystacks
　　Lawrence, David Herbert, 1885-1930.

　　(In his Short novels. London ₁1956₎ v. 1 ₁pt. 1₎ 39 p.)

UCB

18

Wheat, Carl Irving, 1892–
    Mapping the American West, 1540–1857; a preliminary study.

    (*In* American Antiquarian Society, Worcester, Mass. Proceedings. Worcester. 25 cm. v. 64 (1954) p. [19]–194. map)

    Bibliographical footnotes.

    1. Cartography—The West.   i. Title.

E172.A35   vol. 64
Newbery Library
for Library of Congress   [3]†   A 55–2912

19

610.7305   SLOW LEARNING CHILDREN
N938   Jubenville, Charles P.
    Day care centers for severely retarded children in Delaware has [sic] led to unexpected dividends for everyone.
        (In Nursing outlook, v. 8, p. 371–375, July 1960)

20

Q11   U.S. National Museum.
.U55   Proceedings.   v. 1–   1878–
    Washington, U.S. Govt. Print. Off.
    v.   illus.   24cm.

Q11.U55   vol. 99
Library of Congress   [5]   54–1872

21

Q11   Schultz, Leonard Peter, 1901–
.U55   A further contribution to the ichthyology of Venezuela.
v. 99
        (*In* U.S. National Museum. Proceedings. Washington. 24 cm. v. 99 (1952) p. 1–211.   illus.)

    Bibliography: p. 208–211.

    1. Fishes—Venezuela.

Q11.U55   vol. 99
Library of Congress

15

Æschylus.
    ... Nine Greek dramas by Æschylus, Sophocles, Euripides and Aristophanes; translations by E. D. A. Morshead, E. H. Plumptre, Gilbert Murray and B. B. Rogers, with introductions, notes and illustrations. New York, P. F. Collier & son [°1909]

    1 p. l., 466 p., 1 l.   front, 2 pl.   22½ cm.   (The Harvard classics, ed. by C. W. Eliot. [VIII])

    CONTENTS.—The house of Atreus (Aeschylus) tr. by E. D. A. Morshead.—Prometheus bound (Aeschylus) tr. by E. H. Plumptre.—Œdipus, the king (Sophocles) ; Antigone (Sophocles) tr. by E. H. Plumptre.—Hippolytus (Euripides) : The Bacchae (Euripides) tr. by Gilbert Murray.—The frogs (Aristophanes) tr. by B. B. Rogers.

                (Continued on next card)

[58⁴⁵]   9—25219

16

Æschylus.   ... Nine Greek dramas ... [°1909]   (Card 2)

    I. Sophocles.   II. Euripides.   III. Aristophanes.   IV. Morshead, Edmund Doidge Anderson, tr.   v. Plumptre, Edward Hayes, 1821–1891, tr.   VI. *Murray, Gilbert, 1866–   VII. Rogers, Benjamin Bickley, 1828–1919, tr.

PA3626.A2N5   9—25219
——— Copy 2.   AC1.A4
Library of Congress   [57†²]

17

Marguerite d'Angoulême, *Queen of Navarre*, 1492–1549.
    La duchesse jalouse et l'amant fidèle.

    (*In* Les Œuvres libres.   Paris.   18 cm.   [Nouv. sér.] no 144 (1958) p. [255]–274)

    I. Title.

[PQ1141.O4   new ser., no. 144]   A 59–3060

Northwestern Univ.
for Library of Congress   [1]

LC

Z682
.B7   LIBRARY SCHOOLS AND TRAINING.
      Leigh, Robert Devore, 1890-1961.
         The education of librarians.

         (In Bryan, A. I.   The public librarian.   New
      York, 1952.   23cm.   p. 299-425)

27

LC

Z682
.B7   Leigh, Robert Devore, 1890-1961.
         The education of librarians.

         (In Bryan, A. I.   The public librarian.   New
      York, 1952.   23cm.   p. 299-425)

26

25

Z682   LIBRARY SCHOOLS AND TRAINING
.B7   Bryan, Alice Isabel, 1902–
         The public librarian; a report of the Public Library In-
      quiry, by Alice I. Bryan, with a section on the education of
      librarians by Robert D. Leigh.   New York, Columbia Uni-
      versity Press, 1952.

         xxvii, 474 p.   diagrs., tables.   23 cm.

24

Z682   Leigh, Robert Devore, 1890-1961.
.B7   Bryan, Alice Isabel, 1902–
         The public librarian; a report of the Public Library In-
      quiry, by Alice I. Bryan, with a section on the education of
      librarians by Robert D. Leigh.   New York, Columbia Uni-
      versity Press, 1952.

         xxvii, 474 p.   diagrs., tables.   23 cm.

         1. Librarians—U. S.   2. Library administration.   I. Social Science
      Research Council.   Public Library Inquiry.   II. Title.

                                                           52—8829

23

Z682
.B7   Bryan, Alice Isabel, 1902–
         The public librarian; a report of the Public Library In-
      quiry, by Alice I. Bryan, with a section on the education of
      librarians by Robert D. Leigh.   New York, Columbia Uni-
      versity Press, 1952.

         xxvii, 474 p.   diagrs., tables.   23 cm.

         1. Librarians—U. S.   2. Library administration.   I. Social Science
      Research Council.   Public Library Inquiry.   II. Title.

      Z682.B7   023   52—8829

      Library of Congress $_{[}a54v^2 10_{]}$

22

      Leigh, Robert Devore, 1890-1961. (auth anal)
      Library schools and training   (subj anal)

026.61
K523a
    Tews, Ruth M.
Keys, Thomas Edward, 1908–
    Applied medical library practice. With chapters by Catherine Kennedy ₍and₎ Ruth M. Tews. Springfield, Ill., Thomas ₍1958₎

    xix, 495 p. illus., port., diagrs., facsims. 24 cm.

33

026.61
K523a
    MEDICINE - PERIODICALS
Keys, Thomas Edward, 1908–
    Applied medical library practice. With chapters by Catherine Kennedy ₍and₎ Ruth M. Tews. Springfield, Ill., Thomas ₍1958₎

    xix, 495 p. illus., port., diagrs., facsims. 24 cm.

32

026.61
K523a
Keys, Thomas Edward, 1908–
    Applied medical library practice. With chapters by Catherine Kennedy ₍and₎ Ruth M. Tews. Springfield, Ill., Thomas ₍1958₎

    xix, 495 p. illus., port., diagrs., facsims. 24 cm.

    Includes bibliographies.
    "Abstract journals: their use in medical references;historical summary;list of current titles ₍by₎ Catherine Kennedy": p. 57-77;"The patients' library ₍by₎ Ruth M. Tews": p. 97-134.
    1. Medical libraries. I. Title.

    Z675.M4K48 1958   026.61   58—8422

    Library of Congress   ₍60x5₎

31

    Kennedy, Catherine   (auth anal)
    Medicine - Periodicals   (subj anal)
    Tews, Ruth M.   (auth anal)
    Hospital libraries   (subj anal)

30

026.61
K523a
    Kennedy, Catherine
Keys, Thomas Edward, 1908–
    Applied medical library practice. With chapters by Catherine Kennedy ₍and₎ Ruth M. Tews. Springfield, Ill., Thomas ₍1958₎

    xix, 495 p. illus., port., diagrs., facsims. 24 cm.

    Includes bibliographies.

29

026.61
K523a
    HOSPITAL LIBRARIES
Keys, Thomas Edward, 1908–
    Applied medical library practice. With chapters by Catherine Kennedy ₍and₎ Ruth M. Tews. Springfield, Ill., Thomas ₍1958₎

    xix, 495 p. illus., port., diagrs., facsims. 24 cm.

    Includes bibliographies.
    "Abstract journals: their use in medical references;historical summary;list of current titles ₍by₎ Catherine Kennedy": p. 57-77;"The patients' library ₍by₎ Ruth M. Tews": p. 97-134.
    1. Medical libraries. I. Title.

    Z675.M4K48 1958   026.61   58—8422

    Library of Congress   ₍60x5₎

28

823.08
H321t   **Haycraft, Howard,** 1905–   *ed.*
        A treasury of great mysteries, edited by Howard Hay-
        craft and John Beecroft. New York, Simon and Schuster
        ₁1957₎

        2 v. 22 cm.

1. Detective and mystery stories.   ɪ. Beecroft, John, joint ed.
ɪɪ. Title.

PZ1.H32Tr   57—6099 ‡

Library of Congress   ₍591²10₎

34-
35

Christie, Agatha (Miller) 1891-   (auth anal)
Ambler, Eric, 1909-   (auth anal)
Chandler, Raymond Thornton, 1888-1959. (auth anal)
Du Maurier, Daphne, 1907-   (auth anal)
Title anals

UCB

36

Detective and mystery stories
Beecroft, John, joint ed.
Title
    Author anals
        Christie, Agatha (Miller) 1891-
        Ambler, Eric, 1909-
        Chandler, Raymond Thornton, 1888-1959.
        Du Maurier, Daphne, 1907-
    Title anals

823.08   Christie, Agatha (Miller) 1891-
H321t   **Haycraft, Howard,** 1905–   *ed.*
        A treasury of great mysteries, edited by Howard Hay-
        craft and John Beecroft. New York, Simon and Schuster
        ₁1957₎

        2 v. 22 cm.

        <u>Murder in the Calais coach, by Agatha
        Christie: v. 1, p. 9-146.</u>

1. Detective and mystery stories.   ɪ.
ɪɪ. Title.

PZ1.H32Tr

Library of Congress   ₍591²10₎

37

38

823.08   Murder in the Calais coach
H321t   **Haycraft, Howard,** 1905–   *ed.*
        A treasury of great mysteries, edited by Howard Hay-
        craft and John Beecroft. New York, Simon and Schuster
        ₁1957₎

        2 v. 22 cm.

        <u>Murder in the Calais coach, by Agatha
        Christie: v. 1, p. 9-146.</u>

1. Detective and mystery stories.   ɪ. Beecroft, John, joint ed.
ɪɪ. Title.

PZ1.H32Tr   57—6099 ‡

Library of Congress   ₍591²10₎

```
823.08
H321t  Christie, Agatha (Miller) 1891-
          Murder in the Calais coach.
          (In Haycraft, H., ed.  Treasury of great myster-
       ies.  [1957]  v. 1, p. 9-146)
```

39

```
823.08     Murder in the Calais coach
H321t  Christie, Agatha (Miller) 1891-
          Murder in the Calais coach.
          (In Haycraft, H., ed.  Treasury of great mystery-
       ies.  [1957]  v. 1, p. 9-146)
```

40

```
                                                        LC
823.08
H321t  Christie, Agatha (Miller) 1891-
          Murder in the Calais coach.

          (In Haycraft, Howard, ed.  Treasury of great
       mysteries.  New York [1957]  22cm.  v. 1, p. 9-
       146)
```

41-
42

```
                                                        LC
823.08     Murder in the Calais coach.
H321t  Christie, Agatha (Miller) 1891-
          Murder in the Calais coach.

          (In Haycraft, Howard, ed.  Treasury of great
       mysteries.  New York [1957]  22cm.  v. 1, p. 9-
       146)
```

```
823.08     Murder in the Calais coach
H321t  Christie, Agatha (Miller) 1891-
          Murder in the Calais coach.  (In Haycraft, H.,
       ed.  Treasury of great mysteries.  [1957]  v. 1,
       p. 9-146)
```

43-
45

```
                                                       COL
823.08     Murder in the Calais coach.
H321t  Christie, Agatha (Miller) 1891-
          (In Haycraft, H., ed.  Treasury of great myster-
       ies.  [1957]  v. 1, p. 9-146)
```

```
                                                       UCB
823.08     Murder in the Calais coach
H321t  Christie, Agatha (Miller) 1891-

          (In Haycraft, H., ed.  Treasury of great myster-
       ies.  New York [1957]  v.1, p.9-146)
```

Rebecca
Du Maurier, Daphne, 1907-

Haycraft, Howard,

Du Maurier, Daphne, 1907-
Rebecca v2 p301-576

Haycraft, Howard, 1905-   mysteries; ed. by Howard Haycraft and   ed.

Big sleep
Chandler, Raymond, 1888-   v2 p3-130

Haycraft, Howard,

Chandler, Raymond, 1888-
Big sleep v2 p3-130

Haycraft, Howard, 1905-   ed.
Treasury of great mysteries; ed.
John Beecroft. Simon & Schuster   Howard Haycraft and

2v
Contains 10 short stories, 5 novelettes
full: Murder in the Calais coach, by
E. Ambler; Big sleep, by R. Chandle

1 Mystery and detective stories
(8 author and title anals)

59W5,658

Journey into fear
Ambler, Eric, 1909-   v 1 p437-576

Haycraft, Howard, 1905-

Ambler, Eric, 1909-
Journey into fear v 1 p437-576

Haycraft, Howard, 1905-   ed.
of great mysteries; ed. by Howard Haycraft and

Murder in the Calais coach
Christie, Agatha (Miller) v 1 p9-146

Haycraft, Howard, 1905-   ed.
Treasury of

Christie, Agatha (Miller) 1891-
Murder in the Calais coach v 1 p9-146

Haycraft, Howard, 1905-   ed.
Treasury of great mysteries; ed. by Howard Haycraft and
John Beecroft. Simon & Schuster 1957
2v

e following novels in
Journey into fear, by
by D. Du Maurier

es   I Jt. ed.   II Title
Fic

H. W. Wilson Company

Treasury of great mysteries

Beecroft, John, 1902-   jt. ed.

SHORT STORIES

MYSTERY AND DETECTIVE STORIES

Haycraft, Howard, 1905-   ed.
Treasury of great mysteries; ed. by Howard Haycraft and
John Beecroft. Simon & Schuster 1957
2v

Contains 10 short stories, 5 novelettes and the following novels in
full: Murder in the Calais coach, by A. Christie; Journey into fear, by
E. Ambler; Big sleep, by R. Chandler; Rebecca, by D. Du Maurier

1 Mystery and detective stories   2 Short stories   I Jt. ed.   II Title
(8 author and title anals)   Fic

1-18-57   (W) The H. W. Wilson Company

46-58

Five finger exercise
Shaffer, Peter p75-94
808.82 The best plays of 1959-1960; the Burn

Fiorello! By J. Weidman and G
Weidman, Jerome p250-70
808.82 The best plays of 1959-1960; the Bur

Duerrenmatt, Friedrich
The deadly game p118-37
808.82 The best plays of 1959-1960; the Burn

Duel of angels
Giraudoux, Jean p207-25
808.82 The best plays of 1959-1960; the Burr

The deadly game
Duerrenmatt, Friedrich p118-37
808.82 The best plays of 1959-1960; the Buri

Chayefsky, Paddy
The tenth man p53-74
808.82 The best plays of 1959-1960; the Bur

Camus, Albert
Caligula p138-56
808.82 The best plays of 1959-1960; the Buri

Caligula
Camus, Albert p138-56
808.82 The best plays of 1959-1960; the Burn

The best man
Vidal, Gore p183-206
808.82 The best plays of 1959-1960; the Bur

The Andersonville trial
Levitt, Saul p95-117
808.82 The best plays of 1959-1960; the Buri

Abbott, George, jt. auth.
Fiorello! By J. Weidman and G.
808.82 The best plays of 1959-1960; the Bur
ed. by Louis Kronenberger; illus. v
with drawings by Hirschfeld. Dod
435p illus

Contains the following plays, abridged: The
Five finger exercise, by P. Shaffer; T
S. Levitt; The deadly game, by F. Duerrenm
Toys in the attic, by L. Hellman; The best
angels, by J. Giraudoux; A Thurber carniva
by J. Weidman and G. Abbott

1 Drama   2 Drama—   Collections
ɪ Kronenberger, Louis, ed.   (21 author

60W10,163   ◯   (W) The H. W. Wilson Company

Weidman, Jerome
Fiorello! By J. Weidman and G. Abbott p250-70
808.82 The best plays of 1959-1960; the Burns Mantle yearbook;

Vidal, Gore
The best man p183-206
808.82 The best plays of 1959-1960; the Burns Mantle yearbook;

Toys in the attic
Hellman, Lillian p157-82
808.82 The best plays of 1959-1960; the Burns Mantle yearbook;

A Thurber carnival
Thurber, James p226-49
808.82 The best plays of 1959-1960; the Burns Mantle yearbook;

Thurber, James
A Thurber carnival p226-49
808.82 The best plays of 1959-1960; the Burns Mantle yearbook;

The tenth man
Chayefsky, Paddy p53-74
808.82 The best plays of 1959-1960; the Burns Mantle yearbook;

Shaffer, Peter
Five finger exercise p75-94
808.82 The best plays of 1959-1960; the Burns Mantle yearbook;

Levitt, Saul
The Andersonville trial p95-117
808.82 The best plays of 1959-1960; the Burns Mantle yearbook;

Hellman, Lillian
Toys in the attic p157-82
808.82 The best plays of 1959-1960; the Burns Mantle yearbook;

Giraudoux, Jean
Duel of angels p207-25
808.82 The best plays of 1959-1960; the Burns Mantle yearbook;
ed. by Louis Kronenberger; illus. with photographs, and
with drawings by Hirschfeld. Dodd 1960
435p illus

Contains the following plays, abridged: The tenth man, by P. Chayefsky;
Five finger exercise, by P. Shaffer; The Andersonville trial, by
S. Levitt; The deadly game, by F. Duerrenmatt; Caligula, by A. Camus;
Toys in the attic, by L. Hellman; The best man, by G. Vidal; Duel of
angels, by J. Giraudoux; A Thurber carnival, by J. Thurber; Fiorello!
by J. Weidman and G. Abbott

1 Drama   2 Drama—   Collections 3 Theater—Yearbooks
ɪ Kronenberger, Louis, ed.   (21 author and title anals)   808.82

60W10,163   ◯   (W) The H. W. Wilson Company

59-79

574
C437

Children's guide to knowledge. ₍New York₎ Published for the Parents' Institute by special arrangement with Maxton Publishers ₍1953₎

258 p. illus. (part col.) 27 cm.

CONTENTS.—Birds, by L. M. Henderson.—Dogs, by L. M. Henderson.—Flowers, by I. Wilde.—Insects, by S. Barlowe.—Trees, by V. Swenson.—Horses, by E. J. Dreany.—Fishes, by D. Kay.—Stars, by S. Barlowe.

1. Natural history——Juvenile literature.   ɪ. Henderson, Luis M.

QH48.C56   574   54–552

Library of Congress   ₍5₎

80

UCB

81

Anals
    Henderson, Luis M.
    Wilde, Irma
    Barlowe, Sy
    Swenson, Valerie
    Dreany, E   Joseph
    Kay, Dorothea
Subj anals: see contents note

UCB

574
C437

Children's guide to knowledge. ₍New York₎ Published for the Parents' Institute by special arrangement with Maxton Publishers ₍1953₎

258 p. illus. (part col.) 27 cm.

CONTENTS.—Birds, by L. M. Henderson.—Dogs, by L. M. Henderson.—Flowers, by I. Wilde.—Insects, by S. Barlowe.—Trees, by V. Swenson.—Horses, by E. J. Dreany.—Fishes, by D. Kay.—Stars, by S. Barlowe.

82

1. Natural history——Juvenile literature.   ɪ. Henderson, Luis M.

QH48.C56   574   54–552

Library of Congress   ₍5₎

574
C437

NATURAL HISTORY

Children's guide to knowledge. ₍New York₎ Published for the Parents' Institute by special arrangement with Maxton Publishers ₍1953₎

258 p. illus. (part col.) 27 cm.

CONTENTS.—Birds, by L. M. Henderson.—Dogs, by L. M. Henderson.—Flowers, by I. Wilde.—Insects, by S. Barlowe.—Trees, by V. Swenson.—Horses, by E. J. Dreany.—Fishes, by D. Kay.—Stars, by S. Barlowe.

1. Natural history—Juvenile literature.   ɪ. Henderson, Luis M.

QH48.C56   574   54–552

Library of Congress   ₍5₎

83

574
C437   Henderson, Luis M.
          Birds.
          (In Children's guide to knowledge. ₍1953₎
        p. ₍4₎-42)

574   BIRDS
C437   Henderson, Luis M.
          Birds.
          (In Children's guide to knowledge. ₍1953₎
        p. ₍4₎-42)

84-
85

LC

574
C437   Henderson, Luis M.
          Birds.

          (In Children's guide to knowledge. ₍New York,
        1953₎ 27cm. p. ₍4₎-42)

LC

574   BIRDS.
C437   Henderson, Luis M.
          Birds.

          (In Children's guide to knowledge. ₍New York,
        1953₎ 27cm. p. ₍4₎-42)

86-
87

574
C437   Henderson, Luis M.
          Birds. (In Children's guide to knowledge.
        ₍1953₎ p. ₍4₎-42)

574   BIRDS
C437   Henderson, Luis M.
          Birds. (In Children's guide to knowledge.
        ₍1953₎ p. ₍4₎-42)

COL

574   BIRDS.
C437   Henderson, Luis M.
          (In Children's guide to knowledge. ₍1953₎
        p. ₍4₎-42)

88-
90

189

VII.

VII.　Works related　(1-85)

  A.　Abridgments　(1-2)

    1.　Original author　(1)
    2.　Adaptor　(2)

  B.　Adaptations　(3-10)

    1.　Original author　(3-4)
    2.　Adaptor/paraphraser　(5-10)
      a.　Personal name　(5-8)
      b.　Corporate name　(9-10)
      c.　Title:　see III-B

  C.　Commentaries, criticism, etc.　(11-17)

    1.　Commentator/author of critical study　(11-17)
    2.　Text:　see III-C-D

  D.　Concordance　(18)

  E.　Dramatizations and novelization　(19-22)

  F.　Editions of same work　(23-36)

    1.　Combined　(23-24)　see also VII-P
    2.　Multiple　(25-36)

  G.　Indexes, etc.　(37-39)

    1.　Monographs　(37)
      a.　Independent publication　(37)
      b.　Dependent publication:　see X-C
    2.　Serials　(38-39)
      a.　Independent publication　(38-39)
      b.　Dependent publications:　see II-B; IV-B
        (1)　Conventional note
        (2)　Informal note

  H.　Librettos　(40-42)　see also X-F-G

  I.　Reprints, offprints, issues, etc.　(43-45)

    1.　Independent entries　(43-45)
    2.　Dependent entries:　see X-D

  J.　Revisions　(58)　access also through Index

VII.   Works related (continued)

   K. Selections, excerpts, extracts (46-48)

       1. Individual author (46)
       2. Multiple authorship (47-48)
       3. Bible: see III-C
       4. Sacred literature: see III-C

   L. Sequel (49-50)

   M. Supplements, continuations, etc. (51-55)

       1. Independent publications (51-52)
       2. Dependent works (53-55)
           a. Monographs: see also III-A
           b. Serials: see IV-B
           c. Styles
               (1) Body of entry (53)
               (2) Note (52)
               (3) "Dash" entry (53-55) see also IV-B; VIII-A
                   (a) Personal name (53-55)
                   (b) Corporate name: see VIII-A
                   (c) Title: see IV-B

   N. Titles changed (59-63)

       1. Entry for one title (61) see also III-A
       2. Entries for both titles (59-60,62-63)

   O. Translations from and/or into (56-57) access also through Index

   P. Works bound together: variant styles: LC/typed (64-85)
          see also IX-E

       1. Personal authors (64-70,73-76,84-85)
       2. Corporate author (82-83)
       3. Uniform heading and personal author (77-78)
           a. Title page with verso of independent volume (71-72)
           b. Title pages with verso of works bound together (79-81)

Dumas, Alexandre, 1802–1870.
 The three musketeers; a new translation by Jacques La Clercq, edited and abridged by the translator especially for the Illustrated junior library. Illustrated by Norman Price and E. C. Van Swearingen. New York, Grosset & Dunlap [1953]

 302 p. illus. 24 cm. (Illustrated junior library)

 "Special edition."—Copyright application.

 1. France—Hist.—Louis XIII, 1610–1643—Fiction. I. Le Clercq, Jacques Georges Clemenceau, 1898– ed. and tr. II. Title.

PZ3.D89Th 80   ◯   843.76   53–3495 ↕

Library of Congress   [2]

1

2

Laube, Herbert David
 The story of Jean Valjean, extracted from Les miserables, abbreviated and recast. Geneva, N. Y., Press of W. F. Humphrey, 1928.
 64p. 20cm.

 I. Hugo, Victor Marie, comte, 1802-1885. Les miserables II. Title: Jean Valjean

◯

Melville, Herman, 1819–1891.
 Moby Dick. Adapted for young readers by Felix Sutton, illustrated by H. B. Vestal. New York, Grosset & Dunlap [1956]

 69 p. illus. 29 cm.

 I. Sutton, Felix. II. Title.

PZ7.M5166Mo ◯   56—58632 ↕

Library of Congress [58d5]

3

4

Lanson, Gustave, 1857–1934.
 Manuel illustré d'histoire de la littérature française [par] G. Lanson [et] P. Tuffrau. Éd. complétée pour la période 1919–1950. [Paris] Hachette [°1953]

 984 p. illus. 20 cm. (Classiques Hachette)

 Adapted for school use from Lanson's Histoire de la littérature française.
 Includes bibliographies.

 1. French literature—Hist. & crit. I. Tuffrau, Paul, 1887– joint author.
   Full name: Achille Alexandre Gustave Marie Lanson.

PQ116.L3 1953 ◯   55–2310 ↕

Library of Congress [2]

Chrestien *de Troyes, 12th cent.*
　　The story of the Grail. Translated by Robert White Linker. ₍2d ed.₎ Chapel Hill, University of North Carolina Press ₍1960, ᶜ1952₎

xx, 188 p.　24 cm.

Translation based on the Old French text edited by Alfons Hilka. Bibliography : p. ₍187₎–188.

　　ɪ. Perceval (Romances, etc.)　ɪɪ. Grail.　Legend.　ɪɪɪ. Linker, Robert White, tr.

PQ1447.E5L5　1960　　　　841.1　　　　　　61—396

Library of Congress　　　　　　　₍61h15₎

5

6

Malory, *Sir* **Thomas,** *15th cent.*
　　Le morte Darthur; the story of King Arthur & of his noble knights of the Round Table.　First printed by William Caxton, now modernised, as to spelling and punctuation, by A. W. Pollard.　Illustrated with wood engravings by Robert Gibbings.　New York, Printed for the Heritage Press ₍1955₎

vii, 757 p.　illus.　28 cm.

　　ɪ. Pollard, Alfred William, 1859–　　ed.　ɪɪ. Arthur, King (Romances, etc.)　ɪɪɪ. Title.

PR2043.P7　1955　　　　[398.22]　823.2　　　55–14494

Library of Congress　　　　　　₍10₎

Lamb, Charles, 1775–1834.
　　Tales from Shakespeare ₍by₎ Charles and Mary Lamb, edited by the Rev. Alfred Ainger, ᴍ. ᴀ., revised by H. Y. Moffett, illustrated by Maud and Miska Petersham.　₍New York₎ The Macmillan company ₍ᶜ1932₎

xix, 441 p.　incl. front., plates.　17 cm.　(*Half-title:* New pocket classics)

　　"Published October, 1907; revised edition with illustrations published May, 1932."

　　ɪ. Shakespeare, William.　Paraphrases, tales, etc.　ɪɪ. Lamb, Mary Ann, 1764–1847, joint author.　ɪɪɪ. Ainger, Alfred, 1837–1904, ed.　ɪᴠ. Moffett, Harold Young.　ᴠ. Title.

PR2877.L3　1932　　　　[823.79]　822.33　　　32—13918

Library of Congress　　　　　　₍59h1₎

7

8

Watson, Jane (Werner) 1915–
　　The Iliad and the Odyssey; the heroic story of the Trojan War ₍and₎ the fabulous adventures of Odysseus.　Adapted from the Greek classics of Homer by Jane Werner Watson. Pictures by Alice and Martin Provensen.　New York, Simon and Schuster ₍1956₎

96 p.　illus.　33 cm.　(A Giant golden book, 756.　De luxe ed.)

　　ɪ. Homerus.　Paraphrases, tales, etc.　ɪɪ. Title.

PZ8.1.H75 I Wat　　　　　　　　56—14219　‡

Library of Congress　　　　　　₍58k10₎

Disney (Walt) Productions.
    Walt Disney's Lady. Authorized ed. Based on the Walt Disney motion picture "Lady and the Tramp." Pictures by the Walt Disney Studio; adapted by Allan Hubbard and Gene Wolfe. Racine, Wis., Whitman Pub. Co., °1954 ᵢi. e. 1955ᵢ

    unpaged. illus. 17 cm. (Tell-a-tale books)

9

    ɪ. Title: Lady.

    PZ10.3.D632Lad 4   55–27083 ↕

Disney (Walt) Productions.
    Walt Disney's Sleeping beauty. Based on the Walt Disney motion picture, told by Jane Werner Watson. Pictures by the Walt Disney Studio, with many of the original backgrounds and color sketches from the film production. Additional art adapted by Eyvind Earl and Julius Svendsen. New York, Simon and Schuster ᵢ1957ᵢ

    57 p. illus. 34 cm. (A Giant golden book, 757)

10

    ɪ. Watson, Jane (Werner) 1915–   ɪɪ. Title: Sleeping beauty.

    PZ8.D632Se

    Library of Congress   57—14184 ↕
                              ᵢ59f7ᵢ

COMMENTARIES,
CRITICISM, ETC.

11

Grant, Frederick Clifton, 1891–
    Translating the Bible. Greenwich, Conn., Seabury Press, 1961.

    183 p. illus. 22 cm.

    "Published to commemorate the 350th anniversary of the King James version of the Holy Bible."

    1. Bible—Hist. 2. Bible. English—Versions. 3. Bible—Criticism, Textual. ɪ. Title.

    BS450.G67   220.52   61—5794 ↕

Morgan, George Campbell, 1863–1945.
    The unfolding message of the Bible; the harmony and unity of the Scriptures. ᵢWestwood, N. J.ᵢ Revell ᵢ1961ᵢ

    416 p. 22 cm.

12

    1. Bible—Criticism, interpretation, etc.   ɪ. Title.

    BS481.M65   220.6   61–9842 ↕

    Library of Congress   ᵢ10ᵢ

Ibn ʿAttar, Judah, 1655–1733.

מנחת יהודה. מקנאם. דפום פ. ۷נۘۖ۰י. צאייאג, תרנ"ן.

Meknès ₁1939/40₁

136 l. 22 cm.

Commentary on the Pentateuch.

13

1. Bible. O. T. Pentateuch—Commentaries. ɪ. Title.
Title transliterated: Minḥat Yehudah.

gx to 1. Pentateuch (Book of the Old

BS1225.I 29 Testament) 59–57989 ‡

Library of Congress ₁8₁

14

Haraszti, Zoltán, 1892–
The enigma of the Bay Psalm book. ₁Chicago₁ University of Chicago Press ₁1956₁

xiii, 143 p. port., facsims. 20 cm.

Companion volume to The Bay Psalm book, a facsimile reprint of the first edition of 1640, published in 1956.
Bibliographical references included in "Notes" (p. 119–139)

1. Bible. O. T. Psalms. English—Paraphrases—Bay Psalm book.
2. Bay Psalm book. ɪ. Title.

BS1440.B415H3 223.5 56—5128

Library of Congress ₁61n2₁

Claudel, Paul, 1868–1955.
Paul Claudel interroge le Cantique des cantiques. Paris, Egloff ₁1948₁

531 p. 21 cm.

Includes Latin text and French translation of the Song of Solomon.

15

1. Bible. O. T. Song of Solomon—Commentaries. ɪ. Bible.
O. T. Song of Solomon. Latin. 1948. ɪɪ. Bible. O. T. Song of Solomon. French. 1948.

Full name: Paul Louis Charles Marie Claudel.

BS1485.C62 223.9 A 50—1564

Illinois. Univ. Library
for Library of Congress ₁a58b½₁†

16

Gordis, Robert, 1908–
The Song of songs: a study, modern translation, and commentary. New ʃYork, Jewish Theological Seminary of America, 1954.

xii, 108 p. 24 cm. (Texts and studies of the Jewish Theological Seminary of America, v. 20)

Bibliography: p. 99–106.

1. Bible. O. T. Song of Solomon—Commentaries. ɪ. Bible.
O. T. Song of Solomon. English. 1954. Gordis. (Series: Jewish Theological Seminary of America. Texts and studies, v. 20)

BS1485.G63 223.9 54—765

Library of Congress ₁61f½₁

Solages, Bruno de, 1895–
    A Greek synopsis of the Gospels; a new way of solving the Synoptic problem. English ed. translated from the French text by J. Baissus. With a pref. by Cardinal Tisserant. Leyden, Brill, 1959.

    1128 p. diagrs. (part col.) 25 cm.

    1. Bible. N. T. Gospels—Criticism, interpretation, etc. 2. Bible. N. T. Gospels—Harmonies. I. Title.

    BS2555.5.S6   226.07   60–4007

17

CONCORDANCE

Ellison, John William, 1920–
    Nelson's complete concordance of the Revised standard version of the Bible. Compiled under the supervision of John W. Ellison. New York, Nelson [°1957]

    2157 p. 28 cm.

    1. Bible—Concordances, English. 2. Bible. English—Versions—Revised standard. I. Nelson (Thomas) and Sons, inc. II. Title.

    BS425.E4 1957   220.2   57—7122

    Library of Congress   [59t⁴20]

18

DRAMATIZATIONS

Anderson, Robert Woodruff, 1917–
    All summer long, a drama in two acts. Adapted from the novel A wreath and a curse, by Donald Wetzel. New York, S. French [1955]

    138 p. illus. 20 cm.

    I. Title.

    PS3501.N34A75   812.5   55—3621 ‡

19

Thomas, Dylan, 1914–
    The doctor and the devils. From the story by Donald Taylor. [Norfolk, Conn.] New Directions [1953]

    138 p. 20 cm.

    "Dramatic story, written in the form of a film scenario."

    I. Taylor, Donald Fraser. II. Title.

    [PN1997]   *822.9 792   53—12848

    Printed for U. S. Q. B. R.
    by Library of Congress   [54f5]

20

Wouk, Herman, 1915–
    The Caine mutiny court-martial; a drama in two acts by Herman Wouk, based on his novel The Caine mutiny. [Acting ed.] New York, French [1955]

96 p. illus. 19 cm.

1. World War, 1939–1945—Drama. I. Title.

PS3545.O98C3 1955   812.5   55–33705 ‡

21

813
K672m Klein, Charles, 1867–1915.
    The music master; novelized from the play as produced by David Belasco; illus. with scenes from the photoplay, a William Fox production. New York, Grosset & Dunlap [1909]
    341p. illus. 20cm.

I. Belasco, David, 1854–1931. II. Title

NOVELIZATION

22

EDITIONS OF
SAME WORK

Hansemann, David Justus Ludwig, 1790–1864.
    Die Eisenbahnen und deren Aktionäre in ihrem Verhältniss zum Staat. Leipzig, Renger'sche Verlagsbuchhandlung, 1837.

iv, 163 p. fold. tables. 22 cm.

—— —— Microfilm copy (negative) in the Library of Congress.

Imperfect: pages 76–111 not filmed.

Microfilm 1813 HE

1. Railroads and state—Germany. 2. Railroads—Early works to 1850. I. Title.

A 59–3849

Bureau of Railway   Economics. Library
for Library of Congress   [8]†

23

025.33
Sel7L7 Sears, Minnie Earl, 1873–1933.
    List of subject headings; with Practical suggestions for the beginner in subject heading work. 7th ed. by Bertha Margaret Frick. New York, H. W. Wilson Co., 1954.

xxviii, 589 p. 26 cm.

"First–fifth editions had title: List of subject headings for small libraries."

025.33
Sel7L8 ---- ---- 8th ed. by Bertha Margaret Frick. New York, Wilson, 1959.
    610p. 27cm.

1. Subject headings. 2. Classification, Decimal. I. Frick, Bertha Margaret, 1894– ed.

Z695.S43 1954   025.33   53—5511

Library of Congress   [550*20]

24

025.33
Sel72l4

Sears, Minnie Earl, 1873–1933.
List of subject headings for small libraries, including practical suggestions for the beginner in subject heading work, edited by Minnie Earl Sears. 4th ed, rev., with the addition of decimal classification numbers, by Isabel Stevenson Monro. New York, The H. W. Wilson company, 1939.

2 p. l., [iii]-xxvi, 516 p. 26 cm.

"Directions for use" on lining-paper.
Note on slip inserted between pages iv and v.
For other issues of this edition, see

1. Subject headings. 2. Classification, Decimal.   I. Monro, Isabel
Stevenson.   Latest edition stamped

Library of Congress   Z695.S43 1939

39—27691

025.33
Sel72l5

Sears, Minnie Earl, 1873–1933.
List of subject headings for small libraries, including Practical suggestions for the beginner in subject heading work, edited by Minnie Earl Sears. 5th ed., with the addition of decimal classification numbers by Isabel Stevenson Monro. New York, The H. W. Wilson company, 1944.

xxviii, 536 p. 26 cm.

"Directions for use" on lining-paper.

1. Subject headings. 2. Classification, Decimal.   I. Monro, Isabel
Stevenson.   Latest edition stamped

Library of Congress   Z695.S43 1944

44—40213

025.33
Sel72l5

Monro, Isabel Stevenson

Sears, Minnie Earl, 1873–1933.
List of subject headings for small libraries, including Practical suggestions for the beginner in subject heading work, edited by Minnie Earl Sears. 5th ed., with the addition of decimal classification numbers by Isabel Stevenson Monro. New York, The H. W. Wilson company, 1944.

xxviii, 536 p. 26 cm.

"Directions for use" on lining-paper.

For other editions, see author

1. Subject headings. 2. Classification, Decimal.   I. Monro, Isabel
Stevenson.

Library of Congress   Z695.S43 1944
[49q²10]   44—40213

025.3

28

25

29

26

30

27

025.33
Sel72l

Sears, Minnie Earl, 1873–1933.
List of subject headings for small libraries, compiled from lists used in nine representative small libraries, edited by Minnie Earl Sears. New York, The H. W. Wilson company; London, Grafton & co., 1923.

xii, 183 p. 26¹⁄₂ᵐ.

1. Subject headings.   Latest edition stamped

Library of Congress   Z695.S43

23—26243

025.33
Sel72l2

Sears, Minnie Earl, 1873–1933.
List of subject headings for small libraries, compiled from lists used in nine representative small libraries, edited by Minnie Earl Sears. 2d ed., rev. and enl. New York, The H. W. Wilson company, 1926.

x p., 1 l., 415 p. 26 cm.

"First edition 1923."

1. Subject headings.   Latest edition stamped

Library of Congress   Z695.S43 1926

26—13593   025.3

025.33
Sel72l3

Sears, Minnie Earl, 1873–1933.
List of subject headings for small libraries, compiled from lists used in nine representative small libraries, edited by Minnie Earl Sears. 3d ed., rev. and enl., including a new section, Practical suggestions for the beginner in subject heading work. New York, The H. W. Wilson company, 1933.

xxviii, 453 p. 26 cm.

"Practical suggestions for the beginner in subject heading work" issued also separately with cover-title.

1. Subject-headings.   Latest edition stamped

Library of Congress   Z695.S43 1933 [50¹²3]

33—27143   025.3

31

025.33
Sel7*l*8

SUBJECT HEADINGS
Sears, Minnie Earl, 1873–1933.
    List of subject headings; with Suggestions for the beginner in subject heading work. 8th ed. by Bertha Margaret Frick. New York, Wilson, 1959.

610 p. 27 cm.

"First-fifth editions had title: List of subject headings for small libraries."

For other editions, see author

1. Subject headings. 2. Classification, Decimal. 1. Frick, Bertha Margaret, 1894– ed.

Z695.S43 1959   025.33   59—6607

34

32

025.33
Sel7*l*8

CLASSIFICATION, DECIMAL
Sears, Minnie Earl, 1873–1933.
    List of subject headings; with Suggestions for the beginner in subject heading work. 8th ed. by Bertha Margaret Frick. New York, Wilson, 1959.

610 p. 27 cm.

"First-fifth editions had title: List of subject headings for small libraries."

For other editions, see author

1. Subject headings. 2. Classification, Decimal. 1. Frick, Bertha Margaret, 1894– ed.

Z695.S43 1959   025.33   59—6607

35

33

025.33
Sel7*l*8

Frick, Bertha Margaret, 1894–   ed.
Sears, Minnie Earl, 1873–1933.
    List of subject headings; with Suggestions for the beginner in subject heading work. 8th ed. by Bertha Margaret Frick. New York, Wilson, 1959.

610 p. 27 cm.

"First-fifth editions had title: List of subject headings for small libraries."

For other editions, see author

1. Subject headings. 2. Classification, Decimal. 1. Frick, Bertha Margaret, 1894– ed.

Z695.S43 1959   025.33   59—6607
[60g*30*]
Library of Congress

36

025.33
Sel7*l*6

Sears, Minnie Earl, 1873–1933.
    List of subject headings. 6th ed. by Bertha Margaret Frick. With Practical suggestions for the beginner in subject heading work, by Minnie Earl Sears. New York, H. W. Wilson Co., 1950.

xxx, 558 p. 26 cm.

"First-fifth editions had title: List of subject headings for small libraries."

"Directions for use" on lining paper.

1. Subject headings. 2. Classification, Decimal. 1. Frick, Bertha Margaret, 1894– ed.   **Latest edition stamped**

Z695.S43 1950   025.33   50—6615

025.33
Sel7*l*7

Sears, Minnie Earl, 1873–1933.
    List of subject headings; with Practical suggestions for the beginner in subject heading work. 7th ed. by Bertha Margaret Frick. New York, H. W. Wilson Co., 1954.

xxviii, 589 p. 26 cm.

"First-fifth editions had title: List of subject headings for small libraries."

1. Subject headings. 2. Classification, Decimal. 1. Frick, Bertha Margaret, 1894– ed.   **Latest edition stamped**

Z695.S43 1954   025.33   53—5511

025.33
Sel7*l*8

Sears, Minnie Earl, 1873–1933.
    List of subject headings; with Suggestions for the beginner in subject heading work. 8th ed. by Bertha Margaret Frick. New York, Wilson, 1959.

610 p. 27 cm.

"First-fifth editions had title: List of subject headings for small libraries."

1. Subject headings. 2. Classification, Decimal. 1. Frick, Bertha Margaret, 1894– ed.

Z695.S43 1959   025.33   59—6607
[60g*30*]
Library of Congress

INDEXES, ETC.

37

Baker, Arthur Ernest, 1876–1941.
　A Shakespeare commentary ...　New York, F. Ungar Pub.
Co. [1957]
　　2 v. (9, 964 p.)　fold. geneal. table (inserted)　26 cm.

1. Shakespeare, William—Dictionaries, indexes, etc.　ɪ. Title.

[   ] 1957　　　○　　822.33　　　　57—9168
[   ]ongress　　　　[59p5]

38

The Classical quarterly.　(Indexes)
　General index to volumes I-XXXII.　London, J.
Murray; New York, G. E. Stechert [1939?]
　36p.　28cm.
　Cover title.

39

Clapp, Jane
　Art in Life.　New York, Scarecrow Press, 1959.
　504p.　23cm.
　"This index ... designed ... to provide immedi-
ate reference to reproductions of paintings and
graphic arts in Life from its first issue, November 23, 1936 through 1956."

　1. Art - Indexes　I. Life (Chicago)　(Indexes)
II. Title

○

40

Loewe, Frederick, 1904–
　[My fair lady. Libretto. English]

　My fair lady; a musical play in two acts, based on Pyg-
malion by Bernard Shaw.　Adaptation and lyrics by Alan
Jay Lerner.　New York, Coward-McCann [1956]
　　186 p.　21 cm.

　1. Musical revues, comedies, etc.—Librettos.　ɪ. Lerner, Alan
Jay, 1918–　　My fair lady.　ɪɪ. Title.

ML50.L825M9　1956　○　782.8　　　　56—11519

Library of Congress　　　　[60y³10]

Puccini, Giacomo, 1858–1924.
　[Turandot. Libretto. German]

　Turandot; lyrisches Drama in drei Akten und fünf Bil-
dern [von] Giuseppe Adami [und] Renato Simoni.　Deutsche
Übertragung von Alfred Brüggemann.　Musik von Giacomo
Puccini.　Leipzig, Neuyork, G. Ricordi [19—]
　　63 p.　20 cm.

　[1. Operas—Librettos]　ɪ. Adami, Giuseppe, 1878–　Turandot.
ɪɪ. Simoni, Renato, 1875–　Turandot.　ɪɪɪ. Title.

ML50.P965T76　　　　○　　　　54–43173

Library of Congress　　　　[³]

LIBRETTOS

41

[Kheraskov, Mikhail Matveevich] 1723–1807.

Добрые солдаты; опера комическая, сочиненная на российскомъ языкѣ. Изд. 2. Въ Москвѣ, Иждивеніемъ Н. Новикова, въ Унив. тип., 1782.

64 p.   20 cm.

The composer is not mentioned.

I. Title.   *Title transliterated:* Dobrye soldaty.

ML50.K516D6   1782   ◯

Library of Congress   [2]

42

54–54717

REPRINTS,
OFFPRINTS,
ISSUES, ETC.

Barton, Albert Olaus.

Lincoln-Douglas debates, seventy-first anniversary, August 27, 1929; Freeport unveils a Lincoln statue.   Springfield? 1930]

8 p.   port.   23 cm.

"Reprinted from the Journal of the Illinois State Historical Society, volume 22, no. 4, January, 1930."

1. Freeport, Ill.   Lincoln statue.   2. Lincoln-Douglas debates, 1858.
3. Lincoln, Abraham, Pres. U. S.—Anniversaries, etc.

E457.7.B3   ◯   923.173   53–52188

43

Sayers, Frances (Clarke) 1897–

The belligerent profession.   Ann Arbor, 1950.

141–144 p.   26 cm.   (William Warner Bishop lectureship series, 2d, 1948)

"Reprinted from the Michigan alumnus quarterly review, vol. LVI, no. 14."

1. Librarians.   I. Title.   (Series)

Z682.S28   ◯   020.69   50–62742

44

Wheat, Carl Irving, 1892–

Mapping the American West, 1540–1857; a preliminary study.   Worcester, Mass., American Antiquarian Society, 1954.

[19]–194 p.   map.   25 cm.

"Reprinted from the Proceedings of the American Antiquarian Society for April 1954."
Bibliographical footnotes.

1. Cartography—The West.   I. Title.

GA408 1540.W4W4   ◯   016.91278   55–31007

Library of Congress   [1]

45

Emmanuel, Pierre.
  Qui est cet homme; ou, Le singulier universel. **Paris, Egloff** [1947]
  353 p. 19 cm.
  Sequel: L'ouvrier de la onzième heure.

  I. Title. II. Title: Le singulier universel.

PQ2609.M58Q5   848.91   50-38429

49

46

Emmanuel, Pierre.
  L'ouvrier de la onzième heure. Paris, Éditions du Seuil [1953]
  248 p. 20 cm.
  Sequel to the author's Qui est cet homme.

  I. Title.

Wisconsin. Univ. Libr. [1]   A 56-5865
for Library of Congress

50

47

Garey, Howard B
  The historical development of tenses from late Latin to Old French. Baltimore, Linguistic Society of America [1955]
  107 p. diagrs. 26 cm. (Language dissertation no. 51)
  Supplement to Language; journal of the Linguistic Society of America, v. 31, no. 1, pt. 2, Jan.–Mar. 1955.
  "Yale University dissertation."
  Bibliography: p. 105–107.

  1. Latin language, Postclassical—Tense. 2. French language—Old French—Tense. I. Language. Supplement. II. Title. (Series)

PA2250.G3   479   55-3622

Library of Congress   [10]

51

48

Dickens, Charles, 1812–1870.
  Comic scenes from Dickens, selected with an introd. by Bernard N. Schilling. Hamden, Conn., Shoe String Press, 1955.
  318 p. illus. 23 cm.
  CONTENTS.—From The Pickwick Club.—From The old Curiosity Shop.—From Martin Chuzzlewit.—From David Copperfield.

  I. Schilling, Bernard Nicholas, ed. II. Title.

PR4553.S34   823.83   55-3516 ‡

PG3237
.E5N3

Pushkin, Aleksandr Sergeevich, 1799–1837.
  Three Russian poets, selections from Pushkin, Lermontov and Tyutchev in new translations by Vladimir Nabokov ... Norfolk, Conn., New directions [1944]
  37, [3] p. 22½ cm. (The Poets of the year. [1943])

  1. Russian poetry—Translations into English. 2. English poetry—Translations from Russian. I. Lermontov, Mikhail IÜr'evich, 1814–1841. II. Tīūtchev, Fedor Ivanovich, 1803–1873. III. Nabokov, Vladimir Vladimirovich, 1899– tr. IV. Title.

PG3237.E5N3   891.71082   45-35068
              [61i2]

Library of Congress

Giles, Hermann Harry, 1901–   *ed.*
  Playwrights present problems of everyday life, a book of excerpts from well-known dramas, edited by H. H. Giles and Robert J. Cadigan. [1st ed.] New York, Harper [1942]
  xiii, 290 p. 22 cm.
  Bibliography: p. [275]–290.

  1. American drama (Selections: Extracts, etc.) I. Cadigan, Robert J., joint ed. II. Title.

PS634.G5   808.82   42-24972 rev*
              [r55g2]

Library of Congress

Walch, John Weston, 1902–
Complete handbook on foreign trade policy. Portland, Me., ᶜ1954.
2 v. Illus. 28 cm.
Includes bibliographies.
Contents.—v. 1. The basic handbook.—v. 2. The debate handbook.
——— Supplement on foreign trade policy. Portland, Me., ᶜ1955.
101 p. 28 cm.
Includes bibliographies.

HF1455.W28 Suppl.

1. U. S.—Foreign economic relations. 2. U. S.—Commercial policy. I. Title: Foreign trade policy.

HF1455.W28   337.91   55–3882 rev

52   55

Lamb, Charles, 1775–1834.
Contos de Shakespeare ₍por₎ Charles & Mary Lamb. 2. ed. Tradução de Mario Quintana. Porto Alegre, Livraria do Globo ₍1946₎
₍4₎ 1., ₍7₎–283 p. Illus. (part col.) 23 cm.

1. Lamb, Mary Ann, 1764–1847, joint author. II. Shakespeare, William. Paraphrases, tales, etc. III. Quintana, Mario, tr. IV. Title.

PR2877.L43 1946   [823.79] 822.33   48–23157*

53   56

Williams, Tennessee, 1914–
Un tramway nommé Désir. Adaptation de Jean Cocteau d'après la traduction de Paule de Beaumont. Couverture et lithographies de Jean Cocteau. ₍Paris₎ Bordas, 1949.
218 p. illus. (1 col.) 20 cm.

I. Cocteau, Jean, 1889–   II. Title.

Real name: Thomas Lanier Williams.

PS3545.I 5365S817   812.5   53–33996

Library of Congress   ₍3₎

54   57

Shaw, Charles Bunsen, 1894–1962.
A list of books for college libraries, 1931–38, prepared by Charles B. Shaw ... Chicago, American library association, 1940.
ix, 284 p. 11. 27 cm.
Classified, with index.
"This is a supplement to, not a revision of, A list of books for college libraries, the publication prepared under the aegis of the Advisory group on college libraries of the Carnegie corporation of New York and published by the American library association in 1931."—Introd.
1. Bibliography—Best books. 2. Libraries, University. I. Carnegie corporation of New York. Advisory group on college libraries. A list of books for college libraries. II. American library association. III. Title: College libraries, A list of books for.

Z1035.C27 1931   Suppl.   016   40—27354

Grace, Melania, *Sister,* 1898–
Books for Catholic colleges, a supplement to Shaw's list of books for college libraries. Compiled under the auspices of the Catholic Library Association by Sister Melania Grace and Gilbert C. Peterson. Chicago, American Library Association, 1948.
x, 184 p. 29 cm.

——— ₍Supplement₎ 1948/49–
Chicago, American Library Association.
v. 28 cm.

(Continued on next card)

Z1035.G72

Grace, Melania, *Sister,* 1898–   Books for Catholic colleges ... 1948. (Card 2)
Compiled 1948/49–   under the auspices of the Catholic Library Association by Sister Melania Grace and others.

1. Bibliography—Best books. 2. Libraries, University and college. 3. Libraries, Catholic. I. Shaw, Charles Bunsen, 1894–1962. A list of books for college libraries. II. Peterson, Gilbert Charles, 1907– III. Catholic Library Association. IV. American Library Association. V. Title.

Z1035.G7   016   ₍57r55r₃*₁0₎   48—11124*

Library of Congress

203

Colombo, Cristoforo.
Four voyages to the New World; letters and selected documents. Translated and edited by R. H. Major. Introd. by John E. Fagg. Bi-lingual ed. New York, Corinth Books [1961]

x, 240 p. facsim. 19 cm. (The American experience series, AE5)

First published in 1847 under title: Select letters of Christopher Columbus, with other original documents relating to his four voyages to the New World.

1. America—Disc. & explor.—Spanish. I. Title.

E114.M24 1961   973.15   61-8150

58 | **61**

Kilbracken, John Raymond Godley, *baron,* 1920–
A peer behind the curtain. London, V. Gollancz, 1959.

240 p. illus. 22 cm.

American ed. (Boston, Houghton Mifflin) has title: Moscow gatecrash.

1. Russia—Descr. & trav.—1945–   2. Russia—Soc. condit.—1945–
I. Title.

DK28.K52   914.7   59-3246 ‡

59 | **62**

Kilbracken, John Raymond Godley, *baron,* 1920–
Moscow gatecrash; a peer behind the curtain. Boston, Houghton Mifflin, 1959.

240 p. 22 cm.

London ed. (Gollancz) has title: A peer behind the curtain.

1. Russia—Descr. & trav.—1945–   2. Russia—Soc. condit.—1945–
I. Title.

DK28.K52 1959a   914.7   59-8858 ‡
[25]
Library of Congress

60 | **63**

Andrews, Ethan Allen, 1787-1858.
A Latin dictionary founded on Andrews' edition of Freund's Latin dictionary. Rev., enl., and in great part rewritten by Charlton T. Lewis and Charles Short. Oxford, Clarendon Press [1955]

2019 p. 26 cm.

First published in 1850 under title: A copious and critical Latin-English lexicon.

1. Latin language—Dictionaries—English. I. Freund, Wilhelm, 1806-1894. II. Lewis, Charlton Thomas, 1834-1904. III. Short, Charles, 1821-1886.

PA2365.E5A7 1955   473.2   56—58003

928.2
F228
Farjeon, Eleanor, 1881-
A nursery in the nineties; with many illustrations. London, Gollancz, 1935.
528p. ports.(part.col.) 21cm.
Includes music
American ed. (New York, Stokes) has title: Portrait of a family.
An account of the author's family.

1. Farjeon family. I. Title

928.2
F228
1936
Farjeon, Eleanor, 1881-
Portrait of a family; with many illustrations. New York, Stokes Co., 1936.
456p. ports.(part.col.) 22cm.
Includes music
London ed. (Gollancz) has title: A nursery in the nineties.
An account of the author's family.

1. Farjeon family. I. Title

Coto Fernández, Rubén.

Para los gorriones. San José de Costa Rica, J. García Monge, 1922.

133 p. 19 cm. (Repertorio americano. Biblioteca)

Bound with Escobar, J. I. Escritos. San José de Costa Rica, 1922; López, Ismael. Cesarismo teocrático. San José de Costa Rica, 1922; and Chacón y Calvo, J. M. Ensayos sentimentales. San José de Costa Rica, 1923.

64 — 67

Escobar, José Ignacio, 1848–1938.

Escritos. Selección y prólogo del Dr. Diego Mendoza. San José de Costa Rica, J. García Monge, 1922.

87 p. 15 cm. (Repertorio americano. Biblioteca)

Bound with Coto Fernández, Rubén. Para los gorriones. San José de Costa Rica, 1922.

65 — 68

López, Ismael, 1880–

Cesarismo teocrático, por Cornelio Hispano [pseud.] San José de Costa Rica, J. García Monge, 1922.

75 p. 15 cm. (Repertorio americano. Biblioteca)

Bound with Coto Fernández, Rubén. Para los gorriones. San José de Costa Rica, 1922.

66 — 69

Chacón y Calvo, José María, 1893–

Ensayos sentimentales. San José de Costa Rica, J. García Monge, 1923.

163 p. 15 cm. (Repertorio americano. Biblioteca)

Bound with Coto Fernández, Rubén. Para los gorriones. San José de Costa Rica, 1922.

I. Title.

PQ7489.C6P3

Library of Congress [3]

55–52354

70

Rogier, Léon.

Achille Millien. Paris, C. Vanier, 1860.

119 p. 18 cm. (Les Poètes contemporains)

Bound with Millien, Achille. Légendes d'aujourd'hui. Paris, 1870 and Millien, Achille. Musettes et clairons. 2. ed. Paris, 1867. Binder's title: Miscelánea 23.

1. Millien, Achille, 1838–1927.

PQ2364.M65Z8

55–48954

Millien, Achille, 1838–1927.

Légendes d'aujourd'hui, poèmes, suivis de Lieds et sonnets. Paris, Garnier frères, 1870.

226 p. 18 cm.

Bound with Rogier, Léon. Achille Millien. Paris, 1860.

I. Title. II. Title: Lieds et sonnets.

Full name: Jean Étienne Achille Millien.

PQ2364.M65Z8

55–48955

Millien, Achille, 1838–1927.

Musettes et clairons. 2. éd. rev. et augm. Paris, J. Tardieu, 1867.

viii, 170 p. 18 cm.

Bound with Rogier, Léon. Achille Millien. Paris, 1860.

I. Title.

Full name: Jean Étienne Achille Millien.

PQ2364.M65Z8

Library of Congress [3]

55–48956

71-
72

Printed May, 1893. Reprinted January, July, 1894;
October, 1896; July, 1897; October, 1898; November,
1899; September, 1900; July, 1901 : February, 1902;
June, 1903; July, 1904; February, 1905; January, 1906;
March, December, 1907; November, 1908; October, 1909;
January, 1911; November, 1912; November, 1913; October,
1914; September, 1915 May, 1916; February, 1917.

GREEK-ENGLISH LEXICON

TO THE

NEW TESTAMENT

AFTER THE LATEST AND BEST AUTHORITIES

BY

W. J. HICKIE, M.A.

ST. JOHN'S COLLEGE, CAMBRIDGE: LATE ASSISTANT MASTER
IN DENSTONE COLLEGE

NEW YORK
THE MACMILLAN COMPANY
LONDON: MACMILLAN & CO., LTD.
1917

73

PA881
.H5
Hickie, William James
  Greek-English lexicon to the New Testament,
after the latest and best authorities. New York,
Macmillan, 1917.
  213,16p. 16cm.
  "Aids to the study of the New Testament" 16p.
at end.

74

BS1965
1935
Hickie, William James
  Greek-English lexicon to the New Testament,
after the latest and best authorities. New York,
Macmillan, 1935.
  213p. 23cm.
  Bound with Bible. N.T. Greek. 1935. Westcott.
The New Testament in the original Greek. New York,
1935.

77

BS1965
1935
Bible. N.T. Greek. 1935. Westcott.
  The New Testament in the original Greek; the
text rev. by Brooke Foss Westcott and Fenton John
Anthony Hort. [Student's ed. with lexicon] New
York, Macmillan, 1935.
  618p. 23cm.
  Bound with Hickie, W. J. Greek-English lexicon
to the New Testament. New York, 1935.

75

PA881
.H5
Hickie, William James
  Greek-English lexicon to the New Testament,
after the latest and best authorities. New York,
Macmillan, 1917.
  213,16p. 16cm.
  "Aids to the study of the New Testament" 16p.
at end.
BS1965
1935
---- ---- New York, Macmillan, 1935.
  213p. 23cm.
  Bound with Bible. N.T. Greek. 1935. Westcott.
The New Testament in the original Greek. New York,
1935.

78

gx New Testament
gx Greek New Testament
I. Westcott, Brooke Foss, Bp. of Durham, 1825-1901, ed.
II. Hort, Fenton John Anthony, 1828-1892, joint ed.

76

1. Greek language, Biblical - Dictionaries - English

79

THE NEW TESTAMENT

IN THE ORIGINAL GREEK

THE TEXT REVISED BY

BROOKE FOSS WESTCOTT D.D.

AND

FENTON JOHN ANTHONY HORT D.D.

New York
THE MACMILLAN COMPANY
1935

81

Printed May, 1893.   Reprinted January, July, 1894; October, 1896; July, 1897; October, 1898; November, 1899; September, 1900; July, 1901; February, 1902; June, 1903; July, 1904; February, 1905; January, 1906; March, December, 1907; November, 1908; October, 1909; January, 1911; November, 1912; November, 1913; October, 1914; September, 1915; May, 1916; February, 1917.

* PRINTED IN THE UNITED STATES OF AMERICA *

80

GREEK-ENGLISH LEXICON

TO THE

NEW TESTAMENT

AFTER THE LATEST AND BEST AUTHORITIES

BY

W. J. HICKIE, M.A.

ST. JOHN'S COLLEGE, CAMBRIDGE: LATE ASSISTANT MASTER IN DENSTONE COLLEGE

NEW YORK

THE MACMILLAN COMPANY

LONDON: MACMILLAN & CO., LTD.

1935

960.3
C737a Committee on Africa, the War, and Peace Aims.
         The Atlantic Charter and Africa from an American
       standpoint; a study. The application of the "eight
       points" of the Charter to the problems of Africa,
       and especially those related to the welfare of the
       African people living south of the Sahara, with
       related material on African conditions and needs.
       New York, 1942.
         xi,168p. 24cm.
         Bibliography: p. 144-150.
         On cover: Africa
         Bound with Smith, E. W., comp. Events in African
       history. New York, ◯ 1942.

82

◯
Cataloger's name or initials

83

1. Atlantic declaration, August 14, 1941
2. World War, 1939-1945 - Africa
3. World War, 1939-1945 - Peace
4. Africa - Politics
I. Title

960.3
C737a Smith, Edwin William, 1876-   comp.
         Events in African history; a supplement to The
       Atlantic Charter and Africa from an American
       standpoint. New York, Committee on Africa, the
       War, and Peace Aims, 1942.
         67p. map. 24cm.
         Bound with Committee on Africa, the War, and
       Peace Aims. The Atlantic Charter and Africa from
       an American standpoint. New York, 1942.

84

◯

◯
Cataloger's name or initials

85

1. Africa - History - Chronology
I. Committee on Africa, the War, and Peace Aims.
     The Atlantic Charter and Africa from an American
     standpoint.

VIII. Relationships in the catalog (1-97)

    A. Works related by main/added entries/notes/references (1-23)

        1. Cataloging codes (1-9)
        2. LC/union catalogs (10-23)
        3. References: see II-H
        4. Corporate body under successive names: NLM study:
           see App. H.

    B. Works related by subject: Sears and LC headings (24-58)
       specific access through Index

        1. Main entries
        2. Subject entries
        3. References: see also I-E

WORKS RELATED BY
MAIN/ADDED ENTRIES
NOTES

RELATIONSHIPS
IN THE CATALOG

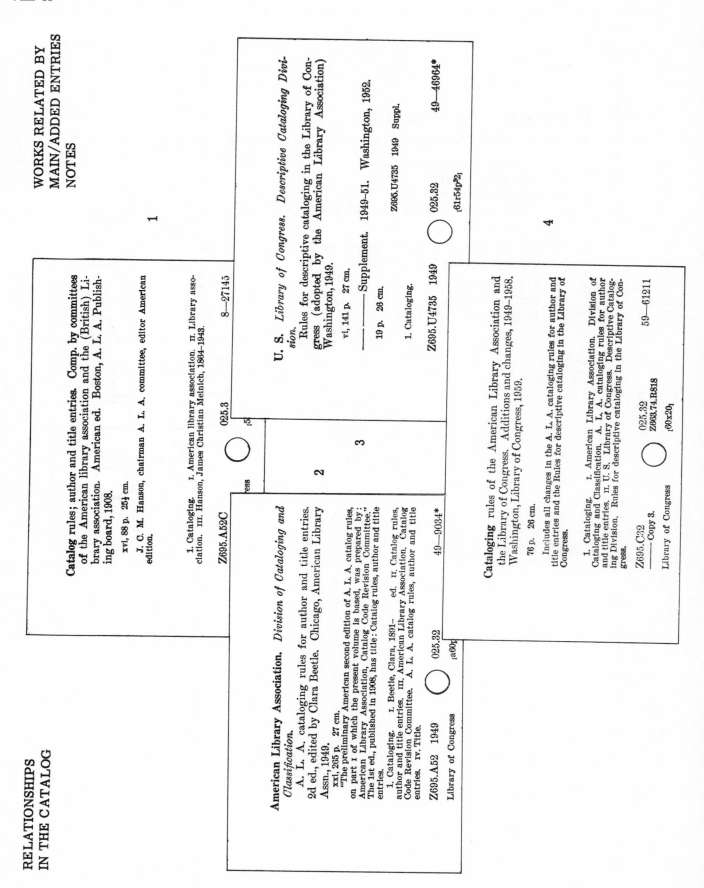

1

Catalog rules; author and title entries. Comp. by committees of the American library association and the (British) Library association. American ed. Boston, A. L. A. Publishing board, 1908.

xvi, 88 p. 25½ cm.

J. C. M. Hanson, chairman A. L. A. committee, editor American edition.

1. Cataloging. I. American library association. II. Library association. III. Hanson, James Christian Meinich, 1864–1943.

Z695.A52C   025.3   8–27145

2

American Library Association. *Division of Cataloging and Classification.*

A. L. A. cataloging rules for author and title entries. 2d ed, edited by Clara Beetle. Chicago, American Library Assn., 1949.

xxi, 265 p. 27 cm.

"The preliminary American second edition of A. L. A. catalog rules, on part I of which the present volume is based, was prepared by:" American Library Association, Catalog Code Revision Committee.

The 1st ed., published in 1908, has title: Catalog rules, author and title entries.

1. Cataloging. I. Beetle, Clara, 1891– ed. II. Catalog rules, author and title entries. III. American Library Association. Catalog Code Revision Committee. A. L. A. catalog rules, author and title entries. IV. Title.

Z695.A52 1949   025.32   49–9034*

Library of Congress   ⟨a60p⟩

3

U. S. *Library of Congress. Descriptive Cataloging Division.*

Rules for descriptive cataloging in the Library of Congress (adopted by the American Library Association) Washington, 1949.

vi, 141 p. 27 cm.

—— Supplement. 1949–51. Washington, 1952.

19 p. 26 cm.

1. Cataloging.

Z695.U4735 1949   025.32   49–46964*

Z695.U4735 1949 Suppl.

⟨61r54p²₂⟩

4

Cataloging rules of the American Library Association and the Library of Congress. Additions and changes, 1949–1958. Washington, Library of Congress, 1959.

76 p. 26 cm.

Includes all changes in the A. L. A. cataloging rules for author and title entries and the Rules for descriptive cataloging in the Library of Congress.

1. Cataloging. I. American Library Association. Division of Cataloging and Classification. A. L. A. cataloging rules for author and title entries. II. U. S. Library of Congress. Descriptive Cataloging Division. Rules for descriptive cataloging in the Library of Congress.

Z695.C32   025.32   59–61211

—— Copy 3.   Z663.74.R818

Library of Congress   ⟨60x20⟩

Lubetzky, Seymour.
Code of cataloging rules: author and title entry. An unfinished draft for a new edition of cataloging rules prepared for the Catalog Code Revision Committee. With an explanatory commentary by Paul Dunkin. [n. p.] American Library Association, 1960.

xv, 86 p. 28 cm.

At head of title: American Library Association, Resources and Technical Services Division, Cataloging and Classification Section, Catalog Code Revision Committee.

1. Cataloging. I. American Library Association. Cataloging and Classification Section. Catalog Code Revision Committee. II. Title.

Z695.L872   025.32   60–2990

7

5

Lubetzky, Seymour.
Code of cataloging rules: bibliographic entry and description. A partial and tentative draft for a new edition of bibliographic cataloging rules, prepared for the Catalog Code Revision Committee. [n. p.] 1958.

iv, 71 p. 27 cm.

At head of title: American Library Association, Resources and Technical Services Division, Cataloging and Classification Section, Catalog Code Revision Committee.

1. Cataloging. I. American Library Association. Cataloging and Classification Section. Catalog Code Revision Committee. II. Title.

Z695.L873   025.32   59–455

Library of Congress   [2]

Institute on Catalog Code Revision, McGill University, 1960.
Working papers. Sponsored by Cataloging and Classification Section of the Resources and Technical Services Division, American Library Association, Cataloguing Section of the Canadian Library Association [and] McGill University. Chicago [American Library Association] 1960.

1v.(various pagings) 28cm.

1. Lubetzky, Seymour. Code of cataloging rules: author and title entry   2. Cataloging – Congresses

(Continued on next card)

8

6

Institute on Cataloging Code Revision, *Stanford University, 1958.*
Working papers. Stanford, Calif., 1958.

1 v. (various pagings) 28 cm.

"Papers ... based on the draft for a new cataloging code prepared by Seymour Lubetzky for the Catalog Code Revision Committee of the Cataloging and Classification Section [American Library Association]"

1. Lubetzky, Seymour. Code of cataloging rules.

Z695.L8733   025.3206379473   59–457

Library of Congress   [2]

Institute on Catalog Code Revision, McGill University, 1960. (Card 2)

I. American Library Association.

CLSU IU NN LU ICU CLU FTaSU CU CSt MiU TxU

9

10

A **Catalog** of books represented by Library of Congress printed cards issued to July 31, 1942. Ann Arbor, Mich., Edwards Bros., 1942–46.

167 v. 29 cm.

At head of title: The Association of Research Libraries.

——Supplement: cards issued August 1, 1942–December 31, 1947. Ann Arbor, J. W. Edwards, 1948.

42 v. 29 cm.

Z881.A1C312

1. Bibliography—Universal catalogs. 2. Catalogs, Library. 3. American literature—Bibl.—Catalogs. I. Association of Research Libraries. II. U. S. Library of Congress.

Z881.A1C3   018.1   43—3338*

11

U. S. *Library of Congress.*

Library of Congress catalog; a cumulative list of works represented by Library of Congress printed cards. Books: authors. Jan. 1947–1955. Washington.

46 v. 29 cm.

Printed in 9 monthly issues, 3 quarterly cumulations, annual cumulations for four years and a quinquennial in the fifth.

Annual vol. for 1947 not issued as all the cards for this year appeared in the Supplement to the Catalog of books represented by Library of Congress printed cards. Cf. Introd.

Title varies: 1947–49, Cumulative catalog of Library of Congress printed cards.—1950–52, The Library of Congress author catalog ...

Compiled and edited by the Catalog Maintenance Division.

(Continued on next card)   47—32682*

12

U. S. *Library of Congress.*   Library of Congress catalog ... (Card 2)

Cumulative vols. for 1948–52 published in Ann Arbor, Mich, by J. W. Edwards.

Supplements Catalog of books represented by Library of Congress printed cards.

Beginning with 1953, entries for Maps and atlases, Films, and Music and phonorecords form separate parts of the Library of Congress catalog.

Superseded by the National union catalog; a cumulative author list ...

Issue for 1948 includes supplement: Army Medical Library. Catalog cards. Apr./Dec. 1948.

Catalog for 1948–52, v. 24 : Films.

(Continued on next card)   47—32682*

(a58r56g*20)

13

U. S. *Library of Congress.*   Library of Congress catalog ... (Card 3)

1. Catalogs, Library. 2. Catalogs, Union. 3. American literature—Bibl.—Catalogs. 4. Moving-pictures — Catalogs. 5. Music — Bibl. — Catalogs. I. U. S. National Library of Medicine. II. A Catalog of books represented by Library of Congress printed cards. Supplement. III. U. S. Library of Congress. Cumulative catalog of Library of Congress printed cards. IV. U. S. Library of Congress. Author catalog. V. Title.

Z881.U49A2   47—32682*

——3d set.   Z663.7.L5

14

U. S. *Library of Congress.*

Library of Congress catalog—Books: subjects; a cumulative list of works represented by Library of Congress printed cards. Jan./Mar. 1950– Washington.

v. 29 cm.

Printed in 3 quarterly issues (for Jan./Mar., Apr./June, and July/Sept.); an annual cumulation for four years and a quinquennial in the fifth.

Title varies: 1950–52, The Library of Congress subject catalog ... 1953–55, Library of Congress catalog; a cumulative list of works represented by Library of Congress printed cards—Books: subjects.

Compiled and edited by Catalog Maintenance Division.

(Continued on next card)

15

U. S. *Library of Congress.*   Library of Congress catalog— (Card 2)
Books: subjects ... Jan./Mar. 1950–

Cumlative vols. for 1950–54 published in Ann Arbor, Mich. by J. W. Edwards.

Beginning with 1953, entries for Motion pictures and filmstrips, Music and phonorecords form separate parts of the Library of Congress catalog. Entries for Maps and atlases were issued separately 1953–55.

1. Catalogs, Subject. I. U. S. Library of Congress. Catalog Maintenance Division.

Z881.A1U375   017.1   50—60682 rev 3

——3d set.   Z663.7.L52

Library of Congress   (r59w²19)

WORK RELATED BY
MAIN/ADDED ENTRIES
NOTES

16

U. S. *Library of Congress.*
    Library of Congress catalog; a cumulative list of works represented by Library of Congress printed cards. Maps and atlases. 1953-55. Washington.
    3 v. 29 cm.
    Semiannual, with an annual cumulation.
    Compiled and edited by the Catalog Maintenance Division.
    Formerly included in the Library's Author catalog and its Subject catalog.
    Beginning with 1956 included in the National union catalog; a cumulative author list representing Library of Congress printed cards and titles reported by other American libraries; and in the Library's Catalog—books: subjects.
    1. Maps—Bibl.—Catalogs. 2. Atlases—Bibl.—Catalogs. I. U. S. Library of Congress. Catalog Maintenance Division.
Z881.A1C327   016.912   53—60010 rev
——— 3d set.   Z663.35.L45
——— 7th set.   Z6009.U5
Library of Congress

17

U. S. *Library of Congress.*
    Library of Congress catalog: Motion pictures and film-strips; a cumulative list of works represented by Library of Congress printed cards. 1953– Washington.
    v. 29 cm.
    Quarterly (Jan./Mar.-July/Sept.) with annual and quinquennial cumulations.
    Formerly included in the Library's Author catalog and its Subject catalog.
    Title varies: 1953, **Library of Congress catalog; a cumulative list of works represented by Library of Congress printed cards: Films.**—1954-55, Library of Congress catalog; a cumulative list of works
                          (Continued on next card)

18

U. S. *Library of Congress.* (Card 2)   Library of Congress catalog
    represented by Library of Congress printed cards: Modern pictures and filmstrips.
    Compiled and edited by the Library's Catalog Maintenance Division.
    Quinquennial cumulations issued as vols. of the quinquennial cumulations of the National union catalog.
    1. Moving-pictures—Catalogs. 2. Filmstrip—Catalogs. I. U. S. Library of Congress. Catalog Maintenance Division. II. Title.
Z881.U49A25   Z663.7.L54   53—60011
——— 3d set.   PN1998.U617
——— 7th set.
Library of Congress   [60r58g*3]

19

U. S. *Library of Congress.*
    Library of Congress catalog: Music and phonorecords; a cumulative list of works represented by Library of Congress printed cards. 1953– Washington.
    v. 29 cm.
    Semiannual with annual and quinquennial cumulations. Cards for music were formerly included in the Library's Author catalog and its Subject catalog.
    Title varies slightly.
    Compiled and edited by the Library's Catalog Maintenance Division.
                          (Continued on next card)
                          53—60012
[62r58q1]

20

U. S. *Library of Congress.* (Card 2)   Library of Congress catalog
    Quinquennial cumulations issued as volumes of the quinquennial cumulations of the National union catalog.
    1. Music—Bibl.—Catalogs. 2. Phonorecords—Catalogs. 3. Catalogs, Library. I. U. S. Library of Congress. Catalog Maintenance Division. II. Title.
Z663.37.A3   53—60012
ML136.U5L45
——— 3d set.
——— 7th set.
Library of Congress   [62r58q1]

21

The **National** union catalog, 1952–1955 imprints; an author list representing Library of Congress printed cards and titles reported by other American libraries. Compiled by the Library of Congress under the auspices of the Committee on Resources of American Libraries of the American Library Association. Ann Arbor, Mich., J. W. Edwards, 1961.

30 v. 29 cm.

At head of title: The Library of Congress catalogs.

"Supplements the published National union catalog for materials of 1956 and later imprint by providing in published form a record of the monographic materials for the imprint years 1952 through 1955."

1. Catalogs, Union. 2. American literature—Bibl.—Catalogs. I. U. S. Library of Congress. II. Title: The Library of Congress catalogs.

Z881.A1U374   018.1   60–53635 rev

Library of Congress   ₍r61k4₎

22

The **National** union catalog; a cumulative author list representing Library of Congress printed cards and titles reported by other American libraries. 1956–
Washington, Library of Congress.

v. 28 cm.

Printed in 9 monthly issues, 3 quarterly cumulations, annual cumulations for four years and a quinquennial in the fifth.

In 1958 a cumulation, covering 1956–57 entries and entries in the 1953–55 annual vols. of the Library of Congress catalog ... —Books: authors, was published in Ann Arbor, Mich. by J. W. Edwards.

At head of title, 1956–   The Library of Congress catalogs.

Supersedes Library of Congress catalog; a cumulative list of works represented by Library of Congress printed cards—Books: authors.

Compiled by the Processing Dept. of the Library of Congress (with the cooperation of the Committee on Resources of American Libraries

(Continued on next card)

56–60041 rev 3

₍r59d⁴9₎

23

The **National** union catalog ...   (Card 2)

(called July 1956–Oct. 1957 Board of Resources of American Libraries) of the American Library Association, July 1956–

Includes entries for maps and atlases.

Quinquennial cumulations include the quinquennial cumulations of Library of Congress catalog: Music and phonorecords, and Library of Congress catalog: Motion pictures and filmstrips.

1. Catalogs, Union. 2. American literature—Bibl.—Catalogs. I. U. S. Library of Congress. Processing Dept. II. Title: The Library of Congress catalogs.

Z881.A1U372   018.1   56–60041 rev 3
——— 3d set.   Z663.7.L512

Library of Congress   ₍r59d⁴9₎

ADDRESSES
see

24

General subjects with subdivision ADDRESSES AND
ESSAYS, e.g. LIBRARY SCIENCE - ADDRESSES AND
ESSAYS

027.473
Am35ℓ **American Library Association.**
Library service for rural people. ₍Washington₎ U. S.
Dept. of Agriculture ₍1959₎
20 p. illus. 24 cm. (₍U. S. Dept. of Agriculture₎ Farmers'
bulletin no. 2142)

25

1. Library service. 2. Rural libraries. (Series)
S21.A6 no. 2142   027.473   Agr 60–29 rev
U. S. Dept. of Agr. Libr.   1Ag84F no. 2142
for Library of Congress   ₍r60f6₎†

---

010   BIBLIOGRAPHY
St29n **Staveley, Ronald.**
Notes on modern bibliography. London, Library Associa-
tion, 1954.

26

BIBLIOGRAPHY
see also
LIBRARY SCIENCE

27

026.65   BUSINESS LIBRARIES
J632h **Johnson, Herbert Webster,** 1906–
How to use the business library, with sources of business
information, prepared by H. Webster Johnson and Stuart
W. McFarland. ₍2d ed.₎ Cincinnati, South-western Pub.
Co. ₍1957₎
154 p. illus. 22 cm.
First published in 1951 under title: How to use a business library.

28

1. Business libraries. ɪ. McFarland, Stuart W., joint author.
ɪɪ. Title.
Z675.B8J6 1957   026.65   57—12718 ‡
Library of Congress   ₍a58f5₎

217

027.477311　CHICAGO.　PUBLIC LIBRARY.
J59m　　**Joeckel, Carleton Bruns,** 1886–1960.
　　　　　　　A metropolitan library in action; a survey of the Chicago
　　　　　　public library, by Carleton Bruns Joeckel and Leon Carnov-
　　　　　　sky ...　Chicago, Ill., The University of Chicago press ₁1940₎

　　　　　　　xvii, 466 p.　maps (part fold.)　diagrs.　(part fold.)　23½ cm.
　　　　　　(*Half-title:* The University of Chicago studies in library science)

29

027.0421
H249l　　**Harrod, Leonard Montague,** 1905–
　　　　　　　The libraries of Greater London; a guide.　London, Bell,
　　　　　　1951.
　　　　　　　vii, 252 p.　22 cm.

30

　　　　　1. London—Libraries—Direct.　　ɪ. Title.

　　　　　Z791.H3　　　　　　◯　　　　027.042　　　　　52—835

　　　　　Library of Congress　　　　　　₁52e5₎

027.477311
J59m　　**Joeckel, Carleton Bruns,** 1886–1960.
　　　　　　　A metropolitan library in action; a survey of the Chicago
　　　　　　public library, by Carleton Bruns Joeckel and Leon Carnov-
　　　　　　sky ...　Chicago, Ill., The University of Chicago press ₁1940₎

　　　　　　　xvii, 466 p.　maps (part fold.)　diagrs.　(part fold.)　23½ cm.
　　　　　　(*Half-title:* The University of Chicago studies in library science)

31

　　　　　1. Chicago.　Public library.　2. Library surveys.　　ɪ. Carnovsky,
　　　　　Leon, 1903–　　joint author.　ɪɪ. Title.

　　　　　Z733.C531J　　　　　◯　　　　027.47731　　　　40—27038

　　　　　Library of Congress　　　　　　₁61r42y2₎

026.65
J632h　　**Johnson, Herbert Webster,** 1906–
　　　　　　　How to use the business library, with sources of business
　　　　　　information, prepared by H. Webster Johnson and Stuart
　　　　　　W. McFarland.　₁2d ed.₎　Cincinnati, South-western Pub.
　　　　　　Co. ₁1957₎

　　　　　　　154 p.　illus.　22 cm.

　　　　　　　First published in 1951 under title: How to use a business library.

32

　　　　　1. Business libraries.　　ɪ. McFarland, Stuart W., joint author.
　　　　　ɪɪ. Title.
　　　　　Z675.B8J6　1957　　◯　026.65　　　　57—12718 ‡

　　　　　Library of Congress　　　　　₁59k7₎

LIBRARIANSHIP
see
LIBRARY SCIENCE

33

LIBRARIES
see also
BUSINESS LIBRARIES

34

Names of cities with the subdivision LIBRARIES
(e.g. LONDON - LIBRARIES); names of individual
libraries (e.g. Chicago. Public Library); and
headings beginning with the words LIBRARIES and
LIBRARY

LIBRARIES, BUSINESS
see
BUSINESS LIBRARIES

35

027.474   LIBRARIES - NEW ENGLAND
Sh51f **Shera, Jesse Hauk,** 1903–
Foundations of the public library; the origins of the
public library movement in New England, 1629–1855. Chicago, Univ. of Chicago Press [1949]

36

LIBRARIES, RURAL
see
RURAL LIBRARIES

37

LIBRARY SCIENCE
see also
BIBLIOGRAPHY
LIBRARY SERVICE
LIBRARY SURVEYS

38

Headings beginning with the words LIBRARIES and
LIBRARY

020.4
M356o   LIBRARY SCIENCE - ADDRESSES AND ESSAYS

Marshall, John David, *comp.*
     Of, by, and for librarians; further contributions to library literature. Hamden, Conn., Shoe String Press, 1960.

     335 p. 23 cm.

39

027.473   LIBRARY SERVICE
Am35

American Library Association.
     Library service for rural people. [Washington] U. S. Dept. of Agriculture [1959]

     20 p. illus. 24 cm. ([U. S. Dept. of Agriculture] Farmers' bulletin no. 2142)

40

027.477311 LIBRARY SURVEYS
J59m

Joeckel, Carleton Bruns, 1886–1960.
     A metropolitan library in action; a survey of the Chicago public library, by Carleton Bruns Joeckel and Leon Carnovsky ... Chicago, Ill., The University of Chicago press [1940]

     xvii, 466 p. maps (part fold.) diagrs. (part fold.) 23½ cm.
     (*Half-title:* The University of Chicago studies in library science)

41

027.0421   LONDON - LIBRARIES - DIRECTORIES
H249*l*

Harrod, Leonard Montague, 1905–
     The libraries of Greater London; a guide. London, Bell, 1951.

     vii, 252 p. 22 cm.

42

     1. London—Libraries—Direct.   ɪ. Title.

Z791.H3   ◯   027.042   52—835

Library of Congress   [52e5]

020.4
M356o

Marshall, John David, *comp.*
     Of, by, and for librarians; further contributions to library literature. Hamden, Conn., Shoe String Press, 1960.

     335 p. 23 cm.

43

                  and
     1. Library science—Addresses, essays, ~~lectures.~~ ɪ. Title.

Z674.M3   ◯   020.4   60—10701 ‡

Library of Congress   [61v²10]

PUBLIC LIBRARIES
see
LIBRARIES

44

027.473   RURAL LIBRARIES
Am35   **American Library Association.**
Library service for rural people. ₍Washington₎ U. S.

45

027.474
Sh51f   **Shera, Jesse Hauk,** 1903–
Foundations of the public library; the origins of the
public library movement in New England, 1629–1855. Chicago, Univ. of Chicago Press ₍1949₎

xv, 308 p. illus., port., maps, facsims. 24 cm. (The University
of Chicago studies in library science)

"Check list of circulating library book catalogs, New England,
1765–1860" : p. 261–263.
"Selected bibliography" : p. 291–295.

1. Libraries—New England.   ɪ. Title.   (Series : Chicago. University. The University of Chicago studies in library science)

Z731.S55   ◯   027.474   49—8133*

Library of Congress   ₍60d²2₎

46

010
St29n   **Staveley, Ronald.**
Notes on modern bibliography. London, Library Associa-
tion, 1954.

111 p. 23 cm.

1. Bibliography.   ɪ. Title.

Z1001.S8   ◯   010   54–37518 ‡

Library of Congress   ₍1₎

47

SURVEYS, LIBRARY
see
LIBRARY SURVEYS

48

◯

49

CHURCH MUSIC
see also
MUSIC IN CHURCHES

50

ML3082   CHURCH MUSIC - HESSE - MAINZ
.K77   Köllner, Georg Paul, 1902-
Der Accentus Moguntinus; ein Beitrag zur Frage
des "Mainzer Chorals." [Mainz] 1950.
202p. illus. 30cm.

51

ML3082
.K77   Köllner, Georg Paul, 1902-
Der Accentus Moguntinus; ein Beitrag zur Frage
des "Mainzer Chorals." [Mainz] 1950.
202p. illus. 30cm.

1. Church music - Hesse - Mainz

52

MUSIC, RELIGIOUS
see
CHURCH MUSIC

53

MUSIC, SACRED
see
CHURCH MUSIC

ML3001   MUSIC IN CHURCHES
.R8   Routley, Erik
        The church and music; an enquiry into the
    history, the nature, and the scope of Christian
    judgment on music. London, Duckworth ₍1950₎
        225p. 19cm.   54

        MUSIC IN CHURCHES
            see also
        CHURCH MUSIC   55

        RELIGIOUS MUSIC
            see
        CHURCH MUSIC   56

ML3001
.R8   Routley, Erik
        The church and music; an enquiry into the
    history, the nature, and the scope of Christian
    judgment on music. London, Duckworth ₍1950₎
        225p. 19cm.   57

        1. Music in churches

                        ◯

        SACRED MUSIC
            see
        CHURCH MUSIC   58

                        ◯

VIII.

59

PA6296
.D5
1883

De officiis.

Cicero, Marcus Tullius.
 M. Tullii Ciceronis De officiis libri tres. Accedunt in usum juventutis notae quaedam anglice scriptae. Ex editione postrema et emendatissima Valpiana. Philadelphia, Hogan & Thompson; [etc., etc.,] 1883.

60

BJ214
.C6D44

De officiis. Ger.

Cicero, Marcus Tullius.
 Vom rechten Handeln; eingeleitet und neu übers. von Karl Büchler. Zürich, Artemis-Verlag [1963]
 217 p. 18 cm. (Die Bibliothek der alten Welt. Römische Reihe)
 Translation of De officiis.

1. Ethics. I. Title.

BJ214.C6D44 [r56b8]
Library of Congress   54-18258 rev

MH

61

Académie des inscriptions et belles-lettres

Paris

MH

62

Académie diplomatique internationale

Paris

(Index cards)

MH

63

Académie... Paris
 Académie des inscriptions et belles-lettres, Paris
 Les travaux de l'Académie des inscriptions et belles-lettres; histoire et inventaire des publications. Notices rédigées par Adrien Blanchet [et al.] Paris, C.Klincksieck, 1947
 190 p.

LSoc 1621.40

MH

64

Académie... Paris
 Académie des sciences, Paris
 Index biographique des membres et correspondants de l'Académie des sciences du 22 déc.1666 au 15 nov.1954. [2.éd.] Paris, Gauthier-Villars, 1954
 xi, 534 p.

RR 1771.22

MH

65

Académie... Paris
 Académie diplomatique internationale, Paris
 Dictionnaire diplomatique, publié sous la direction de A.-F.Frangulis, avec la collaboration des membres du Bureau, Mm. Vte.de Fontenay [et al.] et la collaboration des membres, des associés et des adhérents de l'Académie. Paris [c1933-57]
 6 v.

RR 4103.4

MH

```
                                      Works   1904
        822.33
66      I       Shakespeare, William, 1564-1616.
        1904       Comedies, histories, and tragedies, faithfully
                reproduced in facsimile from the ed. of 1685.
                London. Methuen. 1904.


                                      Works   Farjeon
        822.33
67      JF      Shakespeare, William, 1564-1616.
                   Complete works; the text and order of the first
                folio with quarto variations & a choice of modern
                readings noted marginally.  The Nonesuch text es-
                tablished 1929 by Herbert Farjeon, with a new
                introd. by Ivor Brown.  ⌐London, Nonesuch Press;
                New York, Random House, 1953⌐


                                      Works   Neilson
        822.33
68      JN      Shakespeare, William, 1564-1616.
                   Complete dramatic and poetic works; edited from
                the text of the early quartos and the first folio,
                by William Allan Neilson.  Boston, Houghton,
                Mifflin, 1906.


                                      Works   Fr   Guizot
        822.33
69      KFrG    Shakespeare, William, 1564-1616.
                   Oeuvres completes; traduction de M. Guizot;
                nouv. ed. entierement revue avec une etude sur
                Shakespeare, des notes sur chaque piece, et des
                notes.  Paris, Didier, 1860-62.


                                      Works   Ger   Schlegel
        822.33
70      KGerS   Shakespeare, William, 1564-1616.
                   Dramatische Werke, übers. von August Wilhelm
                Schlegel.  Berlin, J. F. Unger, 1797-1810.


                                      Selected works   Kittredge
        822.33
71      MK      Shakespeare, William, 1564-1616.
                   Sixteen plays of Shakespeare with full explana-
                tory notes, textual notes, and glossaries, edited
                by George Lyman Kittredge; with a pref. by Arthur
                Colby Sprague.  Boston, Ginn ⌐1946⌐


                                      Selected works   Welles
        822.33
72      MW      Shakespeare, William, 1564-1616.
                   The Mercury Shakespeare; edited for reading and
                arranged for staging by Orson Welles and Roger
                Hill.  New York, Harper ⌐c1939⌐
```

```
                                  Selections  Ger  Rothe
       822.33
73     HGerR  Shakespeare, William, 1564-1616.
                 Shakespeare - Trostbüchlein für viele Lagen des
              Lebens zusammengestellt und übers. von Hans Rothe
              ₍3. Aufl.₎ München, P. List ₍1947₎


                                  As you like it  Burchell
       822.33
74     O3B    Shakespeare, William, 1564-1616.
                 As you like it; edited by S. C. Burchell.  ₍Rev.
              ed.₎ New Haven, Yale University Press ₍1954₎


                                  As you like it  Gollancz
       822.33
       O3G    Shakespeare, William, 1564-1616.
                 Comedy of As you like it; with pref., glossary,
              &c. by Israel Gollancz.  London, J. M. Dent, 1901.


                                  As you like it  Harbage
       822.33
75     O3H    Shakespeare, William, 1564-1616.
                 As you like it; edited by Alfred Harbage.  New
              York, Appleton-Century-Crofts ₍1954₎


76     822.33    SHAKESPEARE, WILLIAM.  AS YOU LIKE IT
       O4S    Sennett, Mabell
                 His erring pilgrimage; a new interpretation of
              As you like it. ₍1st ed.₎ London, Bacon Society
              ₍1949₎


                                  Hamlet  Rolfe
       822.33
77     S7ER   Shakespeare, William, 1564-1616.
                 Tragedy of Hamlet, prince of Denmark; edited
              with notes, by William J. Rolfe.  New York,
              American Book Co. ₍c1906₎


                                  Hamlet  Du  Courteaux
       822.33
78     S7DuC  Shakespeare, William, 1564-1616.
                 Hamlet.  Ingeleid en vertaald door W. Courteaux
              Antwerpen, Nederlandsche Boekhandel, 1958.


                                  Hamlet  Fr  Pourtalès
       822.33
79     S7FrP  Shakespeare, William, 1564-1616.
                 La tragique histoire de Hamlet, prince de
              Danemark; traduite par Guy de Pourtalès, et ornée
              de bois gravés par Raphael Drouart.  Paris,
              Société Littéraire de France, 1923.
```

```
                                        Hamlet  It  Montale
        822.33
80      S7ItM  Shakespeare, William, 1564-1616.
                  Amleto, principe di Danimarca.  ₍Tradotto per
               le scene italiane da Eugenio Montale₎  Milano, E.
               Cederna ₍1949₎


                                        Hamlet  Rus  Pasternak
        822.33
81      S7RusP Shakespeare, William, 1564-1616.
                  Gamlet, prints datskii.  Perevod B. Pasternaka.
               Moskva, Detgiz, 1956.



        822.33   SHAKESPEARE, WILLIAM.  HAMLET
        S8C    Clutton-Brock, Arthur, 1868-1924.
82                Shakespeare's "Hamlet."  London, Methuen ₍1922₎



        821.09   SHAKESPEARE, WILLIAM, 1564-1616.
        D195p  Danby, John Francis
83                Poets on Fortune's Hill; studies in Sidney,
               Shakespeare, Beaumont & Fletcher.  London, Faber
               and Faber ₍1952₎



        822.33   SHAKESPEARE, WILLIAM - BIOGRAPHY
84      BM     Maurice, Martin
                  Master William Shakespeare.  ₍Paris₎ Gallimard
               ₍1953₎


                 SHAKESPEARE, WILLIAM - CRITICISM AND INTERPRE-
        822.33     TATION
85      DC     Capocci, Valentina
                  Genio e mestiere; Shakespeare e la commedia
               dell 'arte.  Bari, H. Laterza, 1950.


                 Shakespeare, William.  Paraphrases, tales,
        823         etc.
86      L165tam Lamb, Charles, 1775-1834.
                  Tales from Shakespeare ₍by₎ Charles and Mary
               Lamb, edited by the Rev. Alfred Ainger, revised
               by H. Y. Moffett; illustrated by Maud and Miska
               Petersham.  ₍New York₎ Macmillan ₍c1932₎


        822.33   SHAKESPEARE, WILLIAM - QUOTATIONS
87      HGerR  Shakespeare, William, 1564-1616.
                  Shakespeare - Trostbüchlein für viele Lagen des
               Lebens zusammengestellt und übers. von Hans Rothe
               ₍3. Aufl.₎ München, P. List ₍1947₎
```

VIII-C

822.33
S7ER Shakespeare, William, 1564-1616.
        Tragedy of Hamlet, prince of Denmark; edited
      with notes, by William J. Rolfe. New York, Ameri-
      can Book Co. [c1906]
        287p. illus. 18cm.

          I. Rolfe, William James, 1827-1910, ed.
        gx Title: Hamlet

88 / 91

822.33
S71tM Shakespeare, William, 1564-1616.
        Amleto, principe di Danimarca. [Tradotto per
      le scene italiane da Eugenio Montale] Milano,
      E. Cederna [1949]
        207p. 21cm.

          I. Montale, Eugenio, 1896-   tr.   gx Title

89 / 92

822.33
S7RusP Shakespeare, William, 1564-1616.
        Gamlet, prints datskii. Perevod B. Pasternaka.
      Moskva, Detgiz, 1956.
        188p. illus. (Shkol'naia biblioteka)

          I. Pasternak, Boris Leonidovich, 1890-
        gx Title
        MH NB NcD

90 / 93

MH

Shakespeare, William.
  Complete works

List of editions with distinctive titles, showing
date of publication of first volume by which cards are
arranged

Aldus Shakespeare   1909
Bankside Shakespeare   1888-1906
Edinburgh folio   1901-1904
India Shakespeare   1928
New Shakespeare series   [1935]
New Readers' Shakespeare (Can.ed.)   [1929?]
Temple Shakespeare   1895
Yale Shakespeare. Rev.ed.   1954

MH

Shakespeare, William, 1564-1616.
  The Yale Shakespeare. Rev.ed. General editors: H.
Kökeritz and C.T.Prouty. [New Haven, Yale UP, 1954-   ]

As you like it   [1954]   13478.3.103
Henry V   [1955]   13478.3.110
Julius Caesar   [1959]   13478.3.116
Measure for measure   [1954]   13478.3.117
Romeo and Juliet   [1954]   13478.3.126
The tempest   [1955]   13478.3.128
Twelfth night   [1954]   13478.3.134

MH
                                  13478.3.117
Shakespeare, William, 1564-1616.
  Measure for measure; edited by Davis Harding. [Rev.
ed.] New Haven, Yale UP [1954]

  131 p. (The Yale Shakespeare)

BIBLE entries are arranged in the following order:
a. Bible. Manuscripts.   **MWelC**
      Arranged by language and under each
      language by parts.
b. Bible as a whole.
    1. Texts.
      Arranged alphabetically by language. A
      polyglot Bible is filed in its alpha-
      betical place.
      Under each language subarranged by:
      a. Date and then by version or editor.
      b. Form division alphabetically (i.e.
         Bible. Language. Paraphrases; Bible.
         Language. Selections). Subarranged by
         date.

AUTHOR CATALOG   (see next card)

(card numbered 1, ref. 94)

---

c. Bible. Old Testament.   **MWelC**
    1. Texts.
      Arranged alphabetically by language.
      Under each language, subarranged by:
      a. Date and then by version or editor.
      b. Form division alphabetically, sub-
         arranged by date.
    2. Parts.
      Under each part arranged by language in
      alphabetical order and further sub-
      arranged by date.
      Groups of books such as the Pentateuch
      filed in alphabetical order.
d. Bible. New Testament, arranged like O.T.
e. Bible (titles, etc.)

AUTHOR CATALOG

(card numbered 2, ref. 95)

BIBLE entries are arranged as follows: **MWelC**
[red]

a. Bible. Manuscripts, arranged by language and
   under each language by parts.

b. Bible as a whole.
    1. Texts arranged alphabetically by language
      and under each language subarranged by
      date and then by version or editor.

c. Bible with form divisions, i.e. Bibliography,
   Commentaries.

SUBJECT CATALOG

(card numbered 1, ref. 96-97)

---

d. Bible. O.T.   **MWelC**
    1. Texts arranged alphabetically by language,
      subarranged by date and then by version
      or editor.
    2. Bible. O.T. with form divisions.
    3. Parts arranged alphabetically by language.
e. Bible. N.T.
      Arranged like O.T.
f. Bible (titles, etc.)

SUBJECT CATALOG

(card numbered 2)

IX. Works of special type and special collections (1-68)

    A. Theses and dissertations: comparative styles (1-15)

        1. Typescript, etc. (1-15)
        2. Microfilms; microcard: LC: see X-E

    B. Technical reports (16-27)

        1. ASTIA (16-19)
        2. Mitre Corporation Library: set of cards (20-27)
           a. Agency
           b. Title
           c. Author
           d. Subjects (3)
           e. Numbers assigned by originating agency
           f. Numbers assigned by sponsoring agency (Cambridge
              Research Laboratories)

    C. Works for the blind (28-40)

        1. Books in raised characters (28-40)
           a. Braille: LC sets for distribution to regional libraries
              (28-35)
           b. Moon: separate catalog: Perkins School for the Blind
              Library (36-40)
        2. Talking books: LC: see X-G

Das Gupta, Jayanta Kumar.
A critical study of the life and novels of Bankimcandra.
₍Calcutta₎ Calcutta University, 1937.

xiv, 186 p.   22 cm.

Thesis—University of London.
Bibliography : p. ₍165–183₎

1. Chatterji, Bankim Chandra, 1838–1894.   ɪ. Title.

PK1718.C43Z6   55–47488

1

Dewton, Johannes Leopold, 1905–
Uniform catalog headings for the anonymous literature of
ancient and medieval Roman law.   Urbana, Ill., 1944.

150 l.   28 cm.

Thesis (ᴍ. ѕ. in ʟ. ѕ.)—University of Illinois.
Typescript (carbon copy)
Bibliography : leaves 145–150.

1. Cataloging—Law.   ɪ. Title.

Name originally: Johannes Leopold Deutsch.

Z695.1.L3D4   53–52318

Library of Congress   ₍³⁄₄₎

2

**THESES
DISERTATIONS**

3

CU

308t   Hyde, Robert Lee
1961   A quantitative analysis of the junction capacitance and
251   current- voltage characteristics of tunnel diodes.   [Berkeley]
1961.
vi, 85 ℓ.   diagrs.

Thesis (M.S. in Electrical Engineering) - Univ. of California,
June 1961.
Bibliography: ℓ. 75- 76.

l. Diodes.   I. Title: Tunnel diodes.

CU 62

CU

308t   Wilson, Allan Charles
1961   Control of flavin synthesis by bacteria.   [Berkeley] 1961.
101   vi, 140 ℓ.   diagrs., tables.

Thesis (Ph.D. in Biochemistry) - Univ. of California, Jan. 1960.
Bibliography: ℓ. 132- 140.

1. Flavin.   2. Biosynthesis.   3. Bacteria.

CU 61

4

```
Nucl.                                                    MCM
eng'g    ROBKIN,  Maurice Abraham
Thesis        Eigenvalue matching: an equivalence principle
1961     for nuclear reactors.  M.I.T.  ms. 1961
Ph.D.    [1]+7+203p.  incl. tabs. & diagrs.  30cm.              5

         Supervised by Melville Clark, Jr.

         M.I.T. Nuclear eng'g, Dept. of.  Theses 1961
                                              Ph.D.

            Course XXII
```

```
                                                              MCM

         Nuclear reactors:- Tables, calculations, etc.
         Nuclear reactors:- Neutron flux distribution
         Boltzmann equation
         Eigenvalues
    6    Diffusion
         Computer programming
```

```
                                                  MCM
Physics
Thesis   BROWN,  Howard Howland, Jr.
1961          Precision measurement of the hyperfine
Ph.D.    structure constants of the stable bromine isotopes.
         M.I.T.  ms. 1961  [54]p.  incl. pl., tabs., &
         diagrs.  30cm.

         Supervised by John G. King & J.R. Zacharias

         M.I.T. Physics dept.  Theses 1961 Ph.D.
            Course VIII
```

```
                                                              MCM

         Atoms:- Beams
         Spectrum:- Fine structure
         Bromine:- Isotopes
    8    Resonance, Nuclear
```

```
                                                     CtY
         Heine, Kurt, 1929-
WG            Über den Kernrückstoss in kristallinen
1369     Hexahalogenkomplexen des vierwertigen
         Iridiums.  Köln, 1961.
            80 p.  illus.

            Inaug.-Diss. - Cologne.                           9


         Cdu
```

MH HU 90.6383.15(2 cop)

Jones, Edward Ellsworth
The role of authoritarianism in the perception and evaluation of a prospective leader

Thesis - Harvard, 1953

10 · 13

MH Math 3629.60.40

Karadžić, Lazar
Prilozi proučavanju nekih problema iz teorije redova i jednoznačnih analitičkih funkcija pomoću geometrije Lobačevskog. Beograd, Univerzitet, 1960

51 p. (Publikacije Elektrotehničkog fakulteta Universiteta u Beogradu. Serija: Matematika i fizika, 42 (1960)
Cover title
Disertacija - Belgrade
French summary

11 · 14

MH Slav 8550.47

Radosavović, Ilija
Medjunarodnopravni položaj Crne Gore u drugoj polovini XIX vijeka. Beograd, Univerzitet, 1960

140 p.
Disertacija - Belgrade
English and Russian summaries. Table of contents also in French

12 · 15

CtY

Braum, Franjo, 1914-
Die Beseitigung der Modelldeformationen in Senkrechtaufnahmen durch die Aenderung der relativen oder der innern Orientierung. Zagreb, 1960.
201 p. illus.

Promotionsarbeit - Eidgenössische Technische Hochschule, Zürich.

CtY

Haber, Fritz, 1868-1934.
Experimental-Untersuchungen über Zersetzung und Verbrennung von Kohlenwasserstoffen. München, 1896.
116 p. illus.

Habilitationsschrift - Karlsruhe Technische Hochschule.

CtY

Pannenborg, Albert
Zur Geschichte des Göttinger Gymnasiums. Göttingen, L. Hofer, 1886.
59 p. 25 cm.

"Beilage zum Jubel-Programm des Kgl. Gymnasiums und Realgymnasiums zu Göttingen, 1886."

AD-271 589   Div. 14, 30   U   UNCLASSIFIED
(TISTM/GEC) OTS price $5.60   ASTIA

National Carbon Co., Inc., Cleveland, Ohio.
RESEARCH AND DEVELOPMENT ON ADVANCED GRAPHITE
MATERIALS. VOLUME IV. ADAPTATION OF RADIOGRAPH-
IC PRINCIPLES TO THE QUALITY CONTROL OF GRAPHITE.
Rept. for Apr 58-Oct 60, on Refractory Inorganic
Nonmetallic Materials,
by R. W. Wallouch. Oct 61, 45p. incl. illus.
(Contract AF 33(616)6915, Proj. nos. 7350, 7381,
and 7-817)
(WADD TR 61-72, Vol. 4)   Unclassified report

16-
17

  DESCRIPTORS: (*Graphite, *X rays, *Radiography,
  Sensitivity, Chemical impurities, Distribution.) (X rays, Detectors, Fluorescent
  screens, Photographic film, Ionization chambers, Sheets, Aluminum, Selenium, Coatings.)

Special equipment and techniques were developed
for the radiographic inspection of large size
graphite shapes, as well as for complex multi-
thickness shapes. Because of the low atomic
number of the element C, techniques were used
which discriminated between the transmitted and

UNCLASSIFIED

UNCLASSIFIED

scattered radiation. Various methods are described which have been used for nondestructively
testing graphite and exposure charts relaying exposure time to graphite thickness for various
source voltages were prepared. (Author)

AD-271 597   Div. 10, 25, 30   U   UNCLASSIFIED
(TISTM/GEC) OTS price $4.60   ASTIA

Armour Research Foundation, Chicago, Ill.
FUNDAMENTALS OF LIQUID PROPELLANT SENSITIVITY.
Quarterly rept. no. 2, 13 Sep-13 Dec 61,
by T. A. Erikson and E. L. Grove. 30 Jan 62,
39p. incl. illus. tables (Rept. no. ARF-3197-6)
(Contract NOw 61-0603-c, Proj. C 197)
            Unclassified report

  DESCRIPTORS: (*Liquid rocket propellants,
  *Nitroglycerine, Sensitivity, Detonation,
  Tests.) (Test methods, Vapor pressure,
  Surface tension, Heating, Heat transfer,
  *Photolysis, Xenon lamps, Infrared radiation,
  Ultraviolet radiation, *Photochemical reac-
  tions.) (Absorption, Water.) (Time, Tempera-
  ture, Pressure, Shock tubes.)

The study of liquid propellant sensitivity continued. Positively identified, shock-tube-
initiated detonations of liquid nitroglycerine
were achieved after evacuation of the sample in
the shock tube was eliminated from the test procedure. Apparently evacuation removed volatile

(reverse)
UNCLASSIFIED

UNCLASSIFIED

18-
19

sensitizing agents and thus desensitized the
nitroglycerine sample to the shock-tube test.
In 50 tests with samples that were not desensitized, the time delay was found to decrease
from 100 to 25 microseconds when the Mach number
of the incident shock was raised from about 3 to
5. Photolysis experiments indicated that a light
of an absorptive wavelength caused self-heating
of the nitroglycerine until either decomposition
or detonation occurred, depending on the geomet-
rics of the particular experiment. Measurements
showed that water vapor rapidly contaminated the
surface of nitroglycerine, as indicated by a
change in surface tension, from about 50 to 55
dynes/cm, within a few hours. Over a month of
storage, the surface tension of a sample of
nitroglycerine was observed to increase by about
3 dynes/cm. (Author)

AD-271 597   9   N2

(reverse)
UNCLASSIFIED

20

ANTENNA LAB., OHIO STATE U. RESEARCH FOUNDATION
AF 19(604)7270
ENDFIRE ECHO AREA OF PLASMA CYLINDER CONFIGURATIONS. SCIENTIFIC
REPORT NO. 3. (U) 15 MAY 1961

PETERS, LEON
MD-17,842   **(Agency) MITRE**
2:227.22   CRL-382
6:25.11   OSURF AL-1116-6
15:211.7

MITRE CORPORATION

21

ENDFIRE ECHO AREA OF PLASMA CYLINDER CONFIGURATIONS.
SCIENTIFIC REPORT NO. 3. (U) 15 MAY 1961

ANTENNA LAB., OHIO STATE U. RESEARCH FOUNDATION
AF 19(604)7270
ENDFIRE ECHO AREA OF PLASMA CYLINDER CONFIGURATIONS. SCIENTIFIC
REPORT NO. 3. (U) 15 MAY 1961

PETERS, LEON
MD-17,842   **(Title) MITRE**
2:227.22   CRL-382
6:25.11   OSURF AL-1116-6
15:211.7

22

PETERS, LEON

ANTENNA LAB., OHIO STATE U. RESEARCH FOUNDATION
AF 19(604)7270
ENDFIRE ECHO AREA OF PLASMA CYLINDER CONFIGURATIONS. SCIENTIFIC
REPORT NO. 3. (U) 15 MAY 1961

PETERS, LEON
MD-17,842   **(Author) MITRE**
2:227.22   CRL-382
6:25.11   OSURF AL-1116-6
15:211.7

23

2:227.22

ANTENNA LAB., OHIO STATE U. RESEARCH FOUNDATION
AF 19(604)7270
ENDFIRE ECHO AREA OF PLASMA CYLINDER CONFIGURATIONS. SCIENTIFIC
REPORT NO. 3. (U) 15 MAY 1961

PETERS, LEON
MD-17,842   **(Subject) MITRE**
2:227.22   CRL-382
6:25.11   OSURF AL-116-6
15:211.7

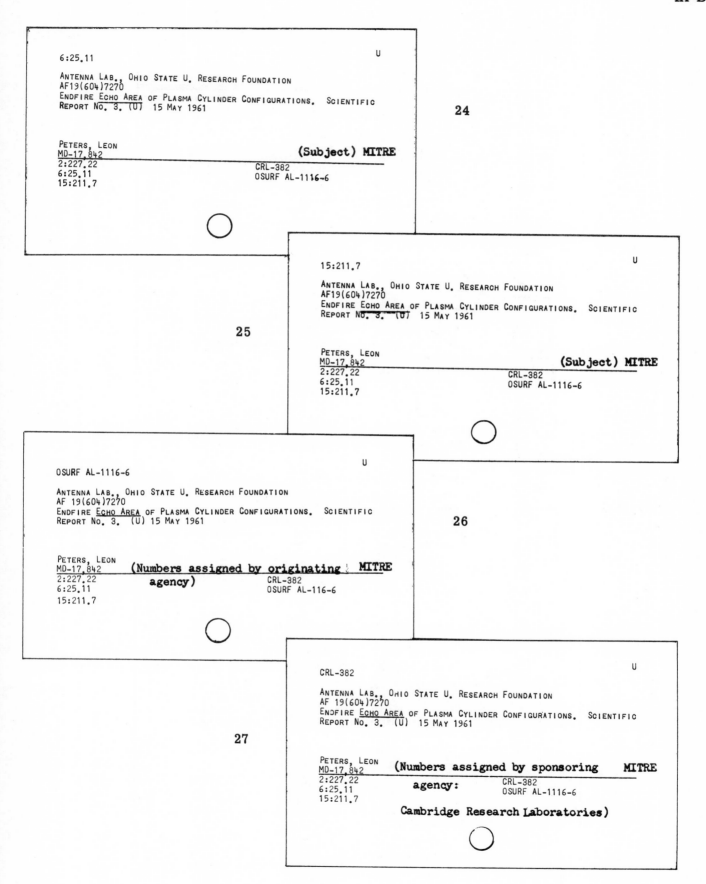

6:25.11   U

Antenna Lab., Ohio State U. Research Foundation
AF19(604)7270
Endfire Echo Area of Plasma Cylinder Configurations. Scientific
Report No. 3. (U) 15 May 1961   24

Peters, Leon
MD-17,842   (Subject) MITRE
2:227.22   CRL-382
6:25.11   OSURF AL-1116-6
15:211.7

25

15:211.7   U

Antenna Lab., Ohio State U. Research Foundation
AF19(604)7270
Endfire Echo Area of Plasma Cylinder Configurations. Scientific
Report No. 3. (U) 15 May 1961

Peters, Leon
MD-17,842   (Subject) MITRE
2:227.22   CRL-382
6:25.11   OSURF AL-1116-6
15:211.7

OSURF AL-1116-6   U

Antenna Lab., Ohio State U. Research Foundation
AF 19(604)7270
Endfire Echo Area of Plasma Cylinder Configurations. Scientific
Report No. 3. (U) 15 May 1961   26

Peters, Leon
MD-17,842   (Numbers assigned by originating   MITRE
2:227.22   agency)   CRL-382
6:25.11   OSURF AL-116-6
15:211.7

CRL-382   U

Antenna Lab., Ohio State U. Research Foundation
AF 19(604)7270
Endfire Echo Area of Plasma Cylinder Configurations. Scientific
Report No. 3. (U) 15 May 1961   27

Peters, Leon
MD-17,842   (Numbers assigned by sponsoring   MITRE
2:227.22   agency: CRL-382
6:25.11   OSURF AL-1116-6
15:211.7

          Cambridge Research Laboratories)

92
Juvenile

28

AERONAUTICS—HIST.

Reynolds, Quentin James, 1902–
    The Wright brothers, pioneers of American aviation.
ₜ*Braille, grade 2*ₜ New York, Random House, ᶜ1950;
ₜprinted by theₜ American Printing House for the Blind,
Louisville, Ky., 1953.

    1 v. 30 cm. (Landmark books)

    For grades 4–6.

92
Juvenile

29

Reynolds, Quentin James, 1902–
    The Wright brothers, pioneers of American aviation.
ₜ*Braille, grade 2*ₜ New York, Random House, ᶜ1950;
ₜprinted by theₜ American Printing House for the Blind,
Louisville, Ky., 1953.

    1 v. 30 cm. (Landmark books)

    For grades 4–6.

    1. Aeronautics—Hist. 2. Wright, Orville, 1871–1948. 3. Wright,
Wilbur, 1867–1912.

92
Juvenile

30

WRIGHT, ORVILLE, 1871–1948.

Reynolds, Quentin James, 1902–
    The Wright brothers, pioneers of American aviation.
ₜ*Braille, grade 2*ₜ New York, Random House, ᶜ1950;
ₜprinted by theₜ American Printing House for the Blind,
Louisville, Ky., 1953.

    1 v. 30 cm. (Landmark books)

    For grades 4–6.

    1. Aeronautics—Hist. 2. Wright, Orville, 1871–1948. 3. Wright,
Wilbur, 1867–1912.

92
Juvenile

31

WRIGHT, WILBUR, 1867–1912.

Reynolds, Quentin James, 1902–
    The Wright brothers, pioneers of American aviation.
ₜ*Braille, grade 2*ₜ New York, Random House, ᶜ1950;
ₜprinted by theₜ American Printing House for the Blind,
Louisville, Ky., 1953.

    1 v. 30 cm. (Landmark books)

    For grades 4–6.

    1. Aeronautics—Hist. 2. Wright, Orville, 1871–1948. 3. Wright,
Wilbur, 1867–1912.

B R 59–20

Library of Congress

411

ALPHABET.

Ogg, Oscar.
    The 26 letters. ₍*Braille, grade 2*₎ New York, T. Y. Crowell Co., ᶜ1948; printed for the Library of Congress ₍at the₎ American Printing House for the Blind, Louisville, Ky., 1960.

    2 v. 30 cm.

    Summary: Describes the growth and development of the alphabet, from cave drawings and hieroglyphics to the modern linotype.

    1. Writing—Hist. 2. Alphabet. ɪ. Title.

B R 60–190

32

411

Ogg, Oscar.
    The 26 letters. ₍*Braille, grade 2*₎ New York, T. Y. Crowell Co., ᶜ1948; printed for the Library of Congress ₍at the₎ American Printing House for the Blind, Louisville, Ky., 1960.

    2 v. 30 cm.

    Summary: Describes the growth and development of the alphabet, from cave drawings and hieroglyphics to the modern linotype.

    1. Writing—Hist. 2. Alphabet. ɪ. Title.

B R 60–190

Library of Congress

33

411

    The 26 letters.

Ogg, Oscar.
    The 26 letters. ₍*Braille, grade 2*₎ New York, T. Y. Crowell Co., ᶜ1948; printed for the Library of Congress ₍at the₎ American Printing House for the Blind, Louisville, Ky., 1960.

    2 v. 30 cm.

    Summary: Describes the growth and development of the alphabet, from cave drawings and hieroglyphics to the modern linotype.

    1. Writing—Hist. 2. Alphabet. ɪ. Title.

34

411

    WRITING—HIST.

Ogg, Oscar.
    The 26 letters. ₍*Braille, grade 2*₎ New York, T. Y. Crowell Co., ᶜ1948; printed for the Library of Congress ₍at the₎ American Printing House for the Blind, Louisville, Ky., 1960.

    2 v. 30 cm.

    Summary: Describes the growth and development of the alphabet, from cave drawings and hieroglyphics to the modern linotype.

    1. Writing—Hist. 2. Alphabet. ɪ. Title.

B R 60–190

Library of Congress

35

F	Country of the pointed fir 5v. **MWatP**	
	Jewett, Sarah Orne	

36

B	Grandma Moses 3v. **MWatP**	
	Moses, Anna Mary	

37

F	Jewett, Sarah Orne **MWatP**	
	Country of the pointed fir 5v.	
	BIA 1960 Gift of Mrs. Nelson	

cop.

4026-30

1. title

38

B	Moses, Anna Mary **MWatP**	
	Grandma Moses, my life's history	
	edited by Otto Kallir 3v.	
	BIA 1953 LC c.1948	

cop.

3871-73   1. title   2. MOSES, ANNA MARY

39

B	MOSES, ANNA MARY **MWatP**	
	Moses, Anna Mary	
	Grandma Moses, my life's history,	
	edited by Otto Kallir 3v.	
	BIA 1953 LC c.1948	

cop.

3871-73

40

IX. Works of special type and special collections (continued from page 231)

    D. Incunabula (41-47)

    E. "Rare books; treasure room collection" (48-68)

        1. Broadsides (48-52)
        2. Original works: 16th century (53-59, 62)
        3. Facsimile works: 17th century (60-61, 63-64)
           a. Reprint (60-61)
           b. Photostat (63-64)
        4. Miniature books (65-68)

SPECIAL COLLECTIONS

INCUNABULA

44 / 41

MH

Cortesius, Thomas Alexander, 1464?-1491.
[Begins, sig.[a]3r:] Alexandri Cortesii: De laudibus Matthiae Corvin. regis Hung. ac Bohem. liber .1.
[Rome,Eucharius Silber,after 1 June 1485]
4°. [50]p. 19.5cm.
Hain 5774; GW 7794; Collijn (Uppsala) 452.
Signatures: [a-b8,c,d4] ([a]1 blank).
This copy agrees with that described by Collijn; GW transcribes the caption on [a]3r as ending "liber primvs."
In verse.
Paste-paper boards.   MH61-1974

Inc 3816.5

---

45 / 42

MH-AH

RARE BOOK ROOM
604.7 H74.4os 1494

Holkot, Robertus, d.1349.
Opus super Sapientiam Salomonis.
Ropertus holkot super libros Sapietie.
[Hagenau,Heinrich Gran,1494]
f°. [483]p. 31cm.
Hain *8761; Proctor 3181; BMC III.683; Stillwell H263.
Signatures: A8,B6,a8,b6,c8,d-e6,f-x8.6.6.6, y6,z8,A-C6,D-I8.6.6.6.6,M6.
Colophon: Hoc opus ... impssum in imperiali oppido Hagenowe. Anno incarnationis dnice
(See next card)   MH61-3276

---

46 / 43

MH-AH

RARE BOOK ROOM
604.7 H74.4os 1494

Holkot, Robertus, d.1349.
Opus super Sapientiam Salomonis.
Ropertus ... [1494]   (Card 2)
millesimoqdringentesimononagesimoquarto.
Contemporary blind-stamped calf over wooden boards (repaired); corner-bosses & clasps wanting.

MH61-3276

MH

[Amaseo, Girolamo, 1468?-1517]
Vaticinivm qvo praedicitvr vniversvm orbem terrarvm christianae religionis imperivm svbitvrvm.
[Venice,Aldo Manuzio,1499]
4°. [24]p. 21.5cm.
Hain 895; Proctor 5573; GW 1596; BMC V.561; Stillwell A488.
Signatures: a8,b4.
Colophon: M.CCCCLXXXXVIIII. die .xx. septem-bris.
(See next card)   MH61-706

Inc 5573

MH

[Amaseo, Girolamo, 1468?-1517]   Vaticinivm ... [1499]   (Card 2)
Caption on a2r: Hieronymi Amasei vtinensis ... poema ad Accursium Mainerid euenionensem ...
Full 19th cent. brown morocco, bound for Edward Herbert, 2d earl of Powis.
Another copy.   20.5cm.
Vellum.

WKR 2.3.2

MH

Baptista Mantuanus, 1448-1516.
In Robertum Severinatem panegyricum carmen.
Baptiste mantuani vatis excellstissimi in preconid Roberti Seuerinatis panegyricd carme cui quodd pulcerrind epygrne Henrici bebelij ad adolescetes scholasticos adheret ...
[Deventer,Jacobus de Breda,1497?]
4°. [32]p. 20cm.
GW 3258; Campbell 240; Nijhoff-Kronenberg 182.
Signatures: a6,b4,c6.
Printer's mark (Juchhoff 29) on t.-p. & verso of last leaf.
Full modern morocco.   MH61-2167

Inc 9093.5

50

MH

An answer to the pretended reasons of some drapers, mercers, haberdashers, grocers, and hosiers, &c. against pedlars, hawkers, & pettychapmen, humbly offered to the consideration of the high-court of Parliament.
London:Printed in the year,1675.

broadside. 44.5x27.5cm., mounted & bd.to 66cm.

No.B29 of the Marquess of Bute broadsides

MH58-1040

*pEB65 A100 B675b v.3

51

MH-BA

Kress Room

Reasons for making the duties easie upon the trade to Africa ... [London, 1698]
broadside. 30.5 x 20 cm.

Indorsed.
Refers to a proposed duty of ten per cent to be paid to the Royal African company of England.

1.Royal African company of England. 2.Gt. Brit. - Commerce -Africa.

52

MH-BA

Kress Room

Sherman, Roger Minott, 1773-1844.
To the Hon. Elisha Phelps, Controller of public accounts, Hartford, Conn. [Hartford, S.Babcock, printer, 1832]
broadside. 48 x 30.5 cm.

In two columns.

1.Bank notes - Connecticut. 2.Banks and banking - Connecticut.

47

Lancelot.
Lancelot du Lac. Paris, Antoine Vérard, 1 July 1494—[1504]

3 v. woodcuts. f°. 35 cm.

The second edition (45-line page)
Printer's device at end of the third volume.
Hain. Repertorium (with Copinger's Supplement) 9850 (variations); Macfarlane, John. Antoine Vérard, 168; Chantilly. Musée Condé. Le cabinet des livres antérieurs au milieu du xvI siècle, 1067.
Autograph of Marcus Fuggerus on the inside front cover.

I. Arthur, King (Romances, etc.)

Incun. 1494.L3 Rosenwald Coll.
55-3638

Library of Congress (2)

48

[Virginia company of London]
A declaration for the certaine time of drawing the great standing lottery. London, Imprinted by F. Kyngston, for W. Welby, 1615.

broadside. 52 x 40¼ fold. to 41¾ (In Brown university. Library. John Carter Brown library. Three proclamations concerning the lottery for Virginia, 1613-1621. Providence, R. I., 1907)

Facsimile.

1. Virginia—Hist.—Colonial period. I. Title.

F229.B879
8-5307

Library of Congress

49

MH

*pEB65 A100 B675b v.5

Advice to Whiggs: or, A challenge to the Jacobites; and all such as are ill-affected to the present government, and endeavour the ruine of the Protestant interest, to muster up their arguments, and vindicate themselves, if they can.
London:Printed in the year, 1702[i.e.1701].

broadside. 38.5x29.5cm., mounted & bd.to 66cm.
Narcissus Luttrell's copy, priced & dated in his hand "1d 9.Dec. 1701." and annotated: a silly poem.

No. C16 of the Marquess of Bute broadsides.

MH58-1314

56

Boccaccio, Giovanni, 1313–1375.

Ioannis Boccatii de Certaldo insigne opvs De claris mulieribus ... Bernae Helvet. excudebat M. Apiarius [1539]

6 p. l., lxxxi numb. l., [2] p. illus. 29 cm.

Colophon: Excvsvm Bernae Helvet. per Mathiam Apiarium. Anno M.D.XXXIX.

Printer's mark on t.-p. and on last page.

The 14 woodcut illustrations are mostly signed I. K., accompanied by a short dagger in a sheath, some have the initials only, and some are unsigned. They are by an unknown German artist, though erroneously attributed by many authorities to Jakob Kerver or Jakob Koebel. *cf.* Nagler, Monogrammisten, v. 3, p. 1021, no. 2682.

1. Woman—History and condition of women. 2. Woman—Biog.
i. Title: De claris mulieribus.

PQ4274.D4 1539

21-18150 rev 2

57

BX890
B735
[illeg.]

Bonaventura, ~~originally Giovanni Fidanza~~ Saint, cardinal, ~~bp. of Albano,~~ 1221–1274.

S.Ancti bonauēture doctoris seraphici breuiloquiũ theologie: quo omnis laus. magistro iohanne gerson teste: lōge inferior est. [Parisiis, 1505?]

[312] p. 15 ^{cm}.

Colophon: ¶Doctoris seraphici sancti Bonauēture ordinis fratrũ minorum] tractatus de septem gradibus contemplationũ / finit: nuperrime summa diligētia castigatus Impressusq̃. Parrhisii per Gaspardum philippe. Expēsis viirabilis viri Johānis Petit / In vico scti Jacobi moram trahentis / apud leonē argenteum.

(Continued on next card)

11-3396

58

Bonaventura, ~~originally Giovanni Fidanza~~ Saint, cardinal, ~~bp. of Albano,~~ 1221–1274. Sancti Bonauēture doctoris seraphici Breuiloquiũ theologie ... [1505?] (Card 2)

Printer's mark of Jehan Petit on t.-p., and of Gaspard Philippe at end.

Signatures: a-n in eights, o in four, p-v in eights.

Includes: Doctoris Seraphici beati Bonauenture tractatus qui lignũ vite dicitur. eiusdē Expositio orationis dominice. s. pater noster. Et laudismus de sancta cruce: ab eodē (cordis de visceribus) editus. ... (Eiusdem Itinerarius mentis in deũ. Cuius optuscuii immo operis imēsi (magistro Johāne gerson teste) laus superior est oīe mortalium. ... Tractat⁹ (vt fertur) sancti Bonauenture de septē gradib⁹ cōtēplationis, q̄p̄ nō redoleat stilũ ei⁹

11-3396

Library of Congress

53

Bianchi, Marco Antonio, 1498–1548.

Tractatvs de indiciis homicidii ex proposito comissi & de alijs indicijs homicidij & furti ad legem finalem ff. de quaestionibus. Venetiis, Apud I. A. Vauafforem cognomine Guadagninum, 1546.

112 l. 16 cm.

Bound with Bruni, Francesco. Tractatvs de indiciis et tortvra. Lvgdvni, 1553.

1. Homicide (Roman law) 2. Larceny (Roman law) 3. Criminal investigation (Roman law)

53-51912

54

Boccaccio, Giovanni, 1313–1375.

Il Decamerone di m. Giovanni Boccaccio di nvovo emendato secondo gli antichi essemplari, per givdicio et diligenza di piv avtori con la diuersità di molti testi posta per ordine in margine, & nel fine con gli epitheti dell' autore, cō la espositione de prouerbi et lvoghi difficili, che nell' opera si contengono, con tauole & altre cose notabili & molto utili alli studiosi della lingua uolgare ... In Vinegia, Appresso G. Giolito de Ferrari, 1548.

6 p. l., 502, [8] p. 1 l., [52] p. woodcuts. 22½ ^{cm}.

(Continued on next card)

6-8208 Revised

55

Boccaccio, Giovanni, 1313–1375. Il Decamerone ... 1548. (Card 2)

Printer's marks on t.-p. and p. 502.

Appended ([54] p. at end) with special t.-p.: Dichiaratione di m. Francesco Sansovino di tvtti i vocaboli, detti proverbi, e lvoghi difficili, che nel presente libro si trouano. Con l'avtorita di Dante, del Villani, del Cento, e d'altri antichi. Aggivntevi alcvne annotationi de lvoghi, dichiarando le historie da lui brevemente toccate. E nel fine vna parte delle voci con i loro piv proprj epitheti. Con i nomi delle casate piv antiche in Firenze ...

i. Sansovino, Francesco, 1521–1586, ed.

PQ4287.A2 1548 [+42b2]

Library of Congress

6-8208 Revised

Card 62

Masuccio *Salernitano. 15th cent.*
Nouellino de Masuccio Salernitano. [Venetia, Impresso per Bertholomio de Zannis da Portese, 1503]

64 l. 53 woodcuts. 29 cm.

Signatures: A–K⁶, L⁴.
Bound in early nineteenth century Italian blind-stamped calf; gilt back (for Count Gaetano Melzi)

PQ4630.M26N59 Rosenwald Coll.

55–3429

Card 63

Shakespeare, William, 1564–1616.
The || Tragicall Historie of || Hamlet, Prince of Denmarke. || By William Shakespeare. || Newly imprinted and enlarged to almost as much || againe as it was, according to the true and perfect || Coppie. || [*Printer's device*] At London, || Printed by I. R. for N. L. and are to be sold at his || shoppe vnder Saint Dunstons Church in || Fleetstreet. 1604. [San Marino, Calif., 1932]

facsim.: 51 l. 22ᵐᵐ.

(Continued on next card)

[3]

Pho 36–5

Card 64

Shakespeare, William, 1564–1616. The || Tragicall Historie of || Hamlet ... [1932] (Card 2)

"Photostat facsimile [positive] reproduced from the copy in the Henry E. Huntington library."
Printed matter on one side of double leaves (except the last) folded at top.
Collation of original (based on the facsimile): [10], p. 17ᶜᵐ. Signatures: 1 leaf unsigned, B–N⁴, O² (O² wrongly marked G⁴) "First edition", in manuscript on t-p.

I. Title. II. Title: Hamlet.

Title from Stanford Univ. Univ. Printed by L. C.

[3]

Pho 36–5

Card 59

Bruni, Francesco. *16th cent.*
Tractatvs de indiciis et tortvra, Francisci Bruni de S. Seuerino, item & Guidonis de Suzaria Mantuani, & Baldi de Periglis Perusini. Cvm additionibvs Lvdouici Bolognini Bononieñ nunc multis in locis emendati & restituti in gratiam eorum, quibus ad regimen Reipublicæ usui erunt. Indicem copiosissimum in calce reposuimus. Lvgdvni, Apud G. Rouillium, 1553.

266 p. 16 cm.

Bound with Bianchi, M. A. Tractatvs de indiciis homicidii. Venetiis, 1546.

1. Criminal investigation. 2. Torture. I. Guido da Suzzara, 13th cent. II. Baldo degli Ubaldi, 1327?–1400. III. Bolognini, Ludovico, 1447 (ca.)–1508.

53–51916

Card 60

Shakespeare, William, 1564–1616.
The || Tragicall Historie of || Hamlet || Prince of Denmarke || By William Shake-speare. || As it hath beene diuerse times acted by his Highnesse ser- || uants in the Cittie of London: as also in the two V- || niuersities of Cambridge and Oxford, and else-where. || [*Printer's device*] At London printed for N. L. and Iohn Trundell || 1603. [Facsimile reprint, 1858]

1 p. l., [63] p. 21ᵐᵐ.

Signatures: 1 p. l., B–I⁴.
Collation: title (verso blank); text: B–I⁴ (last verso blank)

(Continued on next card)

[42c1]

20–3649

Card 61

Shakespeare, William, 1564–1616. The || Tragicall Historie of || Hamlet ... 1603 [1858] (Card 2)

Manuscript not on fly-leaf: "40 copies. Presented by his Grace The Duke of Devonshire to the Library of Congress, Washington. This facsimile was made by the direction, and at the expence of the late Duke of Devonshire. J. Payne Collier. Maidenhead Berkshire Sept. 1858."
The original copy (now the Huntington) lacks the last leaf, which was supplied from the only other copy known, that in the British museum. of. Bartlett & Pollard Census of Shakespeare's plays in quarto, 1916, p. 1, etc.

I. Collier, John Payne, 1789–1883, ed.

Library of Congress PR2750.B67 1858

[42c1]

20–3649

Famous men of Britain. Philadelphia, Loomis and Peck, 1847.

191 p. illus. 80 mm. (Miniature juveniles)

1. Gt. Brit.—Biog. 2. Bibliography—Microscopic and miniature editions.

DA28.4.F3 1847   58–51072

65

Gavaldá, Antonio C

Curiosidades del Quijote (rarezas, extravagancias, vocablos, monedas, juegos y otra porción de zarandajas por el estilo) comentarios. Ilus. de C. Campañá. [Barcelona, Editorial Símbolo, 1952]

178 p. 69 mm. (Colección Microliber)

"Edición numerada de 300 ejemplares ... Ejemplar 95."

1. Cervantes Saavedra, Miguel de. Don Quixote. 2. Bibliography—Microscopic and miniature editions.   I. Title.

PQ6353.G36   53–17236

Library of Congress   [¾]

66

Thoreau, Henry David, 1817-1862.
  Wild apples; history of the apple tree. Worcester [Mass.] A. J. St. Onge, 1956.
  94p. 77mm.

  1. Apple 2. Bibliography - Microscopic and miniature editions - Specimens I. Title

SB363.T55   55-22837

67

U. S. President, 1961-   (Kennedy)
  The inaugural address, delivered at the Capitol, Washington, January 20, 1961. Worcester, A. J. St. Onge [1961]
  30p. port. 68mm.
  "A limited edition of this book has been printed from Lutetia type on 'Antiqua' paper by Joh. Enschedé en Zonen, Haarlem, Holland."

  1. U. S. - Foreign relations - 1961-
  2. Bibliography - Microscopic and miniature editions - Specimens

LCA   J82.D91 Jan.20a   973.922

68

X.   Nonbook materials (1-224)

    A. Art photographs and slides: treatment by

        1. Boston. Museum of Fine Arts.
            a. Art photographs (1-12)
                (1) Catalog
                    (a) Main entry (author/artist) with tracing and accession
                          numbers
                    (b) Subject entries
                    (c) Location of original
                (2) Shelf list: see XI-B
            b. Slides (18-19)
                (1) Charge cards: identification of each slide, filed behind
                    slides
                (2) Shelf list: see XI-B
        2. Harvard University. William Hayes Fogg Art Museum.
            a. Art photographs (13-17)
                (1) Catalog
                    (a) Main entry (author/artist) with tracing
                    (b) Location of original
                (2) Label on photograph
                (3) Charge card, clipped to photograph
                (4) Shelf list: see XI-B
            b. Slides (20-24)
                (1) Catalog
                  (a) Main entry (author/artist) with tracing
                  (b) Subject entry: national school of painting
                (2) Label on slide
                (3) Charge card, filed behind slide
                (4) Shelf list: see XI-B

    B. Manuscripts (25-29)

        1. Facsimile (25)
        2. Calendar (26)
        3. Personal papers, etc. (27-29)
        4. Boxed material (29)

    C. Maps, globes, atlases, etc. (30-67)

        1. LC style: main entry by:
            a. Cartographer, title, etc. (30-36)
            b. Government agencies (37-51)
            c. Commercial agencies (52-58)
            d. Society (59-62)
        2. Printed forms (63-65)
        3. Boggs & Lewis style (66-67)

NONBOOK MATERIALS

ART PHOTOGRAPHS

```
                                          MBMu

763      Dallin, Cyrus Edwin.
D1            Appeal to the Great Spirit.
B5



         Sculpture.
            Boston.   Museum of Fine Arts.          1


                        ◯
```

```
    15733 .1
     9519 .1
     8952 .2                                         2
    21008 .3    Animals.   Horses.
                Indians.   North America.

                (Boston.   Museum of Fine Arts.)
```

```
Animals.   Horses.
                                          MBMu

763_____ Dallin.
D1            Appeal to the Great Spirit.
B5                Boston.   Museum.
```
3

```
Indians.   North America.
                                          MBMu

763_____ Dallin.
D1            Appeal to the Great Spirit.
B5                Boston.   Museum.
```
4

```
                                          MBMu

Boston.   Museum of Fine Arts.   (red)

763   |      | Dallin.   (underlined in red)
D1    | B5   |   Appeal to the Great Spirit.
```
5

```
                        ◯
```

```
                                              MBMu
841        Eyck, Jan van.
Ey3            Portrait of Giovanni Arnolfini and
Gel               of Giovanna Cenani, his wife.


           Painting.
              London.   National Gallery.                6


                         ◯
```

```
  4975     Animals.   Dogs.
 81258 (red) Arnolfini, Giovanni.   15th cent.           7
  9578)    Costume.   15th cent.
           Marriage customs and rites.

           (London.   National Gallery.)
```

```
Animals.  Dogs.
                                              MBMu
841        Eyck, J. van.
Ey3            Portrait of Giovanni Arnolfini and         8
Gel               of Giovanna Cenani, his wife. c.
                  London.   National Gallery.     (red)
```

```
Arnolfini, Giovanni.   15th cent.
                                              MBMu
841        Eyck, J. van.
Ey3            Portrait of Giovanni Arnolfini and         9
Gel               of Giovanna Cenani, his wife. c.
                  London.   National Gallery.     (red)
```

```
Costume.   15th cent.
                                              MBMu
841        Eyck, J. van.
Ey3            Portrait of Giovanni Arnolfini and        10
Gel               of Giovanna Cenani, his wife.  c.
                  London.   National Gallery.     (red)
```

```
Marriage customs and rites.
                                              MBMu
841        Eyck, J. van.
Ey3            Portrait of Giovanni Arnolfini and        11
Gel               of Giovanna Cenani, his wife.  c.
                  London.   National Gallery.     (red)
```

```
                                              MBMu
           London.   National Gallery.  (red)
841                Eyck, J. van.  (underlined in red)    12
Ey3    Gel         Portrait of Giovanni Arnolfini and
                      of Giovanna Cenani, his wife.


                         ◯
```

```
                                              MH-FA

374.1        Patinir, Joachim de
P 274
38Je
                 St. Jerome in a rocky landscape

                 London, National Gallery, 4826




   (buff)                        ◯
```

Fogg Art Museum	NUMBER	374.1
Harvard University		P 274
		38Je

AUTHOR Patinir, Joachim de
SUBJECT St. Jerome in a rocky
landscape

PLACE London, National Gallery, 4826
PHOTOGRAPHER National Gallery neg.

```
London, National Gallery
```

```
                                              MH-FA

             LONDON, NATIONAL GALLERY  (red)
374.1        Patinir, Joachim de
P 274
38Je
                 St. Jerome in a rocky landscape

                 London, National Gallery, 4826




   (buff)                        ◯
```

```
   374.1   P 274   38Je




 charge card

                            (yellow)
```

16-17

13-15

```
763    Dallin      Appeal to the
D1664              Great Spirit
W1                        30398




        SLIDE LIBRARY
      MUSEUM OF FINE ARTS
           BOSTON
```

18

19

```
763    Dallin, C.   Appeal to the Great Spirit
D1664                              34941
W1










                    Slide Library

        MUSEUM OF FINE ARTS, BOSTON
```

MH-FA

374.1
P 274
38Je

Patinir, Joachim de

20

St. Jerome in a rocky
landscape

London, National Gallery

London, National
Gallery photograph

21   **Painting, Flemish, 16th century. Patinir, Joachim de**

MH-FA

PAINTING, FLEMISH, 16TH CENTURY. PATINIR, JOACHIM DE *(red)*

374.1   Patinir, Joachim de
P 274
38Je

22

St. Jerome in a rocky
landscape

London, National Gallery

374.1   P 274   38Je

23

charge card

(yellow)

Label on slide

24

FOGG ART MUSEUM OF HARVARD UNIVERSITY
Patinir, Joachim de   374.1
St. Jerome in a rocky landscape   P 274
London, National Gallery, 4826   38Je

MANUSCRIPTS

Washington, Booker Taliaferro, 1859?–1915.
Papers, 1882–1942.

443 ft. (ca. 300,000 items)

In Library of Congress, Manuscript Division.
Educator, author, leader in the advancement of the Negro race. Eleven large correspondence series, with MSS. of books, articles and speeches, printed matter, scrapbooks, reports, and documents. Photos. Much material relates to Tuskegee Institute, Hampton Institute, the National Negro Business League, and the General Education Board. Important correspondents include William H. Baldwin, Wallace Buttrick, Andrew Carnegie, George Washington Carver, James C. Clarkson, James H. Dillard, Frederick Douglass, William E. B. DuBois, Charles W. Eliot, T. Thomas Fortune, Hollis B. Frissell, Abraham Grant, Leigh Hunt, Seth Low, Fred R. Moore, Robert R. Moton, E.

(Continued on next card)

MS 59–4

27

Washington, Booker Taliaferro, 1859?–1915. Papers, 1882–1942. (Card 2)

Gardiner Murphy, Robert C. Ogden, Walter Hines Page, George F. Peabody, John D. Rockefeller, Theodore Roosevelt, Julius Rosenwald, Emmett J. Scott, Anson Phelps Stokes, William Howard Taft, Victor H. Tulane, and Oswald Garrison Villard. Also described in the Library's Quarterly Journal of current acquisitions, v. 2, no. 2 (Feb. 1945) p. 23–31.
Information on literary rights available in repository. Gift of the Trustees of Tuskegee Institute, 1943 and 1945.

1. Negroes. I. Tuskegee Institute. II. Hampton Institute, Hampton, Va. III. National Negro Business League. IV. General Education Board.

MS 59–4

28

Ashley, Frederick William, 1863–1942.
Material for a history of the Library of Congress, 1939.

7 boxes.

In Library of Congress, Manuscript Division.
Librarian and scholar; Superintendent of the Reading Room and Chief Assistant Librarian of Congress. MSS. for a Library history. Unpublished register in the library.

1. U. S. Library of Congress—Hist.

Library of Congress [61b1]
MS 59–1 rev

29

Orthodox Eastern church. *Liturgy and ritual. Menologion.*
Il menologio di Basilio II (cod. vaticano greco 1613) ... Torino, Fratelli Bocca, 1907.

xxii, 123 p., 1 l. *and* atlas (facsims.) 2 p. l., xv, 362, 362a–433 p. 49ᶜᵐ. (*Half-title:* Codices e vaticanis selecti phototypice expressi ivssv Pii PP. X consilio et opera cvratorvm Bibliothecae vaticanae. (Series maior) vol. VIII)

"Exemplar e centvm qvae perfecta svnt N. 36."

1. Manuscripts, Greek—Facsimiles. 2. Basilius II, surnamed Bulgaroktonos, emperor of the East, d. 1025. I. Vatican. Biblioteca vaticana. Mss. (Graec. 1613)

Z114.C65 vol. 8
[45r36g1]
7–27008
Library of Congress

25

U. S. *Library of Congress. Manuscripts Division.*
Calendar of the letters of Alexander Baring, 1795–1801. Prepared from microfilms in the Manuscripts Division. Library of Congress, by Ruth Anna Fisher. [Washington] 1954.

82 l. facsims. 27 cm.

Typescript.

1. Ashburton, Alexander Baring, 1st baron, 1774–1848. 2. Real property—Maine. 3. Maine—Descr. & trav. 4. U. S.—Descr. & trav.—1783–1848. I. Fisher, Ruth Anna, 1888– II. Title.

Z663.34.C3
[2]
54–1543
Library of Congress

26

Anville, Jean Baptiste Bourguignon d', 1697–1782.
    Twelve maps of antient geography, drawn by the sieur Danville, and designed for the explanation of Mr. Rollin's Antient history of the Egyptians, Carthaginians, Assyrians, Babylonians, Medes, and Persians, Macedonians, and Grecians. London, Printed for J. and P. Knapton, 1750.

30

    [2] l., 12 fold. col. maps. 35 cm.

    1. Geography, Ancient—Maps.   ɪ. Rollin, Charles, 1661–1741. Histoire ancienne des Égyptiens. ɪɪ. Title.

G1033.A58 1750

Map 61–205

Library of Congress   [8]

31

Everyman's Classical atlas. With an essay on the development of ancient geographical knowledge and theory by J. Oliver Thomson. [3d ed.] London, J. M. Dent; New York, Dutton [1961]

    lxx, 125 p. illus., maps (part col.) 20 cm. (Everyman's reference library)

    First ed. published in 1907 under title: Atlas of ancient and classical geography.

    1. Classical geography—Maps.   ɪ. Thomson, James Oliver, ed.

G1033.A8 1961

Map 62–131

Congress   [10]

Map
912
.755
F946

Fry, Joshua, 1700 (ca.)–1754.
    The Fry & Jefferson map of Virginia and Maryland; a facsimile of the first edition in the Tracy W. McGregor Library, with an introd. by Dumas Malone. Princeton, Published for the Harry Clemons Publication Fund of the University of Virginia by Princeton University Press, 1950.

32

    21, [3] p. plate, col. map on 4 fold. sheets. 32 cm.
    In portfolio.
    "Checklist of eighteenth-century editions of the Fry & Jefferson map": p. 13–[19]
    "Three hundred copies ... published, the first hundred copies being for presentation to Harry Clemons by a group of his friends."
    Bibliography: p. 21–[22]

    1. Virginia—Maps.   2. Maryland—Maps.   ɪ. Jefferson, Peter, 1708–1757.   ɪɪ. Malone, Dumas, 1892–

GA408 1751.F7M3   912.755   Map 50—834

Library of Congress   [50b3]

33

Klepešta, Josef.
    Mondkarten, erstes und letztes Viertel; mit einem interessanten Beitrag über Wissenswertes vom Mond [von] Josef Klepešta und Ladislav Lukeš. [1. deutschsprachige Ausg.] Prag, Zentralverwaltung Geodäsie und Kartographie, 1959.

    31 p. illus., 2 fold. maps (in pocket) 30 cm.

    "Landung der sowjetischen Rakete auf dem Mond": leaf inserted.
    In portfolio.
    Scale 1:5,000,000.

    1. Moon—Photographs, maps, etc.   ɪ. Lukeš, Ladislav J., joint author. ɪɪ. Title.

G3192.M6 1959.K54

Map 61–174

Library of Congress   [3]

Peterson, Donald William, 1925–
Geologic map of the Haunted Canyon quadrangle, Arizona. Washington, U.S. Geological Survey, 1960.
col. map 58 x 49 cm. on sheet 76 x 127 cm. fold. to 30 x 24 cm. (U. S. Geological Survey. Geologic quadrangle maps of the United States. GQ–128)
Scale 1 : 24,000.
Issued in envelope.
Caption title, and title on envelope: Geology of the Haunted Canyon quadrangle, Arizona.
"Contour interval 40 feet."
"Prepared in cooperation with the Corps of Engineers, U. S. Army."
Includes text and 3 col. cross sections.
1. Geology—Arizona—Maps. I. Title: Haunted Canyon quadrangle, Arizona. (Series)

G3701s.C5 var.U5   GQ–128

Library of Congress [3]   Map 61–217

34

Tanner, Henry Schenck, 1786–1858.
United States of America. 2d ed.   Philadelphia, 1880.
col. map 115 x 153 cm.
Scale ca. 1 : 2,000,000.
Prime meridian: Washington.
"Engraved by H. S. Tanner, assisted by E. B. Dawson, W. Allen & J. Knight."
With 16 inset maps including "Oregon and Mandan Districts," statistical tables and profiles of railroads and canals.

1. U. S.—Maps.

G3700 1830.T3   **Map 62–80**

35

Wilson, Lee Jerome.
Gas pipeline map of Brazoria Co.   Houston, Tex. [1954]
map 102 x 96 cm.
Scale 1 : 99,999 ; 1 inch=3,000 varas.
Blue line print.
Shows ownership of non-urban real property.
Pipe-line data added to a map issued by the Texas General Land Office; compiled by G. C. Morriss, drawn by Eltea Armstrong.
Inset: [Brazoria County, showing chief oil and gas fields]

1. Brazoria Co., Tex.—Maps. 2. Gas, Natural—Texas—Pipe lines—Maps. 3. Real property—Brazoria Co., Tex.—Maps. I. Texas. General Land Office.

G4033.B7 1954.W5   **Map 54–1291**

Library of Congress [3]

36

U. S. *Coast and Geodetic Survey.*
Status of horizontal control, United States.
[Washington]
col. maps 62 x 99 cm.
Scale 1 : 5,000,000.
"Albers equal area projection, standard parallels 29½° and 45½°."
"Base map by United States Geological Survey."
Issued also with "Completed reconnaissance."
Insets: Alaska.—Hawaii.—Canal Zone.—Puerto Rico and Virgin Islands.

1. Triangulation—U. S.—Maps.

G3701.B33 year.U48   Map 60–284

37

U. S. *Coast and Geodetic Survey.*
Status of vertical control, United States.
[Washington]
col. maps 62 x 99 cm.
Scale 1 : 5,000,000.
"Albers equal area projection, standard parallels 29½° and 45½°."
"Base map by United States Geological Survey."
Insets: Alaska.—Hawaii.—Canal Zone.—Puerto Rico and Virgin Islands.

1. Leveling—U. S.—Maps.

G3701.B32 year.U48   Map 60–285

38

U. S. *Coast and Geodetic Survey.*
Index map—control leveling, State of Maine.
Washington.
col. maps 76 x 51 cm.
Scale ca. 1:665,000.
"Base map by United States ... Geological Survey."

1. Leveling—Maine—Maps.

G3731.B32 1960.U6   Map 61–187

Library of Congress [3]

39

U.S. *Office of Education. Division of Vocational Education.*
Basic preparatory programs for practical nurses by States and changes in number of programs from 1957 to 1958. Washington [U. S. Govt. Print. Off., 1959]
sheet. map. 27 cm.

1. Practical nursing—U. S.   I. Title.

U.S. Dept. of Health, Education, and Welfare.   Library
RT62

HEW 59-14

43

U.S. *Post Office Dept.*
Post route map, Michigan. [Washington]
col. maps 126 x 87 cm.
Scale ca. 1:570,240.
Each issue includes index of "Counties in Michigan."
Insets: [Western part of Northern Peninsula]—Detroit and vicinity [ca. 1:21,120]

1. Postal service—Michigan—Maps. 2. Michigan—Maps.

G4121.P8 year.U6

Map 55-300

44

Washington, D. C. *National Arboretum.*
Plant hardiness zone map. [Prepared by the U. S. National Arboretum, Agricultural Research Service, U. S. Dept. of Agriculture in cooperation with the American Horticultural Society. Washington, U. S. Govt. Print. Off., 1960]
col. map 49 x 73 cm. fold to 28 x 19 cm. (U. S. Dept. of Agriculture. Miscellaneous publication no. 814)
"Approximate scale 1: 7,500,000."
Text, table, and map on verso.

1. U. S.—Climate—Maps.   I. Title.   (Series)

S21.A46 no. 814   G3701.C82 1960.W8
——— Copy 3.   [3]
Library of Congress

Map 60-60

45

U.S. *Army Map Service.*
South Carolina photo maps 1:25,000: Fort Jackson and vicinity. Washington, 1951–
maps 56 x 48 cm. (Its A. M. S. V046A)
Scale ca. 1:25,000.
"Transverse Mercator projection."
"Heights in feet."
Issued mostly on versos of corresponding topographic sheets of South Carolina 1:25,000 (A. M. S. V846)
Marginal maps: Index to adjoining sheets.

1. Fort Jackson, S. C.—Maps.   (Series)

G3914s.F7 25.U5

Map 53-1079

40

U.S. *Geological Survey.*
Index to maps of Massachusetts, Rhode Island, and Connecticut. Washington.
col. maps 49 x 71 cm. fold. to 27 x 22 cm.
Scale 1:500,000; approximately 1 inch equals 8 miles.
Title on outside when folded: Index to topographic mapping in Massachusetts, Rhode Island, and Connecticut.
Text and lists of maps on verso (5 p.)

1. Massachusetts—Maps, Topographic—Indexes. 2. Rhode Island—Maps, Topographic—Indexes. 3. Connecticut—Maps, Topographic—Indexes.

G3721.A2 year.U6

Map 53-720

41

U.S. *National Park Service.*
The national park system, eastern United States. [Washington] U.S. Govt. Print. Off., 1954.
col. map 74 x 59 cm. fold. to 21 x 10 cm.
Scale ca. 1:4,600,000.
Text on verso.
Inset: [Puerto Rico and Virgin Islands]

1. National parks and reserves—U. S.—Maps.   I. Title: Eastern United States.

G3706.G52 1954.U5

Map 55-202
Library of Congress   [3]

42

Czechoslovak Republic. *Ústřední správa geodesie a karto-*
grafie.
Školní atlas československých dějin. [Odpovědný redaktor: Jan Musílek.] 1. vyd.] Praha, 1959.
44 p. of col. maps, 18 p. 31 cm.

1. Czechoslovak Republic—Historical geography—Maps.
i. Musílek, Jan, ed. ii. Title.

G1946.S1C9 1959

Map 61-213

46

Czechoslovak Republic. *Ústřední správa geodesie a karto-*
grafie.
Malý atlas sveta. [Hlavný redaktor Antonín Koláčný.
2. doplněné slovenské vyd.] Bratislava, Správa geodézie a
kartografie na Slovensku, 1959.
2 v. col. maps (part fold.) 22 x 30 cm.
Bibliography: v. 1, 11th prelim. page.

1. Atlases, Slovak. 2. Geography, Economic—Maps. i. Koláčný,
Antonín, ed. ii. Slovakia. Správa geodézie e kartografie. iii. Title.

G1019.C9902 1959

Map 61-215

47

France. *Direction de la documentation.*
Carte agricole de l'Afrique. Paris [1958]
col. map 85 x 79 cm. fold. to 30 x 20 cm. (*Its* Carte no. 80)
Scale 1:10,000,000.
At head of title: Présidence du conseil, Secrétariat général du gou-
vernement. Direction de la documentation. Ministère des finances et
des affaires économiques, Institut national de la statistique et des
études économiques.
Title from verso, outside when folded.
Shows land types by color, and principal crops by symbols.
Inset: Elavage [showing relief and types of livestock]

1. Agriculture—Africa—Maps. i. France. Institut national de
la statistique et des études économiques. (Series)

G8201.J1 1958.F7

[3]

Library of Congress

Map 61-178

48

Maryland. *Maryland-National Capital Park and Planning*
Commission.
Street map of Montgomery County. Compiled by Ad-
vance Planning Section. 1st ed., March 1960. Silver Spring,
Md., [1960.
4 col. maps 101 x 123 cm.
Scale 1:24,000; 1"=2,000'.
Inset: Sheet index.
——A street index by census tracts for Montgomery County,
Maryland, Jan. 1960. Silver Spring, Md. [1960]
56 p. map. 28 cm.
"Addendum ... Jan. 1, 1959–Nov. 30, 1959" (7 l. inserted)
G3843.M6 1960.M3 Index
1. Montgomery Co., Md.—Maps.

G3843.M6 1960.M3

Map 60-57

49

Tennessee. *Highway Planning Survey Division.*
General highway map[s] ... Tennessee. Prepared by the
Tennessee State Highway Dept., Highway Planning Survey
Division in cooperation with the U. S. Dept. of Commerce,
Bureau of Public Roads. [Nashville] 19
maps on sheets 46 x 61 cm.

Scale ca. 1:126,720.
"Polyconic projection."
Each county map includes insets at enlarged scale, ca. 1:31,680.

1. Tennessee—Road maps.

G3961s.P2 126.T4

Map 61-183

50

Vermont. *State Geologist.*
Centennial geologic map of Vermont. Compiled and
edited under the direction of Charles G. Doll, State Geologist,
by Charles G. Doll [and others. Montpelier] Vermont Geological Survey, Vermont Development Dept., 1961.
col. map 104 x 144 cm.
Scale 1:250,000.
"Contour interval 100 feet."
Includes 6 col. cross sections.
Insets: Index map of Vermont (ca. 1:100,000)—Metamorphic map
of Vermont (ca. 1:860,000)—Tectonic map of Vermont (ca. 1:860,000)
1. Geology—Vermont—Maps. i. Doll, Charles George, 1888–

G3751.C5 1961.V4

[1]

Library of Congress

Map 62-54

51

Map Corporation of America.
Map and directory of information, Tri-city area, Pasco, Richland, Kennewick; and Walla Walla, Washington; with indexed streets. Latest ed. Boston, Map Corporation of America; distributed by Buchanan News Agency, Pasco [1959]

3 maps on sheet 56 x 72 cm. fold. to 23 x 11 cm.
Scales vary.
Cover title.
CONTENTS.—recto. Map of Pasco, Washington; Map of Kennewick, Washington. (ca. 1:14,400)—verso. Map of Richland, Washington. (ca. 1:12,000) Map of Walla Walla, Washington. (ca. 1:20,000)

1. Pasco, Wash.—Maps. 2. Richland, Wash.—Maps. 3. Kennewick, Wash.—Maps. 4. Walla Walla, Wash.—Maps.

G4284.P3 1959.M3

Library of Congress [3]

Map 61-180

52

55

Master Maps, ltd., *London*.
Route map of the coronation of Her Majesty, Queen Elizabeth II, Head of the Commonwealth. [London, 1953]

col. map 49 x 73 cm.

Pictorial map, not drawn to scale.
Coats of arms of London boroughs in margin.
On verso: The royal family [text, ports., and geneal. table]—The British Commonwealth of Nations represented at the coronation [with coats of arms]

1. London—Maps, Pictorial. 2. Elizabeth II, Queen of Great Britain, 1926- —Coronation—Maps.

G5754.L7A5 1953.A3

Map 53-694

53

56

Metsker Maps.
Atlas of Clark County, Washington. Nov. 1961. Seattle [1961]

36 (i. e. 40) l. (chiefly maps (part fold.)) 37 x 45 cm.

Blue line print.
Previous editions (1929 and 1937) by C. F. Metsker.
Scale of township maps 1:31,680 or 2 in.=1 mile, and 1:15,840 or 4 in.=1 mile.

1. Clark Co., Wash.—Maps. 2. Real property—Clark Co., Wash.—Maps. I. Metsker, Charles Frederick, 1881- Atlas of Clark County, Wash.

G1488.C5M42 1961

Library of Congress [1]

Map 62-187

54

57

Aero Service Corporation, *Philadelphia*.
The Aero 12" relief globe in true raised relief. Philadelphia, °1960.

col. globe 31 cm. in diameter.

Scale 1:42,134,400: 1 inch=665 miles.
Vinyl plastic; mounted on fixed semi-meridian with metal base.
Colored to show generalized land use.

1. Globes.

G3171.C18 1960.A3

Library of Congress [3]

Map 61-77

Goode, John Paul, 1862-1932.
Rand McNally regional atlas. [Edited by Edward B. Espenshade, Jr. Abridged ed. of Goode's World atlas] 2d ed. Chicago, Rand McNally, °1962.

64 p. (p. 2-51 col. maps) 29 cm.

1. Atlases. I. Espenshade, Edward Bowman, 1910- ed. II. Title.

G1019.G66 1962

912

Map 62-188

Hammond (C. S.) and Company, inc.
The march of civilization in maps and pictures; a graphic reference book covering man's development and conquests from 3000 B.C. to the present day. 1949- Maplewood, N. J.

v. illus. (part col.) maps (part col.) 32 cm.

Includes Atlas of the Bible lands, Historical atlas, American history atlas; also The races of mankind, by Henry Field.

1. Geography, Historical—Maps. 2. Bible—Geography—Maps. 3. U. S.—Historical geography—Maps. I. Title.

G1030.H34

912

Library of Congress [10]

Map 62-8

58

Road atlas of U. S., Mexico, and S. Canada; with Rand-McNally maps. Baltimore, I. & M. Ottenheimer, c1954.

177 p. maps. 15 cm.

Cover title: Road atlas with Rand McNally maps.

1. U. S.—Road maps. I. Rand, McNally and Company. II. Ottenheimer, I. and M., Baltimore.

G1201.P2R62 1954

Map 54–915

59

National Geographic Society, *Washington, D. C. Cartographic Section.*

The Great Lakes region of the United States and Canada. Washington, 1953.

col. map 68 x 104 cm.

Scale 1:2,027,520 or 32 miles to the inch. "Albers conical equal-area projection, standard parallels 38° and 48°."

"James M. Darley, chief cartographer; nomenclature by A. D. Grazzini; transportation by W. Chamberlin; physiography by J. J. Brehm and A. E. Holdstock; compiled by R. J. Darley (and others) typography by C. E. Riddiford."

(Continued on next card)

Map 54–89 rev

60

National Geographic Society, *Washington, D. C. Cartographic Section.* The Great Lakes region of the United States and Canada. 1953. (Card 2)

Issued with the National geographic magazine, v. 104, no. 6, Dec. 1953.

With 4 insets.

—— Index. With 11,959 place names. Washington, 1953.

36 p. 26 cm.

G3312.G7 1953.N3 Index

1. Great Lakes region—Maps. 2. Northeastern States—Maps. I. Darley, James Morrison.

G3312.G7 1953.N3

Library of Congress [54c3]

Map 54–89 rev

61

National Geographic Society, *Washington, D. C. Cartographic Division.*

Africa. Compiled and drawn in the Cartographic Section of the National Geographic Society; Albert H. Bumstead, chief cartographer. Washington, 1935.

col. map 77 x 72 cm.

Scale 1:11,721,600 or 185 miles to 1 inch. "Azimuthal equal-area projection (pole of projection at latitude 15° north, longitude 20° east)"

Issued with the National geographic magazine, v. 67, no. 6, June 1935.

Insets: Airways and relief.—Cape Verde Islands.

62

National Geographic Society, *Washington, D. C. Cartographic Division.* Africa. 1935. (Card 2)

—— Index to the new map of Africa including adjacent portions of Europe and Asia. Washington, 1935.

35 p. 26 cm.

G8200 1935.N3 Index

1. Africa—Maps. I. Bumstead, Albert Holt, 1875–1940.

G8200 1935.N3

Library of Congress [3]

Map 62–75

63

TITLE		
DATE		
PUBLISHER		

SCALE		SIZE		COLOR
ONE UNIT				BLACK & W.
ORIGINAL	SET			
PHOTOSTAT	SERIES			COPIES
PRESS RUN	DIAGRAMMATIC			LANGUAGE
PHOTOGRAPH	SHEETS			
SOURCE				

ADMINISTRATION	DISEASE	POWER	TOPOGRAPHY
AGRICULTURE	GEODETIC	PROJECTIONS	CONTOURS
AIR COMMUNICATIONS	GEOLOGY	POPULATION	HACHURES
ASTRONOMY	MINERALS	DISTRIBUTION	OTHER RELIEF
BOUNDARIES	PETROLEUM	ETHNOGRAPHIC	DRAINAGE
CARTOGRAPHY	HISTORY	RELIGIOUS	VEGETATION
CITY PLAN	INDUSTRY	RAILROADS	WATER SUPPLY
CLIMATE	LAND USE	RECREATION	WATERWAYS
REGION	MILITARY	ROADS	CANALS
PRECIPITATION	NAT'L PARKS & RES.	SOILS	DEPTH
TEMPERATURE	PHOTOGRAPHY, AERIAL	TELECOMMUNICATIONS	FACILITIES
COMMERCE	GROUND	TRANSPORTATION	

VERSO:

REMARKS:

NhD

Card 64

```
G          Tennessee                    SCALE 1: 500,000   SIZE 40½×66
3961                                    ORIGINAL   | ONE UNIT | ✓ COLOR
H1     SUBJECT                          PHOTOSTAT  | SET      | BLACK & WHITE
F59    TITLE  Mineral resources and     PRESS RUN  | SERIES   |
       mineral industries of            PHOTOGRAPH | DIAGRAMMATIC | LANGUAGE
       Tennessee *                                               Eng.
PUBLISHER Tennessee. Dept of Conservation   SOURCE
          and Commerce. Div of Geology 1959
```

64

AGRICULTURE		✓ GEOLOGY		POWER		TOPOGRAPHY	
AIR COMMUNICATIONS		✓ MINERALS		RAILROADS		CONTOURS	
✓ BOUNDARIES		PETROLEUM		TYPE		HACHURES	
CITY PLAN		✓ INDUSTRY		GUAGE		OTHER RELIEF	
CLIMATE		AREA		FACILITIES		DRAINAGE	
REGION		✓ PLANT					
PRECIPITATION		✓ TYPE					
TEMPERATURE		MILITARY					
HISTORICAL		POPULATION					
BOUNDARIES		DISTRIBUTIO					
COMMUNICATIONS		ETHNOGRAPHI					
MILITARY		RELIGIOUS					

REMARKS:
* By Wm. D. Hardeman ?
Robert A. Miller. (Assistec
Stuart W. Maher & Robe
Hershey)

Card 65

65

```
G      Mines and Mineral              SCALE 1: 500,000   SIZE 40½×66
3961   resources - Tennessee          ORIGINAL   | ONE UNIT | ✓ COLOR
H1     SUBJECT                        PHOTOSTAT  | SET      | BLACK & WHITE
F59    TITLE  Mineral resources and   PRESS RUN  | SERIES   |
       mineral industries of          PHOTOGRAPH | DIAGRAMMATIC | LANGUAGE
       Tennessee *                                             Eng.
PUBLISHER Tennessee. Dept of Conservation   SOURCE
          and Commerce. Div. of Geology 1959
```

AGRICULTURE		✓ GEOLOGY		POWER		TOPOGRAPHY	
AIR COMMUNICATIONS		✓ MINERALS		RAILROADS		CONTOURS	
✓ BOUNDARIES		PETROLEUM		TYPE		HACHURES	
CITY PLAN		✓ INDUSTRY		GUAGE		OTHER RELIEF	
CLIMATE		✓ AREA		FACILITIES		DRAINAGE	
REGION		✓ PLANT		ROADS		WATERWAYS	
PRECIPITATION		✓ TYPE		SURFACE		CANALS	
TEMPERATURE		MILITARY		MILEAGE		NAVIGABILITY	
HISTORICAL		POPULATION		OTHER		DEPTH	
BOUNDARIES		DISTRIBUTION		RECREATION		FACILITIES	
COMMUNICATIONS		ETHNOGRAPHIC		TELECOMMUNICATIONS	✓	OTHER Hydroelectric plants	
MILITARY		RELIGIOUS		VEGETATION	✓	steam plants	

REMARKS:
* By Wm. D. Hardeman +
Robert A. Miller (Assisted by
Stuart W. Maher & Robert E.
Hershey)

MBU

Card 66 / 67

66

```
630cba
1916U
        United States relief map.  Compiled by Henry
      Gannett.  Engraved by U. S. G. S.  Ed. of 1916
      reprinted 1934.  ⌈Washington, D. C., 1934⌉

        1:7,000,000.  43x70cm.  Polyconic proj.

        At top of sheet: Department of the Interior.
      U. S. Geological Survey.
        Physical map showing relief by contour lines and
      green and brown layer tints; drainage in blue;
      cities.

                        ◯  (Continued on next card)
```

67

```
        1. U. S. - Physical maps - 1916.  I. U. S.
      Geological Survey.
                                    Boggs & Lewis
```

X.

X. Nonbook materials (continued from page 247)

D. Films (68-82)

  1. Motion pictures (68-74) see also App. C
  2. Filmstrips (75-82)

E. Microforms: monographs and serials; personal and corporate
     entries (83-128) see also VII-F; X-F

  1. Microfilms (83-113)
     a. Reproductions (83-97, 101, 112-113)
     b. Originals (98-99, 102-111)
     c. Form referral cards (100)
  2. Microcards (114-116)
     a. Originals (117-125)
     b. Reproductions (126-128)

F. Music scores (129-148) see also III-D

  1. Orchestral (129-133)
  2. Chamber (134)
  3. Keyboard (135-136)
  4. Opera, etc. (137-138)
  5. Librettos (137-138) see also VII-H
  6. Choral (139-145)
  7. Musical revues, comedies, etc. (146)
  8. Songs (147-148)

G. Phonorecords (149-213) see also III-A; App. C

  1. Orchestral (149-161, 175-177)
  2. Chamber (162-174)
  3. Keyboard (178-181)
  4. Opera/libretto (182-184) see also VII-H
  5. Choral (185-190)
  6. Musical revues, comedies, etc. (191-192) /libretto:
       see VII-H
  7. Folk music (193-194)
  8. Jazz, experimental, etc. (195-197)
  9. Nonmusical (198-202)
  10. Talking books for the blind: LC cards for regional
       libraries (203-213)

H. Phonotapes: comparative styles (214-224)

  1. Music (214-218)
  2. Readings (219, 221)
  3. Interview (220)
  4. Lecture (222-224)

Film
919.1
In2 **Indonesia—new nation of Asia** (*Motion picture*) Encyclopædia Britannica Films, 1959.

16 min., sd., color, 16 mm.

With film guide.
Summary: An Indonesian teacher tells the story of his country.
Traces the history of Indonesia from Dutch rule through independence; shows life in crowded cities and in the homes of village families; examines the natural resources, religions, art, and industries of
the country, pointing out how the living standards are improving.
Credits: Collaborator, Peter Gosling.

——— Another issue. b&w.

1. Indonesia.   I. Encyclopædia Britannica Films, inc.

                                                        919.1   Fi A 59–508

Encyclopædia Britannica ◯ Films
for Library of Congress   [2]

68

Partners in progress (*Motion picture*) Southern Bell Telephone and Telegraph Co., 1949. Made by Charles D. Bee-
land Film Productions.

20 min., sd., color, 16 mm.

Summary: Tells the story of farm progress in the South and of the
strides made by Southern Bell in providing telephone service for
rural areas.

1. Farms—Southern States.   2. Telephone—Southern States.
I. Southern Bell Telephone and Telegraph Company.

                                              630.975   Fi A 56–121

Southern Bell Telephone ◯ and Telegraph Co.
for Library of Congress   [2]

69

The sea: Background for literature (*Motion picture*) Coronet Instructional Films, 1958.

11 min., sd., color, 16 mm.

Kodachrome.
With teachers' guide.
Summary: Presents a study of literature revealing many aspects
of the sea. Includes excerpts from The rime of the Ancient Mariner,
Crossing the bar, and Mutiny on the Bounty, and re-enacts key scenes
from Captains courageous, Two years before the mast, the Journals
of Captain Cook, Treasure Island, and Moby Dick.
Credits: Collaborator, Robert O. Pooley.

——— Another issue. b&w.

1. Sea in literature.   I. Coronet Instructional Films.

                                           809   Fi A 58–430

Coronet Instructional ◯ Films
for Library of Congress   [3]

70

Water—sculptor of the land (*Motion picture*) WGBH–
TV. Released by NET Film Service, 1956.

30 min., sd., b&w, 16 mm.   (Discovery)

Summary: Describes how water changes the face of the earth. Explains the formation and distinguishing characteristics of the common
sedimentary rocks such as limestone, sandstone, shale, and conglomer-
ate. Tells how fossils of living things serve as guides to the history
of life on the earth.

1. Erosion.   2. Rocks, Sedimentary.   3. Paleontology.   I. Boston.
Television station WGBH–TV.   II. National Educational Television
Film Service.   Series: Discovery, series 1 (Motion picture)

                                       551.35   Fi A 60–1247

National Educational ◯ Television Film Service
for Library of Congress   [2]

71

FILM		MBSi
F 1 (red)	The Titan; story of Michelangelo (Motion picture) Contemporary Films, 1950. 1 hr. 7 min., sd., b&w., 16 mm. Summary: Photographs of works of the Italian Renaissance artist including "David", "Moses", The Medici monument, the ceiling of the Sistine Chapel and the "Last Judgement". Also includes some works of Da Vinci, Giotto and Botticelli. Credits: Producer, Robert Snyder; narrator, Frederic March.	

72

Michelangelo

73

FILM		MBSi
F 1 (red)	Michelangelo. (red) The Titan. For further information see The Titan.	

74

FILMSTRIP		MBSi
FS4 (red)	Reference materials (Filmstrip) Chicago Teach- ers College, 1954. 31 fr., color, 35 mm. and disc: 1 s., 12 in., 33⅓ rpm. 10 min. (Know your library) Summary: Pictorial survey of a wide range of reference materials. Designed for college students, but with its casual commentary is better adapted to high school level.	

75

76

77

FILMSTRIP

78

Reference books
 Chicago Teachers College

FILMSTRIP		MBSi
FS4 (red)	Reference books. (red) Reference materials (Filmstrip)	

FILMSTRIP		MBSi
FS4 (red)	Chicago Teachers College. Reference materials (Filmstrip) For further information see Reference materials (Filmstrip)	

More national parks in the West (*Filmstrip*) Eye Gate House, 1960.

38 fr., color, 35 mm. (Our national parks, no. 5)

With teachers manual.
Summary: Shows views of Crater Lake National Park in Oregon, Mount Rainier National Park in Washington, and Olympic National Park in northwest Washington.

1. Crater Lake National Park. 2. Mount Rainier National Park. 3. Olympic National Park. ɪ. Eye Gate House, inc. Series: Our national parks (Filmstrip) no. 5.

Eye Gate House   917.9   Fi A 60–2310
for Library of Congress   [2]

79

80

Remodeling the elementary school library (*Filmstrip*) Committee on Planning School Library Quarters of the Buildings and Equipment Section, Library Administration Division of the American Library Association, 1961. Made by the Board of Education of Baltimore County.

63 fr., color, 35 mm.

Eastman color.
Prepared by the Dept. of Library Services, Engineering, and Audio-Visual Aids.
With manual.

81

Remodeling the elementary school library (*Filmstrip*) (Card 2)

Summary: Explains how the school system in Baltimore County, Md., has developed a plan to provide adequate facilities for central libraries in existing elementary schools. Shows how unused space is converted into a library, with views before and after completion of the library. Describes equipment needed in a library, and includes plans and working drawings for the use of space and equipment. With captions.

1. School libraries. 2. Library architecture. ɪ. American Library Association. Library Administration Division. Buildings and Equipment Section.

American Library   027.8222   Fi A 61–2865
for Library of Congress   Association   [2]

A space trip to the moon (*Filmstrip*) Jam Handy Organization, 1961.

30 fr., color, 35 mm. (First adventures in space, no. 6)

Summary: Captioned drawings picture the probable clothing and transportation needed to make a trip to the moon. Discusses known conditions on the moon and their effect upon man.

1. Space flight to the moon—Juvenile films. ɪ. Jam Handy Organization, inc. Series: First adventures in space (Filmstrip) no. 6.

Jam Handy Organization   j 629.4   Fi A 61–2839
for Library of Congress   [2]

82

MB

*Microfilm
AN2
.M4B66   Boston post. Nov. 9, 1831, Nov. 8-9, 1832,
              Jan. 4, 1834, Jan. 6, 1834-Dec. 27, 1850,
              Aug. 1, 1936-Jan. 31, 1941, Mar. 1, 1944-
              Oct. 4, 1956. Boston [etc.] 1936-56.
              256 reels.
              Microfilm copy (positive) for Nov. 9, 1831-
            June 30, 1937, made by Recordak Corp., New
            York; for July 1, 1937-Jan. 31, 1941, made
            by Graphic Service Corp., Boston; for Mar.
            1944-Oct. 4, 1956, made by Recordak Corp.,
            Boston Branch.
                (Continued on   next card)

83

*Microfilm
AN2
.M4B66   Boston post ... (Card 2)
                Collation of the original: 323 v. illus.
            (part col.) ports. 33-58cm.
                Daily and Sunday.
                Ceased publication with Oct. 4, 1956 issue.

84

85

MB

*Microfilm
AN2
.M4B63   Boston Sunday advertiser. May 1, 1938-Aug.
              27, 1939, Jan. 2, 1944- *to date*
                                              (pencil)
              Boston [etc.] 1938- *to date*
              reels.
              Microfilm copy (positive) for May 1, 1938-
            Aug. 27, 1939, made by Graphic Service Corp.,
            Boston; for Jan. 2, 1944-Nov. 25, 1951, made
            by Recordak Corp., Boston Branch; for Dec. 2,
            1951-   made by Micro-Photo Service
            Bureau, Cleveland, Ohio.
to date   (Continued   on next card)
NLC
                                              (over)

86   x *Boston advertiser. Sunday
                edition* (pencil)

87

*Microfilm
AN2
.M4B63   Boston Sunday advertiser ... (Card 2)
                Collation of the original: v. illus.
            (part col.) ports. 31-54cm.

Boston. *City Council.*
   The Railroad Jubilee; an account of the celebration commemorative of the opening of railroad communication between Boston and Canada, September 17th, 18th, and 19th,
1852. Boston, J. H. Eastburn, city printer, 1852.

   (American culture series, 63 : 1)

   Microfilm copy (positive) made in 1956 by University Microfilms,
Ann Arbor, Mich.
   Collation of the original : 288 p. fold. map, tables.

      1. Boston—Railroad Jubilee, 1851. 2. Boston—Comm. 3. Rail-
roads—U. S.—Hist.   I. Title.

Microfilm 01291 reel 63, no. 1 E   Mic 59–7761

Library of Congress   ⟨1⟩

88

89

Margaret Percival in America, a tale edited by a New
England minister. Being a sequel to Margaret Percival, a
tale ⟨by Elizabeth Missing Sewell and⟩ edited by William
Sewell. 2d ed. Boston, Phillips, Sampson, 1850.

   (American culture series, 149 : 5)

   Microfilm copy (positive) made in 1960 by University Microfilms,
Ann Arbor, Mich.
   Collation of the original, as determined from the film : 284 p.

      I. Hale, Edward Everett, 1822–1909, ed.

Microfilm 01291 reel 149, no. 5 E   Mic 61–7213

Library of Congress   ⟨1⟩

Collections, historical and miscellaneous, and monthly literary journal. v. 1–3; Apr. 1822–Nov./Dec. 1824. Concord,
N. H., Hill and Moore.

   2 reels. (American periodical series : 1800–1825. 93–94)

   Collation of the original : 3 v.
   Bimonthly (irregular) 1822; monthly, 1823–24.
   Title varies : v. 1, Collections, topographical, historical & biographical relating principally to New-Hampshire.
   Edited by J. Farmer and J. B. Moore.
      1. New Hampshire—Hist.—Period.   I. Farmer, John, 1789–1838,
ed. II. Moore, Jacob Bailey, 1797–1853, ed. III. Title: Collections,
topographical, historical & biographical.   (Series: American periodical series : 1800–1850. 93–94)

Microfilm 01104 no. 93–94 AP   Mic 56–4824

Library of Congress   ⟨1⟩

90

91

The **Southern** literary journal and magazine of arts. v. 1–3,
Sept. 1835–Feb. 1837; new ser., v. 1–4, Mar. 1837–Dec. 1838.
Charleston, S. C., Printed by Burges & James ⟨etc.⟩

   3 reels. (American periodical series : 1800–1850. 574–576)

   Microfilm copy (positive) by University Microfilms, Ann Arbor,
Mich.
   Collation of the original : 6 v.
   Monthly.
   Title varies : 1835–37, The Southern literary journal and monthly
magazine.
   Editors : 1835–37, D. K. Whitaker.—1838, B. R. Carroll.
   New ser., v. 2, Sept.–Dec. 1837, never published.
      I. Whitaker, Daniel Kimball, 1801–1881, ed. II. Carroll, Barthol-
omew Rivers, ed. III. Title: The Southern literary journal and
monthly magazine.   (Series)

Microfilm 01104   no. 574–576 AP   Mic 61–7441

Library of Congress   ⟨1⟩

Microfilm
Z715
.A5

American Library Association. Division of Cataloging and Classification. Committee on Administration.
Multiple order forms used by American libraries, edited by Edwin B. Colburn. Chicago, Microphotographic Laboratories, University of Chicago Libraries, 1949.
Microfilm copy (positive) of typescript in the University of Chicago Libraries.
Collation of the original, as determined from the film: [2,250 l. illus.

98

1. Library science - Forms, blanks, etc.
2. Libraries - Order dept.
I. Colburn, Edwin Belcher, 1915-   ed.
II. Title

99

LC

The microfilms of this series which are in the library are separately listed under the author.

100

Bruner, Leon James, 1931-
Low-temperature internal friction in face-centered cubic and body-centered cubic metals. [Chicago, Dept. of Photoduplication, University of Chicago Library] 1960.
Microfilm copy (positive of a reprint from the Physical review, vol. 118, no. 2, April 15, 1960).

101

1. Dislocations in metals.
Microfilm 6749 QC
Chicago. Univ. Libr.
for Library of Congress
Mic 62-7092 †
[1]†

92

MICROFILM
M 7
(red)
Cutter, Charles Ammi.   MBS1
Rules for a dictionary catalogue; 2d ed., with corrections and additions. Washington, Govt. Print. Off., 1889.
Microfilm copy, made in 1956, of the original in the Harvard College Library, by Harvard College Library. Negative.
Collation of the original: 133p.   (U.S. Bureau of Education. Special report on public libraries. pt.II)

93

Cataloging
Catalogs, Dictionary
t

94

MICROFILM
M 7   MBS1
Cataloging.   (red)

95

MICROFILM
M 7   MBS1
Catalogs, Dictionary.   (red)

96

MICROFILM
M 7   MBS1
Rules for a dictionary catalogue; 2d ed.
Cutter, Charles Ammi.   (red)

For further information see
Cutter, Charles Ammi.

97

U. S. *Congress. House. Committee on the Judiciary.*
Testimony before the House Committee on the Judiciary on international copyright, Washington, D. C., February 8, 1890. Washington, Govt. Print. Off., 1890.
Microfilm copy (positive)
Collation of the original, as determined from the film: 40 p.

1. Copyright—U. S. 2. Copyright, International.
Microfilm 945
Library of Congress   [1]
Mic 62-7048

X-E

Margulies, Moritz, 1910–
Die Beziehungen zwischen Österreich-Ungarn und Russland in der Zeit Andrassys. [Wien, 1949]

Microfilm copy (negative) made by the Photo Section, Vienna University Library.
Collation of the original, as determined from the film: 382 l.
Diss.—Vienna.
Vita.
Bibliography: leaves 826–830.

1. Austria—For. rel.—Russia. 2. Russia—For. rel.—Austria. I. Title.

Microfilm 6685 DB   Mic 62–7051

Library of Congress   [1]

105

Sherwood, Edward Torrence, 1915–
Swazi personality and the assimilation of Western culture. Chicago [Dept. of Photoduplication, University of Chicago Library] 1961.

Microfilm copy (positive) of typescript.
Collation of the original: 409 l.
Thesis—University of Chicago.
Includes bibliography.

1. Swazi (African tribe) 2. Assimilation (Sociology) 3. Acculturation. I. Title.

Microfilm 6895 DT   Mic 62–7095 ‡

Chicago. Univ. Libr.
for Library of Congress   [1]†

106

Redcar, Eng. St. Peter's Church.
Parish churchyard records of St. Peter's, Redcar, Yorkshire, 1801–1952; compiled by A. S. Maxwell. [Wakefield, Yorkshire, Micro Methods, 1961?]

Microfilm copy (positive) of typescript.
Collation of the original, as determined from the film: [1], 13 l.
"A transcript of the records compiled by S. Cramer ... and an index, compiled by A. S. Maxwell."—Letter from Micro Methods, ltd.

1. Registers of births, etc.—Redcar, Eng. I. Maxwell, A. S. II. Cramer, Sidney.

Microfilm 6949 CS   Mic 62–7056

Library of Congress   [1]

107

102

el Hadidi, Taher Abdel Razzak, 1923–
Heat transfer mechanisms in porous media containing oil and water. Ann Arbor, University Microfilms [1956]

([University Microfilms, Ann Arbor, Mich,] Publication no. 14,900)
Microfilm copy (positive) of typescript.
Collation of the original: 186 l. illus.
Thesis—Pennsylvania State University.
Abstracted in Pennsylvania. State University. Abstracts of doctoral dissertations. v. 18 (1955) p. 370–371.
Bibliography: leaves 185–186.

1. Oil field flooding. 2. Heat—Transmission. 3. Fluid dynamics. I. Title. II. Title: Porous media containing oil and water.

Microfilm AC–1 no. 14,900   Mic 59–7434

Pennsylvania. State University. Library
for Library of Congress   [1]†

103

Shelly, James Harold, 1932–
The decision and synthesis problems in semimodular switching theory. Ann Arbor, Mich., University Microfilms [1959]

Microfilm copy (positive) of typescript.
Collation of the original: vi, 93 l.
Thesis—University of Illinois.
Abstracted in Dissertation abstracts, v. 20 (1959) no. 5, p. 1813–1814.
Published also as Digital Computor Laboratory, University of Illinois, Report no. 88.
Vita.
Bibliography: leaves 90–92.

1. Switching theory. 2. Electronic calculating-machines—Circuits. I. Title.

Microfilm AC–1   no. 59–4569   Mic 59–4569

Illinois. Univ. Library
for Library of Congress   [1]†

104

Sherry, Richard, ca. 1506–ca. 1555.
A critical edition of Richard Sherry's A treatise of schemes and tropes [by] Herbert William Hildebrandt. Ann Arbor, Mich., University Microfilms [1958]

Microfilm copy (positive) of typescript.
Collation of the original: 2 v. facsims.
H. W. Hildebrandt's thesis—University of Wisconsin.
Abstracted in Dissertation abstracts, v. 19 (1958) no. 5, p. 1188.
Vita.
Includes bibliography.

1. Sherry, Richard, ca. 1506–ca. 1555. A treatise of schemes and tropes. 2. Rhetoric—1500–1800. I. Hildebrandt, Herbert William, 1931– II. Title: A treatise of schemes and tropes.

Microfilm AC–1 no. 58–5347   Mic 58–5347

Wisconsin. Univ. Library
for Library of Congress   [1]†

267

MICROFILM		
M 24	Oldham, Ellen M **MBSi**	
(red)	Early women printers in the United States.	
	Microfilm copy of typewritten manuscript.	108
Negative.		
	Collation of the original: 98ℓ.	
	Seminar paper, Library Science S220, Simmons	
College, 1957.		
	Includes bibliography.	
	◯	

Women as printers	109
t	

MICROFILM		
M 24	Women as printers. (red) **MBSi**	
(red)	Oldham, Ellen M	
	Early women printers in the United States.	110
	For further information see	
	Oldham, Ellen M	

MICROFILM		
M 24	Early women printers in the United States.	111
(red)	Oldham, Ellen M **MBSi**	
	For further information see	
	Oldham, Ellen M	

Kuybyshev, Russia. Khudozhestvennyĭ muzeĭ.
 И. И. Шишкин, 1832–1898; к 125-летию со дня рождения.
 ₁Выставка. Составитель каталога А. Д. Павлова; текст
предисл. А. Н. Михранян. Куйбышев₁ 1957.
 Microfilm copy (negative) made in 1959 by Fundamental'naͭ
biblioteka obshchestvennykh nauk of the Akademiͭ nauk SSSR.
 Collation of the original, as determined from the film : 11 p. 2 illus.,
port.

 1. Shishkin, Ivan Ivanovich, 1831–1898.   I. Pavlova, A. D.
                                    Title transliterated: I. I. Shishkin.

Microfilm Slavic 1766 ND   Mic 62–7004

112-
113

Russia (*1923–   U. S. S. R.*) *Ministerstvo lesnoĭ promysh-
lennosti.   TSentral'noe bi͡uro tekhnicheskoĭ informat͡sii.*
 Механизация погрузочно-разгрузочных работ на лесо-
заготовках; сборник статей. Москва, Гослесбумиздат,
1956.

 Microfilm copy (negative)
 Collation of the original, as determined from the film : 73 p. illus.

 1. Lumber—Transportation. 2. Loading and unloading. 3. Cranes,
derricks, etc.   I. Title.
                Title transliterated: Mekhanizat͡sii͡a pogruzochno-
                        razgruzochnykh rabot na lesozagotovkakh.

Microfilm Slavic 1594 SD   Mic 62–7013

Library of Congress   ◯   ₁₂₁

0 2 5 . 3 4   Cataloging of moving-pictures.   Z 6 9 5 . 6 4
Daughtry, Bessie.   [Card 1 (of 3)—p. i-iii. 1-31]
Cataloging, arrangement and storage of motion pictures, filmstrips, and 2" x
2" slides. Rochester, NY., University of Rochester Press for the Association
of College and Reference Libraries, 1954.   (iii, 81 l. illus., charts. 28cm
ACRL Microcard series, no.20) Master's paper, Florida State University, 1948.
Bibliography: l. 80-81.

114

0 2 5 . 3 4   Cataloging of moving-pictures.   Z 6 9 5 . 6 4
Daughtry, Bessie.   [Card 2 (of 3)—p. 32- 71]
Cataloging, arrangement and storage of motion pictures, filmstrips, and 2" x
2" slides. Rochester. N.Y.. 1954.

115

0 2 5 . 3 4   Cataloging of moving-pictures.   Z 6 9 5 . 6 4
Daughtry, Bessie.   [Card 3 (of 3)—p. 72-73, 75-79, Biblio. 80-81]
Cataloging, arrangement and storage of motion pictures, filmstrips, and 2" x
2" slides. Rochester. N.Y., 1954.

116

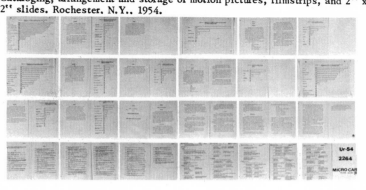

Daughtry, Bessie.
    Cataloging, arrangement and storage of motion pictures,
filmstrips, and 2" x 2" slides. Rochester, N. Y., University
of Rochester Press for the Association of College and Reference Libraries, 1954.

    3 cards. 7½ x 12½ cm. (ACRL microcard series, no. 20)

    Microprint copy of typescript.
    Collation of the original: iii, 81 l. illus. 28 cm.
    Bibliography : leaves 80–81.

    1. Cataloging of moving-pictures. 2. Cataloging of filmstrips.
(Series: Association of College and Reference Libraries. ACRL
microcard series, no. 20)

Microcard Z695.64   Micp 55–16
Library of Congress   [1]

117

Association of College and Research Libraries.
  ACRL microcard series, 1–99: abstracts of titles included
in the series which is published under the auspices of the
Association of College and Research Libraries. Rochester,
N. Y., University of Rochester Press, 1959.

  2 cards. 7½ x 12½ cm. (*Its* ACRL microcard series, no. 100)

  Microprint copy.
  Collation of the original: ii, 91 l. 28 cm.

  1. Library science—Abstracts. (Series)

Microcard Z665

Library of Congress   ◯ [2]

118

119

120

121

122

123

MICROCARD   MBSi
025.6   Diebold (John) & Associates, inc., New York.
(red)   Preliminary study of library circulation
         systems for the Council on Library Resources.
         [N.Y.] 1959.
            1 card. 7½x12½cm.

            Microprint copy of typescript.
            Collation of the original: 1,2,5,11,11 l.
fold. tables, 28cm.

         (Microcards arranged by call number in shelf
         list order - separate file)
                    ◯

Libraries. Circulation, loans
Council on Library Resources
t

MICROCARD   MBSi
025.6   Libraries. Circulation, loans.   (red)
(red)   Diebold (John) & Associates, inc., New York.

MICROCARD
025.6   Council on Library Resources.   MBSi
(red)   Diebold (John) & Associates, inc., New York.

MICROCARD   MBSi
025.6
(red)   Preliminary study of library circulation
             systems.
         Diebold (John) & Associates, inc., New York.

             For further information see
         Diebold (John) & Associates, inc., New York.

Microcard
GN4
  .M5   **Microcard** publications of primary records in culture and
         personality. v. 1–
         Madison, Microcard Foundation, 1956–

            v. (microcards) illus. 7½–12½ cm.

            Editor: v. 1–   B. Kaplan.
            "Under the sponsorship of the Committee on Primary Records,
         Division of Anthropology and Psychology, National Academy of
         Sciences-National Research Council."

         1. Anthropology—Collections.   I. Kaplan, Bert, 1919–   ed.

Microcard GN4   ◯   Micp 56–30

Library of Congress   ◯ [2]

124

Wright, Elizabeth V
 Elinor Wylie: a critical survey and bibliographical study. West Salem, Wis., Microcard Corp., 1956.

 5 cards. 7½ x 12½ cm.

 Microprint copy of typescript.
 Collation of the original: 178 l. 26 cm.
 Thesis—Loyola University.
 Bibliography: leaves 101–172.

 1. Wylie, Elinor (Hoyt) 1885–1928.

 Microcard PS3545.Y45

 Micp 59–11

 Library of Congress ⟨1⟩

125

126

Coferati, Matteo.
 Il cantore addottrinato; ovvero, Regole del canto corale, oue con breue, e facil metodo s'insegna la pratica de' precetti più necessari del canto fermo; il modo di mantenere il coro sempre alla medesima altezza di voce; di ripigliare doue resta l'organo; d'intonare molte cose, che fra l'anno si cantano; e in particolare tutti gl'inni. Firenze, Il Vangelisti, 1682. ⟨Rochester, N. Y.⟩ U⟨niversity of⟩ R⟨ochester Press, 19⟩57.

 8 cards. 7½ x 12½ cm.

 Microprint copy made from the original in the Library of Congress.

 (Continued on next card)

127

Coferati, Matteo. Il cantore addottrinato ... ⟨19⟩57.
 (Card 2)

 Collation of the original: ⟨40⟩, 306 p. illus., coat of arms, music. 15 cm.
 "Dell'origine, e progressi del canto ecclesiastico, discorso proemiale di Francesco Cionacci": prelim. page ⟨23⟩–⟨40⟩

 1. Chants (Plain, Gregorian, etc.)—Instruction and study—To 1800. I. Cionacci, Francesco, 1633–1714. II. Title.

 Microcard MT860

 Micp 59–8

 Library of Congress ⟨1⟩

Heylyn, Peter, 1599–1662.
 Ecclesia restaurata; or, The history of the Reformation of the Church of England ... With the life of the author, by John Barnard. Edited by James Craigie Robertson. Cambridge, 1849. ⟨Madison, Wis., Microcard Foundation, 1957?⟩
 21 cards. 7½ x 12½ cm.
 Microprint copy.
 Collation of the original: 2 v. facsims.
 Edition of 1849 printed for the Ecclesiastical History Society.
 "Editions of some works to which reference is made": v. 1, p. ⟨xv⟩–xvii. Bibliographical footnotes.
 1. Reformation—England. 2. Church of England—Hist. I. Ecclesiastical History Society, London. II. Title.

 Microcard BR375

 Micp 57–20

 Library of Congress ⟨1⟩

128

Beethoven, Ludwig van, 1770–1827.
₍Symphony, no. 3, op. 55, E♭ major₎

ɪɪɪᵉ ₍i. e. Troisième₎ symphonie, "Héroïque," op. 55, mi♭ majeur. Paris, Heugel ₍1951₎

miniature score (174 p.) 19 cm.

Analysis in English and German, by Marc Pincherle (₍4₎ p.) inserted.

1. Symphonies—Scores.

M1001.B4 op.55.H4 1951a M 55–307

129

Bartók, Béla, 1881–1945.
₍Concerto, violin (1907–8)₎

Violin concerto no. 1 (op. posth.) London, New York, Boosey & Hawkes ₍ᶜ1959₎

miniature score (64 p.) 19 cm. (Hawkes pocket scores, no. 710)
Duration : 21 min.

1. Concertos (Violin)—Scores.

M1012.B292C6 M 59–1183

Library of Congress ₍8₎

130

MB

M1013
.B88 Busoni, Ferruccio Benvenuto, 1866 1924.
op.35a [Concerto, violin, op. 35a, D major:
1954 arr.]
Konzert für Violine und Orchester, D dur, D major, Op. 35a. Ausg. für Violine und Klavier. Leipzig, Breitkopf & Härtel [1954, c1899]
score (35 p.) and part. 31 cm. (Edition Breitkopf, Nr. 5210)
Publisher's pl. no.: 22222.
1. Concertos (Violin) - Solo with piano.
NLC

131

MB

M1004
.B47C6 Berlioz, Hector, 1803-1869.
1950 [Le corsaire. Overture]
Ouverture du Corsaire, op. 21. London E. Eulenberg; New York, Eulenburg Miniature Scores [195-?]
miniature score (62 p.) 19cm. (Edition Eulenburg, no. 621)
Publisher's pl. no.: E. E. 3721.

1. Overtures--Scores. I. Title: Le corsaire.
NLC

132

Rachmaninoff, Sergei, 1873–1943.
 [Symphonic dances, op. 45]

Symphonic dances. [Op. 45] New York, C. Foley [°1941]

score (148 p.) 35 cm.

1. Orchestral music—Scores.   I. Title.

M1047.R12   op. 45   ◯   M 55–2192

Library of Congress   [3]   133

Stravinskiĭ, Igor' Fedorovich, 1882–
 [Histoire du soldat. Suite; arr.]

L'histoire du soldat (The soldier's tale) ; for violin, clarinet, and piano. Arr. by the composer. New York City,
International Music Co. [196–?] Pl. no. 1548.

score (28 p.) and   parts. 31 cm.

CONTENTS.—The soldier's march.—The soldier's violin.—A little
concert.—Tango-waltz-ragtime.—The devil's dance.

1. Suites (Piano, clarinet, violin), Arranged.   I. Title. II. Title:
The soldier's tale.

M324.S   ◯   M 60–2862

Library of Congress   [3]   134

Byrd, William, 1542 or 3–1623.

Parthenia [by] William Byrd, John Bull [and] Orlando
Gibbons. Transcribed and edited by Thurston Dart. London, Stainer & Bell [1960]

40 p. 33 cm.

"A critical edition ... first published in 1612–13, comprising eight
pieces by William Byrd, seven by John Bull, and six by Orlando
Gibbons."
Errata (leaf) inserted.

1. Harpsichord music—To 1800.   I. Bull, John, d. 1628. II. Gibbons, Orlando, 1583–1625. III. Dart, Thurston, 1921–   ed. IV. Title.

M21.B9P3   1960   M 60–2034

Library of Congress   ◯   [3]   135

Schumann, Robert Alexander, 1810–1856.
 [Songs. Selections; arr.]

Lieder und Gesänge, für das Pianoforte zu 2 Händen,
übertragen von Max Schultze. Braunschweig, H. Litolff;
Boston, A. P. Schmidt [18—] Pl. no. 12096.

39 p. 31 cm. (His Compositionen; neue kritisch durchgesehene
Ausg.)
Collection Litolff, No. 1697.
Cover title: Lieder ohne Worte.
For piano.

1. Piano music, Arranged.   I. Title: Lieder ohne Worte.

M38.5.S   ◯   M 53–1288

Library of Congress   [3]   136

137

Menotti, Gian Carlo, 1911–

[The unicorn, the gorgon, and the manticore. English]

The unicorn, the gorgon, and the manticore; or, The three Sundays of a poet. A madrigal fable for chorus, ten dancers, and nine instruments. [195–]

1 v. (various pagings) 35 cm.

Holograph, in pencil, with additions (primarily piano acc.) in red ink.

Libretto by the composer.

Published: New York, G. Ricordi, c1977.

Commissioned by the Elizabeth Sprague Coolidge Foundation in the Library of Congress.

—Vocal scores with piano.

1. Masques with music   I. U.S. Elizabeth Sprague Coolidge Foundation.   II. Title.   III. Title: The three Sundays of a poet.

Library of Congress

ML29c.M5   62–35166/M

140

Orthodox Eastern Church. *Liturgy and ritual. Hirmologion.*

The hymns of the Hirmologium. Transcribed by Aglaïa Ayoutanti and Maria Stöhr. Rev. and annotated by Carsten Høeg, with the assistance of Jørgen Raasted. Copenhagen, Munksgaard, 1952–

v. facsims. 27 cm. (Monumenta musicae Byzantinae. Transcripta. v. 6)

Greek words.

Transcription in modern notation of all the hirmi occurring in the Hirmologium Athoum. Includes also the variants in other mss, in the original notation and in transcription, for at least one canon of each mode.

138

Orthodox Eastern Church. *Liturgy and ritual. Hirmologion.* 1952–

(Card 2)

The hymns of the Hirmologium.

CONTENTS.—pt. 1. The first mode. The first plagal mode.

1. Music, Byzantine.   2. Church music—Orthodox Eastern Church.   3. Hymns, Greek.   I. Ayoutanti, Aglaïa.   II. Stöhr, Maria.   III. Høeg, Carsten, 1896–   ed.   IV. Athos (Monasteries) Iveron. Mss. (470)   v. Title.   (Series)

M2.B99T7   vol. 6, etc.   783.9   M 53–1690

Library of Congress   [3]

141

Talma, Louise, 1906–

[The Alcestiad. English]

The Alcestiad; opera in 3 acts. Text by Thornton Wilder. [1960]

Microfilm (negative) of holograph. At end: Finished December 24, 1960, in the Phi Beta Studio of the MacDowell Colony, Peterborough, New Hampshire. Louise Talma.

Collation of the original: score (561 l.)

1. Operas—Scores.   I. Wilder, Thornton Niven, 1897–   II. Title.

Alcestiad.   The

Microfilm M–86   Mic 62–7170/M

139

Brahms, Johannes, 1833–1897.

[Ein deutsches Requiem. German]

A German requiem, for soli, chorus, and orchestra (organ ad lib.) Op. 45. London, E. Eulenburg; New York, Eulenburg Miniature Scores [195–?]

Pl. no. 10444.

miniature score (265p.) port., facsim. 19cm.

(Edition Eulenburg, no. 969)

Edition Peters, Nr. 3671a

Reissued from Peters plates.

Includes English and German words printed as text.

1. Requiems –   Scores   I. Title

M2010.B8 op.45.E8   M 55–764

142

Bach, Johann Sebastian, 1685–1750.

[Chorales. Selections]

Choräle; eine Auswahl Bach'scher Choralsätze für den Gottesdienstlichen Gebrauch. 5. Aufl. Krs. Moers, Verlag Singende Gemeinde Vluyn, 1958.

close score (48 p.) 28 cm.

1. Chorales.

M2138.B17C555   M 59–1120

Library of Congress   [3]

143

[Book of anthems and hymns. Newburyport? Mass., ca. 1780]

score (40 p.) 21 x 28 cm.

L. C. copy imperfect: t. p. wanting.
Erroneously ascribed to Daniel Bayley as comp. in Evans (Amer. bibl. 18311) with reconstructed title: A collection of anthems and hymn tunes. Cf. also Music Library Association. Notes, 2d ser., June 1947, p. 292-295.
Photocopy (negative) of p. 1, letter from Irving Lowens, dated May 25, 1953, concerning the publication, and detached copy of the Notes article laid in.

1. Choruses, Sacred (Mixed voices), Unaccompanied.
I. Lowens, Irving, 1916-

M1.A1B   M 54-2678

144

Foss, Lukas, 1922-
[Song of songs. English]

Song of songs; Biblical solo cantata for soprano (or mezzo) and orchestra. Text from the Song of Solomon. New York, C. Fischer [1960]

score (98 p.) 27 cm. (Carl Fischer study score series, no. 14)
Duration: 26 min., 45 sec.

CONTENTS.—Awake, O north wind.—Come my beloved.—By night on my bed.—Set me as a seal.

1. Solo cantatas, Sacred (High voice)—Scores. 2. Song of Solomon (Music) I. Title.

                                               Real name: Lukas Fuchs.

M2103.F7S68   M 60-2808

145

Hindemith, Paul, 1895-
[A song of music]

Lied von der Musik (George Tyler) Für dreistimmigen Frauenchor (SSA) mit Klavier oder Streichorchester. A song of music; chorus for women's voices (SSA) with piano or string orchestra. Mainz, B. Schott's Söhne [°1958]

score (11 p.) 28 cm.
English and German words.
Duration : 2 min.

1. Choruses, Secular (Women's voices, 3 pts.) with string orchestra—Scores. I. Title. II. Title: A song of music.

M1543.5.H53S6   M 61-69

Library of Congress   [8]

146

Styne, Jule, 1905-
[Gypsy. Piano-vocal score. English]

Gypsy. Lyrics by Stephen Sondheim. Book by Arthur Laurents, suggested by the memoirs of Gypsy Rose Lee. Piano reduction by Robert Noeltner. New York, William-son Music & Stratford Music Corp.; Chappell, sole selling agent [1960]

192 p. 31 cm.

1. Musical revues, comedies, etc.— Vocal scores with piano. I. Sondheim, Stephen. II. Laurents, Arthur. Gypsy. III. Title.

M1503.S937G9 1960   M 60-2804

Library of Congress   [8]

147

Wolf, Hugo, 1860-1903.
[Italienisches Liederbuch]

Songs on Italian lyrics by Heyse and Geibel, for voice and piano. German and English texts. [English translation by Lily Henkel] Original key. New York, International Music Co. [1948]

3 v. port. 27 cm.

1. Songs with piano. I. Heyse, Paul Johann Ludwig von, 1830-1914. II. Geibel, Emanuel, 1815-1884. III. Title.

                                       Full name: Hugo Philipp Jakob Wolf.

M1620.W85 I 62 1948   M 54-1853

148

African song sampler. [Delaware, Ohio, °1958]

34 p. illus. 17 x 18 cm. (Song samplers for good group singing, no. 8)

Cover title.
In part unacc. melodies ; in part close score.
English words, or words in the original language with English translation.

1. Folk-songs, African.

M1830.A35   M 59-1110

Library of Congress   [8]

275

AUTHORITY FILE

PHONORECORDS

MBS1

Mendelssohn-Bartholdy, Felix.
  Symphony, no.4, op.90, A major.

x Mendelssohn-Bartholdy, Felix. Italian symphony.
x Italian symphony.

152

MBS1

Mendelssohn-Bartholdy, Felix.
  Symphony, no.5, op.107, D major.

x Mendelssohn-Bartholdy, Felix. Reformation symphony.
x Reformation symphony.

153

Pd I
7
(**red**)   **MBS1**

Mendelssohn-Bartholdy, Felix.
  [Symphony, no.4, op.90, A major]
Symphony no.4, in A, op.90 (Italian) Symphony no.5, in D minor [i.e. major] op.107 (Reformation) RCA Victor LM 2221.
  2 s.
  Boston Symphony Orchestra; Charles Munch, conductor.

149

Mendelssohn-Bartholdy, Felix
  Symphony, no.5, op.107, D major

150

Pd I
7
(**red**)   **MBS1**

Mendelssohn-Bartholdy, Felix.
  Symphony, no.5, op.107, D major.

For further information see entry under composer.

151

PHONORECORD CATALOG

MBS1

Villa-Lobos, Heitor.
[Bachianas brasileiras, no.4, piano; arr.]
Bachianas brasileiras, no.4 [and 7] Angel
Records ANG. 35674.
2 s.

Orchestre national de la Radiodiffusion
française, the composer conducting.

Pd I
2
(red)

154 / 158

Villa-Lobos, Heitor
Bachianas brasileiras, no.7, orchestra
t

155 / 159

MBS1

Villa-Lobos, Heitor.
Bachianas brasileiras, no.7, orchestra.

For further information see entry under composer.

Pd I
2
(red)

156 / 160

MBS1

Bachianas brasileiras, no.4 [and 7]
Villa-Lobos, Heitor.
Bachianas brasileiras, no.4, piano; arr.

For further information see entry under composer.

Pd I
2
(red)

157 / 161

MBS1

Mendelssohn-Bartholdy, Felix
Italian symphony
see
Mendelssohn-Bartholdy, Felix
Symphony, no.4, op.90, A major.

MBS1

Italian symphony
see
Mendelssohn-Bartholdy, Felix
Symphony, no.4, op.90, A major.

MBS1

Mendelssohn-Bartholdy, Felix
Reformation symphony
see
Mendelssohn-Bartholdy, Felix
Symphony, no.5, op.107, D major.

MBS1

Reformation symphony
see
Mendelssohn-Bartholdy, Felix
Symphony, no.5, op.107, D. major.

PHONORECORD NAME
AUTHORITY FILE

PHONORECORD TITLE
AUTHORITY FILE

162

M̌ CC P CH HS   MBr

Budapest String Quartet.

Thompson 46

163

M̌ CC P CH HS   MBr

Debussy, Claude, 1862-1918.

Thompson

164

M̌ CC P CH HS   MBr

Ravel, Maurice, 1875-1937.

Thompson

(√ in pencil)

165

M̌ CC P CH HS   MBr

Debussy, Claude, 1862-1918.
[Quartet, strings, G minor, op. 10]

Kolodin

166

M̌ CC P CH HS   MBr

Ravel, Maurice, 1875-1937.
[Quartet, strings, F major]

Thompson

278

PHONORECORD
DIVIDED CATALOG

COMPOSER/PERFORMER

SUBJECT

Card 171 (MBr)

G R25m Ravel, Maurice, 1875-1937.
[Quartet, strings, F major]
Quartet in F major. Columbia, ML 5245.
1 s. 12" 33 1/3 rpm microgroove.

Budapest String Quartet (J. Roismann and
A. Schneider, violins; B. Kroyt, viola; M.
Schneider, 'cello)
Reverse side: Debussy. Quartet, strings,
G minor, op. 10.

Card 167

G R25m Budapest String Quartet.
Debussy, Claude, 1862-1918.
[Quartet, strings, G minor, op. 10]
Quartet in G minor, op. 10. Columbia,
ML 5245.

Card 172

Quartets (red)
Budapest String Quartet

Card 173 (MBr)

G R25m Quartets (red)
Debussy, Claude, 1862-1918.

Card 174 (MBr)

G R25m Ravel, Maurice, 1875-1937.
[Quartet, strings, F major]
Quartet in F major. Columbia, ML 5245.
1 s. 12" 33 1/3 rpm microgroove.

Budapest String Quartet (J. Roismann and
A. Schneider, violins; B. Kroyt, viola; M.
Schneider, 'cello)
Reverse side: Debussy. Quartet, strings,
G minor, op. 10.

Card 168

G R25m Budapest String Quartet.
Ravel, Maurice, 1875-1937.
[Quartet, strings, F major]
Quartet in F major. Columbia, ML 5245.
1 s. 12" 33 1/3 rpm microgroove.

Card 169

G R25m Debussy, Claude, 1862-1918.
[Quartet, strings, G minor, op. 10]
Quartet in G minor, op. 10. Columbia,
ML 5245.
1 s. 12" 33 1/3 rpm microgroove.

Budapest String Quartet (J. Roismann and
A. Schneider, violins; B. Kroyt, viola; M.
Schneider, 'cello)
Reverse side: Ravel. Quartet, strings,
F major.

Card 170

Quartets (red)
Budapest String Quartet
Debussy, Claude, 1862-1918
[Quartet, strings, G minor, op. 10]

---

175 / 178

LP M[red]

MFm

Chopin, Frédéric Francois
[Concerto, piano, no. 2, op. 21, F min]
Piano concerto No. 2 in F minor, Opus 21.
Vox PL–7100, 1951
1½ s. 12 in. 33⅓ rpm.

Guiomar Novaes, piano; Vienna Symphony Orchestra; Otto Klemperer, conductor.

Side 2: his Fantasy, op. 49, F minor.

---

176 / 179

A. Chopin. Fantasy, op. 49, F minor

---

177 / 180

LP

MFm

Chopin, Frédéric Francois
[Fantasy, op. 49, F min]
Fantasia in F minor, Op. 49   Vox PL–7100, 1951
½ s. 12 in. 33⅓ rpm.

Guiomar Novaes, piano; Vienna Symphony Orchestra; Otto Klemperer, conductor.
[red]
(On side 2 of his Concerto, piano, no. 2, op. 21, F minor)

175

Beethoven, Ludwig van, 1770–1827.
[Symphony, no. 3, op. 55, Eb major] *Phonodisc.*

Symphony, no. 3, in E-flat major, op. 55 (Eroica) Columbia ML 4228. [¹1949]
2 s. 12 in. 33⅓ rpm. microgroove. (Columbia masterworks)
Philharmonic-Symphony Orchestra of New York; Bruno Walter, conductor.
Program notes on slipcase.

1. Symphonies.   I. Philharmonic-Symphony Society of New York. II. Walter, Bruno, 1876–

R A 55–176

176

Schubert, Franz Peter, 1797–1828.
[Symphony, D. 759, B minor] *Phonodisc.*

Symphony no. 8, in B minor, "Unfinished." Vanguard VRS–445. [1954]

1 s. 12 in. 33⅓ rpm. (Vanguard recordings for the connoisseur)
Vienna State Opera Orchestra; Felix Prohaska, conductor.
Recorded in the Brahmssaal of the Musik Verein, Vienna, 1953. Microgroove.
Program notes by S. W. Bennett on slipcase.
With: Mozart, J. C. W. A. Symphony, K. 550, G minor.

1. Symphonies.   I. Vienna. Operntheater. Orchester.   II. Prohaska, Felix.

R 54–444

177

Mozart, Johann Chrysostom Wolfgang Amadeus, 1756–1791.
[Symphony, K. 550, G minor] *Phonodisc.*

Symphony no. 40, in G minor, K. 550. Vanguard VRS–445. [1954]

1 s. 12 in. 33⅓ rpm. (Vanguard recordings for the connoisseur)
Vienna State Opera Orchestra; Felix Prohaska, conductor.
Recorded in the Brahmssaal of the Musik Verein, Vienna, 1953. Microgroove.
Program notes by S. W. Bennett on slipcase.
With: Schubert, F. P. Symphony, D. 759, B minor.

1. Symphonies—To 1800.   I. Vienna. Operntheater. Orchester.   II. Prohaska, Felix.

R 54–445

Library of Congress   [1]

Menotti, Gian Carlo, 1911–
[Amahl and the night visitors. Selections; arr.]

Highlights from Amahl and the night visitors. RCA Victor ERA–120. [1952?]

2 s. 7 in. 45 rpm.

Title from slipcase.

Soloists, chorus, and orchestra; Thomas Schippers, conductor.

"Recorded under the personal direction of Mr. Menotti, with the original cast of the NBC television production. Extended play."

Synopsis on slipcase.

CONTENTS.—Don't cry, mother dear.—Entrance of the Kings, march.—Have you seen a child?—Shepherds' chorus.—All that gold—Shepherds' dance.

1. Operas—Excerpts. I. Schippers, Thomas. II. Title: Amahl and the night visitors.

R 53–603

181
184

Händel, Georg Friedrich, 1685–1759.
[Utrecht Te Deum] *Phonodisc.*

Utrecht Te Deum. Coronation anthem, Let thy hand be strengthened. Haydn Society HSL 2046. [°1952]

2 s. 12 in. 33⅓ rpm.

Ruth Guldbaek, Valborg Garde, soprano; Else Brems, Dagmar Schou, alto; Ole Walbom, Volmer Holbøll, tenor; Einar Nørby, bass; Søren Sørenson, organ; Chorus of the Danish State Radio; Chamber Orchestra of the Danish State Radio; Mogens Wöldike, conductor.

Recorded in the concert hall of the Danish State Radio Building, Copenhagen, Dec. 1951.

Duration: 39 min.

Microgroove.

(Continued on next card)

182
185

Händel, Georg Friedrich, 1685–1759.
[Utrecht Te Deum] *Phonodisc.*

Utrecht Te Deum … (Card 2)

Program notes by Karl Geiringer on slipcase.

1. Choruses, Sacred (Mixed voices) with orchestra—To 1800. 2. Te Deum laudamus (Music) I. Händel, Georg Friedrich, 1685–1759. Coronation anthems. Let thy hand be strengthened. II. Statsradiofoniens kor, Copenhagen. III. Statsradiofoniens symfoniorkester, Copenhagen. IV. Wöldike, Mogens. V. Title. VI. Title: Coronation anthem, Let thy hand be strengthened. VII. Title: Let thy hand be strengthened.

Library of Congress [a55b1]

R 54–748

183
186

Widor, Charles Marie, 1845–1937.
[Symphonies, organ. Selections; arr.]

Six movements from the organ symphonies. Adapted and arr. by Stanley E. Saxton. [n. p.] H. Flammer [1960]

35 p. 31 cm.

1. Symphonies (Organ)—Excerpts, Arranged. 2. Organ music, Arranged.

M12.W49S98

M 61–147

Puccini, Giacomo, 1858–1924.
[Turandot. Italian] *Phonodisc.*

Turandot. [The last duet and the finale] completed by Alfano. London OSA 1308 (OS. 25068–25070) [1959]

6 s. 12 in. 33⅓ rpm. microgroove. stereophonic.

Starring Inge Borkh, Renata Tebaldi, sopranos, and Mario del Monaco, tenor, with supporting soloists; Chorus and Orchestra of the Accademia di santa Cecilia, Rome; Alberto Erede, conductor. Automatic sequence.

Program notes and synopsis by Dyneley Hussey and libretto by Giuseppe Adami and Renato Simoni, with English translation (20 p.) laid in container.

(Continued on next card)

Puccini, Giacomo, 1858–1924.
[Turandot. Italian] *Phonodisc.*

Turandot. (Card 2)

1. Operas. I. Alfano, Franco, 1876– II. Borkh, Inge. III. Tebaldi, Renata. IV. Monaco, Mario del. V. Rome (City) Accademia di santa Cecilia. Coro. VI. Rome (City) Accademia di santa Cecilia. Orchestra stabile. VII. Erede, Alberto, 1910– VIII. Puccini, Giacomo, 1857–1924. Turandot. Libretto. English & Italian. IX. Title.

Library of Congress [1]

R 59–924

Mozart, Johann Chrysostom Wolfgang Amadeus, 1756–1791.
[Works, chorus. Selections] *Phonodisc.*
Motets. (Card 2)
CONTENTS—Continued.
tus sit Deus, K. 66ᵃ (117)—Benedicite angeli, from Convertentur sedentes, by L. Mozart.—Offertorium de B. V. Maria: Alma Dei creatoris, K. 272ᵃ (277)—Regina coeli laetare, K. 321ᵇ (276)
1. Offertories (Music) 2. Graduals (Music) 3. Part-songs, Sacred—To 1800. I. Raugel, Felix, 1881– II. Mozart, Leopold, 1719–1787. Convertentur sedentes. Benedecite angeli. (Series)
R 54—1043

190
187

G
L827m
Loewe, Frederick, 1904–
[My fair lady. Selections] *Phonodisc.*
My fair lady. Book, and lyrics: Alan Jay Lerner. Columbia OL 5090. [1956]
2 s. 12 in. 33⅓ rpm. microgroove. (Columbia masterworks)
Starring Rex Harrison and Julie Andrews, with chorus and orchestra; Franz Allers, conductor.
Program notes by George B. Dale on slipcase.
1. Musical revues, comedies, etc. I. Harrison, Rex. II. Andrews, Julie. III. Title.
R 56—227

191
188

Hoffnung Interplanetary Music Festival, *London, 1958.*
Hoffnung Interplanetary Music Festival, 1958. [*Phonodisc*] Angel Records ANG. 35800. [1959]
2 s. 12 in. 33⅓ rpm. microgroove.
As presented by Gerard Hoffnung with various vocal and instrumental groups, at the Royal Festival Hall, Nov. 2–22, 1958.
Program notes ([8] p.) inserted in slipcase.
1. Vocal music. 2. Instrumental music. 3. Wit and humor, Musical. I. Hoffnung, Gerard.
Library of Congress [1]
R 59—1534

192
189

G
H41m
Haydn, Joseph, 1732–1809.
[Mass, C major (1782?)] *Phonodisc.*
Missa Sanctae Caeciliae. Haydn Society HSL 2028. [1951]
4 s. 12 in. 33⅓ rpm.
Serial no. on album cover: HSLP 2028.
Rosl Schwaiger, soprano; Sieglinde Wagner, alto; Herbert Handt, tenor; Walter Berry, bass; Akademie Chorus of Vienna; Vienna Symphony Orchestra; Hans Gillesberger, conductor.
Recorded in the Mozartsaal of the Konzerthaus, Vienna, Dec. 1950. Microgroove. Automatic sequence.

G
H41m
Haydn, Joseph, 1732–1809.
[Mass, C major (1782?)] *Phonodisc.*
Missa Sanctae Caeciliae. (Card 2)
Program notes by H. C. Robbins Landon on album cover. Text, with English translation (leaf laid in)
1. Masses—To 1800. I. Schwaiger, Rosl. II. Wagner, Sieglinde. III. Handt, Herbert. IV. Berry, Walter. V. Akademie-Kammerchor, Vienna. VI. Wiener Symphoniker. VII. Gillesberger, Hans. VIII. Title.
Full name: Franz Joseph Haydn.
R 54—771
Library of Congress [1]

Mozart, Johann Chrysostom Wolfgang Amadeus, 1756–1791.
[Works, chorus. Selections] *Phonodisc.*
Motets. Haydn Society AS-G (AS-34) [1954]
(L'Anthologie sonore, v. 7, record 4)
2 s. 12 in. 33⅓ rpm.
Soloists, chorus, and orchestra of L'Anthologie sonore; Maurice Duruflé, organ; Félix Raugel, conductor.
Program notes on slipcase.
CONTENTS.—Offertorium de tempore: misericordias Domini, K. 205ᵃ (222)—Graduale ad festum B. Maria virginis: Sancta Maria mater Dei, K. 273.—Lacrymosa, K. 93ᶜ (Anh. 21)—Jubilate, from Benedic-
(Continued on next card)
[a54b1]
R 54—1043

Grimes, Anne, comp.

Ballads of Ohio. [Phonodisc] Folkways Records FH 5217. [1957]

2 s. 12 in. 33⅓ rpm. microgroove.

Title on slipcase; Ohio State ballads.
Sung by the compiler, with dulcimer acc.
Program notes by the compiler, edited by Kenneth S. Goldstein, and texts ([16] p.) inserted in slipcase.

1. Folk-songs, American—Ohio. 2. Ballads, American—Ohio.
I. Title. II. Title: Ohio State ballads.

R 58-214

Library of Congress [1]

193

African tribal music and dances. [Phonodisc] Esoteric ES-513. [1952]

2 s. 12 in. 33⅓ rpm.

Sonar Senghor and his troupe.
"The instruments used in this recording are called: tama, banta, tcha tcha, gamba, tin tin, baba, and sabar."
Recorded Sept. 1952.
Microgroove.
Program notes by Jerry Newman on slipcase.
CONTENTS.—Sicco.—Toffi.—Ibonga.—Gnoubi gnibi.—Dianka bl.—Sibi saba.—Sindhio.—Didrenouo.—Bonomollo.—Sammsamounn.—Sougnou mbtaye.—Ndolo.—Sabar.—Badunde.—Ndonga.—Changoo.—Sammsamounn.—Mbtalaya.—Miva.

1. Folk-songs, African. 2. Dance music, African. I. Senghor, Sonar.

R 54-313

Library of Congress [1]

194

Hawkins, Coleman.

Coleman Hawkins, a documentary. [Phonodisc] Riverside RLP 12-117—12-118. [1956?]

4 s. 12 in. 33⅓ rpm. microgroove. (Jazz archives series)

"The life and times of a great jazzman, newly recorded in his own words."
Automatic sequence.
Notes concerning the recording, made during the summer of 1956, on slipcase.

1. Jazz music—U. S. 2. Jazz musicians. I. Title.

R 61-625

195

Badings, Henk, 1907–

[Works, concrete music. Selections] Phonodisc.

Capriccio for violin and other works. Epic BC 1118. [1961]

2 s. 12 in. 33⅓ rpm. microgroove. stereophonic.

Title from slipcase.
Electronic music derived from apparatus in the Philips studios, Eindhoven, Holland.
Program notes by Badings and Dick Raaijmakers on slipcase.
Includes Contrasts, by Dick Raaijmakers (4 min., 48 sec.)
CONTENTS.—Capriccio for violin and two sound tracks (7 min., 25 sec.)—Genese, music for five audio-frequency oscillators (9 min., 57 sec.)—Evolutions, ballet suite (13 min., 47 sec.)

1. Concrete music. 2. Violin music. 3. Suites (Concrete music) I. Raaijmakers, Dick. Tweeklank.

R 60-1397

[1]

196

Fassett, James H

Music and bird songs. [Sounds from nature with commentary and analysis. Phonodisc] Cornell University Records CH 973. [195-]

2 s. 10 in. 33⅓ rpm. microgroove.

Re-recorded from the intermission broadcast of the Philharmonic-Symphony Orchestra of New York, May 25, 1952.
Includes "the voices of ten birds and six frogs ... at their natural speed; then some are slowed down, as much as eight times."
Descriptive notes on slipcase.

1. Bird-song. 2. Sound production by animals. 3. Frogs. I. Title.

R 61-361

Library of Congress [1]

197

Chaucer, Geoffrey, *d.* 1400.
The pardoner's prologue and tale. The nun's priest's tale.
[*Phonodisc*] Caedmon TC–1008. [1952]

2 s. 12 in. 33⅓ rpm. microgroove.

Read in Middle English by Robert Ross.
From the author's Canterbury tales.
Descriptive notes on slipcase. Text of portions recorded ([15] p.)
inserted in slipcase.

I. Ross, Robert. II. Title. III. Title: The nun's priest's tale.

R A 55–275

California. Univ. Libr
for Library of Congress   [1]

198

199

Yeats, William Butler, 1865–1939.
The only jealousy of Emer. [A poetic play for masked
dancers with original] music by Lou Harrison. Esoteric
ES–506. [195–]
2 s. 12 in. 33⅓ rpm.
"This performance ... is based upon one given by students and in-
structors in the Summer Workshop in Dance and Drama at Reed Col-
lege in Oregon in the summer of 1949. Double casts were employed,
speaking voices were located in the pit, the masked dancers on the stage."
The music is performed by flute, violoncello, celesta, piano, and
double bass, the composer conducting.
Recorded Feb. 1951.
Microgroove.
Program notes by Barry Ulanov and synopsis on slipcase.
I. Harrison, Lou,   1917–   The only jealousy of
Emer. II. Title.

R 54–539

Library of Congress   [1]

PHONODISC

Pd 4   MBSi
(red)   Folk music lecture. [Phonodisc] Folkways Records FD 2A   c1956.
2s. 7in. 33⅓rpm.   microgroove.

To illustrate article Folk music, by Moses
Asch. Music Library Association. Notes, Dec. 1956,
p.29–32.

Folk music

200–
201

PHONODISC

Pd 4   Folk music. (red)   MBSi
(red)   Folk music lecture.

For further information see
Folk music lecture.

202

Fiction

Mutiny on the Bounty.

Nordhoff, Charles Bernard, 1887–
Mutiny on the Bounty, by Charles Nordhoff and James Norman Hall. [*Phonodisc.*] Washington, Library of Congress; manufactured by American Foundation for the Blind, New York. AFB 57–388—57–400.
26 s. 12 in. 33⅓ rpm. microgroove.

213

Fiction

Madden, Donald.

Nordhoff, Charles Bernard, 1887–

212

Fiction

Hall, James Norman, 1887–1951, joint author.

Nordhoff, Charles Bernard, 1887–
Mutiny on the Bounty, by Charles Nordhoff and James Norman Hall. [*Phonodisc.*] Washington, Library of Congress; manufactured by American Foundation for the Blind, New York. AFB 57–388—57–400.
26 s. 12 in. 33⅓ rpm. microgroove.

211

Fiction

BLIGH, WILLIAM, 1754–1817—FICTION.

Nordhoff, Charles Bernard, 1887–
Mutiny on the Bounty, by Charles Nordhoff and James Norman Hall. [*Phonodisc.*] Washington, Library of Congress; manufactured by American Foundation for the Blind, New York. AFB 57–388—57–400.
26 s. 12 in. 33⅓ rpm. microgroove.

210

Fiction

BOUNTY (SHIP)

Nordhoff, Charles Bernard, 1887–
Mutiny on the Bounty, by Charles Nordhoff and James Norman Hall. [*Phonodisc.*] Washington, Library of Congress; manufactured by American Foundation for the Blind, New York. AFB 57–388—57–400.

209

Fiction

Nordhoff, Charles Bernard, 1887–
Mutiny on the Bounty, by Charles Nordhoff and James Norman Hall. [*Phonodisc.*] Washington, Library of Congress; manufactured by American Foundation for the Blind, New York. AFB 57–388—57–400.
26 s. 12 in. 33⅓ rpm. microgroove.
Talking book, solely for the use of the blind.
Donald Madden, reader.
Edition used for the recording: Boston, Little, Brown, 1932. Recorded in 1957.
Manual sequence.
1. Bounty (Ship) 2. Bligh, William, 1754–1817—Fiction. I. Hall, James Norman, 1887–1951, joint author. II. Madden, Donald. III. Title.

Library of Congress

T B 57–127

208

207 206 205 204 203

TALKING BOOKS
FOR THE BLIND

329

Candidates 1960.

Sevareid, Arnold Eric, 1912– *ed.*
Candidates 1960; behind the headlines in the presidential race. [*Phonodisc.*] Washington, Library of Congress; manufactured by American Foundation for the Blind, New York. AFB 59–1301—59–1315.

329

Cannon, John, 1921–

Sevareid, Arnold Eric, 1912– *ed.*
Candidates 1960; behind the headlines in the presidential race. [*Phonodisc.*] Washington, Library of Congress; manufactured by American Foundation for the Blind, New York. AFB 59–1301—59–1315.

329

CAMPAIGN LITERATURE, 1960.

Sevareid, Arnold Eric, 1912– *ed.*
Candidates 1960; behind the headlines in the presidential race. [*Phonodisc.*] Washington, Library of Congress; manufactured by American Foundation for the Blind, New York. AFB 59–1301—59–1315.

329

PRESIDENTS—U. S.—ELECTION—1960.

Sevareid, Arnold Eric, 1912– *ed.*
Candidates 1960; behind the headlines in the presidential race. [*Phonodisc.*] Washington, Library of Congress; manufactured by American Foundation for the Blind, New York. AFB 59–1301—59–1315.

329

Sevareid, Arnold Eric, 1912– *ed.*
Candidates 1960; behind the headlines in the presidential race. [*Phonodisc.*] Washington, Library of Congress; manufactured by American Foundation for the Blind, New York. AFB 59–1301—59–1315.
30 s. 12 in. 33⅓ rpm. microgroove.
Talking book, solely for the use of the blind.
John Cannon, reader.
Edition used for the recording: New York, Basic Books [1959] Recorded in 1959.
Manual sequence.
1. Presidents—U. S.—Election—1960. 2. Campaign literature, 1960. I. Sevareid, Arnold Eric, 1912– II. Cannon, John, 1921– III. Title.

Library of Congress

T B 60–31

PHONOTAPES

---

1 CU

TS47

Mozart, Johann Chrysostom Wolfgang Amadeus, 1756-1791.
  ₍Serenade, wood-winds & 2 horns, K.384a (388) C minor₎ Phonotape.
  Serenade in C minor, K.388. Berkeley, Calif., University of California, Department of Music, 1953.
  1 reel (7 in.) 7 1/2 in. per sec.

  Plastic; single track.
  For 2 oboes, 2 clarinets, 2 horns, and 2 bassoons.
  Members of the University of California Symphony; David Boyden, conductor.

(See next card)

216   214

---

2 CU

TS47

Mozart, Johann Chrysostom Wolfgang Amadeus, 1756-1791.
  ₍Serenade, wood-winds & 2 horns, K.384a (388) C minor₎ Phonotape. (Card 2)
  Serenade in C minor, K.388. 1953.

  Recorded from the Artists concert broadcast, April 17, 1953, by radio station KPFA, Berkeley, Calif.

₍TS = 7" reel₎

  1. Suites (2 bassoons, 2 clarinets, 2 horns, 2 oboes) - To 1800. I. California. University, Berkeley. Orchestra. II. Boyden, David Dodge, 1910-   III. California. University, Berkeley. Department of   Music.

217

CU

TS58

Shifrin, Seymour, 1926-
  ₍Quartet, strings₎
  String quartet. ₍Berkeley, Calif., University of California, Department of Music, 1953₎
  1 reel (7 in.) 7 1/2 ips.

  Plastic tape; single track.
  Nathan Rubin, Gerald Ogle, violin; Helen Best, viola; Helen Stross, violoncello.
  Recorded from the KPFA broadcast, June 9, 1953.

  1. String quartets. I. Rubin, Nathan.
  II. Ogle, Gerald. III. Best, Helen.
  IV. Stross, Helen

CU-Mu 53-631   23 Jun 53

215   218

MiU

TAPE
RGP
144

Piston, Walter, 1894-
  ₍Concerto, viola₎ Phonotape.
  Concerto for viola and orchestra. New York, American International Music Fund.
  2/3 reel (7 in.) 7½ in. per sec. (The Recording guarantee project, season 1957-58)
  Title from publisher's catalog.
  Joseph de Pasquale, viola; Boston Symphony Orchestra; Charles Munch, conductor.
  Plastic; single track.
  With this is: Warren, E.R. Crystal lake.

MiU

TAPE
RGP
144

Warren, Elinor Remick, 1906-
  ₍Crystal Lake₎ Phonotape.
  Crystal Lake. New York, American International Music Fund.
  1/3 reel (7 in.) 7 1/2 in. per sec. (The Recording guarantee project, season 1958-59)
  Title from publisher's catalog.
  Indianapolis Symphony Orchestra; Izler Solomon, conductor.
  Plastic; single track.
  With: Piston, Walter. Concerto, viola.

PHONOTAPES

219
222

Healey, Denis Winston, 1917-
The crisis of the Western alliance.
[Phonotape] Wellesley College, 1961.
1 reel 7in. 3 3/4 ft. per sec. (Barnette Miller Foundation lecture)

Lecture given at Wellesley College, Feb. 21, 1961.

MWelC

(DIVIDED CATALOG: AUTHOR/TITLE)

220
223

T 3
Healey, Denis Winston, 1917-
The crisis of the Western alliance.
[Phonotape] Wellesley College, 1961.
1 reel. 7in. 3 3/4 ft. per sec. (Barnette Miller Foundation lecture)

Lecture given at Wellesley College, Feb. 21, 1961.

MWelC

(POPE ROOM CATALOG)

221
224

1. North Atlantic Treaty Organization.
I. Title.

2TF1
De La Mare, Walter John, 1873-
[Walter De La Mare reading his own poems.
Phonotape] Toronto, Ross, Court & Co., 1955]
1 reel(5 in.) 7 1/2 in. per sec.

Phonotape copy of private recordings made for the author by His Master's Voice (O.B. 6132-O.B. 6135) in the possession of Ross, Court & Co.
Plastic tape; single track.
Collation of original discs: 8 s. 12 in.?
Contents.- A bunch of grapes.- The buckle.- Some.- The silver penny.- Nod.- England.- The song of shadows.- The mermaids.- Music.- All that's past.- Snowing.- Farewell.- Epitaph.

CU

2TF2
Kirkegaard, Preben
[The UN story. Phonotape. 1957]
2 reels(5 in.) 7 1/2 in. per sec.

Recording of an interview by Ruth Pennell Dec. 10, 1957, for a radio broadcast.
Plastic tape; single track.

[TF = 5" reel]

1. United Nations. I. Pennell, Ruth. II. Title.

CU

2TS1
Menander, of Athens.
Dyskolus. [Phonotape] Ardmore, Pa., Taben Recordings [1959?]
1 reel(7 in.) 3 3/4 in. per sec.

Translated into English and narrated by L.A. Post.
Plastic; dual track.

["2" precedes nonmusic]

1. Greek drama. 2. Drama readings. I. Post, Levi Arnold, 1889- II. Title.

CU

XI.   Shelf list (1-96)

    A. Official record

        1. Inventory record

            a. Accession and/or copy/volume number: access through Index
            b. Missing and withdrawn records (27,36)
        2. Business information (46,55,62,87,92)
        3. Statement of holdings for series and serials (2-3,6,53,59,64-65,67)
        4. Authority record for fiction, juvenile works, etc. with tracing of references (47-48)

    B. Types of entries: LC/Wilson/typed, etc. cards: unit card vs. brief styles

        1. Monographs and serials
        2. Biography: subject headings for individual biography (18,38,44-45)
        3. Nonbook materials, etc.: comparative arrangements (68-96)
            a. Art photographs and slides (68-73)
            b. Films and filmstrips (74-76)
            c. Microfilms and microcard (77-80)
            d. Broadside (81)
            e. Maps (82-83)
            f. Phonorecords (84-92)
            g. Works for the blind (93-96)
                (1) Talking books (93-94)
                (2) Books in raised characters (95-96)

    C. Call numbers vs. numerical notation vs. location designation

        1. Class numbers
            a. DDC:16 vs. DDC:8, abridged (1-31,33-46,74,82,93,95-96)
            b. LCC (52-56,58-59,62-67,79-80,83)
            c. NLMC (57,60-61)
            d. Other (68-73,75-78,81,84-92)
         2. Book numbers: Cutter vs. LC
            a. Use vs. omission vs. substitutes
            b. Biography: individual vs. collective (18,20,38-42,44-46,96) see also App. A
            c. Fiction (31,33-34,36-38 vs. 32,49,94)
            d. Bible: see App. A
            e. Voluminous authors: see VIII-C; App. A
            f. LC notation (52-56,58-59,62-67,79-80,83)

    D. Reference works: interfiled vs. separated vs. duplicated

    E. Shelflisting for branches (49-51) see also App. C

016.82309
C128c   **California. University.** *University at Los Angeles. Library.*
      College life, an exhibit of the English university novel,
1749–1954, UCLA Library, October 14–November 8, 1959.
₍Los Angeles? 1959₎

1

020.5
C28   **American Library Association.** Division of Cataloging and Classification.
      Catalogers' and classifiers' yearbook. no. ₍1₎–11; 1929–45. Chicago.
      11 no.

no. 1 52225	no. 4 60067	no. 9 72890
91849 cop 2	5 1885	4995 cop 2
2 51027	6 3243	10 3930
385 cop 2	7 5218	5376 cop 2
3 5851	8 8821	11 82457
6842 cop 2		

2

020.5
L616   **Library resources & technical services.**
      Library has:

      v. 1–3   winter 1957 – fall 1958
      v. 3–4   1959 –   1960

3

020.58 **American** library annual.   1955/56–   Bowker 1956–

        v

12-28-56

4

LSR
020.92
W62   **Who's** who in library service; a biographical directory of
professional librarians of the United States and Canada.
3d ed. Dorothy Ethlyn Cole, editor. Prepared under the
direction of the Council on Who's Who in Library Service
for the School of Library Service, Columbia University.
New York, Grolier Society, 1955.

      xxiii, 546 p. 26 cm.

      1. Librar
     II. Columbi

Z720.A4U

Library of

5

025.305
Un3c   **U. S.** *Library of Congress. Processing Dept.*
      Cataloging service. Bulletin 1–*56*
June 1945– *Apr 1961*
Washington.

      56 no. 27 cm. irregular.

      1. Cataloging. 2. Catalogs, Card. I. Title.

    Z695.U437   ◯   025.305   49—238*
    Library of Congress   ₍62i1₎

6

025.33
Sel7*l*

Sears, Minnie Earl, 1873–1933.

    List of subject headings for small libraries, compiled from lists used in nine representative small libraries, edited by Minnie Earl Sears. New York, The H. W. Wilson company; London, Grafton & co., 1923.

    xii, 183 p. 26½ᵐ.

41376

025.33
Sel7*l*2

Sears, Minnie Earl, 1873–1933.

    List of subject headings for small libraries, compiled from lists used in nine representative small libraries, edited by Minnie Earl Sears. 2d ed., rev. and enl. New York, The H. W. Wilson company, 1926.

    x p., 1 l., 415 p. 26 cm.

    "First edition 1923."

78109

025.33
Sel7*l*3

Sears, Minnie Earl, 1873–1933.

    List of subject headings for small lists used in nine representative s Minnie Earl Sears. 3d ed., rev. a section, Practical suggestions for heading work. New York, The H. W

    xxviii, 453 p. 26 cm.

    "Practical suggestions for the beginn issued also separately with cover-title.

81966

025.33
Sel7*l*4

Sears, Minnie Earl, 1873–1933.

    List of subject headings for small tical suggestions for the beginner edited by Minnie Earl Sears. 4th e of decimal classification numbers, by New York, The H. W. Wilson comp

    2 p. l., ₍iii₎–xxvi, 516 p. 26 cm.

    "Directions for use" on lining-paper.
    Note on slip inserted between pages iv
85817
    8 cop 2
    1. Subject headings. 2. Classification, Stevenson.
86014   3 (1941)
    Library of Congress   Z695.S4
    ₍50t²3₎

025.33
Sel7*l*5

Sears, Minnie Earl, 1873–1933.

    List of subject headings for small libraries, including Practical suggestions for the beginner in subject heading work, edited by Minnie Earl Sears. 5th ed., with the addition of decimal classification numbers by Isabel Stevenson Monro. New York, The H. W. Wilson company, 1944.

    xxviii, 536 p. 26 cm.

    "Directions for use" on lining-paper.

    cop 1⁄2

025.33
Sel7*l*6

Sears, Minnie Earl, 1873–1933.

    List of subject headings. 6th ed. by Bertha Margaret Frick. With Practical suggestions for the beginner in subject heading work, by Minnie Earl Sears. New York, H. W. Wilson Co., 1950.

025.33
Sel7*l*7

Sears, Minnie Earl, 1873–1933.

    List of subject headings; with Practical suggestions for the beginner in subject heading work. 7th ed. by Bertha Margaret Frick. New York, H. W. Wilson Co., 1954.

025.33
Sel7*l*8

Sears, Minnie Earl, 1873–1933.

    List of subject headings; with Suggestions for the beginner in subject heading work. 8th ed. by Bertha Margaret Frick. New York, Wilson, 1959.

    610 p. 27 cm.

    "First–fifth editions had title: List of subject headings for small libraries."

    1. Subject headings. 2. Classification, Decimal. ɪ. Frick, Bertha Margaret, 1894– ed.

    Z695.S43 1959   025.33   59–6607

    Library of Congress   ₍30₎

027.7   Lyle, Guy **R**
       The administration of the college library ₍by₎ Guy R.

15

JR
028.5
Am35s   **American Library Association.** *Editorial Committee.*
       Subject and title index to short stories for children. Com-
piled by a subcommittee; Julia F. Carter, chairman. Chicago, American Library Association, 1955.

     vi, 833 p.   25 cm.

     cop 1
       2   Adult

16

R
032
En19   The Encyclopaedia Britannica; a new survey of
      universal knowledge.   Chicago ₍c1959₎
      24v.

17

73719	v. 1	73725	v. 7	73731	v.13	73737	v.19
20	v. 2	6	v. 8	2	v.14	8	v.20
1	v. 3	7	v. 9	3	v.15	9	v.21
2	v. 4	8	v.10	4	v.16	40	v.22
3	v. 5	9	v.11	5	v.17	1	v.23
4	v. 6	30	v.12	6	v.18	2	v.24

131.34092   FREUD, SIGMUND, 1865–1939.
F895d   ₍Doolittle, Hilda₎ 1886–1961.
       Tribute to Freud, by H. D.   With unpublished letters by

18–
19

194
D453*l*   **Lefèvre, Roger,** *of Grenoble.*
       Le criticisme de Descartes.   ₍1. éd.₎   Paris, Presses univer-
sitaires de France, 1958.

     340 p.   23 cm.   (Bibliothèque de philosophie contemporaine. His-
toire de la philosophie et philosophie générale)

hical footnotes.

es, René, 1596–1650.   2. Criticism (Philosophy)

A 59—4195

iv.   Libr.   B1878
Congress   ₍60c2₎

354.42092
Sm97   **Smyth,** *Sir* **John George,** *bart.,* 1893–
       The only enemy; an autobiography.   London, Hutchin-
son ₍1959₎

371.42   Forrester, Gertrude, 1895-
      Occupational literature; an annotated bibliography. 1958 ed.
Wilson, H.W. 1958
     603p

     cop 1
       2   Reference

20–
21

     1   Occupations—Bibliography   2 Professions—Bibliography   ɪ Title
                                                             371.42

     58W2528   (W)   The H. W. Wilson Company

378.73   **American** universities and colleges. 1st-   ed.   American Council on Education 1928-

v

22

378.7446
Si47m   Mark, Kenneth Lamartine, 1874-1958.
     Delayed by fire, being the early history of
Simmons College. ⌐Concord, N. H.⌐ Priv. print.
⌐Rumford Press⌐ 1945.

23

539.721
L   **Lock, W**   **O**
       High energy nuclear physics.   London, Methuen; New
York, Wiley ⌐1960⌐

629.28   New York University. Division of General Education. Center for Safety Education
     Man and the motor car. 6th ed. Prentice-Hall 1959

24-
26

690.5
Ar25   Architectural & engineering news.
     v. 1-
     Nov./Dec. 1958-
     ⌐New York, Hagen Pub. Co.⌐

711.517446
B657+   Boston. City Planning Board.
     Proposed zoning; a report. Boston, 1958.

     cop 1
       2   Msg 5/24/60 (hll)   (pencil)

750.3   **Encyclopedia** of painting; painters and painting of the world
from prehistoric times to the present day; Bernard S.
Myers, editor. Contributing associates: Milton W. Brown
⌐and others⌐. Crown 1955

27-
29

759.13
Sa32w   **Whitney Museum of American Art,** *New York.*
     Attilio Salemme. ⌐Exhibition. Whitney Museum of
American Art, April 14–May 30, 1959. Boston, Institute
of Contemporary Art, 1959⌐
     unpaged. illus. 20 cm.

     1. Salemme, Attilio, 1911–1955.   I. Boston. Institute of Con-
temporary Art.

ND237.S2W47   759.13   59–3337

Library of Congress   ⌐2⌐

808.82 The best plays of 1959-1960; the Bur
        ed. by Louis Kronenberger; illus. w
        with drawings by Hirschfeld. Dodd
        435p illus

jr 808.83 **American Library Association**
        Subject and title index to short stor
        piled by a subcommittee of the A.L.A.
        Julia F. Carter, Chairman. A.L.A. 19
        333p

        cop 1
             2 Adult

        59W5,442   ◯   (W)

Haycraft, Howard, 1905-   ed.
    Treasury of great mysteries; ed. by Howard Haycraft and
John Beecroft. Simon & Schuster 1957
    2v

813
C786Yn   **New York State Historical Association.**
              James Fenimore Cooper, a re-appraisal. Cooperstown,
          N. Y., 1954.

813
K672m   Klein, Charles, 1867-1915.
             The music master; novelized from the play as
         produced by David Belasco; illus. with scenes
         from the photoplay, a William Fox production.
         New York, Grosset & Dunlap ₁1909₎

821
R349   Rhymes without reason, with reasons for rhyming;
         to which are added two prose essays. By the au-
         thor of no other publication!!! London, Rodwell &
         Martin, 1823.

◯

823
L165tam Lamb, Charles, 1775-1834.
            Tales from Shakespeare ₁by₎ Charles and Mary
        Lamb, edited by the Rev. Alfred Ainger, revised
        by H. Y. Moffett; illustrated by Maud and Miska
        Petersham. ₁New York₎ Macmillan ₁c1932₎

        ~~56892~~   Wdn 1/5/54 (LCC)
            3 cop 2
            4   3 Msd 11/26/55 (LCC)   (pencil)

SHELF LIST: DDC

823
L435   **Lawrence, David Herbert,** 1885–1930.
            Short novels. Phoenix ed. London
        2 v. 19 cm.
        CONTENTS.—v. 1. Love among the hayst
        fox. The captain's doll.—v. 2. St. Mawr.
        The man who died.

        Ohio State Univ. Libr.   ◯
        for Library of Congress   ₁59e5₎

843   HUGO, VICTOR MARIE, COMTE, 1802-1885.
H874Wm   **Maurois, André,** 1885–
             Olympio; the life of Victor Hugo; translated from the
         French by Gerard Hopkins. ₁1st American ed.₎ New York,
         Harper ₁1956₎
             xii, 498 p. illus., ports. 25 cm.
             Bibliography: p. 447–458.

             1. Hugo, Victor Marie, comte, 1802–1885.   ɪ. Title.
                Name originally: Émile Salomon Wilhelm Herzog.

         PQ2293.M353 1956a ◯   928.4   55—8026
         Library of Congress   ₁57v²20₎

293

920.073
B727d Bradford, Gamaliel, 1863-1932.
          Damaged souls. Boston, Houghton Mifflin, 1931.

R920
.073   Who's who of American women; a biographical dic-
W62   tionary of notable American women.

  R
920.7
W62   Who's who of American women; a biographical dic-
          tionary of notable living American women.
          v. 1-
          1958-59-
          Chicago, Marquis-Who's who.

39-
42

926.08
L529m Lehrburger, Egon, 1904-
          Men who changed the world; stor
       covery, by Egon Larsen ₁pseud. 2
       Publishers ₁1953₎

          224 p. illus. 22 cm.

          1. Inventors.   ɪ. Title.

          T39.L43   1953   926

          Library of Congress   ₁62r55v1

940.549
C153m Caniff, Milton Arthur, 1907-
          Male call ₁comic strip₎ The first complete
       collection of the uninhibited adventures of every
       GI's dream girl - Miss Lace. New, enl. ed. New
       York, Grosset & Dunlap ₁1959₎

948.905 FREDERIK IX, KING OF DENMARK, 1899-
F873Wp Palsbo, Susanne, ed.
          The daily life of the King of Denmark. Editors: Susanne
       Palsbo ₁and₎ Ernst Mentze. ₁Copenhagen? Press Dept. of

948.905092 FREDERIK IX, KING OF DENMARK, 1899-
F873p Palsbo, Susanne, ed.
          The daily life of the King of Denmark. Editors: Susanne
       Palsbo ₁and₎ Ernst Mentze. ₁Copenhagen? Press Dept. of
       the Ministry for Foreign Affairs, 1957.

          unpaged (chiefly illus.) 26 cm.

43-
45

          cop 1
            2

erik ɪx, King of Denmark, 1899-   ɪ. Mentze, Ernst,
ɪɪ. Title.

₃13   923.1489   58-37631 ‡

₁ Congress   ₍ᵇ₎

B
SMITH
       Handlin, Oscar, 1915-
          Al Smith and his America. ₁1st ed.₎ Boston, Little,
       Brown ₁1958₎

          207 p. 21 cm. (The Library of American biography)

          Includes bibliography.

       c 1   ALANAR   3.50

46

          1. Smith, Alfred Emanuel, 1873-1944.   ɪ. Title.

          E748.S63H16   923.273   57-6446 ‡

          Library of Congress   ₁30₎

SHELF LIST
AUTHORITY RECORD
FOR FICTION

47

```
O'Donovan, Michael                                    MFm




L.C. Catalog  Feb. 1956




see from  O'Connor, Frank, pseud.
                    ◯
```

48

```
                                                      HL

     Brown, Margaret Wise, 1910-1952

              x MacDonald, Golden, pseud.
              x Hay, Timothy, pseud.
                    EA
                    Braille
```

49

```
                                                    E
                                                    HL

  Brown, Margaret Wise, 1910-1952
     The little fireman.    c1938.
```

Main ✓	Sta.	A	F	N	V ✓
		B	T	P ✓	W ✓
Tape	X	C	K ✓	Q	Y
Braille		D ✓	L	R ✓	Z
Moon					
T.B.R.					

◯

50

```
     FIRE DEPARTMENTS
     Title
```

51

```
                                                    HL

              BRANCH SYMBOLS

     S    Stations

     X    Bookmobile

     D    Kailua

     K    Kaimuki

     L    Kaneohe

     P    Kalihi-Palama

     R    Wahiawa

     V    Waialua

     W    Waikiki

     Z    Waipahu
```

◯

HC101
.N45
    Challenge; the magazine of economic affairs. v. 1–
    Oct. 1952–
    ₍New York₎

        v. illus. 20 cm. monthly.

        Title varies: Oct. 1952–Jan. 1954, Challenge magazine.
        Published by the Institute of Economic Affairs, New York University.
    Supersedes the Institute's Popular economics
(Oct. 1950–June 1952)

        1. U. S.—Econ. condit.—Period.   ɪ. New York University. Institute of Economic Affairs.

    HC101.N533   330.5   55–36370

    Library of Congress   ₍5₎

52–
53

54

v.

    7 1958/59
    8 1959/60
    9 1960/61

LC1011
.F7   Freedom and the university; the responsibility of
        the university for the maintenance of freedom in
        the American way of life ₍by₎ Edgar N. Johnson
        ₍and others₎ Ithaca ₍N.Y.₎ Cornell University
        Press, 1950.

R
PC4625
.A4   Alemany y Bolufer, José, 1866–1934.
1954   La fuente; diccionario enciclopédico ilustrado
    de la lengua espanola. Barcelona, R. Sopena
    ₍1954₎

    cop 1 513155 St & H 15.00 Sp Dept
        2   6   "   "   "

55–
56

57

PG3237
.E5N3 Pushkin, Aleksandr Sergeevich, 1799–1837.
      Three Russian poets, selecti...
    Lermontov and Tyutchev in new t...
    Vladimir Nabokov. Norfolk, Co...
    ₍c1944₎

SAMPLE

QV
4
M685ya   MIYAZAKI, Saburō
1935   ₍Yakurigaku, yakugakusei no tame ni₎
      藥理学 藥学生 のために ₍Pharmacol-
      ogy for students₎ Tōkyō, Hakusen Shobō,
      1935.
        8, 11, 676, 43 p. illus., ports.
        1. Pharmacology
      QV4 M685ya   59–7858

      NATIONAL LIBRARY OF MEDICINE

RC321
.J6 **Journal** of clinical and experimental psychopathology &
quarterly review of psychiatry and neurology. v. 1–

July 1939–
ₜWashington, etc., MD Publications, etc.ₕ   58
        v. in   illus. 26 cm. quarterly.

    Official organ of the Association for the Advancement of Psycho-
therapy, July 1944–Apr. 1946.
    Title varies: July 1939–Apr. 1944, Journal of criminal psycho-
pathology.—July 1944–Apr. 1946, Journal of clinical psychopathology
and psychotherapy.—July 1946–Oct. 1950, Journal of clinical psychopathology.—Jan./Mar. 1951–   Journal of clinical and
experimental psychopathology.

                    (Continued on next card)
                                        43—16472*
                    ₜ60r55h1ₕ

cine.

    For statement of holdings, see CENTRAL SERIAL   59
        RECORD

    1. Psychiatry—Period.   ɪ. Branham, Vernon Carnegie, 1889–
ed. ɪɪ. Association for the Advancement of Psychotherapy. ɪɪɪ. Washington Institute of Medicine.

    RC321.J76   43—16472*

    Library of Congress   ₜ60r55h1ₕ

                                                                       60

W 1   Der LEBENSBERATER.
LE312   ₜ1-   Jahrg.ₕ 1957–
            Bern.
                v. illus.
            Supersedes Naturheilkunde.
            1. Naturopathy - Period.
            W1 LE312   59-3596

W   BRITISH Medical Association
21   The medical practitioners' handbook.
B862h   ₜNew & rev. ed.ₕ London, 1958.
1958   285 p.
                1. Medicine as a profession   Title
            W21 B862h   59-3380

                                                                       61

Z675
.U5W5
1956   **Wilson, Louis Round.**
            The university library; the organization, administration,
        and functions of academic libraries, by Louis Round Wilson
        and Maurice F. Tauber. 2d ed. New York, Columbia Uni-
        versity Press, 1956.   MEDICINE

            xiii, 641 p. diagrs., tables. 24 cm. (Columbia University studies
        in library service, no. 8)

            Includes bibliographies.

        11/1/56 B & T 6.00 LS

            1. Libraries, University and college.   ɪ. Tauber, Maurice Fal-
        colm, 1908–   joint author.   (Series)

            Z675.U5W745 1956   027.7   55—11184

            Library of Congress   ₜ59o²10ₕ
                                                                       62

Z731
.A5

American library & book trade annual. 1955/56–1961.
New York, R. R. Bowker.

6 v. 25 cm.

Title varies: 1955/56–1958, American library annual.—1959, American library annual and book trade almanac.

Sponsored by the Council of National Library Associations and the Library journal.

Editors: 1955/56–1961, W. E. Wright and the editorial staff of R. R. Bowker Company.

Vols. for 1958–1960 include indexes cumulative from 1955/56.

Continued by The Bowker annual of library and

book trade information, 1962–

1. Libraries—U. S.—Direct.   I. Wright, Wyllis Eaton, 1903– ed.   II. Bowker (R. R.) Company, firm, publishers, New York.   III. Council of National Library Associations.   IV. Library journal.

Z731.A47   020.58   55—12434
                                                 (PTO)

Library of Congress   [61r61z³30]

63

1955/56
1956/57
1957/58
1959
1960
1961

64

Z731
.A5
LIBRARY HAS:

The Bowker annual of library and book trade information

VOL. OR NO.	PERIOD COVERED			VOL. OR NO.	PERIOD COVERED		
	1962						

HOW ISSUED: annual

65

66

Z6673
.U515

U. S. *Public Health Service.*
Bibliography series. no. 1–
[Washington] 1951–

no. 23–26 cm. (*Its* Publication)

Title varies: no. 1–   Public health bibliography series.
Some no. in rev. editions.

67

Z6673
.U515

U. S. Public Health Service.
Bibliography series.

1	11	21	31	41
2	12	22	32	42
3	13	23	33	43
4	14	24	34	44
5	15	25	35	45
6	16	26	36	46
7	17	27	37	47
8	18	28	38	48
9 ✓	19	29	39	49
10	20	30	40	50

SHELF LIST

MBMu	
841 Ey3 Gel	Eyck, Jan van. Portrait of Giovanni Arnolfini and of Giovanna Cenani, his wife. London. National Gallery. 1434. 33 x 22 in.
4975 81258 9578	cop.1. Gift. 1900. Anderson 18063. cop.2. Craven Masterpieces of Art. 47. cop.3. Medici. 22 x 28 in. copy.

68   71

NONBOOK

MBMu

763
D1664
W1

American Sculpture
Dallin, Cyrus E. 1861-1944
The Appeal to the Great Spirit 1913
Bronze
Outside Museum of Fine Arts, Boston

2x2 Color
BB
30398

69   72

MATERIALS

MBMu

763
D1664
W1

American Sculpture
Dallin, Cyrus E. 1861-1944
The Appeal to the Great Spirit 1913
Bronze
Outside Museum of Fine Arts, Boston

Standard Color
MEC
34941

70   73

MH-FA

374.1
P 274
38Je

Patinir, Joachim de

St. Jerome in a rocky landscape

London, National Gallery, 4826

Photo: National Gallery

Photograph Fund

(buff)

---

neg.

MH-FA

374.1
P 274
38Je

Patinir, Joachim de

St. Jerome in a rocky landscape

London, National Gallery, 4826

Source: National Gallery
Photograph

MBMu

763 .D1 B5		Dallin, Cyrus Edwin. Appeal to the Great Spirit. Boston. Museum.	
15733	.1	cop.1. Front.	
9519	.1	cop.2.	
8952	.2	cop.1. Side.	17x21 in.
21008	.3	cop.1. Three quarter view.	
copy.			

**Film
919.1
In2**

Indonesia—new nation of Asia (*Motion picture*)   Encyclopædia Britannica Films, 1959.

16 min., sd., color, 16 mm.

With film guide.
Summary: An Indonesian teacher tells the story of his country. Traces the history of Indonesia from Dutch rule through independence; shows life in crowded cities and in the homes of village families; examines the natural resources, religions, art, and industries of the country, pointing out how the living standards are improving.
Credits: Collaborator, Peter Gosling.

—— Another issue.   b&w.

1. Indonesia.   I. Encyclopædia Britannica Films, inc.

74

919.1   Fi A 59–508

FILM

**F 1
(red)**   The Titan.   1950.   MBSi   75

FILMSTRIP

**FS4
(red)**   Reference materials.   1954.   MBSi   76

MICROFILM

**M 7
(red)**   Cutter, C.A.   MBSi

Rules for a dictionary catalogue; 2d ed. 1889.

MICROFILM

**M 24
(red)**   Oldham, E.M.   MBSi

Early women printers in the United States.

**Microfilm
Z715
.A5**   American Library Association.   Division of Cataloging and Classification.   Committee on Administration.
Multiple order forms used by American libraries, edited by Edwin B. Colburn.   Chicago, Microphotographic Laboratories, University of Chicago Libraries, 1949.
Microfilm copy (positive) of typescript in the University of Chicago Libraries.

77-
79

80

**Microcard
GN4
.M5**   **Microcard** publications of primary records in culture and personality.   v. 1–
Madison, Microcard Foundation, 1956–

v. (microcards) illus. 7½–12½ cm.

Editor: v. 1–   B. Kaplan.
"Under the sponsorship of the Committee on Primary Records, Division of Anthropology and Psychology, National Academy of Sciences-National Research Council."

1. Anthropology—Collections.   I. Kaplan, Bert, 1919–   ed.

Microcard GN4   Micp 56–30

Library of Congress   [2]

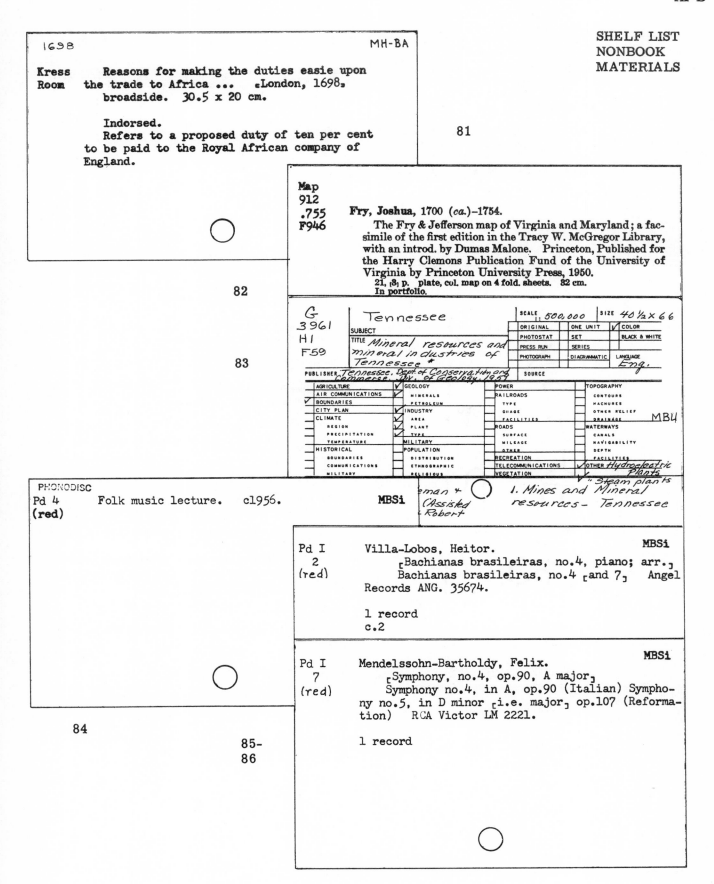

1698   MH-BA

Kress   Reasons for making the duties easie upon
Room   the trade to Africa ... ₍London, 1698₎
             broadside. 30.5 x 20 cm.

             Indorsed.
             Refers to a proposed duty of ten per cent
             to be paid to the Royal African company of
             England.

                                          81

82

Map
912
.755   Fry, Joshua, 1700 (ca.)–1754.
F946   The Fry & Jefferson map of Virginia and Maryland; a fac-
          simile of the first edition in the Tracy W. McGregor Library,
          with an introd. by Dumas Malone.   Princeton, Published for
          the Harry Clemons Publication Fund of the University of
          Virginia by Princeton University Press, 1950.
              21, ₍8₎ p.   plate, col. map on 4 fold. sheets.   82 cm.
              In portfolio.

G   Tennessee   SCALE 1:500,000   SIZE 40½ × 66
3961
H1   SUBJECT   ORIGINAL | ONE UNIT ✓ | COLOR
F59   TITLE Mineral resources and   PHOTOSTAT | SET | BLACK & WHITE
           mineral industries of   PRESS RUN | SERIES
83   Tennessee *   PHOTOGRAPH | DIAGRAMMATIC | LANGUAGE
           PUBLISHER Tennessee. Dept. of Conservation and   Eng.
                     Commerce. Div. of Geology. 1954   SOURCE

AGRICULTURE		GEOLOGY ✓		POWER		TOPOGRAPHY	
AIR COMMUNICATIONS		MINERALS		RAILROADS		CONTOURS	
BOUNDARIES ✓		PETROLEUM		TYPE		HACHURES	
CITY PLAN		INDUSTRY ✓		GUAGE		OTHER RELIEF	
CLIMATE		AREA	✓	FACILITIES		DRAINAGE	MB4
REGION		PLANT	✓	ROADS		WATERWAYS	
PRECIPITATION		TYPE	✓	SURFACE		CANALS	
TEMPERATURE		MILITARY	✓	MILEAGE		NAVIGABILITY	
HISTORICAL		POPULATION		OTHER		DEPTH	
BOUNDARIES		DISTRIBUTION		RECREATION		FACILITIES	
COMMUNICATIONS		ETHNOGRAPHIC		TELECOMMUNICATIONS		OTHER Hydroelectric	✓
MILITARY		RELIGIOUS		VEGETATION		Plants	

                                                   ✓ " Steam plants

PHONODISC   eman +   1. Mines and Mineral
Pd 4   Folk music lecture.   c1956.   MBSi (Assisted   resources – Tennessee
(red)   Robert

                                                        MBSi
          Pd I   Villa-Lobos, Heitor.
          2   ₍Bachianas brasileiras, no.4, piano; arr.₎
          (red)   Bachianas brasileiras, no.4 ₍and 7₎   Angel
                  Records ANG. 35674.

                  1 record
                  c.2

                                                        MBSi
          Pd I   Mendelssohn-Bartholdy, Felix.
          7   ₍Symphony, no.4, op.90, A major₎
          (red)   Symphony no.4, in A, op.90 (Italian) Sympho-
                  ny no.5, in D minor ₍i.e. major₎ op.107 (Reforma-
                  tion)   RCA Victor LM 2221.

84   1 record

                85-
                86

LP   Chopin, Frédéric Francois   MFm
     ₍Concerto, piano, no. 2, op. 21, F min₎
     Piano concerto No. 2 in F minor, Opus 21.
   Vox PL-7100, 1951
     1 record   12 in.   33⅓ rpm.

     Guiomar Novaes, piano; Vienna Symphony Orchestra; Otto Klemperer, conductor.

     Side 2: his Fantasy, op. 49, F minor.

   Merrian Goody 9/57 3.49 FF

87-
88

A.   Chopin.   Fantasy, op. 49, F minor

89

G
H41m   Haydn, Joseph, 1732–1809.
      ₍Mass, C major (1773?)₎ *Phonodisc.*

90

G
H41m   Haydn, Joseph, 1732–1809.
      ₍Mass, C major (1773?)₎ *Phonodisc.*

     Missa Sanctae Caeciliae.   (Card 2)
      Program notes by H. C. Robbins Landon on album cover. Text, with English translation (leaf laid in)

91

G
L827m   Loewe, Frederick, 1904–
      ₍My fair lady. Selections₎ *Phonodisc.*

     My fair lady.   Book, and lyrics: Alan Jay Lerner.   Columbia OL 5090. ₍1956₎
      2 s.   12 in.   33⅓ rpm.   microgroove.   (Columbia masterworks)
      Starring Rex Harrison and Julie Andrews, with chorus and orchestra; Franz Allers, conductor.
      Program notes by George B. Dale on slipcase.

      1. Musical revues, comedies, etc.   ɪ. Harrison, Rex.   ɪɪ. Andrews, Julie.   ɪɪɪ. Title.

                       R 56—227

    Congress   ₍57c1₎

J
R25m   Ravel, Maurice, 1875-1937.   MBr
     ₍Quartet, strings, F major₎

     Quartet in F major.   Columbia, ML 5245.

copy 1   1s   348IM-4My62   (G = 12" 33 1/3)

92

329

Sevareid, Arnold Eric, 1912– *ed.*
 Candidates 1960; behind the headlines in the presidential race. ₍*Phonodisc.* Washington₎ Library of Congress; manufactured by American Foundation for the Blind, New York. AFB 59–1301—59–1315.
 30 s. 12 in. 33⅓ rpm. microgroove.
 Talking book, solely for the use of the blind.
 John Cannon, reader.
 Edition used for the recording: New York, Basic Books ₍1959₎
 Recorded in 1959.
 Manual sequence.
 1. Presidents—U. S.—Election—1960. 2. Campaign literature, 1960. ɪ. Cannon, John, 1921– ɪɪ. Title.

                                        T B 60–31

93

Fiction

Nordhoff, Charles Bernard, 1887–
 Mutiny on the Bounty, by Charles Nordhoff and James Norman Hall. ₍*Phonodisc.* Washington₎ Library of Congress; manufactured by American Foundation for the Blind, New York. AFB 57–388—57–400.
 26 s. 12 in. 33⅓ rpm. microgroove.
 Talking book, solely for the use of the blind.
 Donald Madden, reader.
 Edition used for the recording: Boston, Little, Brown, 1932. Recorded in 1957.
 Manual sequence.
 1. Bounty (Ship) 2. Bligh, William, 1754–1817—Fiction. ɪ. Hall, James Norman, 1887–1951, joint author. ɪɪ. Madden, Donald. ɪɪɪ. Title.

                                        T B 57–127
Library of Congress

94

411

Ogg, Oscar.
 The 26 letters. ₍*Braille, grade 2*₎ New York, T. Y. Crowell Co., ᶜ1948; printed for the Library of Congress ₍at the₎ American Printing House for the Blind, Louisville, Ky., 1960.
 2 v. 30 cm.
 Summary: Describes the growth and development of the alphabet, from cave drawings and hieroglyphics to the modern linotype.
 1. Writing—Hist. 2. Alphabet. ɪ. Title.

                                        B R 60–190

95

92
Juvenile

Reynolds, Quentin James, 1902–
 The Wright brothers, pioneers of American aviation. ₍*Braille, grade 2*₎ New York, Random House, ᶜ1950; ₍printed by the₎ American Printing House for the Blind, Louisville, Ky., 1953.
 1 v. 30 cm. (Landmark books)
 For grades 4–6.
 1. Aeronautics—Hist. 2. Wright, Orville, 1871–1948. 3. Wright, Wilbur, 1867–1912.

                                        B R 59–20
Library of Congress

96

APPENDIX A

Book numbers demonstration (1-46)

I.   Biography: individual vs. collective (1-8) see also XI

II.   Voluminous literary author: texts, criticism, etc. (9-24)

III.   Bible: versions, commentaries, etc. (25-46)

R509.2
A1Am35 American men of science; a biographical directory
            edited by Jacques Cattell. 10th ed.
            Temple, Arizona State University, 1960-

1

530.92
A1H352n Heathcote, Niels Hugh de Vaudrey.
            Nobel prize winners in physics, 1901-1950; with
        a foreword by Herbert Dingle. New York, H.
        Schuman [1953]

2

530.92
M621   Millikan, Robert Andrews, 1868-1953.
            Autobiography. [1st ed.] New York, Prentice-
        Hall [1950]

3

530.92
M621a   Millikan, Robert Andrews, 1868-1953.
            Autobiography; foreword by Sir George Thomson.
        London, Macdonald [1951]

4

   R
610.92
A1Am35 American men of medicine. 3d ed. Farmingdale,
            N. Y., Institute for Research in Biography
            [c1961]

5

780.92
A1G28 m Gelatt, Roland, 1920-
            Music makers, some outstanding musical
        performers of our day. [1st ed.] New York,
        Knopf, 1953.

6

780.92
B455   Berlioz, Hector, 1803-1869.
            New letters, 1830-1868; with introd., notes,
        and English translation by Jacques Barzun. New
        York, Columbia University Press, 1954.

7

780.92
M877m   Mozarteum, Salzburg.
            Mozart-Gedenkstatten in Salzburg mit einem
        Verzeichnis der in Mozarts Geburtshaus
        ausgestellten Gegenstände. [2. Aufl. Salzburg,
        1951]

8

9	811 P752ag	Poe, Edgar Allan, 1809-1849. Selected poems and tales; edited with introd. and notes by Charles Marshall Graves. New York, Silver, Burdett [c1906]
10	811 P752am	Poe, Edgar Allan, 1809-1849. Selected poems; edited with an introd. by Thomas Ollive Mabbott. New York, Macmillan, 1928.
11	811 P752rs	Poe, Edgar Allan, 1809-1849. The raven; illustrated by Gustave Doré; with comment by Edmund C. Stedman. New York, Harper, 1884.
12	811 P752rt	Poe, Edgar Allan, 1809-1849. The raven, The fall of the house of Usher, and other poems and tales; edited by William P. Trent. Boston, Houghton, Mifflin [1897]
13	811 P752rFg	Poe, Edgar Allan, 1809-1849. Le corbeau, traduit par Amand Godoy; orné d'un front. de Mariette Lydis. Paris, Émile-Paul, 1929.
14	811 P752rGe	Poe, Edgar Allan, 1809-1849. Der Rabe; metrisch aus dem Englischen übers. von Carl Theodor Eben, mit einer biographischen Skizze des Dichters. Illus. von David Scattergood. Phil- adelphia, Barclay [1869]
15	811 P752Zb	Booth, Bradford Allen, 1909- A concordance to the poetical works of Edgar Allan Poe, by Bradford A. Booth and Claude E. Jones. Baltimore, Johns Hopkins Press, 1941.
16	813 P752 1902	Poe, Edgar Allan, 1809-1849. Complete works; edited by James A. Harrison. New York, Society of English and French Literature [c1902]

813 P752 1904	Poe, Edgar Allan, 1809-1849. Works; with an introd. by Edwin Markham. ⌐The cameo ed.⌐ New York, Funk & Wagnalls ⌐1904⌐	17
813 P752ac	Poe, Edgar Allan, 1809-1849. Best tales; edited with an introd. by Sherwin Cody. New York, Boni and Liveright ⌐1924⌐	18
813 P752ah	Poe, Edgar Allan, 1809-1849. The book of Poe; tales, criticism, poems; edited with introd. by Addison Hibbard; general introd. by Hervey Allen. Garden City, N. Y., Doubleday, Doran, 1929.	19
813 P752f	Poe, Edgar Allan, 1809-1849. The fall of the house of Usher; engravings on wood by Abner Epstein. New York, Cheshire House, 1931.	20
813 P752fFb	Poe, Edgar Allan, 1809-1849. La chute de la maison Usher, traduction de Ch. Baudelaire; dessins de Combet-Descombes. Paris, Éditions de la Sirène ⌐1919⌐	21
813 P752Vv	Virginia. University. Library. John Henry Ingram's Poe collection at the University of Virginia, by John Carl Miller. Charlottesville, University of Virginia Press, 1960.	22
813 P752Wb	POE, EDGAR ALLAN, 1809-1849. Buranelli, Vincent. Edgar Allan Poe. New York, Twayne Publishers ⌐1961⌐	23
813 P752Yd	Davidson, Edward Hutchins. Poe, a critical study. Cambridge, Mass., Belknap Press of Harvard University Press, 1957.	24

| 25 | 220.52 B471a | Bible. English. 1910. American revised. |
| | | The cross-reference Bible, containing the Old |

| 26 | 220.52 B471au | Bible. English. 1949. Authorized. |
| | | The Holy Bible; alphabetical indexed Bible, con- |

27	220.52 B471c	Bible. English. 1952. Catholic Biblical As-
		sociation.
		The Holy Bible, translated from the original

| 28 | 220.52 B471d 1949 | Bible. English. 1949. Douai. |
| | | New Catholic edition of the Holy Bible, trans- |

| 29 | 220.52 B471d 1952 | Bible. English. 1952. Douai. |
| | | The Holy Bible. Old Testament in the Douay- |

| 30 | 220.52 B471n | Bible. English. 1961. |
| | | The new English Bible. ꞏNew Yorkꞏ Oxford Uni- |

| 31 | 220.52 B471r | Bible. English. 1937. Revised. |
| | | The Holy Bible; the Revised version without the |

| 32 | 220.52 B471rs | Bible. English. 1952. Revised standard. |
| | | The Holy Bible. Revised standard version con- |

| 33 | 220.53 B471l | Bible. German. 1881. Luther. |
| | | Die neue illustrirte Heilige Schrift für häus- |

| 34 | 220.53 B471la | Bible. German. Selections. 1943. Luther. |
| | | Die Botschaft, das Evangelium und andere |

| 35 | 221.52 B471j | Bible. O.T. English. 1928. Jewish Publication Society. |
| | | תורה נביאים וכתובים The Holy Scriptures according to the Masoretic text; a new translation with the aid of previous versions and with constant consultation of Jewish authorities. Philadelphia, Jewish Publication Society of America, 5677-1917 ꞏ1928ꞏ |

221.54 B471d Bible. O.T. French. 1951. Daniel-Rops. La thérapeutique dans l'Ancien Testament. Texte	36
223.1052 B471s Bible. O.T. Job. English. 1947. Stevenson. The poem of Job; a literary study, with a new	37
223.107 C882c Crook, Margaret Brackenbury. The cruel God; Job's search for the meaning of	38
225.5 C727w Colwell, Ernest Cadman, 1901- What is the best New Testament? [Chicago] Uni-	39
225.52 B471r Bible. N.T. English. 1946. Revised standard. The new covenant, commonly called the New Testa-	40
225.52 Sh87u Shroyer, Montgomery J., 1888- Understanding the Scriptures. [A study manual	41
226.052 B471h Bible. N.T. Gospels. English. 1957. Heenan. The word of salvation; translated into English	42

226.1052
B471a Bible. N.T. Gospels. English. Harmonies. 1917.
     American revised.
     A harmony of the synoptic Gospels for historical
	43

226.3 R563p Robinson, James McConkey, 1924- The problem of history in Mark. Naperville,	44
226.3052 B471v Bible. N.T. Mark. English. 1951. Vernon. The Gospel of St. Mark; a new translation in	45

226.307
C235a Carrington, Philip, Abp., 1892-
     According to Mark; a running commentary on the
     oldest Gospel. Cambridge [Eng.] University Press,
     1960.
	46

APPENDIX B

Cataloging process case study: Library of Congress (55-78)

  I. Searching: Descriptive Cataloging Division: step I

  A. Works from Copyright Office; Order Division; Exchange and Gift Division

  B. Priority and limited cataloging slips inserted by selection officer: see I-C

  C. Searching in Official Catalog to see if author established

  D. Report slips inserted by searcher: see I-C

  II. Preliminary cataloging: Descriptive Cataloging Division: step II

  A. Master typed

  B. Preliminary cards duplicated and distributed

  III. Descriptive cataloging: Descriptive Cataloging Division: step III

  A. Name(s) (personal and corporate) established if necessary, and authority card(s) for official catalog made

  B. Descriptive data: body of entry, collation, notes completed

  C. Tracing for added entries indicated

  D. Filing title indicated, if necessary: see I-D

  IV. Subject cataloging and shelflisting: Subject Cataloging Division: step IV

  A. LC class number

  B. LC subject heading(s)

  C. Shelflisting: book number

  D. Certain books sent to Decimal Classification Office, where Dewey number assigned from 16th edition

  E. Books to Labeling Unit, then to shelf

  F. Manuscript card to Editor of Subject Headings, then to Card Division

APPENDIX B (continued)

V. Printing of cards: Card Division: step V

   A. Additions of card number and estimate of number to be printed

   B. Galley proof by the Government Printing Office, LC Branch

   C. Cards printed and cut

VI. Preparation of cards for LC catalogs: Catalog Maintenance Division: step VI

   A. Estimate of number required for LC catalogs put on manuscript card

   B. Cards returned to GPO for overprinting of call numbers and secondary entries

   C. Prepared cards arranged for filing

55

REPORT OF PRELIMINARY CATALOGING SEARCHER

Initials *Elt*   Rev.........................

Date..*30 mar*........ 19.59 USE

This work is NOT in

    Off. Cat.......✓..... Proc. File...........✓.....

L. C. has:

    original..ed.

    translation: Eng.............................

    Fr............. Ger............. Sp.............

    other..

✓ **Author NOT established**.................

     Åberg, Alf

   °*Title*

(Filled out in pencil)

Unadapted cooperative authority
card for another title.................
Form:

Name problem ....

Author ESTABLISHED as:

STEP I - Searching

(Searching report slip revised, 1961; see samples, I-C)
x-ref............. Pseud. x-ref.............

L. C. 0165–29   (6/58)   **(yellow)** ₉₊₀

56-
60

STEP II - Preliminary cataloging

    Entry is reproduced and distributed
as indicated on cards. Variations in distribution depend upon type of entry and
symbols.

To Card Division   **(pink)**

    Åberg, Alf
      Karolinska dagböcker; sammanställda
    och försedda med inledning av Alf Åberg.
    Stockholm, Natur och kultur [1958]
        184 p.   (Levande litteratur)

To Card Division   **(buff)**

    Åberg, Alf
      Karolinska dagböcker; sammanställda
    och försedda med inledning av Alf Åberg.
    Stockholm, Natur och kultur [1958]
        184 p.   (Levande litteratur)

To Card Division   **(buff)**

    Åberg, Alf
      Karolinska dagböcker; sammanställda
    och försedda med inledning av Alf Åberg.
    Stockholm, Natur och kultur [1958]
        184 p.   (Levande litteratur)

Card Division   **(buff)**

    Åberg, Alf
      Karolinska dagböcker; sammanställda
    och försedda med inledning av Alf Åberg.
    Stockholm, Natur och kultur [1958]
        184 p.   (Levande litteratur)

Card Division for series file   **(buff)**

    Åberg, Alf
      Karolinska dagböcker; sammanställda
    och försedda med inledning av Alf Åberg.
    Stockholm, Natur och kultur [1958]
        184 p.   (Levande litteratur)

      e ap 1apr59 asm

To Air Information Division

                                  (buff)

Åberg, Alf
   Karolinska dagböcker; sammanställda
och försedda med inledning av Alf Åberg.
Stockholm, Natur och kultur [1958]
    184 p.   (Levande litteratur)

61-64

To Air Research Division

                                  (buff)

Åberg, Alf
   Karolinska dagböcker; sammanställda
och försedda med inledning av Alf Åberg.
Stockholm, Natur och kultur [1958]

To European Affairs Division

                                  (buff)

Åberg, Alf
   Karolinska dagböcker; sammanställda
och försedda med inledning av Alf Åberg.
Stockholm, Natur och kultur [1958]

To General Reference and Bibliography Division

Åberg, Alf   **(buff)**
   Karolinska dagböcker; sammanställda
och försedda med inledning av Alf Åberg.
Stockholm, Natur och kultur [1958]
    184 p.   (Levande litteratur)

e ap 1apr59 asm

To Loan Division

                                  (buff)

Åberg, Alf
   Karolinska dagböcker; sammanställda
och försedda med inledning av Alf Åberg.
Stockholm, Natur och kultur [1958]

To Orientalia Division

                                  (buff)

Åberg, Alf
   Karolinska dagböcker; sammanställda
och försedda med inledning av Alf Åberg.
Stockholm, Natur och kultur [1958]

To Pan American Union for Revista interamericana de
   bibliografia   **(buff)**
      Åberg, Alf
        Karolinska dagböcker; sammanställda
      och försedda med inledning av Alf Åberg.
      Stockholm, Natur och kultur [1958]

65-68

Remaining cards are for use in Process File. **(six)**
   Åberg, Alf   **(buff)**
     Karolinska dagböcker; sammanställda
   och försedda med inledning av Alf Åberg.
   Stockholm, Natur och kultur [1958]
      184 p.   (Levande litteratur)

e ap 1apr59 asm

Forwarded with book for use of catalogers.

Åberg, Alf
    Karolinska dagböcker; sammanställda
och försedda med inledning av Alf Åberg.
Stockholm, Natur och kultur [1958]
    184 p.   (Levande litteratur)

e ap lapr59 asm NO NOT SET

70

THE LIBRARY OF CONGRESS
DESCRIPTIVE CATALOGING DIVISION

STEP III - Descriptive cataloging

    Name established and authority card is
made for official catalog. Additions made
by descriptive cataloger are typewritten
except proof marks.

THE LIBRARY OF CONGRESS
DESCRIPTIVE CATALOGING DIVISION

STEP IV - Subject cataloging and shelflisting

    Additions made by subject catalogers
are given in pencil.

STEP V - Printing of cards

    Additions made by Card Division are
in ink.

0165-41 (7/60)   gpo

69

THE LIBRARY OF CONGRESS
DESCRIPTIVE CATALOGING DIVISION

STEP II - Preliminary cataloging

    Master is forwarded to Legislative
Reference Service for use there after required number of cards has been duplicated
for cataloging use.

Åberg, Alf
    Karolinska dagböcker; sammanställda
och försedda med inledning av Alf Åberg.
Stockholm, Natur och kultur [1958]
    184 p.   (Levande litteratur)

e ap lapr59 asmk

LC 0165—3 (Rev. 2/58)

314

Åberg, Alf (1916-)

Full name: Alf Robert Edwin Åberg.

√√ Work cat.

√Memo = d.b.
d. Svenskt förf. lex. 1941-50 = full name
No conflict

0165-No. 7—(12/7/53)
msn 4/8/59

Karolinska dagböcker
[1958]

Filing Title

	Initials	Date
Descriptive Cataloger	msn	4/8/59
Reviser		
Subject Cataloger	TSeh	4/10/59
Reviser		
Shelflister	JDB/sl	Apr 24 1959
Decimal Classification		
To P. O.	(ink)	May 13 '59

Cataloger's Notes

Cds.
√ Series

Class. x-ref.

Cat. x-ref.

(In pencil except where indicated ink)

(Reverse copied on new form rev. 10/61)

64-1 (rev. 10/61)

GPO

71

72

73

PT9633
.5
.A2

4+6=10

Åberg, Alf, ed.
Karolinska dagböcker; sammanställda
och försedda med inledning av Alf Åberg.
Stockholm, Natur och kultur [1958]
184 p. 18 cm. (Levande litteratur)

Contents.—Löjtnant Joachim Matthiae Lyths
dagbok, 1703-1722.—Korpralen Erik Larsson
Snepust dagbok och anteckningar, 1701-1721.—
Självbiografiska anteckningar av bataljonspastorn vid Gardet mag. Andreas Westerman,
1705-172..

e ap 1apr59 asmk NOT SET DO NOT

1. Swedish diaries.

I. Title.

Full name: Alf Robert Edvin Åberg.

DDC number	59-33070
3/s	(ink)

Library of Congress

GPO L.C. 1-43

75

PT9633
.5
.A2

Åberg, Alf, *ed.*
  Karolinska dagböcker; sammanställda och försedda med inledning av Alf Åberg. Stockholm, Natur och kultur [1958]
  184 p. 18 cm. (Levande litteratur)
  CONTENTS.—Löjtnant Joachim Matthiae Lyths dagbok, 1708–1722.—Korpralen Erik Larsson Smepust dagbok och anteckningar, 1701–1721.—Självbiografiska anteckningar av bataljonspastorn vid Gardet mag. Andreas Westerman, 1705–1722.

76

PT9633
.5
.A2

SWEDISH DIARIES.

Åberg, Alf, *ed.*
  Karolinska dagböcker; sammanställda och försedda med inledning av Alf Åberg. Stockholm, Natur och kultur [1958]
  184 p. 18 cm. (Levande litteratur)

74

77

PT9633
.5
.A2

Karolinska dagböcker.

Åberg, Alf, *ed.*
  Karolinska dagböcker; sammanställda och försedda med inledning av Alf Åberg. Stockholm, Natur och kultur [1958]
  184 p. 18 cm. (Levande litteratur)
  CONTENTS.—Löjtnant Joachim Matthiae Lyths dagbok, 1708–1722.—Korpralen Erik Larsson Smepust dagbok och anteckningar, 1701–1721.—Självbiografiska anteckningar av bataljonspastorn vid Gardet mag. Andreas Westerman, 1705–1722.

  1. Swedish diaries.   I. Title.

78

PT9633
.5
.A2

Åberg, Alf, *ed.*
  Karolinska dagböcker; sammanställda och försedda med inledning av Alf Åberg. Stockholm, Natur och kultur [1958]
  184 p. 18 cm. (Levande litteratur)
  CONTENTS.—Löjtnant Joachim Matthiae Lyths dagbok, 1708–1722.—Korpralen Erik Larsson Smepust dagbok och anteckningar, 1701–1721.—Självbiografiska anteckningar av bataljonspastorn vid Gardet mag. Andreas Westerman, 1705–1722.

  1. Swedish diaries.   I. Title.

                          Full name: Alf Robert Edvin Åberg.

PT9633.5.A2   59–33070

Library of Congress   [8]

THE LIBRARY OF CONGRESS
DESCRIPTIVE CATALOGING DIVISION

STEP V – Printing of cards

Galley herewith.

Åberg, Alf, *ed.*
  Karolinska dagböcker; sammanställda och försedda med inledning av Alf Åberg. Stockholm, Natur och kultur [1958]
  184 p. 18 cm. (Levande litteratur)
  CONTENTS.—Löjtnant Joachim Matthiae Lyths dagbok, 1708–1722.—Korpralen Erik Larsson Smepust dagbok och anteckningar, 1701–1721.—Självbiografiska anteckningar av bataljonspastorn vid Gardet mag. Andreas Westerman, 1705–1722.

  1. Swedish diaries.   I. Title.

                          Full name: Alf Robert Edvin Åberg.

PT9633.5.A2   59–33070

Library of Congress   [8]

THE LIBRARY OF CONGRESS
DESCRIPTIVE CATALOGING DIVISION

STEP VI – Preparation of cards for LC catalogs

  Estimate of number of cards required for LC catalogs is given in pencil at top of ms. card. Cards are overprinted with call number, subject heading, and title added entry.

(Samples here are typed.)

0185–41 (7/60)   GPO

APPENDIX C

Branch cataloging for nonfiction and fiction and for audio-visual materials:
Boston Public Library Cataloging and Classification Department of the
Division of Home Reading and Community Services (79-97, 97a-1)

I. Preliminary records (79-86)

    A. Quantity book order cards indicating number of copies with branch locations (79, 83)

    B. Cataloger's master copy to be stencilled for mimeographed catalog cards (80, 84)

    C. Quantity slip for sets of cards to be mimeographed (81, 85)

    D. Quantity order record showing call number, forwarded to Book Preparation Department (82)

    E. Correction form slip (86)

II. Catalog records at central and for branches (87-93)

    A. Main entry (with stamp at central only to show branch locations) (87, 93)

    B. Subject headings and added entries (88-90, 94-95)

    C. Shelf list and verso (91-92, 96, 97)

        1. Publisher and price added at branches
        2. Date of accession added at branches
        3. Date of withdrawal (DISCONTINUED stamp) added at branches

III. Catalog records at central and for branches for audio-visual materials (97a-1)

    A. Film (Audio-Visual Department only) (97a-e)

        1. Catalog control card (97a)
        2. Main entry (97b)
        3. Subject heading (97c)
        4. Shelf list and verso (97d-e)

    B. Recordings (97f-1)

        1. Symphonic: main and added entry and reference; shelf list omitted (97f-h)
        2. Folk music: main entry, subject heading, shelf list and verso (97i-1)

Card 79 (buff):

Packard, Vance			Block XI - List 1		
Author			Call Number		
2441 C&H					
The waste makers					
Title			Language, if Foreign		
N. Y.	McKay		c1960 4.50		
Place	Publisher		Date Price		
(checked in pencil)		30			
On Hand New Add. Repl.		Total	Fund		

Date: OCT 10 1960

Branches / Branch or Department

Approved	Asst.	Branch Lib.	Supervisor	Chief of Book Selection	Chief Lib.
AD ✓	BRI ✓	FAN ✓	MAT ✓	OSA ✓	SB ✓
ALL ✓	CHA ✓	GS	MEM ✓	OSC	SE
AV	C SQ ✓	HLS	MT B ✓	OSY ✓	UC ✓
BK I ✓	CON ✓	HP ✓	MT P ✓	PH ✓	WV
BK II ✓	DOR ✓	JP ✓	NE ✓	ROS ✓	WE ✓
BK III ✓	EB	LM ✓	OH ✓	SCH	WR ✓
BI 3	EGL ✓		NOV 23'60 058 (red)		

JUV / YA / XX AD NON / AD FIC

Form No. 881-   BOSTON PUBLIC LIBRARY

79

Card 80:

339
P119w

Packard, Vance Oakley, 1914-
    The waste makers. N. Y., McKay, c1960.
    340 p. 21 cm.

(cataloger's master copy)

Waste (Economics)
U. S.-Economic conditions.   Review copy (red)
Title.   NLC

80

Card 81:

Division of Home Reading Services | No. of cards
Cataloging & Classification Dept. | printed:
Order for mimeographed cards

Author_ Packard _ _ _ _ _ _ _ _ _ _ (typed in red)

Title_ _ Waste makers _ _ _ _ _ _ _ _ _ _ _ _

Main and added entries_ _ 34 _ _ _ _ _ _ _ _ _ _

Shelf list cards _ _ _ _ 39 _ _ _ _ _ _ _ _ _ _

Cataloger _ _ _ _ _ _ _   Date_ 10-13-60 _

81

Card 82 (green):

DIVISION OF HOME READING SERVICES
Quantity Order Record

Author Packard, Vance Oakley   Book no. 339
                                               P119w
Title The waste makers

No. of copies 30

Date of list Block XI-List 1   (typed in red)

(variegated colors to indicate time of order)

82

83

Date APR 25 1961	Paton, Alan		Block V - List 2			
	Author	NEN MAY 2-'61 1140	Call Number			
	Tales from a troubled land					
	Title		Language, if Foreign			
	N. Y.	Scribner	c1961	3.50		
	Place	Publisher	Date	Price		

(buff)

(checked in pencil)   [25]

On Hand	New	Add.	Repl.	Total	Fund

Approved ____ Asst. ____ Branch Lib. ____ Supervisor ____ Chief of Book Selection ____ Chief Lib.

Branches / Branch or Department

AD	✓	BRI	✓	FAN	✓	MAT	✓	OSA	✓	SB		JUV
ALL	✓	CHA		GS		MEM	✓	OSC		SE	✓	YA
AV		C SQ	✓	HLS		MT B		OSY		UC	✓	AD NON
BK		CON		HP	✓	MT P		PH	✓	WV	✓	XX AD FIC
BK I	2	DOR		JP	✓	NE		ROS	✓	WE		
BK II		EB	✓	LM	✓	OH	✓	SCH		WR	✓	
BI		EGL	✓			MAY 19'61 053 (red)						

Form No. 881-   BOSTON PUBLIC LIBRARY

84

P312ta

Paton, Alan.
    Tales from a troubled land. c1961.

(cataloger's master copy)

Africa, South-Fiction.   OS (red)
Title.   LC

85

Division of Home Reading Services | No. of cards
Cataloging & Classification Dept. | printed:
Order for mimeographed cards |

Author_ **Paton**_ _ _ _ _ _ _ _ _ _ _ _ (typed in red)

Title_ _ _ **Tales from a troubled land**_ _ _ _ _ _ _ _

Main and added entries _ _ _ 29 _ _ _ _ _ _ _ _ _ _

Shelf list cards _ _ _ _ _ _ 34 _ _ _ _ _ _ _ _

Cataloger _ _ _ _ _ _ _   Date_ 4-28-61 _

86

BOSTON PUBLIC LIBRARY   (yellow)
DIVISION OF HOME READING & COMMUNITY SERVICES
    Cataloging & Classification Dept.
    Author _____
    Title _____

Please withdraw:
    All cards ....
    Shelf list cards...........
    Duplicates of cards attached..........
Change of entry:

Change numbers in books from _____ to _____

_____   _____
Branch or Dept.   Date

Upper set (cards 93–97)

P312ta

AD✓ BI✓ CON✓ FAN✓ LM✓ MTP OSC SGH W✓✓
ALL✓ BRI✓ DOR HLS MAT✓ NE OSY SB✓ WE
AV CHA✓ EB HP✓ MEM✓ OH✓ PH✓ SE✓ WR✓
BK✓ CSQ✓ JP✓ EGL✓ MTB✓ OS✓ ROS✓ UC✓

Paton, Alan.
    Tales from a troubled land. c1961.

93

(band in red)   P312ta
  Africa, South–Fiction.

94

P312ta

    Tales from a troubled land. c1961.

95

P312ta

Paton, Alan.
    Tales from a troubled land. c1961.

96

Paton, Alan.
    Tales from a troubled land. c1961.
  Africa, South–Fiction.
  Title.   (unit card shelf list)

97

(verso shelf list)   ◯ (date)

(price)   (publisher)

Date of Accession	Date of Withdrawal	Date of Accession	Date of Withdrawal

Form No. 1002—100M.-4-28-'58.

Lower set (cards 87–92)

AD✓ BI✓ CON✓ FAN✓ LM✓ MTP✓ OSC SGH WV✓
ALL✓ BRI✓ DOR✓ HLS MAT✓ NE✓ OSY SB✓ WE✓
AV CHA✓ EB✓ HP✓ MEM✓ OH✓ PH✓ SE✓ WR✓
BK✓ CSQ✓ JP✓ EGL✓ MTB✓ OS✓ ROS✓ UC✓

339
P119w

Packard, Vance Oakley, 1914–
    The waste makers. N. Y., McKay, c1960.

87

(band in red)
  Waste (Economics)

339
P119w

88

(band in red)
  U. S.–Economic conditions.

339
P119w

89

  Waste makers.

339
P119w

Packard, Vance Oakley, 1914–
    The waste makers. N. Y., McKay, c1960.

90

339
P119w

Packard, Vance Oakley, 1914–
    The waste makers. N. Y., McKay, c1960.
    340 p. 21 cm.

91

  Waste (Economics)
  U. S.–Economic conditions.
  Title.   (unit card shelf list)

92

(verso shelf list)   ◯ (date)

(price)   (publisher)

Date of Accession	Date of Withdrawal	Date of Accession	Date of Withdrawal

Form No. 1002—100M.-4-28-'58.

BRANCH CATALOGING:
AUDIO-VISUAL MATERIAL:
FILM

97a

Information about Films for
Cataloging & Classification
Dept.-Home Reading Services

Title __MR. EUROPE AND THE__

__COMMON MARKET__ * Carousel

Release date __1962__

Cost __$250__   Loan

Running time __55 minutes__

B&W? __x__   Color

Subject __Shows how boundaries emphasizing__
__differences between the__
__countries of Western Europe and__
__hindering their economies would__
__be eliminated in a U. S. of__
__Europe.__

Audience __sh--col--ad__

Date __June, 1962__

97b

```
AD    BI    CON   FAN   LM    MTP   OSC   SCH   WV   Film
ALL   BRI   DOR   HLS   MAT   NE    OSY   SB    WE   337
AV✓   CHA   EB    HP    MEM   OH    PH    SE    WR   M678
BK    CSQ   EGL   JP    MTB   OS    ROS   UC
                                                    (green stamp)
```

Mr. Europe and the common market.
N. Y., Carousel, 1962.
55 min--16mm--sd--B&W--sh--col--ad.

97c

European common market (1955--   )

Film
337
M678

(red)

Mr. Europe and the common market.
N. Y., Carousel, 1962.
55 min--16mm--sd--B&W--sh--col--ad.

97d

European common market (1955--   )

97e

$250

Film
337
M678

Mr. Europe and the common market.
N. Y., Carousel, 1962.
55 min--16mm--sd--B&W--sh--col--ad.

Date of Accession	Date of Withdrawal	Date of Accession	Date of Withdrawal

Form No. 1002--200M.-8-15-'57.   (verso shelf list)   BOSTON PUBLIC LIBRARY

BRANCH CATALOGING:
AUDIO-VISUAL MATERIAL:
RECORDINGS

97f

AD✓	Bf	CON✓	FAN	LM	MTP	OSC	SCH	WV✓	Record 33
ALL	Brl✓	DOR✓	HLS	MAT✓	NE✓	OSY	SB✓	WE	785.1
AV✓	CHA✓	EB✓	HP✓	MEM✓	OH	PH	SE	WR	1212ssp
BK	CSQ	EGL✓	JP✓	MTB	OS	ROS✓	UC✓		(green stamp)

Lalo, Edouard, 1823-1892.
  Symphonie Espagnole in D minor, op. 21 [and]
Bruch, M. Concerto no. 1 in G minor for violin
and orchestra, op. 26. Columbia ML 5097.
  2 s. 12" 33 1/3 rpm.

Bruch, Max.
  Concerto no. 1 in G minor for violin and
orchestra, op. 26.
T. R.
  (title reference)

97g

Record 33
785.1
1212ssp

Bruch, Max.
  Concerto no. 1 in G minor for violin and
orchestra, op. 26.
Lalo, Edouard, 1823-1892.
  Symphonie Espagnole in D minor, op. 21 [and]
Bruch, M. Concerto no. 1 in G minor for violin
and orchestra, op. 26. Columbia ML 5097.
  2 s. 12" 33 1/3 rpm.

Bruch, Max.
  Concerto no. 1 in G minor for violin and
orchestra, op. 26.
T. R.
  (title reference)

97h

Symphonie Espagnole in D minor.
  see
Lalo, Edouard, 1823-1892.
  Symphonie Espagnole in D minor, op. 21.

97i

AD✓	BI	CON✓	FAN	LM	MTP	OSC	SCH	WV✓	Record 33
ALL	BRI✓	DOR✓	HLS	MAT✓	NE✓	OSY	SB✓	WE	784.4
AV✓	CHA✓	EB✓	HP✓	MEM✓	OH	PH	SE	WR	G786
BK	CSQ	EGL✓	JP✓	MTB	OS	ROS✓	UC✓		(green stamp)

Great Russian folk dances [and] Hungarian folk
songs and dances. Epic LC 3459.
  2 s. 12" 33 1/3 rpm.
(red band)
Dancing-Folk and national dances.

97j

Record 33
784.4
G786

Great Russian folk dances [and] Hungarian folk
songs and dances. Epic LC 3459.

97k

Record 33
784.4
G786

Great Russian folk dances [and] Hungarian folk
songs and dances. Epic LC 3459.
  2 s. 12" 33 1/3 rpm.
Moiseyev Russian Ballet Company; orchestra
under direction of Sampson Galpérine.
The Hungarian States Folk Ensemble under
direction of Baross Gábor.

Dancing-Folk and national dances.

97l

Date of Accession	Date of Withdrawal	Date of Accession	Date of Withdrawal

Form No. 1002—200M.-3-15-'57. (verso shelf list) BOSTON PUBLIC LIBRARY

APPENDIX D

Classified catalog: Boston University Libraries (98-145)

   I. Authority file in single alphabetic sequence (98-107)

      A. Names (personal, corporate, geographic)

      B. Titles (main entries)

      C. Subjects (names, topics, etc.)

      D. References

  II. Shelf list (108-114)

      A. Control cards

      B. Tracing

         1. Added entries for names, titles, series
         2. Call numbers for subjects

 III. Classified/classed catalog in LC class number sequence (115-123)

 IV. Main catalog in alphabetic sequence (124-145)

      A. Main entries

      B. Added entries

      C. Subject index references

      D. References

AUTHORITY FILE FOR BU CLASSIFIED CATALOG

FISHES QL614-639

Africa QL635 (A-Z)
  East QL635.E3
Anatomy QL634
Atlantic ocean QL621
Bahamas QL631.B3
Bermuda islands QL631.B5
Bibliography Z5971-5975
California, Southern QL628.C2
Canada QL626
Catalogs and collections QL619
Chile QL632.C5

(Continued on next card)

99   101

Lampérez, Blanca de los Ríos
s Ríos de Lampérez, Blanca de los, 1862-

102

MOLINA, TIRSO DE, pseud.
s Tellez, Gabriel, 1570?-1648

PQ6436

100   103

98

AFRICA (CONT'D)   (Card 1a)

British West DT491-518
  (x) British West Africa
  Biography DT504
  Commerce HF3898.W4
→ Economic conditions HC517.W4
  Periodicals HC517.W4A1
Periodicals DT491
Population HB3666.B7
Social conditions HN800.B7
Statistics HA1978.W4

AFRICA (CONT'D)   (Card 2)

Constitutional history JQ1870-3981
Bibliography Z7165.A4
Description and travel DT7-12
Discovery and exploration DT3
East DT361-469
  Antiquities GN865.E2
  Bibliography Z3516
  Church history BR1440
  Climate QC991.E3
  Commerce HF3898.E3
  Economic conditions HC517.E3
  History DT365
  Languages PL8016

(Continued on next card)

BRITISH WEST AFRICA
s Africa, British West

DT491-518

For specific aspects of this subject
consult the references under AFRICA -
BRITISH WEST in this Catalog.

104

NATURAL HISTORY

Addresses, essays, etc. QH81
Africa QH194-195
  Central QH195.C4
  East QH195.E3
  South QH195.S7
Alaska QH199
America QH101
Arctic Ocean QH199
Arctic Regions QH199
Asben QH195.A6
Asia QH179
Australia QH197

(Continued on next card)

108

DT
361
E96

Smith, Arthur Donaldson, 1864-1939.
  Through unknown African countries; the first
expedition from Somaliland to lake Lamu.
Lond., N.Y., E. Arnold, 1896.
  xvi,471p. illus. maps.

  I. Günther, Albert Carl Ludwig Gotthilf, 1830-
1914. Report on a collection of fishes ...
(QL635.E3) II. Title. (QH195.E3)

105

106

Ríos de Lampérez, Blanca de los, 1862-
  x Lampérez, Blanca de los Ríos

PQ6436

107

TELLEZ, GABRIEL, 1570?-1648
  x Molina, Tirso de, pseud.
  x Tirso de Molina, pseud.

PQ6436

TIRSO DE MOLINA, pseud.
  s Tellez, Gabriel, 1570?-1648

PQ6436

109

HC
517
W4
F55

Pedler, F J
  Economic geography of West Africa. London,
New York, Longmans, Green [1955]
  xii, 232 p. illus. (part col.) maps, tables.

  I. Title.

325

SHELF LIST FOR BU
CLASSIFIED CATALOG

110

HF
5468
Z9

Branch stores: Pamphlets.

111

PQ
6065
F10

Ríos de Lampérez, Blanca de los, 1862-
  Del siglo de oro (estudios literarios) con
prólogo del Excmo. Sr. D. Marcelino Menéndez
y Pelayo. Madrid, Rodríguez, 1910.
  xlv, 275p. (Her Obras completas. t.III)

Reprinted in part from various periodicals.

  I. Title. (PQ6436)

112

PQ
6434
D7
F01

Tellez, Gabriel, 1570?-1648.
  Don Gil de las calzas verdes; comedia en
tres actos y en verso por fray Gabriel Téllez
(el maestro Tirso de Molina) ed. with an
introduction, notes and vocabulary by B.P.
Bourland. New York, H. Holt and company,
1901.
  xxvii, 198p. front. (port.) 17cm.

"Bibliographical note": p.xxiii-xxvii.

  I. Bourland, Benjamin Parsons, 1870-
ed. II. Title.

113

PQ
6436
F48

McClelland, Ivy Lillian.
  Tirso de Molina, studies in dramatic
realism. Liverpool, Institute of Hispanic
studies, 1948. 256p. (Liverpool studies in Spanish
vii, 256p. literature: 3d series)

  I. Series.

114

PQ
6436
F49

Revista Estudios.
  Tirso de Molina, ensayos sobre la biografía
y la obra. Madrid, 1949.
  931p. ports.

BU CLASSIFIED CATALOG

115

DT
361
E96

Smith, Arthur Donaldson, 1864-1939.
Through unknown African countries; the first expedition from Somaliland to lake Lamu.
Lond., N.Y., E. Arnold, 1896.
xvi,471p. illus. maps.

---

116   120

Revista Estudios.
Tirso de Molina, ensayos sobre la biografía y la obra. Madrid, 1949.
931p. ports.

PQ
6436
F49

---

117   121

(PQ6436)

PQ
6065
F10

Ríos de Lampérez, Blanca de los, 1862-
Del siglo de oro (estudios literarios) con prólogo del Excmo. Sr. D. Marcelino Menéndez y Pelayo. Madrid, Rodríguez, 1910.
xlv, 275p. (Her Obras completas. t. III)

Reprinted in part from various periodicals.

---

118   122

(QH195.E3)

DT
361
E96

Smith, Arthur Donaldson, 1864-1939.
Through unknown African countries; the first expedition from Somaliland to lake Lamu.
Lond., N.Y., E. Arnold, 1896.
xvi,471p. illus. maps.

---

119   123

(QL635.E3)

DT
361
E96

Günther, Albert Carl Ludwig Gotthilf, 1830-1914.
Report on a collection of fishes made by Dr. A. Donaldson Smith during his expedition to Lake Rudolf.
p. 377-385. (In Smith, A.D. Through unknown African countries. Lond., 1896. Appendix A)

DT
361
E96

Smith, Arthur Donaldson, 1864-1939.
Through unknown African countries; the first expedition from Somaliland to lake Lamu.
Lond., N.Y., E. Arnold, 1896.
xvi,471p. illus. maps.

HC
517
W4
F55

Pedler, F   J
Economic geography of West Africa. London, New York, Longmans, Green [1955]
xii, 232 p. illus. (part col.) maps, tables.

HF
5468
Z9

Branch stores: Pamphlets.

PQ
6065
F10

Ríos de Lampérez, Blanca de los, 1862-
Del siglo de oro (estudios literarios) con prólogo del Excmo. Sr. D. Marcelino Menéndez y Pelayo. Madrid, Rodríguez, 1910.
xlv, 275p. (Her Obras completas. t.III)

Reprinted in part from various periodicals.

PQ
6436
F48

McClelland, Ivy Lillian.
Tirso de Molina, studies in dramatic realism. Liverpool, Institute of Hispanic studies, 1948.
vii, 256p. (Liverpool studies in Spanish literature. 3d series)

124

AFRICA (CONT'D)   (Card 1a)

For material on this subject see the
Classified Catalog

British West   DT491-518
Biography   DT504
Commerce   HF3898.W4
Economic conditions   HC517.W4
Periodicals   HC517.W4A1
Periodicals   DT491
Population   HB3666.B7
Social conditions   HN800.B7
Statistics   HA1978.W4

125

AFRICA (CONT'D)   (Card 2)

For material on this subject see the
Classified Catalog

Constitutional history   JQ1870-3981
Bibliography   Z7165.A4
Description and travel   DT7-12
Discovery and exploration   DT3
East   DT361-469
Antiquities   GN865.E2
Climate   QC991.E3
Commerce   HF3898.E3
Economic conditions   HC517.E3
History   DT365
Languages   PL8016
(Continued on next card)

126

Bourland, Benjamin Parsons, 1870-   ed.
Téllez, Gabriel, 1570?-1648.
   Don Gil de las calzas verdes; comedia en
tres actos y en verso por fray Gabriel Téllez
(el maestro Tirso de Molina) ed. with an
introduction, note and vocabulary by B.P.
Bourland.   New York, H.Holt and company,
1901.
   xxvii, 198p. front. (port.) 17cm.

   "Bibliographical note": p.xxiii-xxvii.

PQ
6434
D7
F01

127

BRITISH WEST AFRICA

   For material on this subject see the
Classified Catalog DT491-518

   For specific aspects of this subject
consult the references under AFRICA -
BRITISH WEST in this Catalog

128

Del siglo de oro (estudios literarios)

Ríos de Lampérez, Blanca de los, 1862-
   Del siglo de oro (estudios literarios) con
prólogo del Excmo. Sr. D. Marcelino Menéndez
y Pelayo. Madrid, Rodríguez, 1910.
xlv, 275p. (Her Obras completas. t.III)

   Reprinted in part from various periodicals.

PQ
6065
F10

129

Don Gil de las calzas verdes.

Téllez, Gabriel, 1570?-1648.
   Don Gil de las calzas verdes; comedia en
tres actos y en verso por fray Gabriel Téllez
(el maestro Tirso de Molina) ed. with an
introduction, notes and vocabulary by B.P.
Bourland.   New York, H. Holt and company,
1901.
   xxvii, 198p. front. (port.) 17cm.

   "Bibliographical note : p.xxiii-xxvii.

PQ
6434
D7
F01

BU MAIN CATALOG

133

Lampérez, Blanca de los Ríos

see

Ríos de Lampérez, Blanca de los, 1862-

134

PQ
6436
F48

Liverpool studies in Spanish literature: 3d series.

McClelland, Ivy Lillian.
Tirso de Molina, studies in dramatic realism. Liverpool, Institute of Hispanic studies, 1948.
vii, 256p. (Liverpool studies in Spanish literature: 3d series)

135

PQ
6436
F48

McClelland, Ivy Lillian.
Tirso de Molina, studies in dramatic realism. Liverpool, Institute of Hispanic studies, 1948.
vii, 256p. (Liverpool studies in Spanish literature: 3d series)

136

MOLINA, TIRSO DE, pseud.

Works by this author are entered in this Catalog under Tellez, Gabriel

For material on this subject see the Classified Catalog PQ6436

130

HC
517
W4
F55

Economic geography of West Africa.

Pedler, F J
Economic geography of West Africa. London, New York, Longmans, Green [1955]
xii, 232 p. illus. (part col.) maps, tables.

131

FISHES

For material on this subject see the Classified Catalog QL614-639

Africa QL635
   East QL635.E3
Anatomy QL634
Atlantic ocean QL621
Bahamas QL631.B5
Bermuda islands QL631.B5
Bibliography Z5971-5975
California, Southern QL628.C2
Canada QL626
Catalogs and collections QL619
Chile QL632.C5

(Continued on next card)

132

DT
361
E96

Günther, Albert Carl Ludwig Gotthilf, 1830-1914.
Report on a collection of fishes made by Dr. A. Donaldson Smith during his expedition to Lake Rudolf.
p. 377-385. (In Smith, A.D., Through unknown African countries. Lond., 1896. Appendix A)

141

DT
361
E96

Smith, Arthur Donaldson, 1864-1939.
Through unknown African countries; the first expedition from Somaliland to lake Lamu. Lond., N.Y., E. Arnold, 1896.
xvi,471p. illus. maps.

142

PQ
6434
D7
F01

Tellez, Gabriel, 1570?-1648.
Don Gil de las calzas verdes; comedia en tres actos y en verso por fray Gabriel Téllez (el maestro Tirso de Molina) ed. with an introduction, notes and vocabulary by B.P. Bourland. New York, H.Holt and company, 1901.
xxvii, 198p. front. (port.) 17cm.
"Bibliographical note": p. xxiii-xxvii.

143

TELLEZ, GABRIEL, 1570?-1648

For material on this subject see the Classified Catalog PQ6436

144

DT
361
E96

Through unknown African countries.
Smith, Arthur Donaldson, 1864-1939.
Through unknown African countries; the first expedition from Somaliland to lake Lamu. Lond., N.Y., E. Arnold, 1896.
xvi,471p. illus. maps.

145

TIRSO DE MOLINA, pseud.

Works by this author are entered in this Catalog under Tellez, Gabriel

For material on this subject see the Classified Catalog PQ6436

BU MAIN CATALOG

137

NATURAL HISTORY
For material on this subject see the Classified Catalog
Addresses, essays, etc. QH81
Africa QH194-195
  Central QH195.C4
  East QH195.E3
  South QH195.S7
Alaska QH199
America QH101
Arctic Ocean QH99
Arctic Regions QH99
Asben QH195.A6
Asia QH179
Australia QH197 (Continued on next card)

138

HC
517
W4
F55

Pedler, F   J
Economic geography of West Africa. London, New York, Longmans, Green [1955]
xii, 232 p. illus. (part col.) maps, tables.

139

PQ
6436
F49

Revista Estudios.
Tirso de Molina, ensayos sobre la biografia y la obra. Madrid, 1949.
931p. ports.

140

PQ
6065
F10

Ríos de Lampérez, Blanca de los, 1862-
Del siglo de oro (estudios literarios) con prólogo del Excmo. Sr. D. Marcelino Menéndez y Pelayo. Madrid, Rodríguez, 1910.
xlv, 275p. (Her Obras completas. t. III).
Reprinted in part from various periodicals.

APPENDIX E

Brieflisting cataloging: University of California Library, Los Angeles
(146-157)

I. Current acquisitions: order (and gift) fanfold (heavy stock) filed
immediately in catalog to record publications received in library
(154-155)

II. Backlog of uncataloged materials: photographic copy of original order
slips filed in catalog (156-157)

III. Backlog of materials accumulating faster than cataloged: photographic
copy of title pages with author entry typed at top filed in catalog
(146-153)

LEWIS GELFAN

THE

Embroidered City

Little, Brown and Company · *Boston* · 1950

LEGES FRANCORVM
SALICAE
ET
RIPVARIORVM,
CVM
ADDITIONIBVS REGVM ET
IMPERATORVM VARIIS,
EX MSSTIS CODICIBVS EMENDATAE,
AVCTAE, ET NOTIS PERPETVIS ILLVSTRATAE:
ACCEDVNT PRAETEREA
I. FORMVLAE VETERES ALSATICAE;
II. G.G. LEIBNITII LIB. DE ORIGINE FRANCORVM,
POSTERIORIBVS CVRIS AVCTIOR, CVM RESPONSIONE AD
OBIECTIONES DOCTORVM QVORVNDAM VIRORVM;
*NNALES FRANCICI REGNI a THEODORO
ARTO EX GREGORIO TVRONENSI, FREDEGARIO,
ALIISQVE COLLECTI;*
V. FRIDERICI ROSTGAARDI EMENDATIONES
OTFRIDINAE,
EX CODICE PALATINO-VATICANO;
OMNIA
OPERA ET STVDIO
JO. GEORGII ECCARDI.

FRANCOF. ET LIPSIAE,
SVMTIBVS NICOLAI FOERSTERI,
ANNO M DCC XX.

A GENERAL
VIEW OF THE WORLD,
COMPRISING A
PHYSICAL, POLITICAL, AND STATISTICAL ACCOUNT
OF ITS
GRAND DIVISIONS,
AMERICA, EUROPE, ASIA, AFRICA AND OCEANICA,
WITH THEIR
EMPIRES, KINGDOMS, REPUBLICS, PRINCIPALITIES, &c.;
Exhibiting the History of Geographical Science and the Progress of Discovery to the present time.
A DESCRIPTION OF THE
MOUNTAINS, RIVERS, LAKES, PLAINS, &c. OF EVERY SECTION;
The principal Beasts, Birds, Fishes and Reptiles; Agricultural and Mineral Productions;
Commerce, Manufactures, Education, Government, Arts, Science, and Literature;
An account of the Manners, Customs, and Condition of the Inhabitants of each Country;
together with a Description of the Chief Cities and Towns.
ILLUSTRATED BY
UPWARDS OF NINE HUNDRED ENGRAVINGS
Of the Principal Vegetable Productions, Animals, Noted Edifices, Curiosities, and Ruins of
Man, in every nation of the Globe.
The whole concluded by a general Statistical Survey of the various Nations in the World;
enumerating the Population of the United States, according to the Census of 1840.

BY S. AUGUSTUS MITCHELL.

PUBLISHED BY
THOMAS, COWPERTHWAIT & CO.,
FOR
JAMES A. BILL.
1845.

ÉGATION ARCHÉOLOGIQUE FRANÇAISE EN AFGHANISTAN. — TOME VIII

recherches archéologiques
n Afghanistan
(1933-1940)
PAR
J. CARL et J. MEUNIÉ
avec des études de R. GHIRSHMAN et J.-C. GARDIN

PARIS — 1959

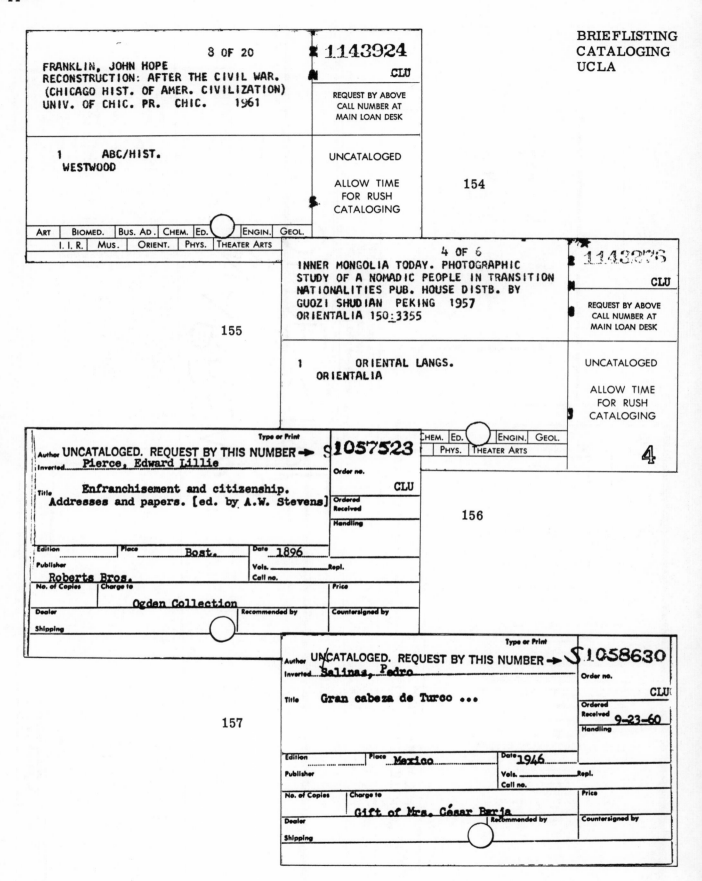

8 OF 20

FRANKLIN, JOHN HOPE
RECONSTRUCTION: AFTER THE CIVIL WAR.
(CHICAGO HIST. OF AMER. CIVILIZATION)
UNIV. OF CHIC. PR. CHIC.   1961

1143924
.CLU

REQUEST BY ABOVE
CALL NUMBER AT
MAIN LOAN DESK

1   ABC/HIST.
WESTWOOD

UNCATALOGED

ALLOW TIME
FOR RUSH
CATALOGING

154

| ART | BIOMED. | BUS. AD. | CHEM. | ED. | | ENGIN. | GEOL. |
| I. I. R. | MUS. | ORIENT. | PHYS. | THEATER ARTS | | | |

155

4 OF 6

INNER MONGOLIA TODAY. PHOTOGRAPHIC
STUDY OF A NOMADIC PEOPLE IN TRANSITION
NATIONALITIES PUB. HOUSE DISTB. BY
GUOZI SHUDIAN PEKING 1957
ORIENTALIA 150:3355

1143276
CLU

REQUEST BY ABOVE
CALL NUMBER AT
MAIN LOAN DESK

1   ORIENTAL LANGS.
ORIENTALIA

UNCATALOGED

ALLOW TIME
FOR RUSH
CATALOGING

| CHEM. | ED. | | ENGIN. | GEOL. |
| PHYS. | THEATER ARTS | | | |

4

Type or Print

Author UNCATALOGED. REQUEST BY THIS NUMBER → S 1057523
Inverted Pierce, Edward Lillie

Order no.

CLU

Title   Enfranchisement and citizenship.
   Addresses and papers. [ed. by A.W. Stevens]

Ordered
Received

Handling

156

Edition	Place Bost.	Date 1896
Publisher Roberts Bros.	Vols.	Repl.
	Call no.	
No. of Copies	Charge to Ogden Collection	Price
Dealer	Recommended by	Countersigned by
Shipping		

157

Type or Print

Author UNCATALOGED. REQUEST BY THIS NUMBER → S 1058630
Inverted Salinas, Pedro

Order no.

CLU

Title   Gran cabeza de Turco ...

Ordered
Received 9-23-60

Handling

Edition	Place Mexico	Date 1946
Publisher	Vols.	Repl.
	Call no.	
No. of Copies	Charge to Gift of Mrs. César Barja	Price
Dealer	Recommended by	Countersigned by
Shipping		

APPENDIX F

Synchronized book processing:* Wayne County Library, Wayne, Michigan

I. Entries in PW and BPR (158-173)

   A. Photographed and enlarged 50% by Xerography

   B. Transferred to masters and reproduced on catalog cards by multilith

II. Changes and adaptations of entries

   A. Deletion of DDC numbers: individual biography

   B. Deletion of fiction numbers

   C. Use of author's name as it appears on book

   D. Addition of title tracing

III. Title entry catalog card as book pocket: values of

   A. Descriptive annotations

   B. Age levels for juvenile books

IV. Standardization of cataloging and classification by use of

   A. LC cataloging

   B. DDC:16th ed.

*Kaiser, Walter H. Synchronized book processing. Library journal 86:752-754, February 15, 1961.

SYNCHRONIZED
BOOK PROCESSING
WAYNE COUNTY

165

The language of animals.

SELSAM, Millicent (Ellis) 1912- *JUV* j591
The language of animals. Illus. by Kathleen Elgin.
New York, Morrow [c.]1962. 96p. 62-7714 bds., 2.75
1. *Animal communication* **I. Title.**
How insects, fish, reptiles, birds and mammals communi-
cate. Ages 12-16.

Ap 62

164

ANIMAL COMMUNICATION

SELSAM, Millicent (Ellis) 1912- *JUV* j591
The language of animals. Illus. by Kathleen Elgin.
New York, Morrow [c.]1962. 96p. 62-7714 bds., 2.75
1. *Animal communication* **I. Title.**
How insects, fish, reptiles, birds and mammals communi-
cate. Ages 12-16.

Ap 62

163

SELSAM, Millicent (Ellis) 1912- *JUV* j591
The language of animals. Illus. by Kathleen Elgin.
New York, Morrow [c.]1962. 96p. 62-7714 bds., 2.75
1. *Animal communication* **I. Title.**
How insects, fish, reptiles, birds and mammals communi-
cate. Ages 12-16.

Ap 62

162

161

MlWC

Alaska harvest.

PEDERSEN, Elsa *JUV*
Alaska harvest. Illus. by Kurt Werth. Nashville,

PEDERSEN, Elsa *JUV*
Alaska harvest. Illus. by Kurt Werth. Nashville,
Abingdon [c.1960] 192p. 61-7042 3.00
I. Title.
A practical young girl faces new responsibility when her
mother becomes ill. Ages 9 and up.

Ap 62

160

159

Experimental biology for boys.

GORAN, Morris Herbert, 1916- *JUV* j574
Experimental biology for boys. New York, Rider

BIOLOGY

GORAN, Morris Herbert, 1916- *JUV* j574
Experimental biology for boys. New York, Rider

158

GORAN, Morris Herbert, 1916- *JUV* j574
Experimental biology for boys. New York, Rider
[c.1961] 113p. illus. (pt. col.) 29cm. (Rider pubn.,
no. 284) 61-18488 bds., 3.45 **I. Title.**
1. *Biology.*
Introduces experimentation in the study of plants and
animals. With 104 experiments. Ages 12-16.

Mr 62

336

MiWC

166

630.1
REHM, George
Requiem for twelve cows. New York, Morrow [c.1962] 189p. 62-11068 3.50
1. Dairying 2. *Farm life*
I. Title.

167

FARM LIFE

630.1
REHM, George
Requiem for twelve cows. New York, Morrow [c.1962] 189p. 62-11068 3.50
1. Dairying 2. *Farm life*
I. Title.

168

Requiem for twelve cows.

630.1
REHM, George
Requiem for twelve cows. New York, Morrow [c.1962] 189p. 62-11068 3.50
1. Dairying 2. *Farm life*
I. Title.
A one-time newspaperman tells of his unsuccessful efforts to run a dairy farm.
Ap 62

169

FIC
PORTER, Katherine Anne
Ship of fools. Boston, Atlantic-Little [c.1945-1962] 497p. 62-9557 6.50
I. Title.
A ship returning from Mexico to Bremerhaven is the microcosm in which a wide variety of passengers live out 27 days of their life. Set in the early 30's.
Ap 62

170

HIS 973.2
MILLER, John Chester, 1907- ed.
The colonial image: origins of American culture, selected, ed., introd., notes by John C. Miller. New York, Braziller [c.]1962. 500p. Bibl. 62-9930 7.50
1. U.S.—Hist.—Colonial period—Sources. 2. U.S.—Soc. life & cust.—Colonial period. I. Title.
Letters, diaries, histories, and memoirs reveal the nature of the peoples who settled in America when the country was in its infancy.
My 62

171

MUSEUMS directory of the United States 069.0587 and Canada. Ed. by Erwin O. Christensen, Washington D.C., American Association of Museums [c.1961] 567p. 26cm. 61-9712 7.50
1. Museums—U.S. 2. Museums—Canada. I. American Association of Museums.
Covers the entire museum field and includes historical societies, aquariums, arboretums, herbariums, botanical gardens, wildlife refuges, and zoos.
Mr 62

172

353
ROURKE, Francis Edward, 1922-
Secrecy and publicity; dilemmas of democracy. Baltimore, Johns Hopkins Press [c.1961] x, 236p. Bibl. 61-10736 5.00
1. Government information—U.S. 2. Executive privilege (Government information)—U.S. 3. Government publicity—U.S. I. Title.
Argues for a completely free press and against the withholding. by governmental agencies, of any information of interest to the public.
Ap 62

173

941.5081
SHAW, George Bernard, 1856-1950.
The matter with Ireland. Ed., introd. by Dan H. Laurence, David H. Greene. New York, Hill & Wang [c.1962] xviii, 308p. front. port. 62-12243 5.00
1. Ireland—Hist.—Addresses, essays, lectures. I. Title.
Collects for the first time all Shaw's writings on Irish problems written between 1886 and 1950.
Ap 62

APPENDIX G

Color band card system for instructional [nonbook] materials: Montgomery
County Public Schools, Division of Instructional Materials, Rockville, Md.
(174-185)

I. Central processing for library materials (book and nonbook) at Instructional Materials Center, available to 130 schools

II. Comprehensive dictionary card catalog file for instructional materials
at Center and in each school library

    A. Contents of card catalogs: multilithed cards for cross media
interfiled

        1. Printed media: books, etc.: white cards
        2. Nonbook media: color band system on catalog cards
          a. Films: red (174-177)
          b. Filmstrips: blue (178-181)
          c. Slides: black
          d. Tapes: green
          e. Records: yellow (182-185)
          f. Art prints: brown
          g. Kits: gray
          h. Maps: magenta
          i. Globes: orange
          j. Charts: light green
          k. Models: purple

    B. Call numbers: Center's inventory control number

**COLOR BAND
CARD SYSTEM**

Film - Red

(MdMCPS)

F
1
    Weather, The
        el,jh,sh   b&w   10 min.   Location: I.M.C.
        Gateway   1951
    Summary: Weather conditions depend upon
    changing conditions of wind, heat, clouds,
    and rain. Knowledge of weather is important
    to modern man and the methods and
    organizations that forecast it are indicated.

174

F
2
    Earth's Rocky Crust
        el,jh,sh   b&w   10 min. Location: I.M.C.
        Encyl. Brit. Film 1943
    Summary: Shows how the forces now changing
    the face of the earth are responsible for
    its present appearance. Rocks and land
    forms are studied through presentation of
    the water cycle, the formation of rocks, and
    the crumbling of rocks.

    1.   Earth   2. Rocks

175

EARTH

F
2
    Earth's Rocky Crust
        el,jh,sh   b&w   10 min. Location: I.M.C.
        Encyl. Brit. Film 1943
    Summary: Shows how the forces now changing
    the face of the earth are responsible for
    its present appearance. Rocks and land
    forms are studied through presentation of
    the water cycle, the formation of rocks, and
    the crumbling of rocks.

176

ROCKS

F
2
    Earth's Rocky Crust
        el,jh,sh   b&w   10 min. Location: I.M.C.
        Encyl. Brit. Film   1943
    Summary: Shows how the forces now changing
    the face of the earth are responsible for
    its present appearance. Rocks and land forms
    are studied through presentation of the
    water cycle, the formation of rocks, and the
    crumbling of rocks.

177

Filmstrips - Blue (on each card)   (MdMCPS)

178   FS   Oral And Written Expression
       1900   ad   Color   Frames: 54   Location: I.M.C.
                   Jam Handy   1956   Accompanies R 4290
             Summary: Shows how oral and written expression
             and reading can be more effectively taught in
             the elementary grades. Demonstrates how class-
             room teachers in the language arts program can
             make use of and develop the many learning
             experiences encountered by children.

             1. English Language - Composition and Exercises

             2. Conversation   ◯   3. Reading

ENGLISH LANGUAGE - COMPOSITION AND EXERCISES

179   FS   Oral And Written Expression
       1900   ad   Color   Frames: 54   Location: I.M.C.
                   Jam Handy   1956   Accompanies R 4290
             Summary: Shows how oral and written expression
             and reading can be more effectively taught in
             the elementary grades. Demonstrates how class-
             room teachers in the language arts program can
             make use of and develop the many learning
             experiences encountered by children.

                              ◯

CONVERSATION

180   FS   Oral And Written Expression
       1900   ad   Color   Frames: 54   Location: I.M.C.
                   Jam Handy   1956   Accompanies R 4290
             Summary: Shows how oral and written expression
             and reading can be more effectively taught in
             the elementary grades. Demonstrates how class-
             room teachers in the language arts program can
             make use of and develop the many learning
             experiences encountered by children.

                              ◯

READING

181   FS   Oral And Written Expression
       1900   ad   Color   Frames: 54   Location: I.M.C.
                   Jam Handy   1956   Accompanies R 4290
             Summary: Shows how oral and written expression
             and reading can be more effectively taught in
             the elementary grades. Demonstrates how class-
             room teachers in the language arts program can
             make use of and develop the many learning
             experiences encountered by children.

                              ◯

Records - Yellow (on each card)   (MdMCPS)

R   Forest Aflame
4236   el   33 1/3 rpm 15 " 2 sides Location:I.M.C.   182
              National Broadcasting Company
        Summary: Shows how forest fires may begin through
        carelessness, and the fast action of a ranger and
        his young companions.

        Where, Oh Where Is Smokey Bear
        Summary: Two boys learn about wildlife conserva-
        tion as they join a ranger in search for Smokey.

        1.   Forest Fires   3. Smokey Bear

        2.   Forests and   ◯   Forestry

        FOREST FIRES

R   Forest Aflame
4236   el   33 1/3 rpm   15" 2 sides Location:I.M.C.   183
              National Broadcasting Company
        Summary: Shows how forest fires may begin through
        carelessness, and the fast action of a ranger and
        his young companions.

        Where, Oh Where is Smokey Bear
        Summary: Two boys learn about wildlife conserva-
        tion as they join a ranger in search for Smokey.

                        ◯

        FORESTS AND FORESTRY

R   Forest Aflame
4236   el   33 1/3 rpm   15" 2 sides   Location:I.M.C.   184
              National Broadcasting Company
        Summary: Shows how forest fires may begin through
        carelessness, and the fast action of a ranger and
        his young companions.

        Where, Oh Where is Smokey Bear
        Summary: Two boys learn about wildlife conserva-
        tion as they join a ranger in search for Smokey.

                        ◯

        SMOKEY BEAR

R   Forest Aflame
4236   el   33 1/3 rpm   15" 2 sides   Location:I.M.C.   185
              National Broadcasting Company
        Summary: Shows how forest fires may begin through
        carelessness, and the fast action of a ranger and
        his young companions.

        Where, Oh Where is Smokey Bear
        Summary: Two boys learn about wildlife conserva-
        tion as they join a ranger in search for Smokey.

                        ◯

APPENDIX H

Corporate body under successive names:* National Library of Medicine study

I. Entry of corporate body under successive names

    A. Values

    B. Limitations

II. Comparative practice of libraries: successive vs. latest form of corporate name heading: monograph or serial

    A. Notes added

    B. History cards required

    C. References involved

*The following six pages of cards have been reproduced, with permission, from the photographic copy distributed by Ruth MacDonald at Stanford University to illustrate her paper: MacDonald, M. Ruth. Entry of corporate body under successive names. Working paper IV. (In Institute on Cataloging Code Revision, Stanford University, 1958. Working papers. Stanford, Calif., 1958. 11p.)

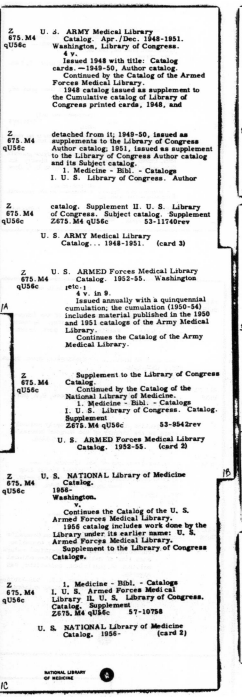

Z
675.M4   U. S. ARMY Medical Library
qU56c   Catalog. Apr./Dec. 1948-1951.
Washington, Library of Congress.
   4 v.
   Issued 1948 with title: Catalog
cards.—1949-50, Author catalog.
   Continued by the Catalog of the Armed
Forces Medical Library.
   1948 catalog issued as supplement to
the Cumulative catalog of Library of
Congress printed cards, 1948, and

Z
675.M4   detached from it; 1949-50, issued as
qU56c   supplements to the Library of Congress
Author catalog; 1951, issued as supplement
to the Library of Congress Author catalog
and its Subject catalog.
   1. Medicine - Bibl. - Catalogs
I. U. S. Library of Congress. Author

Z
675.M4   catalog. Supplement II. U. S. Library
qU56c   of Congress. Subject catalog. Supplement
Z675.M4 qU56c   53-11740rev

   U. S. ARMY Medical Library
     Catalog... 1948-1951.   (card 3)

Z
675.M4   U. S. ARMED Forces Medical Library
qU56c   Catalog. 1952-55. Washington
[etc.]
   4 v. in 9.
   Issued annually with a quinquennial
cumulation; the cumulation (1950-54)
includes material published in the 1950
and 1951 catalogs of the Army Medical
Library.
   Continues the Catalog of the Army
Medical Library.

Z
675.M4   Supplement to the Library of Congress
qU56c   Catalog.
   Continued by the Catalog of the
National Library of Medicine.
   1. Medicine - Bibl. - Catalogs
I. U. S. Library of Congress. Catalog.
Supplement
Z675.M4 qU56c   53-9542rev

   U. S. ARMED Forces Medical Library
     Catalog. 1952-55.   (card 2)

Z
675.M4   U. S. NATIONAL Library of Medicine
qU56c   Catalog.
   1956-
Washington.
   v.
   Continues the Catalog of the U. S.
Armed Forces Medical Library.
   1956 catalog includes work done by the
Library under its earlier name: U. S.
Armed Forces Medical Library.
   Supplement to the Library of Congress
Catalogs.

Z
675.M4   1. Medicine - Bibl. - Catalogs
qU56c   I. U. S. Armed Forces Medical
Library II. U. S. Library of Congress.
Catalog. Supplement
Z675.M4 qU56c   57-10758

   U. S. NATIONAL Library of Medicine
     Catalog. 1956-   (card 2)

NATIONAL LIBRARY
OF MEDICINE

U. S. *National Library of Medicine.*
   Catalog. Apr./Dec. 1948-
Washington, Library of Congress.
    v. in   30 cm.   annual.
   Title varies: Apr./Dec. 1948, Catalog cards—1949-50, Author cata-
log.
   Supplement to the Library of Congress catalog.
   Issued 1948-55 by the library under earlier names: 1948-51, Army
Medical Library; 1952-55, Armed Forces Medical Library.
   Vol. for 1954 is cumulative from 1950, superseding the annual vols.
for 1950-53.
   Beginning with 1951 issued in 2 parts: 1. Authors. 2. Subjects.
   Cumulative vols. for 1950-54 published in Ann Arbor, Mich., by
J. W. Edwards.

     (Continued on next card)
       51-60145 rev 3
   r57rk4]

   1. Medicine—Bibl.—Catalogs   I. U. S. Library of Congress.
II. U. S. Library of Congress. Library of Congress catalog ... Books:
authors. Supplement. III. U. S. Library of Congress. Library of
Congress catalog. Books: subjects. Supplement.

Z6676.U485   —3d set.   Z663.7.C28   51-60145 rev 3
Library of Congress   r57rk4]

---

       *R-WAB
UNITED STATES. Armed forces medical library.
   Catalog; a cumulative list of works represented by
Armed forces medical library cards. 1950/54-
Ann Arbor, J. W. Edwards.   v.   29cm.

RECORD OF HOLDINGS UNDER MAIN ENTRY ONLY
"Will be continued by annual volumes to be issued by the Library of
Congress."
   In 2 parts, Authors and Subjects.
       (Continued)
NN ** S S. SS sN OD, I ED, I   PC, I, 2, I SL MR, I, 2 R, I, 2 (UI,
LCI, XI)   [C]

   Published in cooperation with the Card division and the Catalog
maintenance division of the Library of Congress.

   1. Medicine—Bibl.   2. Bibliography—Catalogues—Libraries, Govt.—U. S.
—D. C.—Washington.   I. United States. Library of Congress.

United States. Armed forces medical library.   *R-WAB
   Catalog; a cumulative list of works represented by   (Cont.)
Armed forces medical library cards.

	Period	Received	t.-p.		To Bndy	From Bndy	NOTES
1950/54	6v.		8/29/56		Bound 9/7/56		
K...5					Rec'd 9-14 56		

Received from bound together.
LIBRARY HAS:

OC OI OS OSA OSDC PCS SL A AS   AH AMB X XS C GB J JB MF MS MU
MUB N O OB P FB FCN FCKS FR R RC RCB I SB SF ST STB T S form 25De [4-24-55 50m]

R016.61   U. S. Armed Forces Medical Library
.U58a   Catalog. Washington, Library of Congress.

   Library has
April-Dec. 1948- √..

   Title varies: Apr.-Dec. 1948, Catalog cards;
1949-50, Author catalog.
   Supplement to the Library of Congress Author
catalog and Subject catalog.
   Issued 1948-51 by the library under its
earlier name: Army Medical Library.

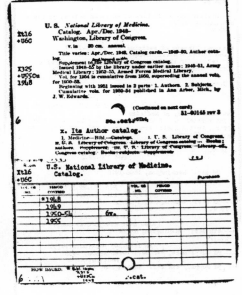

     Copy of permanent serial record card
240.5
Un322   U.S. Army Medical Library.
   Author catalog. Apr./Dec. 1948-

Washington, Library of Congress, 1949-

   Supplement to the U.S. Library of Congress
Author catalog (240.5 Un52Ca)
   First supplement, Apr./Dec. 1948, has title,
Catalog cards, and is included in the 1948
annual cumulation of the U.S. Library of
Congress Cumulative catalog

240.5
Un322   Title varies: 1951-   Catalog.

240.5
Un322   Issuing office varies: 1952-55, U.S. Armed
   Forces Medical Library.
   1956-   U.S. National Library of
   Medicine.

   1. Catalogs, Library.
I. U.S. Library of Congress.
II. U.S. Army Medical Library.
   Catalog.
III. U.S. Armed Forces Medical Library.
   Catalog.
IV. U.S. National Library of Medicine.
   Catalog.

   U. S. *National Library of Medicine.*
Xt16   Catalog. Apr./Dec. 1948-
+U6C   Washington, Library of Congress.
    v. in   30 cm.   annual.
   Title varies: Apr./Dec. 1948, Catalog cards.—1949-50, Author cata-
log.
X32S   Supplement to the Library of Congress catalog.
+U55Ca   Issued 1948-55 by the library under earlier names: 1948-51, Army
1948   Medical Library; 1952-55, Armed Forces Medical Library.
   Vol. for 1954 is cumulative from 1950, superseding the annual vols.
for 1950-53.
   Beginning with 1951 issued in 2 parts: 1. Authors. 2. Subjects.
   Cumulative vols. for 1950-54 published in Ann Arbor, Mich., by
J. W. Edwards.

     (Continued on next card)
       51-60145 rev 3

   x. Its Author catalog.
   1. Medicine—Bibl.—Catalogs.   I. U. S. Library of Congress.
II. U. S. Library of Congress. Library of Congress catalog ... Books:
authors. Supplement. III. U. S. Library of Congress. Library of
Congress catalog. Books: subjects. Supplement.

Xt16   U.S. National Library of Medicine.   Purchase
+U6C   Catalog.

VOL. NO.	PERIOD COVERED	VOL. OR NO.	PERIOD COVERED
*1948			
1949			
1950-54	6v.		
1955			

HOW ISSUED:

---

1. Entry of Corporate Body
Under Successive Names

Card 1 (top left):

```
Z        INDEX-CATALOGUE of the Library of the
675. M4      Surgeon-General's Office, United States
I38          Army.  Authors and subjects. [1st ser.]
             v. 1-16; 2d ser., v. 1-21; 3d ser., v.
             1-10; 4th ser., v. 1-11.  Washington,
             Govt. Print. Off., 1880-1955.
             58 v.
                4th ser., v. 1-10, have title: Index-
             catalogue of the Library of the Surgeon-
             General's Office, United States Army
             (Army Medical Library) Authors and

Z        subjects; 4th ser., v. 11 entitled:
675. M4      Index-catalogue of the Library of the
I38          Surgeon General's Office, United States
             Army (Armed Forces Medical Library)
             Authors and subjects.

Z            1. Medicine - Bibl. - Catalogs
675. M4      I. U. S. Armed Forces Medical Library
I38          II. U. S. Army Medical Library
             III. U. S. Army.  Surgeon-General's
             Office. Library
          Z675. M4 I38              56-7937

          INDEX-CATALOGUE of the Library of the
             Surgeon-General's Office, United States
             Army ...  1880-1955.   (card 3)

| NATIONAL LIBRARY OF MEDICINE
```

Card 2 (middle left):

```
National Library of Medicine      Med 100.21.7
Armed Forces Medical Library
   Catalogue of the library of the Surgeon general's
office, United States Army. With an alphabetical index of
subjects. Washington, 1872

454 p.

  ——Supplement. No.I. List of American medical journals.
Washington, 1872
26 p.

National Library of Medicine     Med 100.21.8
Armed Forces Medical Library
   Catalogue of the library of the Surgeon general's
office. United States Army. Washington, 1872-74

3 v.

                        Med 100.22.1
                     [also Zool.Mus. Howe Lib. Dental Sch.]
National Library of Medicine
   Index-catalogue of the library of the Surgeon-general's
office, United States army. Authors and subjects. Wash-
ington, 1880-95

16 v.
                        Med 100.22.2
                     [also Zool.Mus. Dental Sch.]
—— 2d ser. Washington, 1896-1916
            Card 2        Med 100.22.3
                     [also Howe Lib. Dental Sch.]
—— 3d ser. Washington, 1918-32
10 v.
                        Med 100.22.4
                     [also Howe Lib. Dental Sch.]
—— 4th ser. Washington, 1936-
v. 1-11
            RR 1013.16; Med 100.22.4(3)
—— 2d supplement, 4th ser. Washington, 1938
                     Med.Sch.
—— 3d suppl., 4th ser. Washington, 1941

2
```

Card 3 (middle column, top):

```
United States.  Surgeon General's Office.  Library.
   Index-catalogue of the Library of the Surgeon-General's
Office, United States Army.  Authors and subjects...  Wash-
ington: Govt. Prtg. Off., 1880-95.   16 v.   29cm.

Edited by J. S. Billings.

United States.  Surgeon General's Office.  Library.  Index-
catalogue...  (Continued)
—— Index-catalogue ... Second series ...  Washington:
Govt. Prtg. Off., 1896-1916.   21 v.   29cm.
Edited by R. Fletcher.
—— —— Second copy in * RG-WAB
—— —— Third series ...   Washington: Govt. Prtg. Off.,
1918-32.   10 v.   29cm.

United States.  Surgeon General's Office.  Library.  Index-
catalogue...  (Continued)
—— Alphabetical list of abbreviations of titles of medical peri-
odicals employed in the Index-catalogue of the Library of the Sur-
geon-General's Office, United States Army, from volume I to
volume XVI, inclusive.  Washington: Govt. Prtg. Off., 1895.
282 p.   29½cm.

United States.  Surgeon General's Office.  Library.  Index-
catalogue...  (Continued)
—— —— Fourth series.  v. 1-11.
Washington: Govt. Prtg. Off., 1936-55.  11 v.  29cm.
CONTENTS.—v. 1-11 A— MR.

United States.  Surgeon general's office.  Library.
   Index-catalogue...             (Cont'd)
—— —— Supplement.  no. 1- 3
Washington, 1937, - 41      29 cm.
   Bound with 4th ser., v. 2-3, 6.
               Contents:
no. 1. Synopsis of style with a list of abbreviations
   for serial publications indexed in the fourth series

United States. Surgeon general's office. Library.
   Index-catalogue...             (Cont'd)
Fourth ser., supplement (Cont'd)
no. 1 (cont'd) of the Index-catalogue. [1937]
no. 2. Congresses; tentative chronological and biblio-
   graphical reference list of national and international
   meetings of physicians, scientists, and experts. 1938.
no. 3. Mayer, C.F. Bio-bibliography of xv. century medical
   authors. 1941.
```

Card 4 (middle column, bottom):

```
R610.02    U. S. Surgeon-general's office.  Library
U57           Index-catalogue of the library of the
           Surgeon-general's office, United States
           army.  Authors and subjects ...  Washington,
           Govt. print. off., 1880-95.
              16 v.

           —— 2d ser. ...  Washington, Govt. print.
           off., 1896-1916.
              21 v.
                              see next card
                              1-2344-5 revised

R610.02    U. S. Surgeon-general's office.  Library
U57           Index-catalogue ...  1880-95.

           —— 3d ser. ...  Washington, Govt. print.
           off., 1918-1932.
              10 v.

           —— 4th ser. 1936-
              v. 1-11

4
```

Card 5 (top right):

```
U. S.  National library of medicine.
   Index-catalogue of the library of the Surgeon-general's
office, United States Army.  Authors and subjects ...  Wash-
ington, Govt. print. off., 1880-95.
   16 v.   29½ cm.

      —— 2d ser. ...  Washington, Govt. print. off., 1896-
1916.
   21 v.   29½ cm.
                        Z6676.U6  2d ser.
      —— 3d ser. ...  Washington, U. S. Govt. print. off.,
1918-32.
   10 v.   29½ cm.

                        (Continued on next card)
                                              1-2344 rev 5

"Collection of incunabula and early medical prints in the library
of the Surgeon general's office, U. S. Army": v. 10, p. 1415-1436.
                        Z6676.U6  3d ser.
      —— Index-catalogue of the library of the Surgeon general's
office, United States Army (Army medical library)  Au-
thors and subjects.  4th ser. ...  Washington, U. S. Govt.
print. off., 1936-
   v. 29½ cm.
                        Z6676.U6  4th ser.
   1. Medicine—Bibl.—Catalogs.  2. Medicine—15th-18th cent.—Bibl.
3. Incunabula—Bibl.—Catalogs.

Z6676.U6                                 1-2344 rev 5

Library of Congress  [r57y1]
```

Card 6 (bottom right):

```
                                      Copy of main entry
241.71   U.S. Army Medical Library.
Un38        Index-catalogue of the library of the Surgeon-
         General's office, United States Army.  Authors
         and subjects.  Washington, U.S. Govt. Print.
         Off., 1880-95.
            16 v.

         —— ——— 2d ser. ...  Washington, Govt. Print.
         Off., 1896-1916.
            21 v.
241.71                     2
Un38     —— ——— 3d serv. ...  Washington, U.S. Govt.
         Print. Off., 1918-32.
            10 v.

         "Collection of incunabula and early medical
         prints in the library of the Surgeon General's
         office, U. S. Army": v.10, p. 1415-1436.
241.71                     3
Un38     —— Index-catalogue of the library of the
         Surgeon General's Office, United States Army
         (Army Medical Library)  Authors and subjects.
         4th ser. ...  Washington, U.S. Govt. Print.
         Off., 1936-55.
            11 v.

         Ser. 4 has supplements as follows:
241.71                     4
Un38     suppl. 2 (bound with v.3) U.S. Surgeon General's
         office. Library. Congresses; tentative
         chronological and bibliographical refer-
         ence list of national and international
         meetings of physicians, scientists, and
         experts.
         suppl. 3 (bound with v.6) Mayer, C.F. Bio-biblio-
         raphy of XVI. century medical authors.
         [pt. 1]

6
```

```
2. Entry of Corporate Body
   Under Successive Names
```

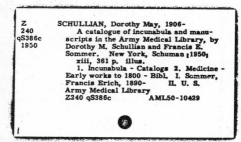

Z
240
qS386c
1950

SCHULLIAN, Dorothy May, 1906-
A catalogue of incunabula and manu-
scripts in the Army Medical Library, by
Dorothy M. Schullian and Francis E.
Sommer. New York, Schuman ₁1950₎
xiii, 361 p. illus.
1. Incunabula - Catalogs 2. Medicine -
Early works to 1800 - Bibl. I. Sommer,
Francis Erich, 1890- II. U. S.
Army Medical Library
Z240 qS386c AML50-10429

1

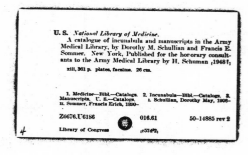

U. S. *National Library of Medicine.*
A catalogue of incunabula and manuscripts in the Army
Medical Library, by Dorothy M. Schullian and Francis E.
Sommer. New York, Published for the hororary consult-
ants to the Army Medical Library by H. Schuman ₁1948₎
xiii, 361 p. plates, facsims. 26 cm.

1. Medicine—Bibl.—Catalogs. 2. Incunabula—Bibl.—Catalogs. 3.
Manuscripts. U. S.—Catalogs. I. Sommer, Francis Erich, 1890-
II. Sommer, Francis Erich, 1890-

Z6676.U6186 016.61 50-14885 rev 2
Library of Congress ₁37d⁴2₎

4

1950

*KAE

United States. Surgeon general's office. Library.
A catalogue of incunabula and manuscripts in the Army medical
library, by Dorothy M. Schullian and Francis E. Sommer₎ New
York, Published for the Honorary consultants to the Army medical library by Henry Schuman, inc. ₁1950?₎ xiii, 361 p. facsims.
26cm.

"Printed by the Anthoensen press, Portland, Maine."

OFF. DOC. CARD
Res.
Mss. Div.
56J786B. 1. Incunabula—Collections —U. S.—Ohio—Cleveland. 2. Manu-
scripts—Collections—U. S.—Ohio —Cleveland. 3. Medicine—Bibl.
I. Schullian, Dorothy May, 1906- II. Sommer, Francis Erich,
1890-
N. Y. P. L. February 5, 1951

2

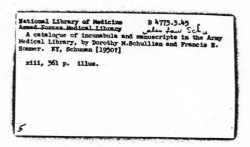

National Library of Medicine B 4773.3.45
Armed Forces Medical Library also law Sch.
A catalogue of incunabula and manuscripts in the Army
Medical Library, by Dorothy M.Schullian and Francis E.
Sommer. NY, Schuman ₁1950?₎

xiii, 361 p. illus.

5

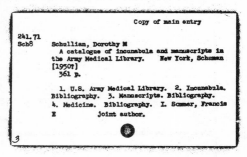

Copy of main entry

241.71
Sch8

Schullian, Dorothy M
A catalogue of incunabula and manuscripts in
the Army Medical Library. New York, Schuman
[1950?]
361 p.

1. U.S. Army Medical Library. 2. Incunabula.
Bibliography. 3. Manuscripts. Bibliography.
4. Medicine. Bibliography. I. Sommer, Francis
E Joint author.

3

U. S. *National Library of Medicine.*
A catalogue of incunabula and manuscripts in the Army
Medical Library, by Dorothy M. Schullian and Francis E.
Sommer. New York, Published for the honorary consult-
ants to the Army Medical Library by H. Schuman ₁1948?₎
xiii, 361 p. plates, facsims. 26 cm.

1. Medicine—Bibl.—Catalogs. 2. Incunabula—Bibl.—Catalogs. 3.
Manuscripts. U. S.—Catalogs. I. Sommer, Francis Erich, 1890-
II. Sommer, Francis Erich, 1890-

Z6676.U6186 016.61 50-14885 rev 2
Library of Congress ₁37d⁴2₎

6

3. Entry of Corporate Body
Under Successive Names

Card 1

A. M. L. [i. e. Army Medical Library]
see
U. S. *National Library of Medicine.*

LIBRARY OF CONGRESS REFERENCE
Users of depository catalogs should note that references may be to Library of Congress secondary entries which do not appear as headings in depository catalogs.

X 51–5897 rev 2
[r57c½]

Card 2

Armed Forces Medical Library, *Washington, D. C.*
see
U. S. *National Library of Medicine.*

LIBRARY OF CONGRESS REFERENCE
Users of depository catalogs should note that references may be to Library of Congress secondary entries which do not appear as headings in depository catalogs.

X 52–15560 rev
[r57b½]

Card 3

Army Medical Library, *Washington, D. C.*
see
U. S. *National Library of Medicine.*

LIBRARY OF CONGRESS REFERENCE
Users of depository catalogs should note that references may be to Library of Congress secondary entries which do not appear as headings in depository catalogs.

X 46–12510 rev 2
[r57c½]

Card 4

National Library of Medicine
see
U. S. *National Library of Medicine.*

LIBRARY OF CONGRESS REFERENCE
Users of depository catalogs should note that references may be to Library of Congress secondary entries which do not appear as headings in depository catalogs.

X 56–8564 rev
[r57b½]

Card 5

Smithsonian Institution. *National Library of Medicine* (Proposed)
see
U. S. *National Library of Medicine.*

LIBRARY OF CONGRESS REFERENCE
Users of depository catalogs should note that references may be to Library of Congress secondary entries which do not appear as headings in depository catalogs.

X 56–8565 rev
[r57c½]

Card 6

U. S. *Armed Forces Medical Library*
see
U. S. *National Library of Medicine.*

LIBRARY OF CONGRESS REFERENCE
Users of depository catalogs should note that references may be to Library of Congress secondary entries which do not appear as headings in depository catalogs.

X 56–18089

Card 7

U. S. *Army. Medical Library*
see
U. S. *National Library of Medicine.*

LIBRARY OF CONGRESS REFERENCE
Users of depository catalogs should note that references may be to Library of Congress secondary entries which do not appear as headings in depository catalogs.

X 46–12506 rev 2
[r57c½]

Card 8

U. S. *Army Medical Library*
see
U. S. *National Library of Medicine.*

LIBRARY OF CONGRESS REFERENCE
Users of depository catalogs should note that references may be to Library of Congress secondary entries which do not appear as headings in depository catalogs.

X 52–15595 rev
[r57b½]

Card 9

U. S. *National Medical Library*
see
U. S. *National Library of Medicine.*

LIBRARY OF CONGRESS REFERENCE
Users of depository catalogs should note that references may be to Library of Congress secondary entries which do not appear as headings in depository catalogs.

X 52–15561 rev
[r57b½]

Card 10

U. S. *War Dept. Army Medical Library*
see
U. S. *National Library of Medicine.*

LIBRARY OF CONGRESS REFERENCE
Users of depository catalogs should note that references may be to Library of Congress secondary entries which do not appear as headings in depository catalogs.

X 46–12508 rev 2
[r57c½]

Card 11

U. S. *Surgeon-General's Office. Library*
see
U. S. *National Library of Medicine.*

LIBRARY OF CONGRESS REFERENCE
Users of depository catalogs should note that references may be to Library of Congress secondary entries which do not appear as headings in depository catalogs.

X 46–12507 rev 2
[r57c½]

Card 12

Washington, D. C. Armed Forces Medical Library
see
U. S. *National Library of Medicine.*

LIBRARY OF CONGRESS REFERENCE
Users of depository catalogs should note that references may be to Library of Congress secondary entries which do not appear as headings in depository catalogs.

X 52–15596 rev
[r57b½]

Card 13

Washington, D. C. Army Medical Library
see
U. S. *National Library of Medicine.*

LIBRARY OF CONGRESS REFERENCE
Users of depository catalogs should note that references may be to Library of Congress secondary entries which do not appear as headings in depository catalogs.

X 46–12509 rev 2
[r57c½]

Card 14

Washington, D. C. National Library of Medicine
see
U. S. *National Library of Medicine.*

LIBRARY OF CONGRESS REFERENCE
Users of depository catalogs should note that references may be to Library of Congress secondary entries which do not appear as headings in depository catalogs.

X 56–18087

Card 15

U. S. *Public Health Service. National Library of Medicine*
see
U. S. *National Library of Medicine.*

LIBRARY OF CONGRESS REFERENCE
Users of depository catalogs should note that references may be to Library of Congress secondary entries which do not appear as headings in depository catalogs.

X 56–18088

4. Entry of Corporate Body Under Successive Names

346

1E

U.S. Armed Forces Medical Library.
    see
    U.S. National Library of Medicine.

U.S. Army. Medical Library
    see
    U.S. National Library of Medicine

U.S. Army Medical Library
    see
    U.S. National Library of Medicine

U.S. Public Health Service. National Library
    of Medicine
    see
    U.S. National Library of Medicine

U.S. Surgeon-General's Office. Library
    see
    U.S. National Library of Medicine

2F

Armed Forces Medical Library
    See National Library of Medicine

Army Medical Library, U.S.
    See National Library of Medicine

U.S. Armed Forces Medical Library
    See National Library of Medicine

U.S. Army Medical Library
    See National Library of Medicine

U.S. National Library of Medicine
    See National Library of Medicine

U.S. Surgeon-general's office. Library
    See National Library of Medicine

3B

Copy of cat. x-ref.
National Library of Medicine, see
U.S. National Library of Medicine.

Copy of cat. history cd.
U.S. Armed Forces Medical Library.

    Name changed, May 1952, from U.S. Army Medical
Library, by Section I of Federal Orders no. 49.
    Name changed Oct. 1, 1956, to U.S. National Library.
of Medicine, in accordance with Public Law 941, 84th
Congress.

3C

Copy of cat. history cd.
U.S. Army Medical Library.

    Name changed, May 1952, to U.S. Armed Forces Medical
Library, by Section I of Federal Orders no. 49.
    Name changed Oct. 1, 1956, to U.S. National Library
of Medicine, in accordance with Public 941, 84th
Congress.

3D

Copy of cat. history cd.
U.S. National Library of Medicine.

    Prior to May 1952 called U.S. Army Medical Library.
Name changed May 1952 to U.S. Armed Forces Medical
Library, by Section I of Federal Orders no. 49.
    Name changed Oct. 1, 1956, from U.S. Armed Forces
Medical Library, in accordance with Public Law 941,
84th Congress.

3F

Copy of cat. x-ref.
U.S. Public Health Service. National Library of
    Medicine, see
U.S. National Library of Medicine.

Copy of x-ref.
U.S. Surgeon-general's office. Library, see
U.S. Army Medical Library.

4H

Armed Forces Medical Library
    see
U. S. Armed Forces Medical Library

Army Medical Library
    see
U. S. Army Medical Library

National Library of Medicine, Washington,
D. C.
    see
U. S. National Library of Medicine

U. S. Armed Forces Medical Library
    see also
U. S. Army Medical Library
U. S. National Library of Medicine

U. S. Army Medical Library
    see also
U. S. Armed Forces Medical Library
U. S. Surgeon-General's Office. Library

U. S. National Library of Medicine
    see also
U. S. Armed Forces Medical Library

U. S. Surgeon-General's Office. Library
    see also
U. S. Army Medical Library

Washington, D. C. National Library of
Medicine
    see
U. S. National Library of Medicine

---

5. Entry of Corporate Body
Under Successive Names

Armed Forces Medical Library, Washington, D. C.

   see

U. S. Armed Forces Medical Library

Army Medical Library, Washington, D. C.

   see

U. S. Army Medical Library

National Library of Medicine, Washington, D. C.

   see

U. S. National Library of Medicine

National Medical Library, Washington, D. C.

   see

U. S. National Library of Medicine

4

U. S. Armed Forces Medical Library

    Established in 1836 as the Library of the
Surgeon-General's Office. Name changed in
1925 to Army Medical Library. On May 9, 1952,
redesignated the Armed Forces Medical Library.
Transferred Oct. 1, 1956, to Public Health
Service as U. S. National Library of Medicine.

   U. S. Armed Forces Medical Library

    see also

U. S. Army Medical Library
U. S. Army. Surgeon-General's Office. Library
U. S. National Library of Medicine

6

U. S. Army Medical Library

    Established in 1836 as the Library of the
Surgeon-General's Office. Name changed in
1925 to Army Medical Library. On May 9, 1952,
redesignated the Armed Forces Medical Library.
Transferred Oct. 1, 1956, to Public Health
Service as U. S. National Library of Medicine.

   U. S. Army Medical Library

    see also

U. S. Armed Forces Medical Library
U. S. Army. Surgeon-General's Office. Library
U. S. National Library of Medicine

8

U. S. Army. Surgeon-General's Office. Library

    Established 1836. Name changed in 1925 to Army
Medical Library. On May 9, 1952 redesignated the
Armed Forces Medical Library. Transferred Oct 1,
1956, to Public Health Service as U. S. National
Library of Medicine.

   U. S. Army. Surgeon-General's Office.
Library

    see also

U. S. Armed Forces Medical Library
U. S. Army Medical Library
U. S. National Library of Medicine

10

U. S. Dept. of Defense. Armed Forces Medical
Library

   see

U. S. Armed Forces Medical Library

11

U. S. War Dept. Army Medical Library

   see

U. S. Army Medical Library

12

U. S. Public Health Service. National
Library of Medicine

   see

U. S. National Library of Medicine

13

U. S. National Library of Medicine

    Established in 1836 as the Library of the
Surgeon-General's Office. Name changed in 1925
to Army Medical Library. On May 9, 1952, redesignated the Armed Forces Medical Library.
Transferred Oct. 1, 1956, to Public Health Service under the above name.

   U. S. National Library of Medicine

    see also

U. S. Armed Forces Medical Library
U. S. Army Medical Library
U. S. Army. Surgeon-General's Office. Library

15

Washington, D. C. National Library of Medicine

   see

U. S. National Library of Medicine

16

Washington, D. C. Army Medical Library

   see

U. S. Army Medical Library

17

Washington, D. C. Armed Forces Medical
Library

   see

U. S. Armed Forces Medical Library

18

---

6. Entry of Corporate Body
Under Successive Names

BIBLIOGRAPHY

PART I: Cataloging course syllabi, etc. listed from information received in response to requests sent to all graduate library schools accredited by the American Library Association.

Atlanta University. School of Library Service. Cataloging and classification I. [Atlanta, n.d.] 47 1.

Bidlack, Russell E. Typewritten catalog cards; a manual of procedure and form, with 125 sample cards. Ann Arbor, Mich., Ann Arbor Publishers, c1959. 35p.

Columbia University. School of Library Service. Sample catalog cards for use in connection with courses in technical services in libraries and organization of materials. 3d ed. New York, 1958. unpaged.

Dean, Hazel. Cataloging manual to supplement the A. L. A. catalog [sic] rules; 2d ed., 1949, and the Library of Congress rules for descriptive cataloging, 1949; for use in connection with Lib. Sci. 494 and 505. Revised by Paul W. Winkler. Los Angeles, School of Library Science, University of Southern California, 1960. 75p.

Dewey, Harry. An introduction to library cataloging and classification. 4th ed., rev. and enl. Madison, Wis., Capital Press [1957] 321p.

---- Specialized cataloging and classification, theory and technique. Madison, Wis., College Typing Co. [1956] 1v. (various pagings)

Dunkin, Paul S. Cataloging manual for course 610:505 and course 610:506. New Brunswick, N. J., Rutgers, The State University, Graduate School of Library Service [1961?] 10p.

Eaton, F. Thelma. Cataloging and classification; an introductory manual. 2d ed. Champaign, Ill., Distributed by the Illini Union Bookstore [1957] 193p.

Markley, A. Ethelyn. Introduction to classification and cataloging, Librarianship 210 [by] Anne Ethelyn Markley, Grete W. Frugé, reviser. Berkeley, University of California Press, 1960. 60p.

---- Special problems in classification and cataloging, Librarianship 214 [by] Anne Ethelyn Markley, Grete W. Frugé, reviser. Berkeley, University of California, 1959. 67p.

Rescoe, A. Stan. Cataloging made easy; a file of card forms to illustrate the cataloging of books and nonbook materials according to existing rules and current practices. 3d ed., rev. New York, Scarecrow Press, c1962. (In press: information furnished by author)

Toronto. University. Ontario College of Education. Library School. Sample cards for use in the course in cataloguing. 2d rev. ed. Toronto, 1960. 66p.

Washington (State) University. School of Librarianship. Sample cards. [Seattle, n.d.] 13 l.

Western Reserve University, Cleveland. School of Library Science. Cataloging rules; rev. [Cleveland] 1960. 34, [2] l.

PART II: Selected list of sources for supplementary exposition and examples of cataloging records, processing, forms, etc.

Akers, Susan G. Simple library cataloging. 4th ed. Chicago, American Library Association, 1954. 250p.

American Library Association. Division of Cataloging and Classification. Committee on Administration. Multiple order forms used by American libraries, edited by Edwin B. Colburn. Chicago, Microphotographic Laboratories, University of Chicago Libraries, 1949. 250 l. (Microfilm (positive) of typescript)

Clarke, Virginia. Non-book library materials; a handbook of procedures for a uniform and simplified system of handling audio-visual aids, vertical file, and other non-book materials in the school library. Denton, Laboratory School Library, North Texas State College [c1953] 155p.

Cornell University. Library. Catalog Dept. Manual of procedures; Robert B. Slocum, editor; Rosamond Danielson [and others] associate editors. Ithaca, N. Y., 1959. 236, [41]p.

[Diversity of cataloging among nations — two representative titles as catalogued in four nations] (Council on Library Resources. Fourth annual report for the period ending June 30, 1960. Washington, D. C. p.[14])

Douglas, Mary P. The teacher-librarian's handbook. 2d ed. Chicago, American Library Association, 1949. 166p.

Fellows, J. Dorcas. Cataloging rules, with explanations and illustrations. 2d ed. rev. and enl. New York, Wilson, 1926. 303p.

Haykin, David J. Subject headings; a practical guide. Washington, U. S. Govt. Print. Off., 1951. 140p.

Herald, Althea C. Processing manual, a pictorial workbook of catalog cards; compiled by Anne M. Crane. Teaneck, N. J. Fairleigh Dickinson University Press, 1961. 88p.

Johnson, Margaret F. Manual of cataloging and classification for small school and public libraries, by Margaret Fullerton Johnson and Dorothy E. Cook. 4th ed. New York, Wilson, 1950. 71p.

Mann, Margaret. Introduction to cataloging and the classification of books. 2d ed. Chicago, American Library Association, 1943. 276p.

Mary Annette, Sister, of the Sisters of the Third Order of St. Francis of the Holy Family. A manual for cataloging school libraries. 4th rev. ed. Ann Arbor, Mich., Edwards Bros., 1961. 97p.

Osborn, Andrew D. Serial publications, their place and treatment in libraries. Chicago, American Library Association, 1955. 309p.

Shachtman, Bella E., ed. Technical services: policy, organization, and coordination. Journal of cataloging & classification, 2:[59]-114, April 1955.

Slocum, Robert B. Sample catalog cards; illustrating solutions to problems in descriptive cataloging. New York, Scarecrow Press, 1962. 190p.

U. S. Library of Congress. Card Division. Handbook of card distribution. 8th ed. Washington, 1954. 82p.

---- Descriptive Cataloging Division. Cooperative cataloging manual for the use of contributing libraries. Washington, U. S. Govt. Print. Off., 1944. 104p.

Wofford, Azile. The school library at work; acquisition, organization, use and maintenance of materials in the school library. New York, Wilson, 1959. 256p.

ADDITIONS AND CORRECTIONS

Page ix: PREFACE: 4th paragraph, division of Sampler; official title for RDC listed on page xx

Page xv: INTRODUCTION: 1st paragraph, 2d sentence, deletion of not

Page xviii: INTRODUCTION: APPENDICES: Appendix C has been extended to include samples for audio-visual materials because these further illustrate simplified practice.
Appendix F, Wayne County Library

Page 8: I-A:33-41: No carbon required

Page 9: Facsimile of copy submitted by Enoch Pratt Free Library

Page 29: I-C:111 (verso top left:): I-C:111a

Page 30: I-C:114: Business Adm. Library, above call number (stamp for departmental library)

Page 39: I-D:151: CBI 1943-48

Page 55: II. F. 2. b. (3) Series: see also II-A; V

Page 56: II. G. 2. e. Supplements: see IV-B-C

Page 67: II-B:48-49, 51-52, 50: arrangement by order of tracing

Page 83: II-H:139-140: arrangement in reverse order

Pages 85, 87-90, 92: II-H:175 (asterisk omitted), 179, 186-187, 191, 209-210: The asterisk indicates that these seven references are traced in the LC Official Catalog (I-D:182), but no unit cards for these have been included. No unit cards are included for Elliot or Elliott (II-H:159).

Page 90: II-H:197: O'Connor, Frank, pseud., see O'Donovan, Michael

Pages 100-101, 105, 108, 111: III-A:4, 11, 25, 36, 47: multiple authorship included in this section to illustrate personal names

Pages 161, 163: IV-B:25 vs. XI-A-E:41; IV-D:38 vs. XI-A-E:6: holdings record (add-to information recorded in pencil) in either main catalog or shelf list, usually not in both

Page 190: VII. A. 2.; B. 2.: Adapter

Page 202: VII-K-L-M: key

Page 204: VII-J, N: key

Page 240: IX-C:39-40: arrangement in reverse order

Page 243: IX-D-E: key

Page 279: X-G:170, 172: tracing for Ravel and Debussy reversed

Page 335: Appendix F. II. A. Deletion of DDC numbers: individual biography: omission of sample

Page 342: Appendix H. II. Comparative practice of libraries: earliest vs. successive vs. latest corporate names: monograph or serial

Page 351: Bibliography. Part II: Journal of cataloging and classification

Pages 360,362,365,366: omission of index references:
   Irregular paging, <u>see</u> Complicated paging
   Numbers, see Volumes/numbers
   Shortened titles, <u>see</u> Partial/shortened titles
   Television stations, <u>see</u> Radio/television stations
The author is aware of several types of notes listed in the outline for which
   no samples appear. Moreover, an analytical entry for an inset map and an
   incomplete monograph set are among the omissions.

Explanation of page numbers versus sample numbers may be
found on page xix, INTRODUCTION: INDEX. The citations represent
a selective listing. "Etc." refers to additional examples either within the section or in other sections of the volume.

358

References
    names, titles, etc.:
        LC official catalog, I-D:171,174-175,181,186
    subject headings:
        authority files, I-E:194-195,197-200;etc.
        dictionary catalog, VIII-B:24,27,33-37;etc.
    subject index:
        classified catalog, App.D:124-125,127,131,
          136-137,143,145
        authority file, App.D:100
    successive title entry, II-H:130,145
    tracing, see Tracing: references
Related works, see Works related
Relationships in the catalog, p.211,VIII-A-B;p.
    224,VIII-C
Religious bodies, II-H:147;III-A:47-48;III-C:
    107,128;III-D:183-190;X-B:25;X-E:107,128;X-
    F:140-141
Religious forenames, p.97,III-A
Religious names in orders, I-D:137;II-H:185;
    III-A:50;III-D:152-153;VII-M:53-54
Reports, II-B:32;III-E:241-242;IV-C:35;IV-D:39-
    43,45-46;etc.
Reprints, III-D:195;IV-F:50;VII-I:43-45;IX-E:
    60-61;X-E:101
Revised editions, II-C:75,96;III-D:184;VII-P:66;
    etc.
Revisions, II-B:22;III-B:87-88;III-D:202;III-E:
    208,227;VII-N:58;VII-P:77;etc.
Roman numerals
    forenames, II-H:147,180;III-A:31,35-36;etc.
    paging, II-B:9,22;II-C:61,72;etc.;III-A-E;etc.
Romanization, I-D:174-175,184-186;V-A-B-C:59,
    see also "Title romanized" notes
Routing slips, I-C:70-71,76-88,95
Rulers, see Sovereigns, rulers, etc.
Russian names, II-E:110;III-A:51,63-65;III-D:
    142;VII-H:42;VIII-C:93;X-F:133-134;etc.

Sacred literature, III-C:138-141
Saints, I-D:129;II-H:139-140;III-A:47-48,51;IX-
    E:57-58
Scale
    atlases, X-C:49,57
    globes, X-C:52
    maps, X-C:33-42,44-48,51,55,59,61,66
Scope notes
    subject headings, I-E:197,203,205,211,216
Scores, X-F:131,133-134,137,143-146, see also
    Close scores; Miniature scores
Searching records, p.1,I-A,C;I-C:89-93,96-114
Secondary entries, p.54-55,II-F
Secondary fullness (abbreviated form) for names,
    see Analytical entries; "Bound with" notes;
    "Contents" notes; Editors: serials; Series
    treatment: combined or abbreviated form

Secular forenames, p.97,III-A
"Secular name" notes, III-A:50
"See also" references
    names, titles, etc., II-H:121-124,130;etc.
    subject headings, I-E:195,197,199;etc.;VIII-
    B:27,34,38;etc.
"See" references
    names, titles, etc.,I-D:171,173,177;etc.;II-
    H:127-129,131-133;etc.
    subject headings, I-E:194,198,200;etc.;VIII-
    B:24,33,35;etc.
Selections, see Excerpts
"Sequel" notes, VII-L:49-50
Sequels, X-E:89
Serbo-Croatian names, see Yugoslav names
Serial publications, p.54-56,II;p.157,IV;p.167,
    V;p.177,VI-B;p.247,X-C;p.260,X-E
    absorbed titles, mergers, unions, etc., II-B:
        46-47,54-55,58;II-H:136,181,188,208;IV-B:
        15-16,22-23
    analytics, VI-B:18-19,21
    bibliographic changes, IV-B:9-10;VIII-A:11-20,
        22-23
    closed entries, see Closed entries: serials
    collections, II-C:95-96;IV-F:48
    contents, IV-B:12,14;IV-C:33;IV-D:42,44;VIII-
        A:12,15-20,23
    continues/continued by notes, II-C:78-84
    duration of publication, IV-B:9,13-14;IV-D:
        46;VIII-A:11;X-E:84
    frequency of publication, II-A:5-6;II-B:54,
        58;IV-B:6,9-11;IV-C:27,32,34;IV-D:36,38-
        39;etc.;VIII-A:14,16-17;etc.;X-E:90-91
    holdings, see Holdings records; Holdings re-
        ferral
    imprint notes, IV-B:18;IV-C:31;VIII-A:12,15,
        22, see also "Imprint varies" notes
    issuing/sponsoring bodies, II-A:6,8;II-B:46,
        53-55,58;II-C:76,84,86,94;IV-B:12-13;V-A-
        B-C:41;X-E:124
    main entries, see Corporate bodies: main and
        added entries for monographs, serials, non-
        book materials, etc.; Titles: main entries
        for monographs, serials, nonbook mate-
        rials, etc., also Title statement: serials
    numbering, IV-B:10;IV-C:27;IV-D:44
    open entries, see Open entries: serials
    organ/official publication, II-B:54-55,58;IV-
        B:9,14-15,17,19
    preliminary cataloging records, I-C:63-79
    report year, IV-D:40-41
    shelf list, XI-A-E:2-4,6,22;etc.
    skeleton catalog cards, II-B:56-57;II-C:87-91;
        IV-C:28
    special numbers, IV-F:51

Titles
  tracing, II-B:10, 35, 64;etc.;III-A-F;VII-B:9-
    10;VII-D;18;etc.;VIII-A:21, 23;etc.;App. F:
    158;etc.
  nonbook materials, X-B-C, E-H
  works of special type, IX-A-C, E
Titles changed, see Changed titles
Titles of nobility, I-D:155-158;II-C:70;II-H:
  220-221, 229-230;III-A:24-33;III-B:87-88;III-
  C:109, 120;III-D:149;VII-N:62;X-B:26
Titles of nobility vs. family names, III-A:27
Titles of office vs. personal names, II-H:147,
  165, 218;III-A:34, 43-49
Tracing
  LC catalog cards, II-A:1, 6;etc.
  references:
    names, titles, etc.:
      authority file, I-D:121-122, 125-126;etc.;
        X-G:152-153
      classified catalog, App. D:105-106
      dictionary catalog, II-A:6;II-B:47, 55;II-
        C:77, 85;III-A:11, 18, 43-49;III-C:104,111,
        127,129;IV-B:16,23;V-A-B-C:60;VII-
        C:13;VIII-C:191-193;X-E:86;App. C:97f-g
      LC official catalog, I-D:165, 167, 170, 179-
        180, 185, 188
      shelf list for fiction, XI-A-E:47-48
    subject headings:
      authority file, I-E:195-196, 199;etc.
    subject index:
      classified catalog, App. D:98
  secondary entries:
    monographs, serials, etc., p. 54-56,II-F-G,
      see also subdivision, tracing under Ana-
      lytical entries; Series; Subject headings;
      Titles;
      classified catalog, App. D:108-109,111-113
  typed catalog cards:
    recto, II-B:10, 17, 32;III-A:14;III-C:109,
      112;III-E:223;IV-B:6;IV-D:40;IV-F:50;VII-
      A:2;VII-E:22;VII-G:39;VII-N:59-60;X-H:
      217-218
    verso, II-B:23-24, 35, 39, 47, 55;II-C:77, 85;
      III-C:116;VII-P:76, 78, 83, 85;X-D:73, 76;X-
      E:93, 99, 109, 120;X-G:150, 159, 170, 172,
      179, 201;X-H:224
  Wilson catalog cards, II-C:64, 71, 75;etc.
Traditional titles, see Anonymous classics
Translation statement, II-E:110;III-A:16, 33, 52;
  III-C:107, 122-123;III-D:184;etc.;VII-O:57;etc.
Translations (from and/or into), p. 191, VII-O
  Arabic, III-C:138
  Danish, III-C:135
  Dutch, VIII-C:78
  English, III-A:16, 33;III-C:107, 118, 120;etc.;
    VI-A:15-16;VII-A-C, K, N-O;VIII-C:91;etc.;

Translations (from and/or into)
  English, X-H:220;etc.
  French, III-A:16, 31;III-C:107-108;VII-A:1;
    VII-B:5;VII-C:15;VII-O:57;VIII-C:69, 79;etc.
  German, I-D:170;III-A:56;III-C:138;VII-H:41;
    VIII-C:60, 70, 73;etc.
  Greek, III-A:56;III-C:126, 136;VI-A:15-16;X-H:
    220
  Hebrew, III-C:126;etc.
  Irish, III-C:118, 120
  Italian, VII-H:41;VII-N:61;VIII-C:80;etc.
  Latin, VII-C:15;VIII-C:60
  Portuguese, VII-O:56
  Russian, II-E:110;III-C:108;VII-K:47;VIII-C:
    81;etc.
Translators
  added entries, III-A:56-58;III-B:88;III-C:108,
    118-120;etc.;VII-A:1;VII-B:5, VII-K:47
Transliteration, III-A:66-67, 74-78, see also
  "Title transliterated" notes
Treasure room collection, p. 241, IX-E
Two-line headings, II-A:3-4, 8;III-A:48;III-B:
  87-88;III-C:109, 133-134;III-D:151, 154-155;etc.
Typed catalog cards
  analytics, VI-A:4, 13-14;etc.
  monographs, II-B:9-20, 22-44;III-A:14;III-C:
    109, 112, 115-117;III-D:145, 155, 160;III-E:
    223;VII-A:2;VII-E:22;VII-G:38-39;VII-N:59-
    60;VII-P:73-75, 77, 82, 84;VIII-C:66-87, 91-
    93;X-E:98
  serials, II-B:46-52, 54-57;II-C:78, 84-85, 87-91;
    IV-B:6-7;IV-C:27-28;IV-D:40, 43;IV-F:50
  series, V-A-B-C:4, 10, 13-14;etc.
  shelf list, XI-A-E:2-3, 17;etc.

Uniform headings/titles, see Anonymous classics;
  Bible; Sacred literature
Unit cards, see Analytical entries; Library of
  Congress catalog cards; Series entries; Typed
  catalog cards; Wilson catalog cards
Unknown, complex, or variable authorship, p. 98,
  III-C
Unnumbered leaves, III-E:233;etc.
Unnumbered pages, III-C:134;III-D:148, 174;etc.
Unpaged works, II-B:17, 21;III-A:17, 36, 43;III-C:
  125;III-D:143, 180;III-E:210;etc.
Unused forenames, I-D:132, 140;II-E:114;II-H:
  141, 169;III-A:9, 13, 41;etc., see also "Full
  name" notes

Variations in authorship and corporate names
  serials, II-B:46, 53;IV-C:32, 34;IV-D:37, 39
Variations in title
  monographs, see Changed titles
  serials, II-C:97;II-H:130-132, 145, 148, 224;IV-
    B:12, see also "Title varies" notes